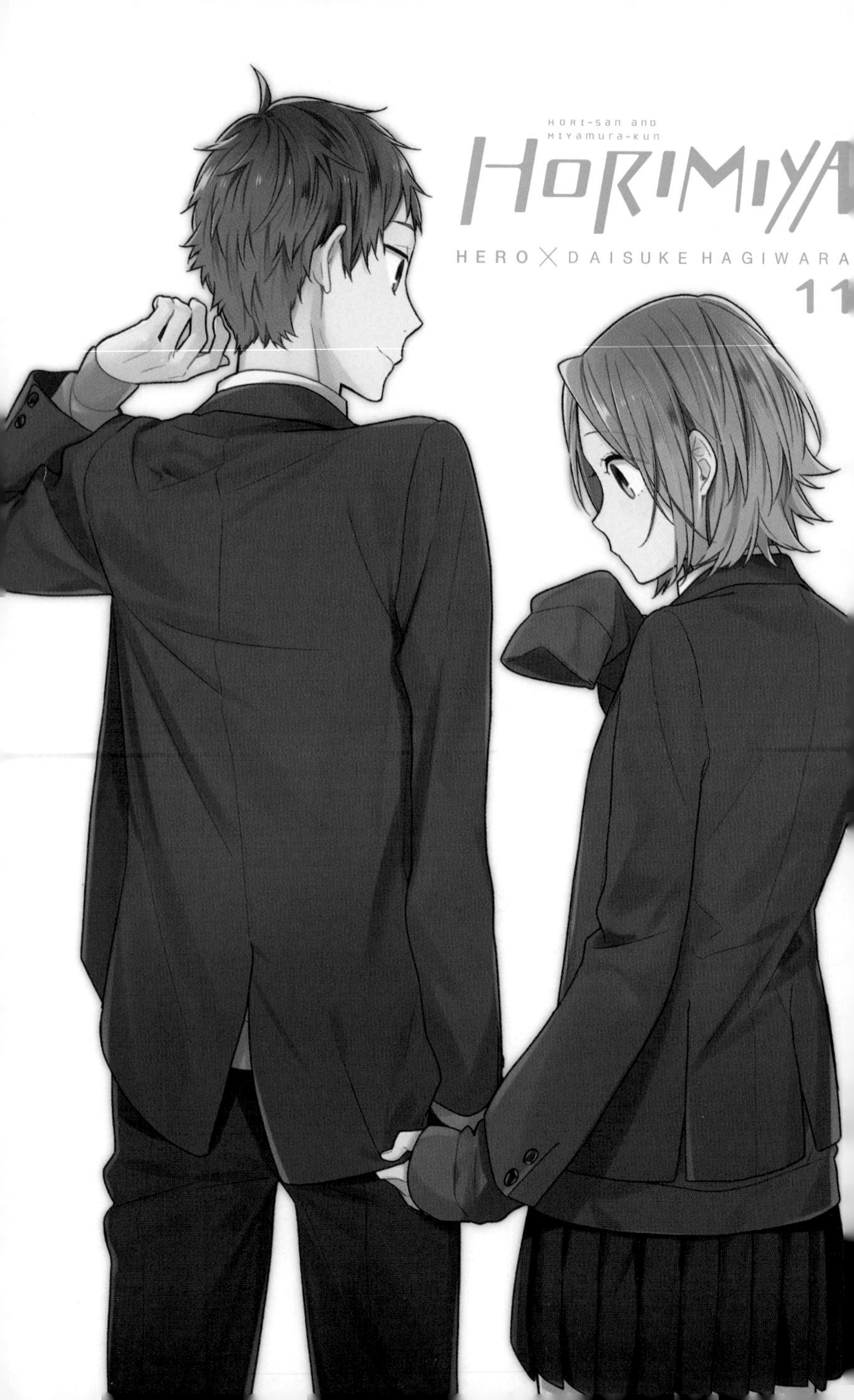
HORI-san and MIYAMURA-kun
HORIMIYA
HERO × DAISUKE HAGIWARA
11

HORI-san and
MIYamura-kun

# HORIMIYA

11

## CONTENTS ★

# Page·72

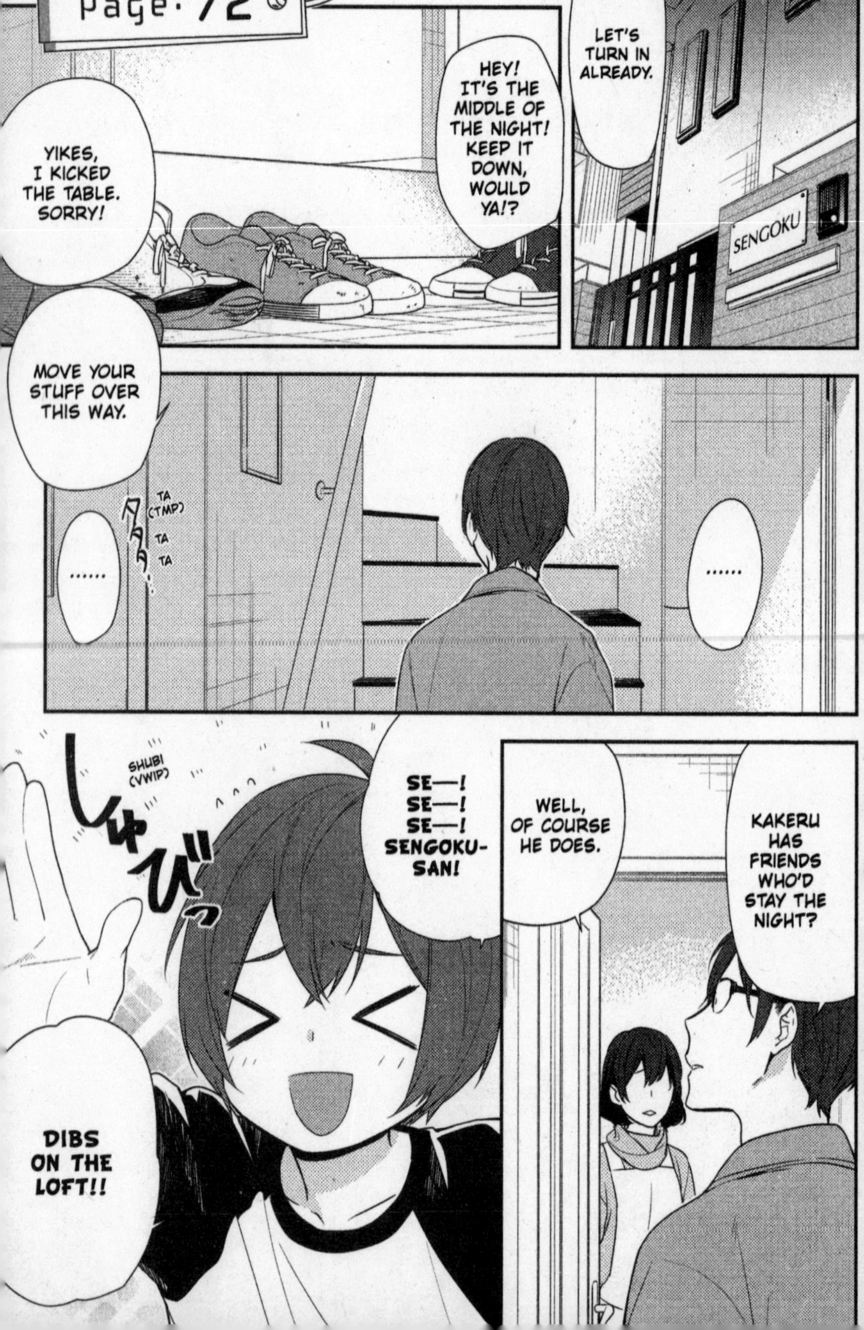
LET'S TURN IN ALREADY.
SENGOKU
HEY! IT'S THE MIDDLE OF THE NIGHT! KEEP IT DOWN, WOULD YA!?
YIKES, I KICKED THE TABLE. SORRY!
MOVE YOUR STUFF OVER THIS WAY.
......
......
TA (TMP) TA TA
KAKERU HAS FRIENDS WHO'D STAY THE NIGHT?
WELL, OF COURSE HE DOES.
SE—! SE—! SE—! SENGOKU-SAN!
SHUBI (VWIP)
DIBS ON THE LOFT!!

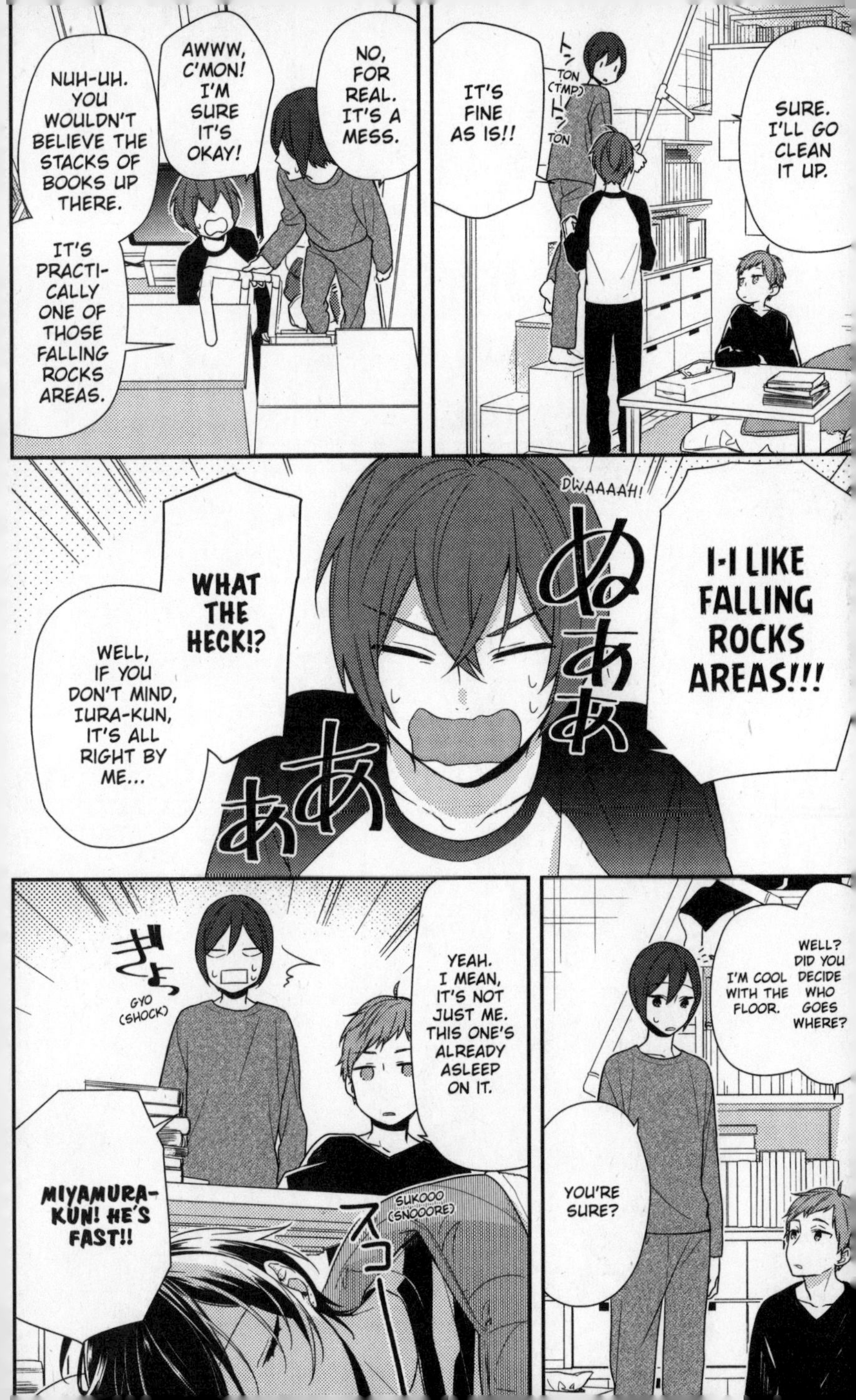

SURE. I'LL GO CLEAN IT UP.
TON (TMP) TON
IT'S FINE AS IS!!
NO, FOR REAL. IT'S A MESS.
AWWW, C'MON! I'M SURE IT'S OKAY!
NUH-UH. YOU WOULDN'T BELIEVE THE STACKS OF BOOKS UP THERE.
IT'S PRACTI-CALLY ONE OF THOSE FALLING ROCKS AREAS.
I-I LIKE FALLING ROCKS AREAS!!!
DWAAAAH!
WHAT THE HECK!?
WELL, IF YOU DON'T MIND, IURA-KUN, IT'S ALL RIGHT BY ME...
WELL? DID YOU DECIDE WHO GOES WHERE?
I'M COOL WITH THE FLOOR.
YOU'RE SURE?
YEAH. I MEAN, IT'S NOT JUST ME. THIS ONE'S ALREADY ASLEEP ON IT.
GYO (SHOCK)
SUKOOO (SNOOORE)
MIYAMURA-KUN! HE'S FAST!!

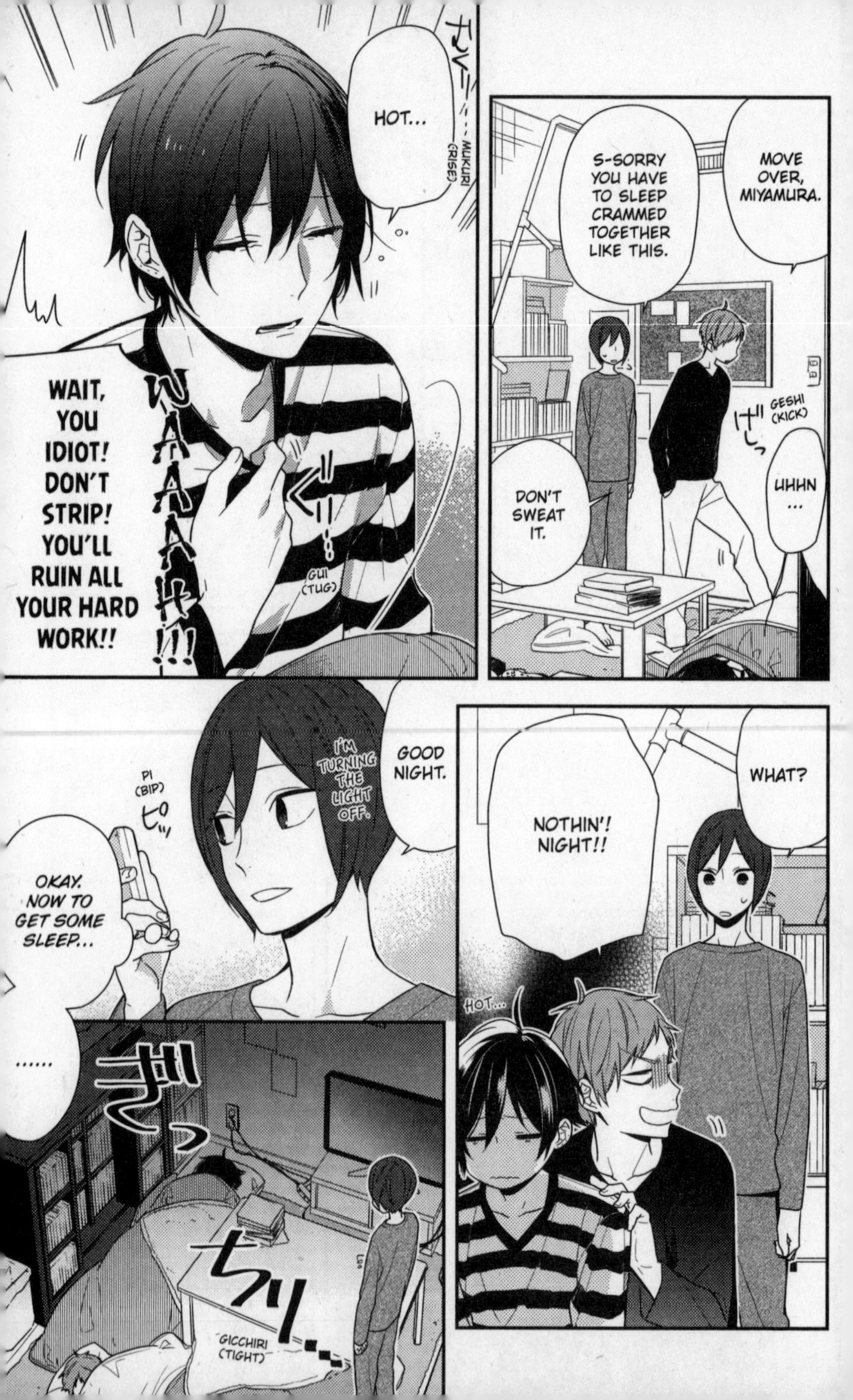
MOVE OVER, MIYAMURA.
S-SORRY YOU HAVE TO SLEEP CRAMMED TOGETHER LIKE THIS.
GESHI (KICK)
UHHN ...
DON'T SWEAT IT.
MUKURI (RISE)
HOT...
GUI (TUG)
WAAAAH!!!
WAIT, YOU IDIOT! DON'T STRIP! YOU'LL RUIN ALL YOUR HARD WORK!!
WHAT?
NOTHIN'! NIGHT!!
HOT...
GOOD NIGHT.
I'M TURNING THE LIGHT OFF.
PI (BIP)
OKAY. NOW TO GET SOME SLEEP...
......
GICCHIRI (TIGHT)

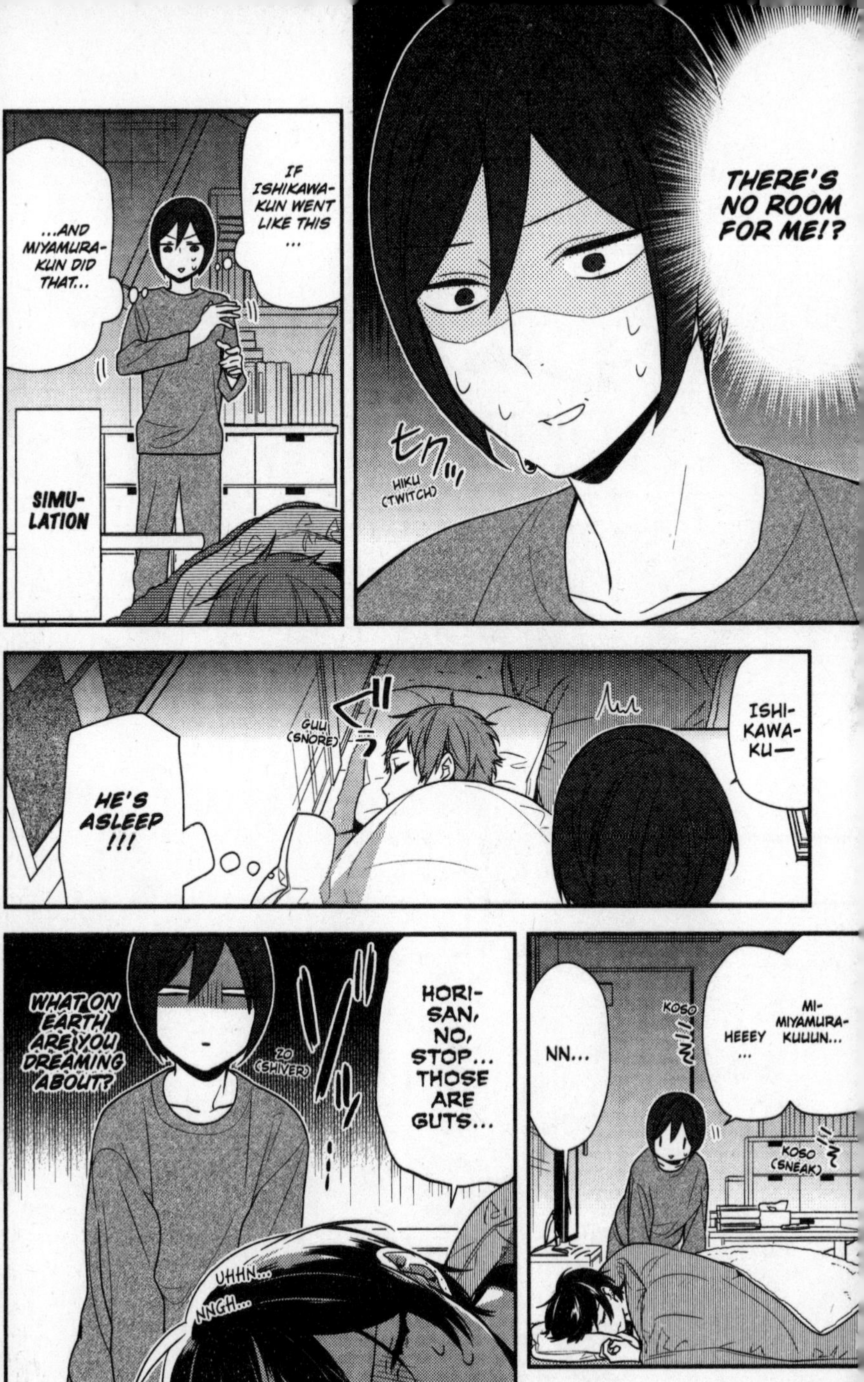
THERE'S NO ROOM FOR ME!?
HIKU (TWITCH)
IF ISHIKAWA-KUN WENT LIKE THIS ...
...AND MIYAMURA-KUN DID THAT...
SIMU-LATION
ISHI-KAWA-KU—
GUU (SNORE)
HE'S ASLEEP !!!
MI-MIYAMURA-KUUUN...
HEEEY ...
KOSO
KOSO (SNEAK)
NN...
HORI-SAN, NO, STOP... THOSE ARE GUTS...
ZO (SHIVER)
WHAT ON EARTH ARE YOU DREAMING ABOUT?
UHHN... NNGH...

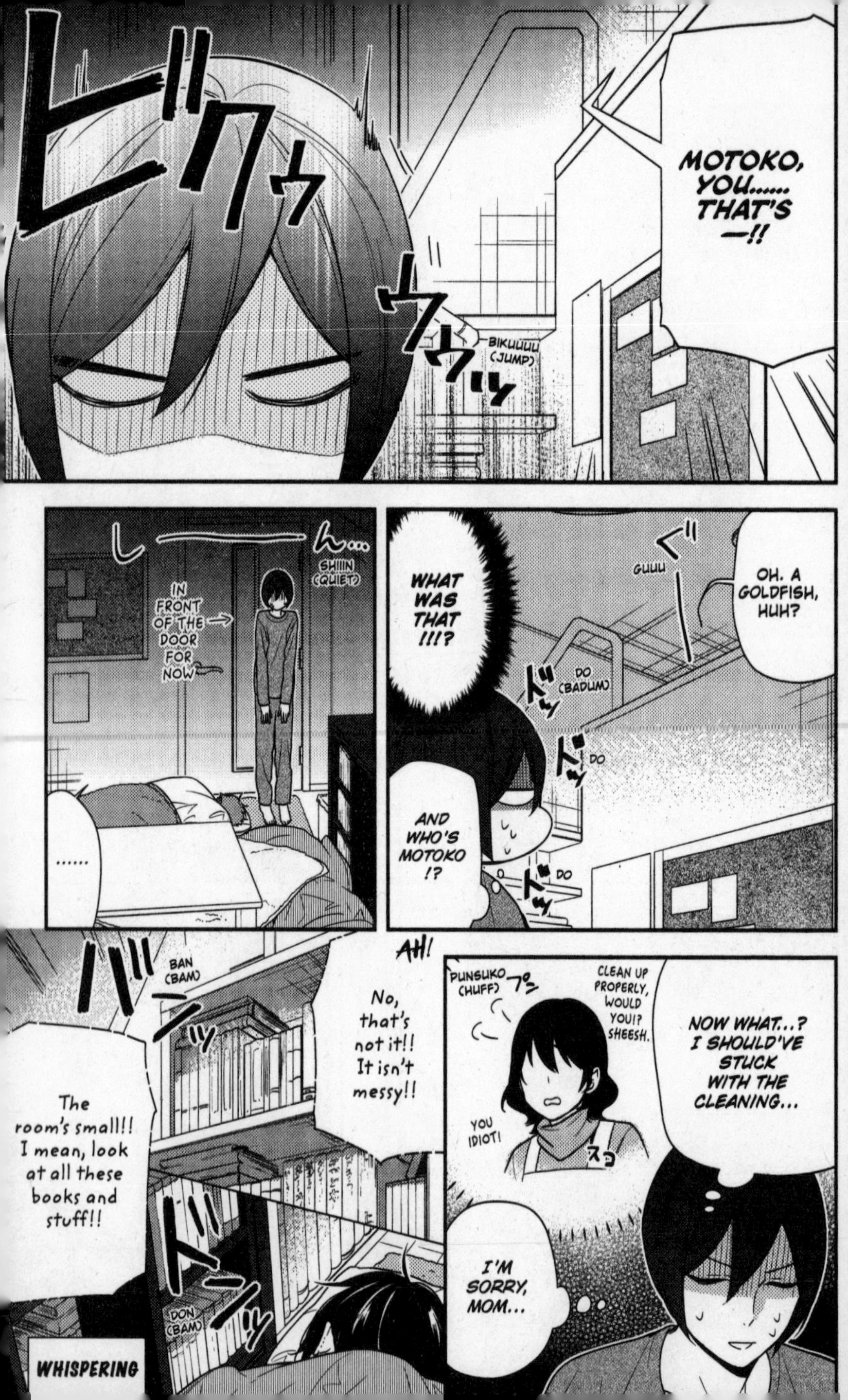

MOTOKO, YOU...... THAT'S —!!
BIKUUUU (JUMP)
OH. A GOLDFISH, HUH?
GUUU
WHAT WAS THAT!!!?
DO (BADUM)
DO
AND WHO'S MOTOKO!?
DO
SHIIN (QUIET)
IN FRONT OF THE DOOR FOR NOW
......
NOW WHAT...? I SHOULD'VE STUCK WITH THE CLEANING...
CLEAN UP PROPERLY, WOULD YOU!? SHEESH.
PUNSUKO (HUFF)
YOU IDIOT!
I'M SORRY, MOM...
AH!
BAN (BAM)
No, that's not it!! It isn't messy!!
The room's small!! I mean, look at all these books and stuff!!
DON (BAM)
WHISPERING

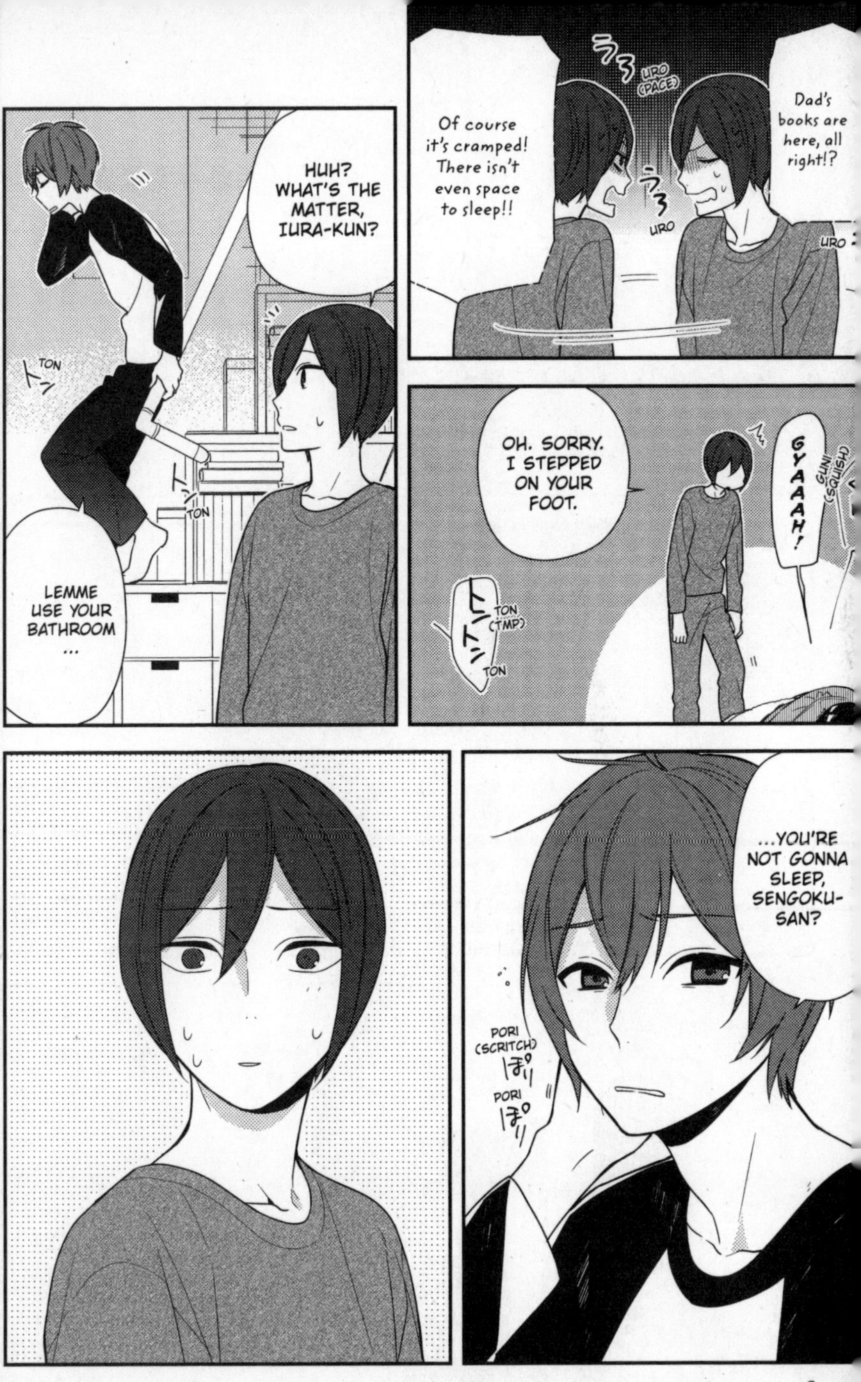
URO (PACE)
Dad's books are here, all right!?
URO
URO
Of course it's cramped! There isn't even space to sleep!!
GUNI (SQUISH)
GYAAAH!
OH. SORRY. I STEPPED ON YOUR FOOT.
TON (TMP)
TON
HUH? WHAT'S THE MATTER, IURA-KUN?
TON
TON
LEMME USE YOUR BATHROOM ...
...YOU'RE NOT GONNA SLEEP, SENGOKU-SAN?
PORI (SCRITCH)
PORI

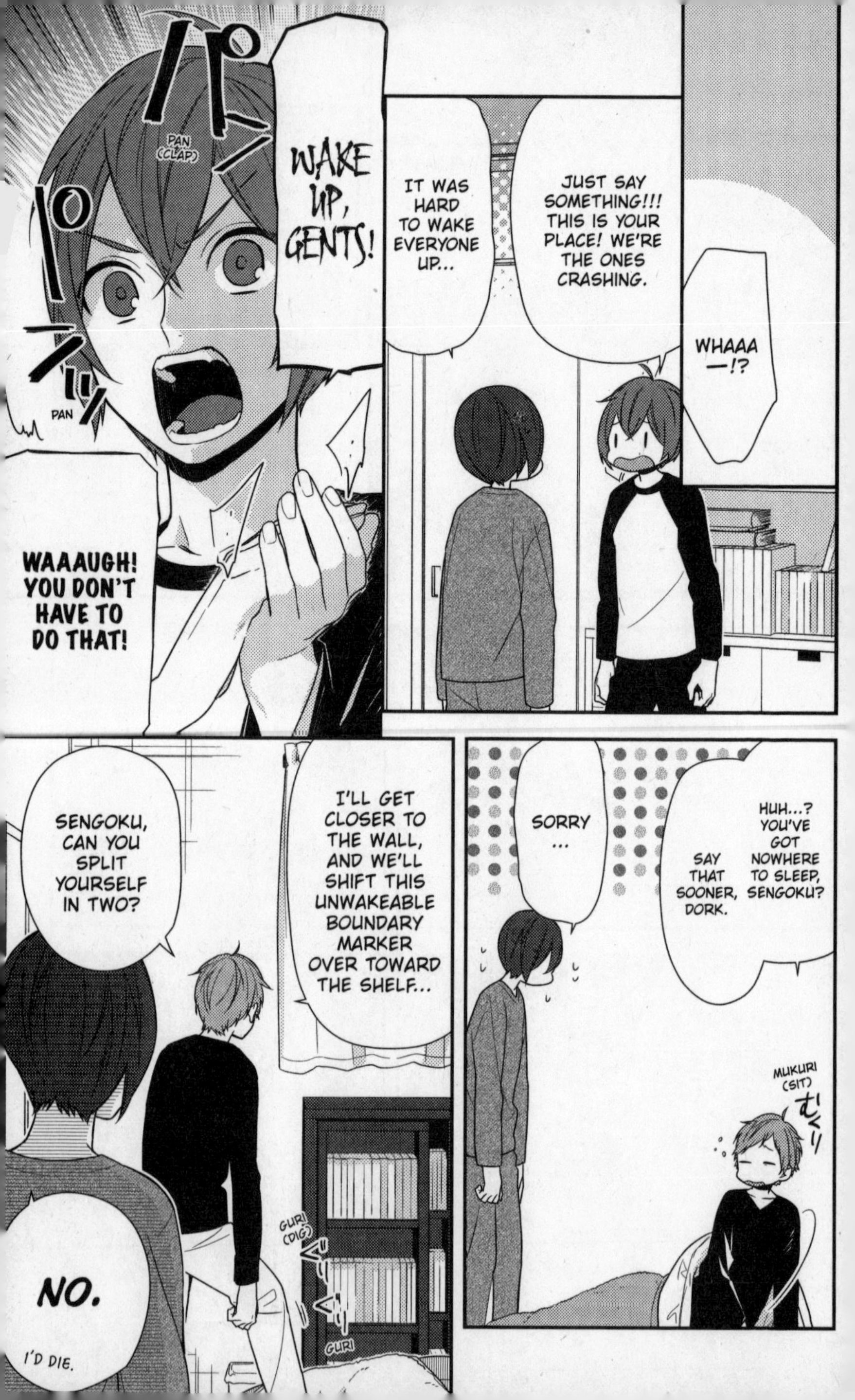
JUST SAY SOMETHING!!! THIS IS YOUR PLACE! WE'RE THE ONES CRASHING.
IT WAS HARD TO WAKE EVERYONE UP...
WHAAA—!?
WAKE UP, GENTS!
PAN (CLAP)
PAN
WAAAUGH! YOU DON'T HAVE TO DO THAT!
HUH...? YOU'VE GOT NOWHERE TO SLEEP, SENGOKU?
SAY THAT SOONER, DORK.
SORRY...
MUKURI (SIT)
I'LL GET CLOSER TO THE WALL, AND WE'LL SHIFT THIS UNWAKEABLE BOUNDARY MARKER OVER TOWARD THE SHELF...
SENGOKU, CAN YOU SPLIT YOURSELF IN TWO?
GURI (DIG)
GURI
NO.
I'D DIE.

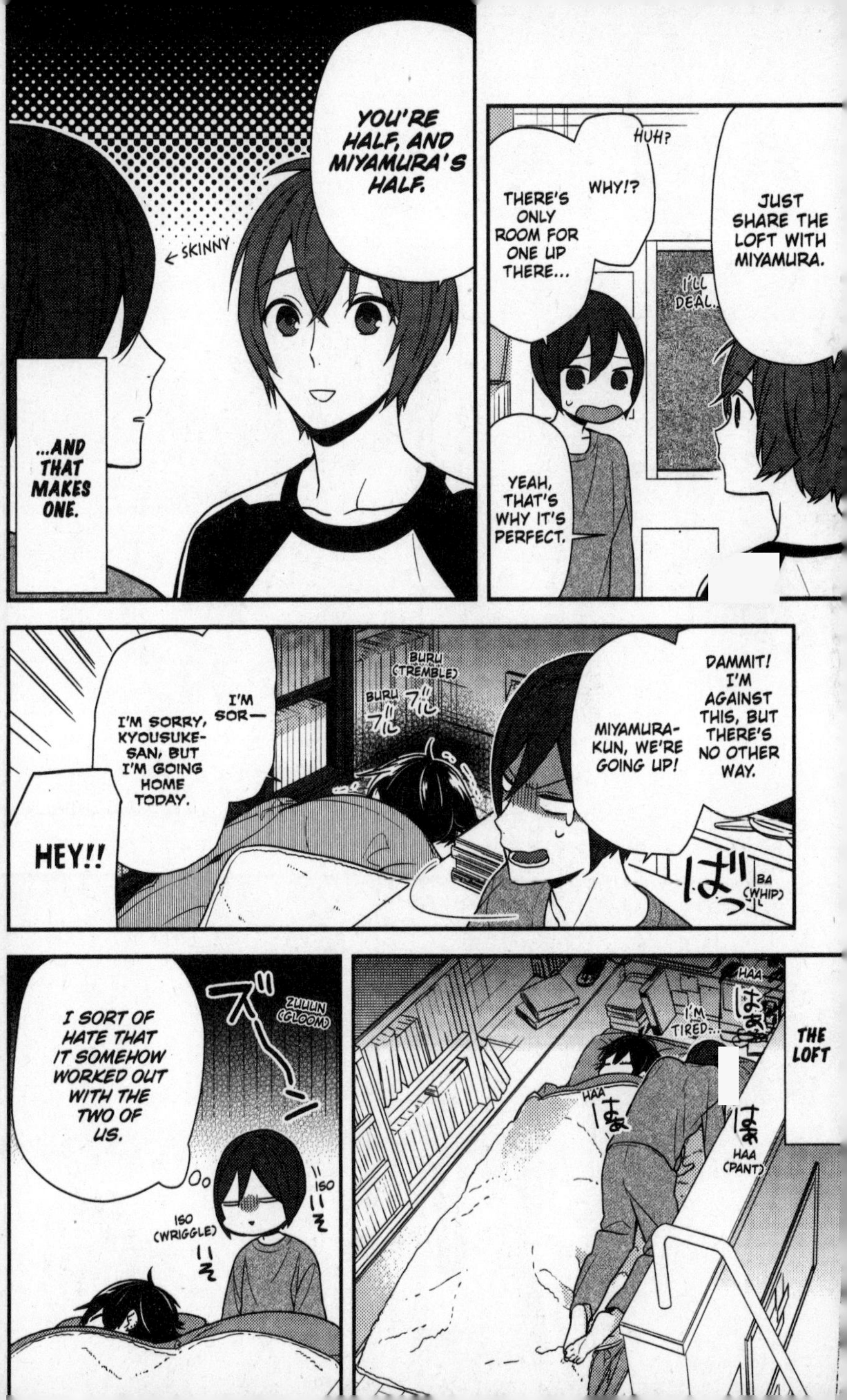
JUST SHARE THE LOFT WITH MIYAMURA.
HUH?
WHY!?
THERE'S ONLY ROOM FOR ONE UP THERE...
I'LL DEAL...
YEAH, THAT'S WHY IT'S PERFECT.
YOU'RE HALF, AND MIYAMURA'S HALF.
← SKINNY
...AND THAT MAKES ONE.
DAMMIT! I'M AGAINST THIS, BUT THERE'S NO OTHER WAY.
MIYAMURA-KUN, WE'RE GOING UP!
BA (WHIP)
BURU (TREMBLE)
BURU
I'M SOR—
I'M SORRY, KYOUSUKE-SAN, BUT I'M GOING HOME TODAY.
HEY!!
THE LOFT
HAA
I'M TIRED...
HAA
HAA (PANT)
ZUUUN (GLOOM)
I SORT OF HATE THAT IT SOMEHOW WORKED OUT WITH THE TWO OF US.
ISO
ISO (WRIGGLE)

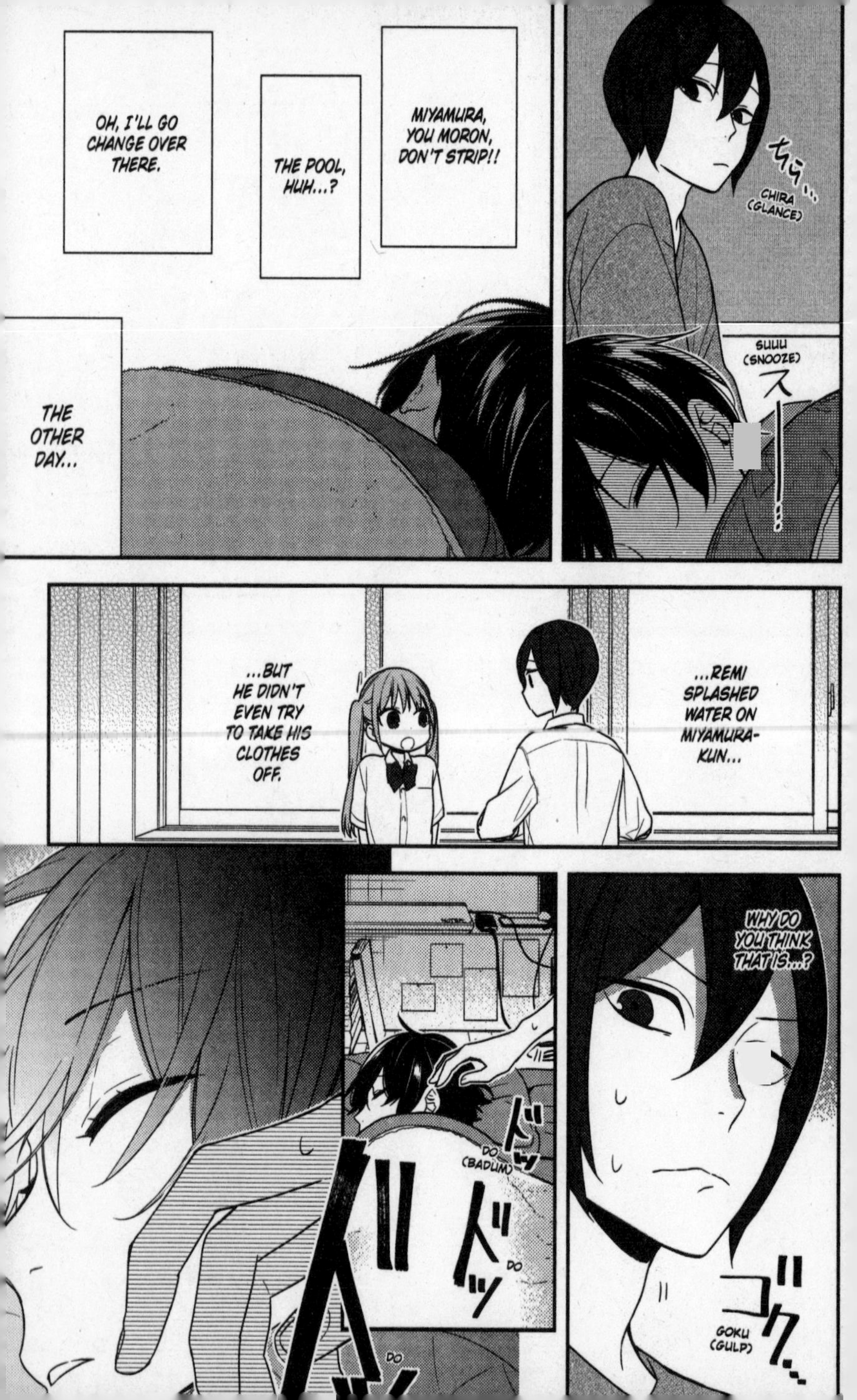
CHIRA (GLANCE)
MIYAMURA, YOU MORON, DON'T STRIP!!
THE POOL, HUH...?
OH, I'LL GO CHANGE OVER THERE.
SUUU (SNOOZE)
THE OTHER DAY...
...REMI SPLASHED WATER ON MIYAMURA-KUN...
...BUT HE DIDN'T EVEN TRY TO TAKE HIS CLOTHES OFF.
WHY DO YOU THINK THAT IS...?
GOKU (GULP)
DO (BADUM)
DO
DO

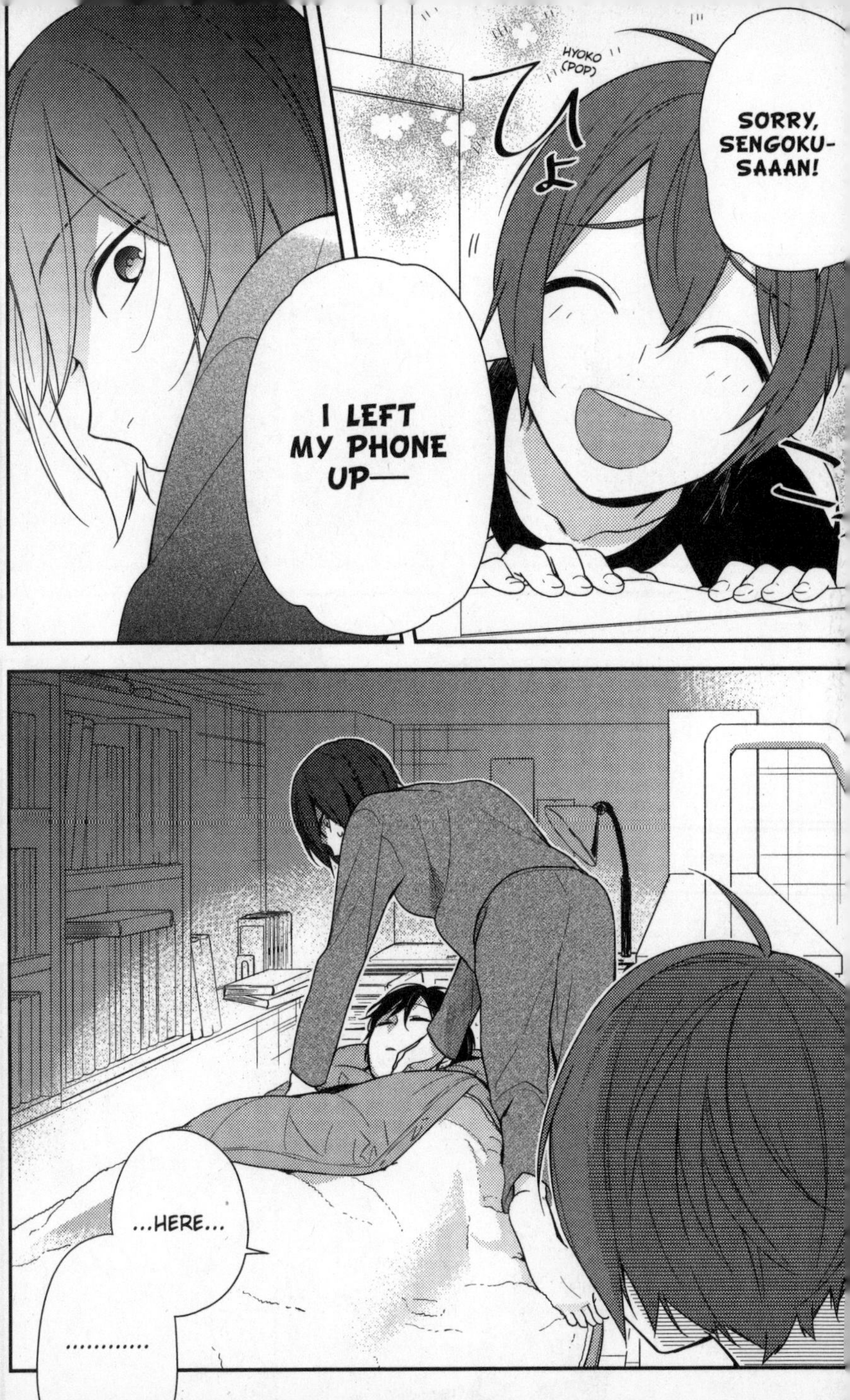
SORRY, SENGOKU-SAAAN!
HYOKO (POP)
I LEFT MY PHONE UP—
...HERE...
............

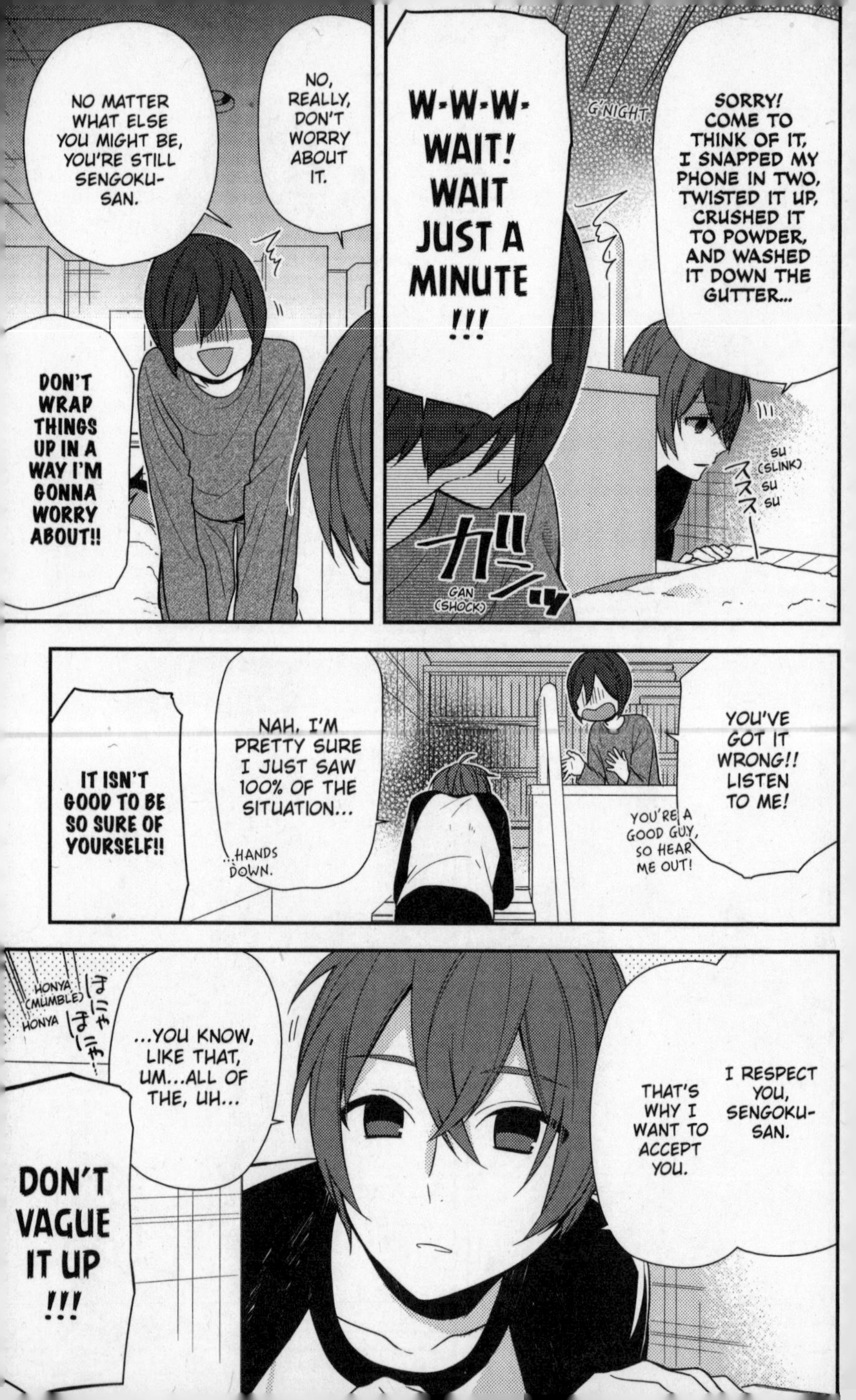
SORRY! COME TO THINK OF IT, I SNAPPED MY PHONE IN TWO, TWISTED IT UP, CRUSHED IT TO POWDER, AND WASHED IT DOWN THE GUTTER...
G'NIGHT.
W-W-W-WAIT! WAIT JUST A MINUTE!!!
SU (SLINK) SU SU
GAN (SHOCK)
NO, REALLY, DON'T WORRY ABOUT IT.
NO MATTER WHAT ELSE YOU MIGHT BE, YOU'RE STILL SENGOKU-SAN.
DON'T WRAP THINGS UP IN A WAY I'M GONNA WORRY ABOUT!!
YOU'VE GOT IT WRONG!! LISTEN TO ME!
YOU'RE A GOOD GUY, SO HEAR ME OUT!
NAH, I'M PRETTY SURE I JUST SAW 100% OF THE SITUATION...
...HANDS DOWN.
IT ISN'T GOOD TO BE SO SURE OF YOURSELF!!
I RESPECT YOU, SENGOKU-SAN.
THAT'S WHY I WANT TO ACCEPT YOU.
...YOU KNOW, LIKE THAT, UM...ALL OF THE, UH...
HONYA (MUMBLE) HONYA
DON'T VAGUE IT UP!!!

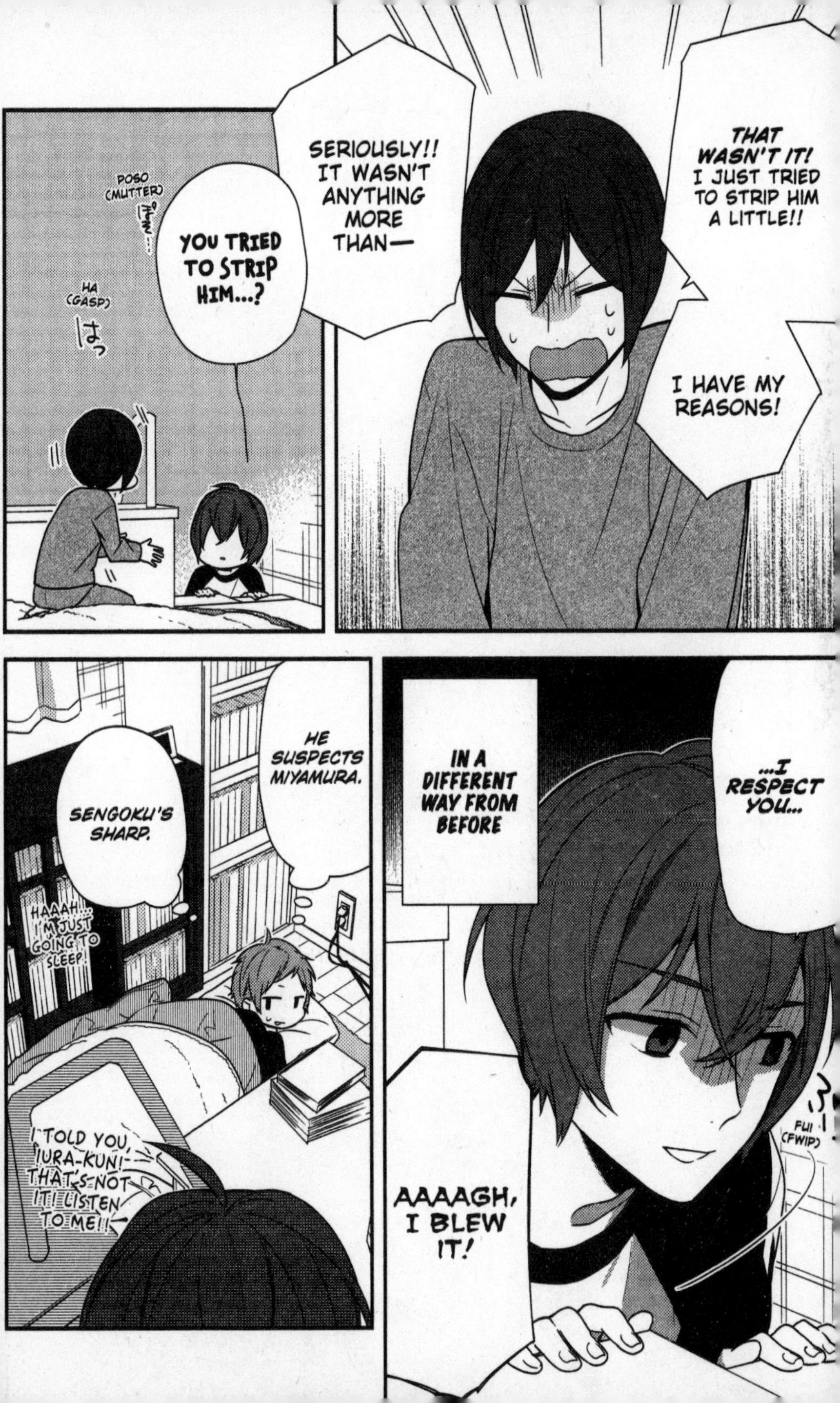
THAT WASN'T IT! I JUST TRIED TO STRIP HIM A LITTLE!!
SERIOUSLY!! IT WASN'T ANYTHING MORE THAN—
I HAVE MY REASONS!
POSO (MUTTER)
YOU TRIED TO STRIP HIM...?
HA (GASP)
はっ
...I RESPECT YOU...
IN A DIFFERENT WAY FROM BEFORE
FUI (FWIP)
AAAAGH, I BLEW IT!
HE SUSPECTS MIYAMURA.
SENGOKU'S SHARP.
HAAAH... I'M JUST GOING TO SLEEP!
I TOLD YOU, IURA-KUN! THAT'S NOT IT! LISTEN TO ME!!

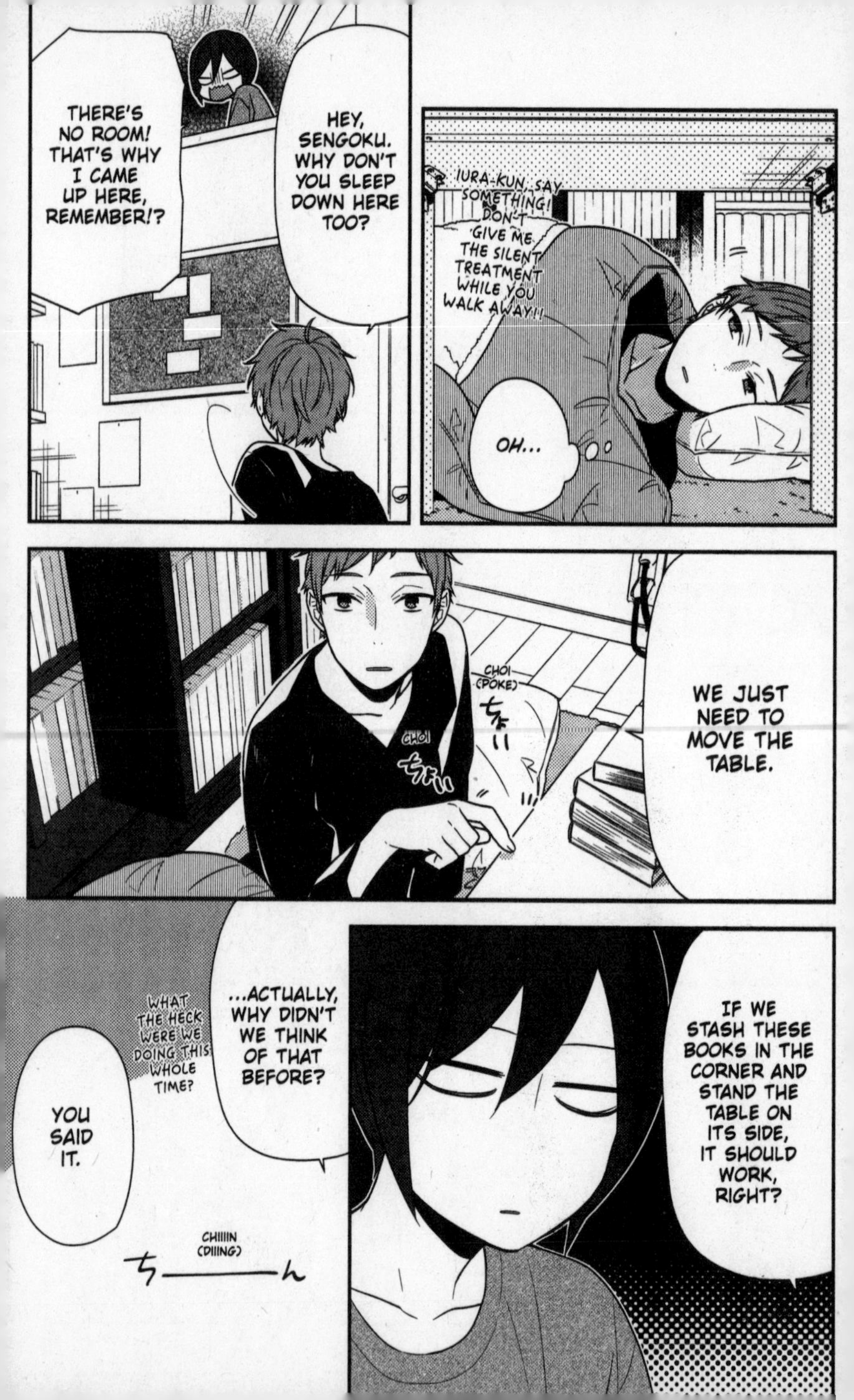
IURA-KUN, SAY SOMETHING! DON'T GIVE ME THE SILENT TREATMENT WHILE YOU WALK AWAY!!
OH...
HEY, SENGOKU. WHY DON'T YOU SLEEP DOWN HERE TOO?
THERE'S NO ROOM! THAT'S WHY I CAME UP HERE, REMEMBER!?
WE JUST NEED TO MOVE THE TABLE.
CHOI (POKE)
CHOI
IF WE STASH THESE BOOKS IN THE CORNER AND STAND THE TABLE ON ITS SIDE, IT SHOULD WORK, RIGHT?
...ACTUALLY, WHY DIDN'T WE THINK OF THAT BEFORE?
WHAT THE HECK WERE WE DOING THIS WHOLE TIME?
YOU SAID IT.
CHIIIN (DIIING)

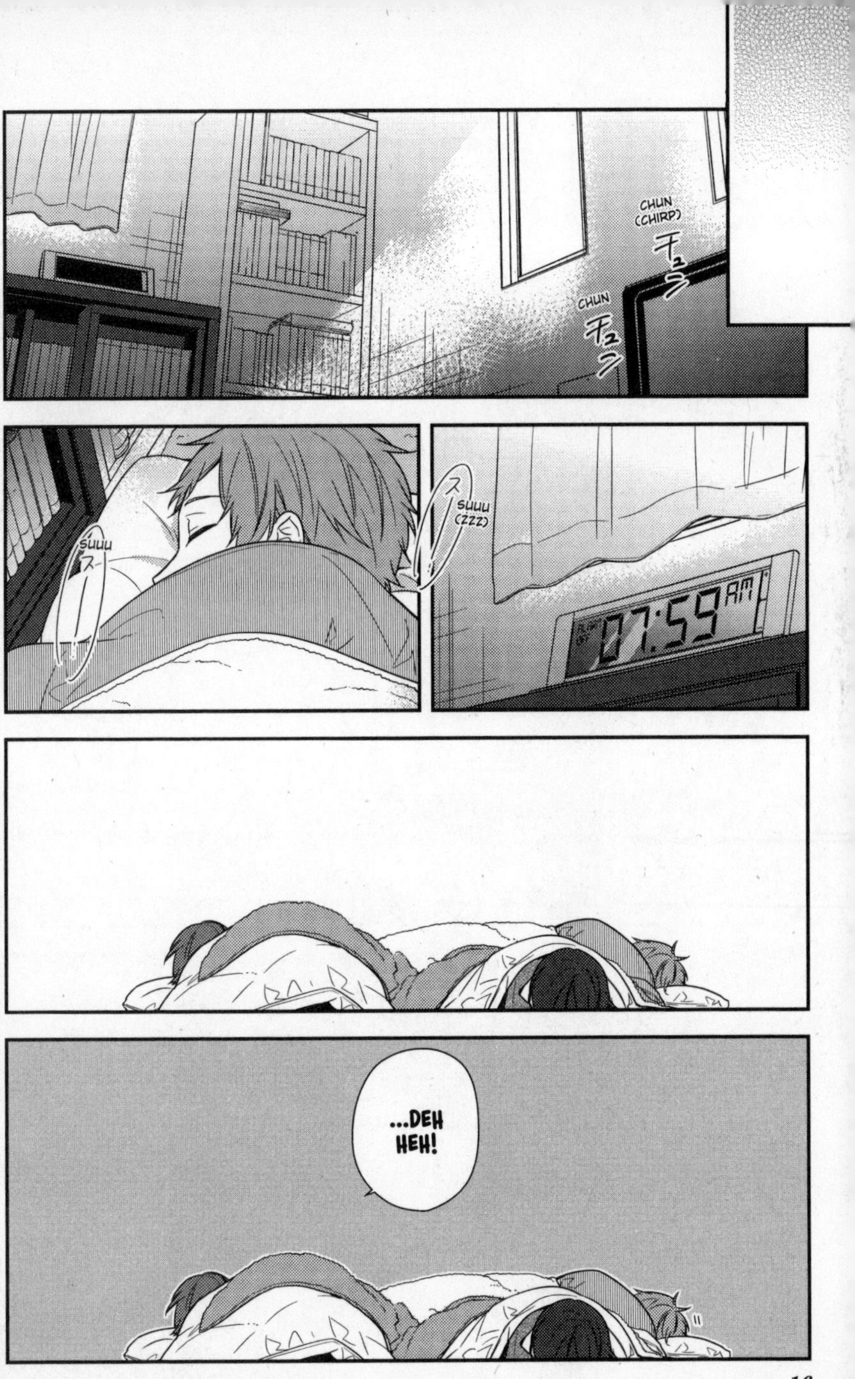
CHUN (CHIRP)
チュン
CHUN
チュン
07:59 AM
SUUU (ZZZ)
スー
SUUU
スー
...DEH HEH!

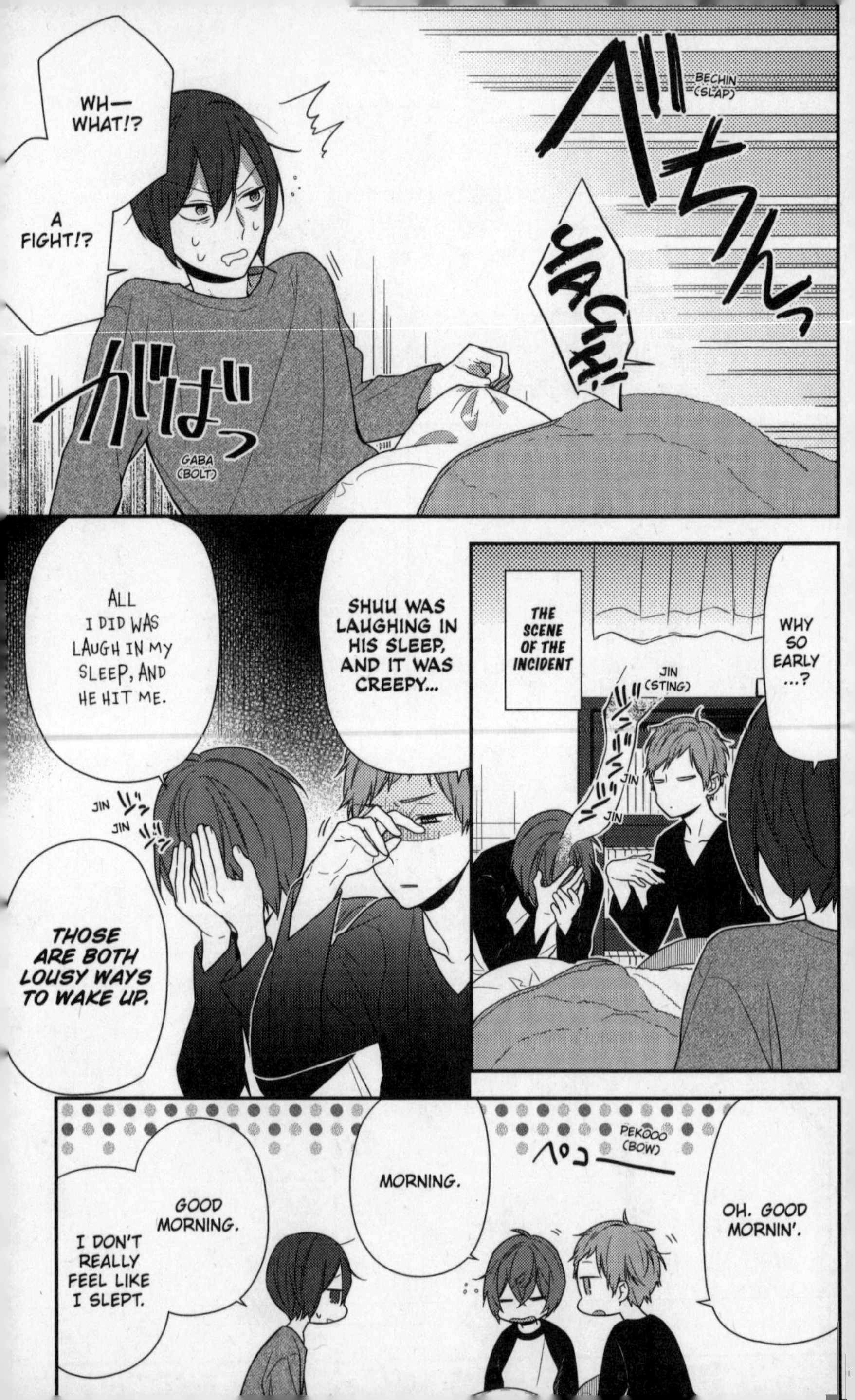
べちんっ
BECHIN (SLAP)
SMACK!
WH— WHAT!?
A FIGHT!?
がばっ
GABA (BOLT)
WHY SO EARLY ...?
THE SCENE OF THE INCIDENT
JIN (STING)
JIN
JIN
SHUU WAS LAUGHING IN HIS SLEEP, AND IT WAS CREEPY...
ALL I DID WAS LAUGH IN MY SLEEP, AND HE HIT ME.
JIN
JIN
THOSE ARE BOTH LOUSY WAYS TO WAKE UP.
OH. GOOD MORNIN'.
ぺこー
PEKOOO (BOW)
MORNING.
GOOD MORNING.
I DON'T REALLY FEEL LIKE I SLEPT.

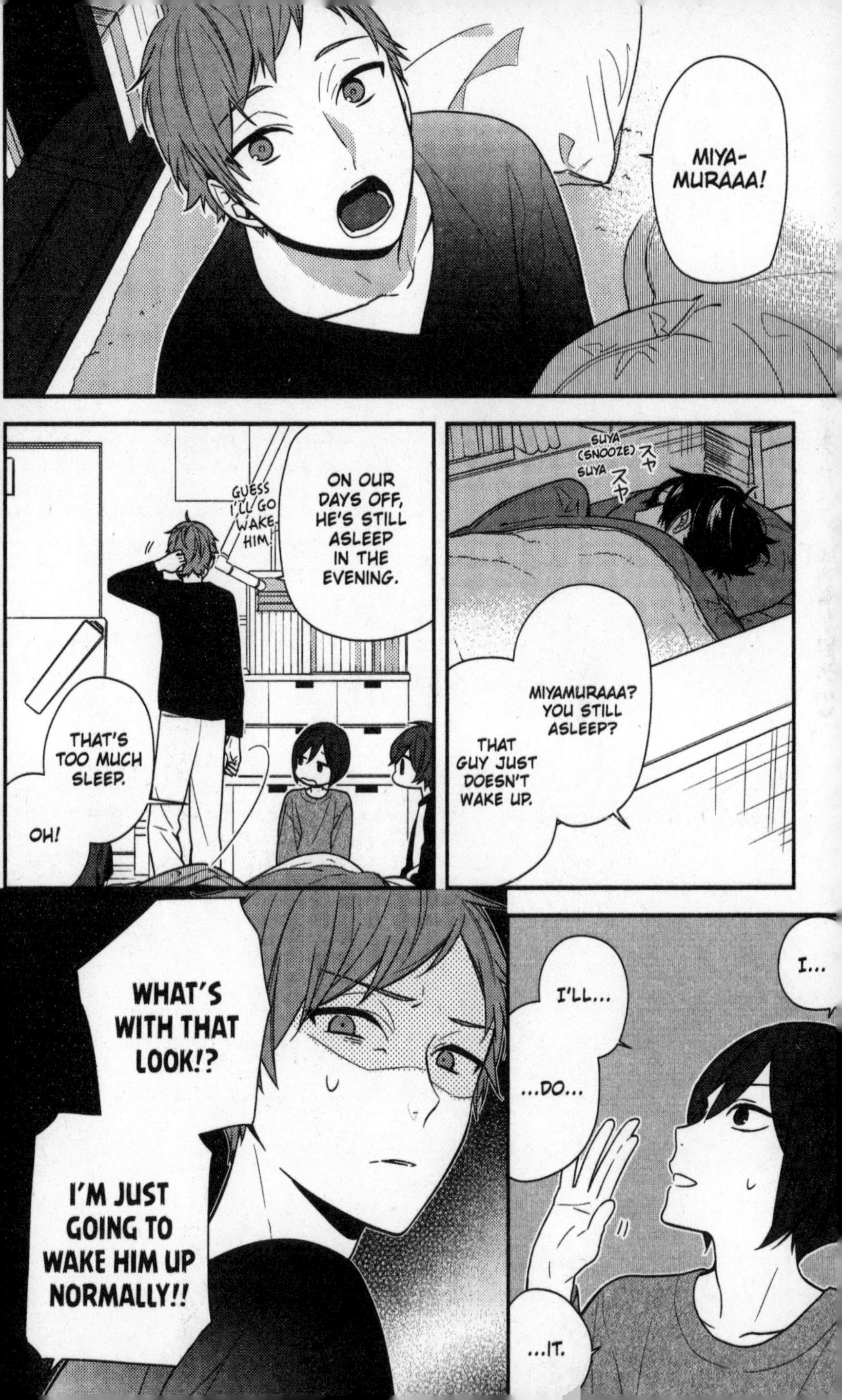
MIYA-MURAAA!
SUYA (SNOOZE) SUYA
スヤスヤ
MIYAMURAAA? YOU STILL ASLEEP?
THAT GUY JUST DOESN'T WAKE UP.
ON OUR DAYS OFF, HE'S STILL ASLEEP IN THE EVENING.
GUESS I'LL GO WAKE HIM!
THAT'S TOO MUCH SLEEP.
OH!
I...
I'LL...
...DO...
...IT.
WHAT'S WITH THAT LOOK!?
I'M JUST GOING TO WAKE HIM UP NORMALLY!!

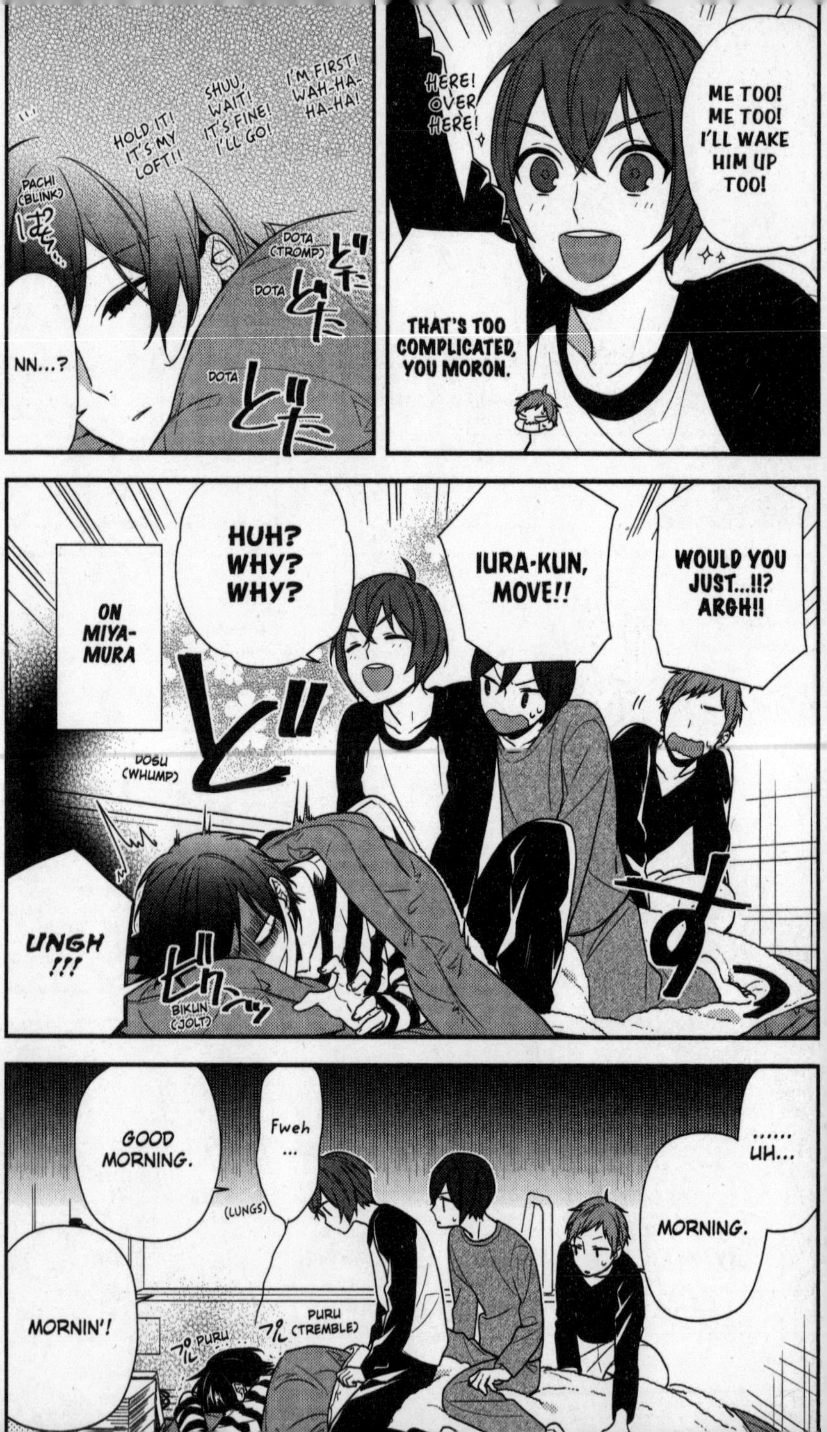
ME TOO! ME TOO! I'LL WAKE HIM UP TOO!
HERE! OVER HERE!
THAT'S TOO COMPLICATED, YOU MORON.
I'M FIRST! WAH-HA-HA-HA!
SHUU, WAIT! IT'S FINE! I'LL GO!
HOLD IT! IT'S MY LOFT!!
...
DOTA (TROMP)
DOTA
DOTA
PACHI (BLINK)
NN...?
WOULD YOU JUST...!!? ARGH!!
IURA-KUN, MOVE!!
HUH? WHY? WHY?
ON MIYAMURA
DOSU (WHUMP)
UNGH!!!
BIKUN (JOLT)
......UH...
MORNING.
Fweh...
(LUNGS)
GOOD MORNING.
PURU (TREMBLE)
PURU
MORNIN'!

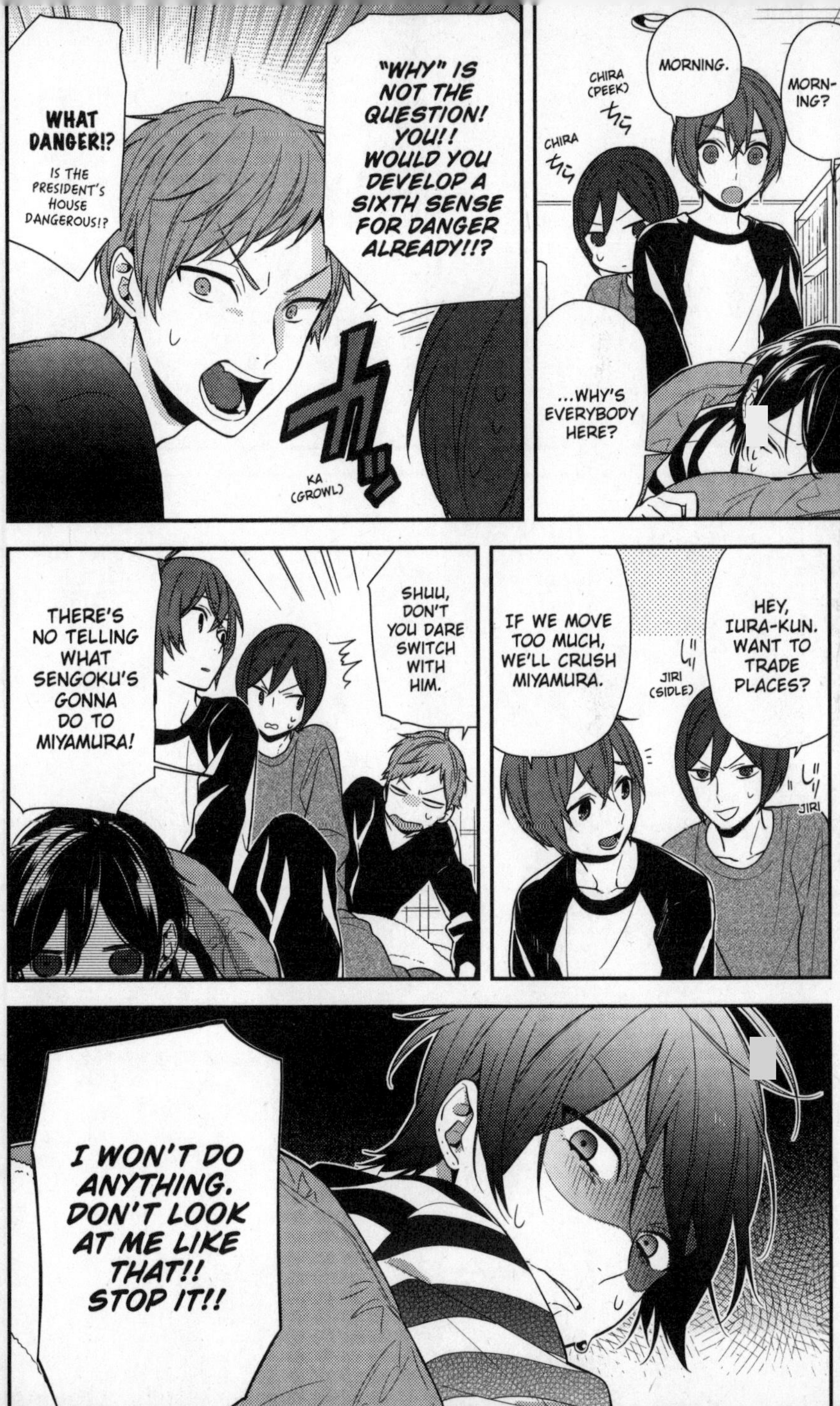

MORN-ING?
MORNING.
CHIRA (PEEK)
CHIRA
...WHY'S EVERYBODY HERE?
"WHY" IS NOT THE QUESTION! YOU!! WOULD YOU DEVELOP A SIXTH SENSE FOR DANGER ALREADY!!?
WHAT DANGER!?
IS THE PRESIDENT'S HOUSE DANGEROUS!?
KA (GROWL)
HEY, IURA-KUN. WANT TO TRADE PLACES?
JIRI (SIDLE)
IF WE MOVE TOO MUCH, WE'LL CRUSH MIYAMURA.
JIRI
SHUU, DON'T YOU DARE SWITCH WITH HIM.
THERE'S NO TELLING WHAT SENGOKU'S GONNA DO TO MIYAMURA!
I WON'T DO ANYTHING. DON'T LOOK AT ME LIKE THAT!! STOP IT!!

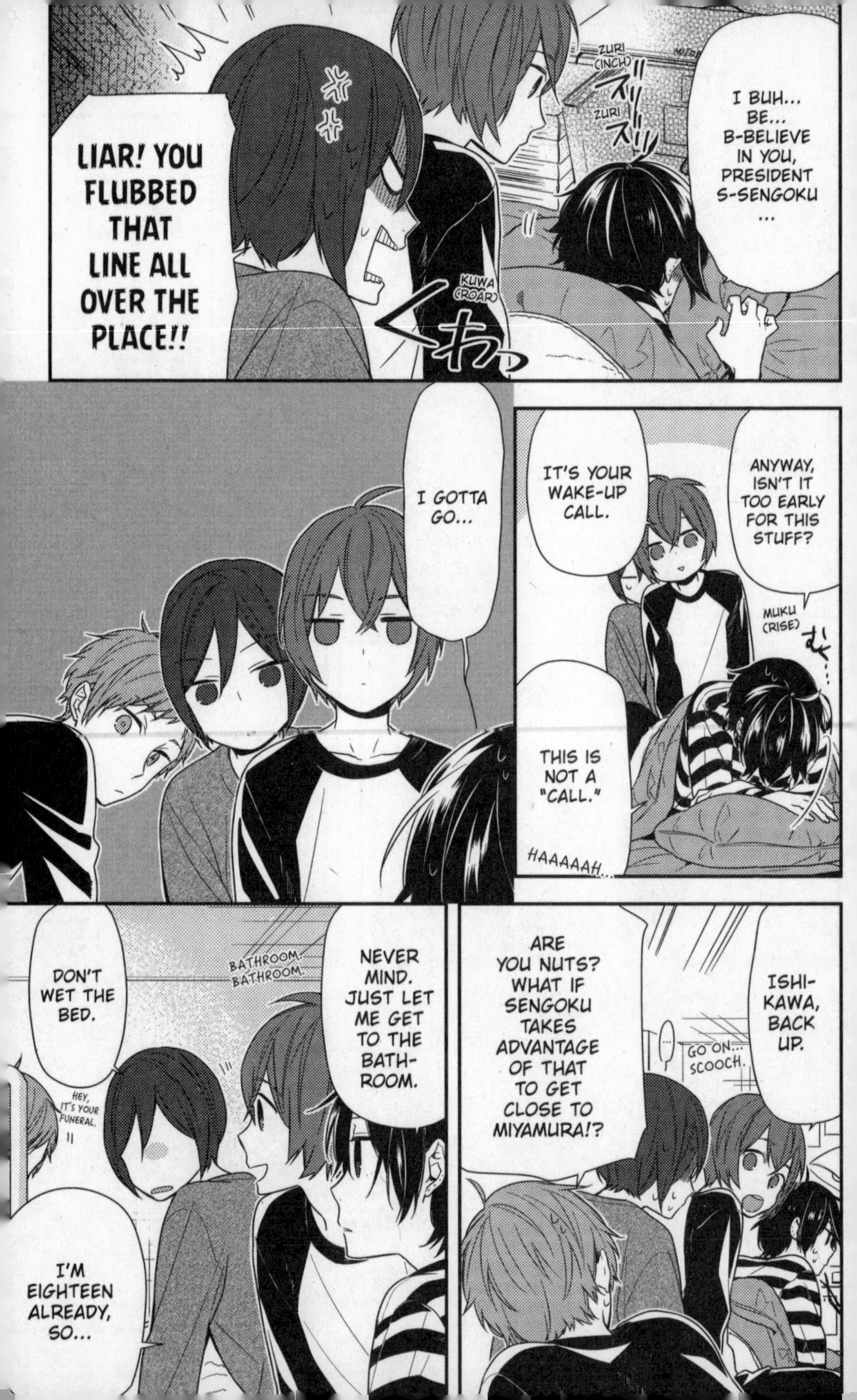
I BUH... BE... B-BELIEVE IN YOU, PRESIDENT S-SENGOKU ...
ZURI (INCH)
ZURI
LIAR! YOU FLUBBED THAT LINE ALL OVER THE PLACE!!
KUWA (ROAR)
ANYWAY, ISN'T IT TOO EARLY FOR THIS STUFF?
IT'S YOUR WAKE-UP CALL.
MUKU (RISE)
THIS IS NOT A "CALL."
HAAAAAH...
I GOTTA GO...
ISHI-KAWA, BACK UP.
ARE YOU NUTS? WHAT IF SENGOKU TAKES ADVANTAGE OF THAT TO GET CLOSE TO MIYAMURA!?
...
GO ON... SCOOCH.
NEVER MIND. JUST LET ME GET TO THE BATH-ROOM.
BATHROOM. BATHROOM.
DON'T WET THE BED.
HEY, IT'S YOUR FUNERAL.
I'M EIGHTEEN ALREADY, SO...

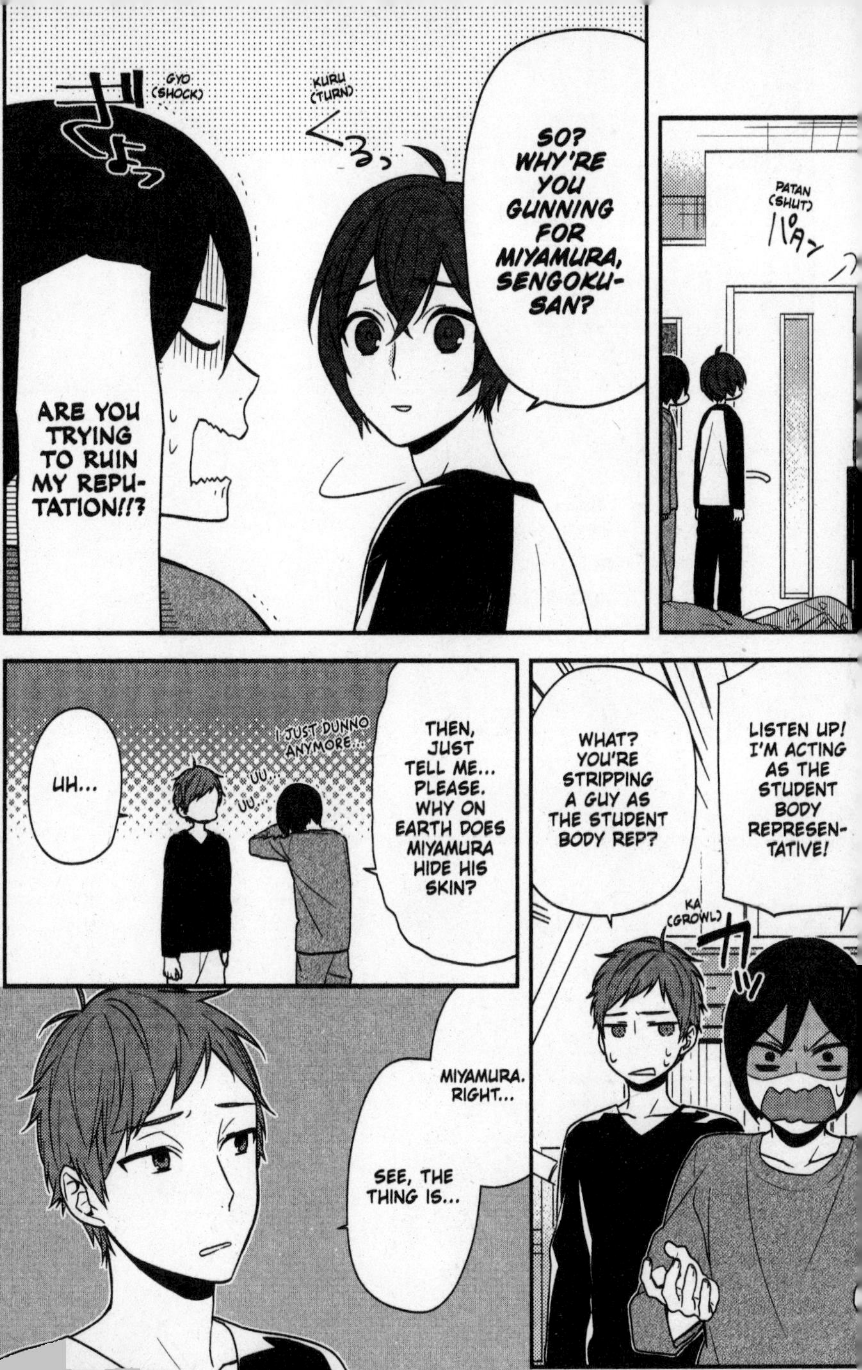
PATAN (SHUT)
SO? WHY'RE YOU GUNNING FOR MIYAMURA, SENGOKU-SAN?
KURU (TURN)
GYO (SHOCK)
ARE YOU TRYING TO RUIN MY REPUTATION!!?
LISTEN UP! I'M ACTING AS THE STUDENT BODY REPRESENTATIVE!
WHAT? YOU'RE STRIPPING A GUY AS THE STUDENT BODY REP?
KA (GROWL)
THEN, JUST TELL ME... PLEASE. WHY ON EARTH DOES MIYAMURA HIDE HIS SKIN?
I JUST DUNNO ANYMORE...
UU... UU...
UH...
MIYAMURA. RIGHT...
SEE, THE THING IS...

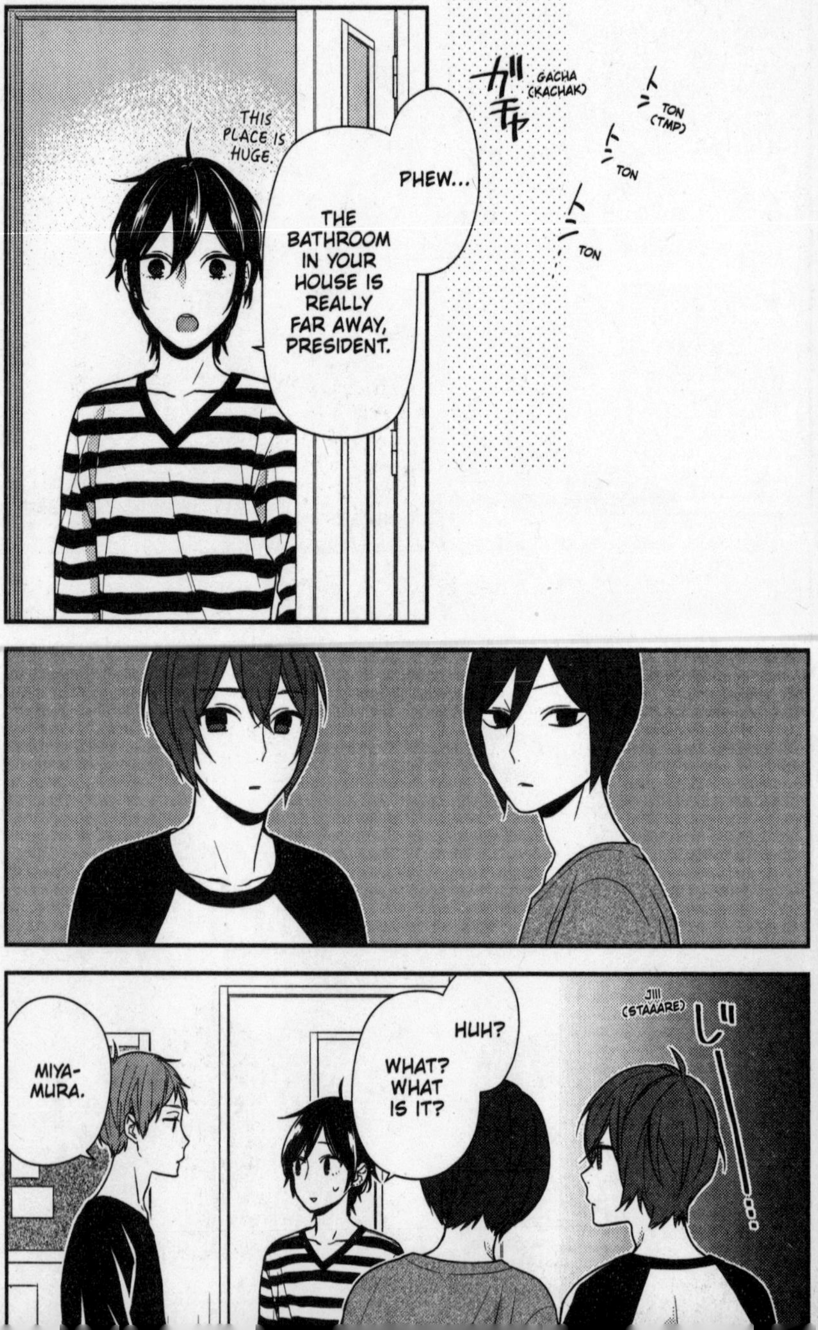

トン
TON (TMP)
トン
TON
トン
TON
ガチャ
GACHA (KACHAK)
PHEW...
THE BATHROOM IN YOUR HOUSE IS REALLY FAR AWAY, PRESIDENT.
THIS PLACE IS HUGE.
JIII (STAAARE)
じーー…
HUH?
WHAT? WHAT IS IT?
MIYA-MURA.

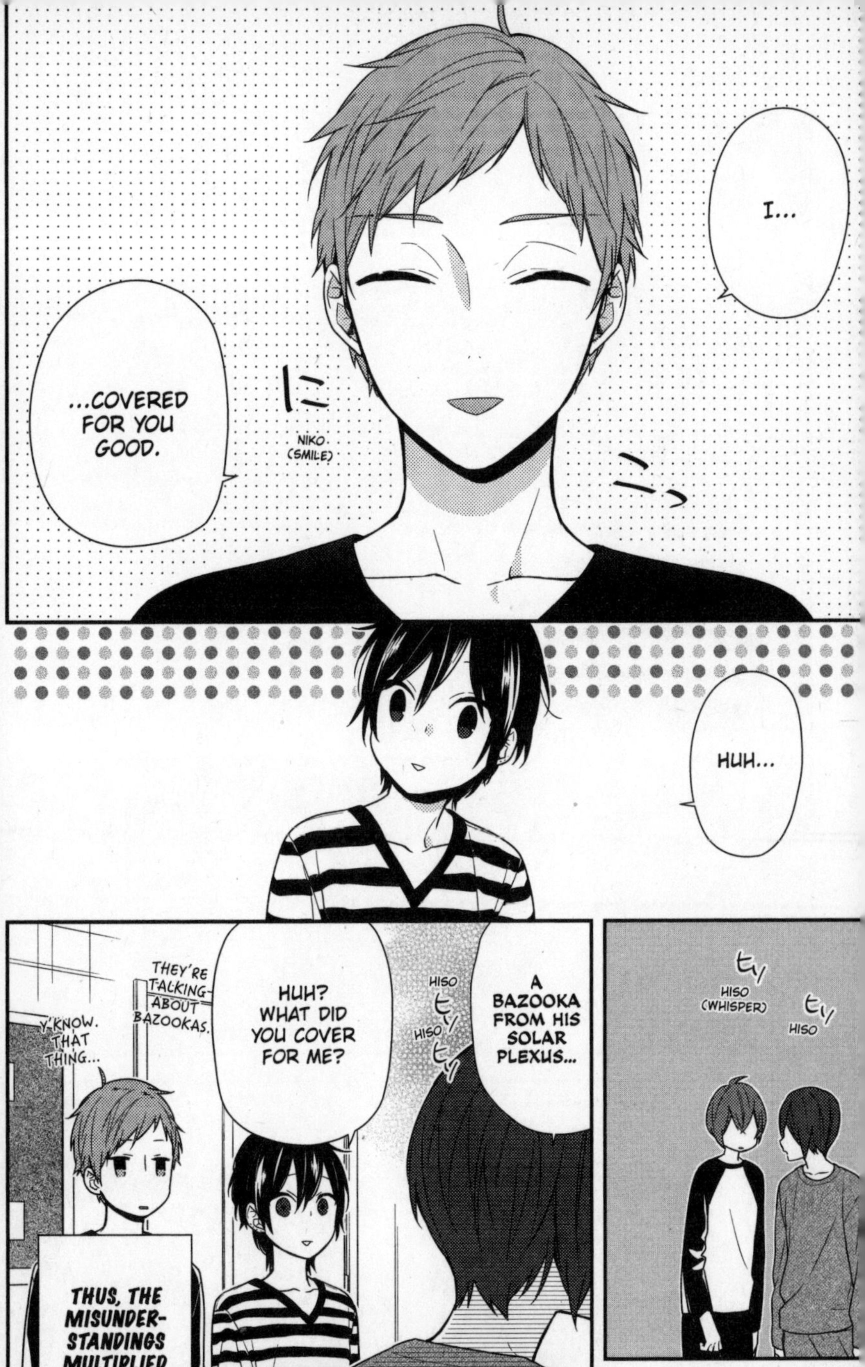
I...
...COVERED FOR YOU GOOD.
NIKO (SMILE)
HUH...
HISO (WHISPER)
HISO
A BAZOOKA FROM HIS SOLAR PLEXUS...
HISO
HISO
HUH? WHAT DID YOU COVER FOR ME?
THEY'RE TALKING ABOUT BAZOOKAS.
Y'KNOW. THAT THING...
THUS, THE MISUNDER-STANDINGS MULTIPLIED.

HORIMIYA

HORIMIYA

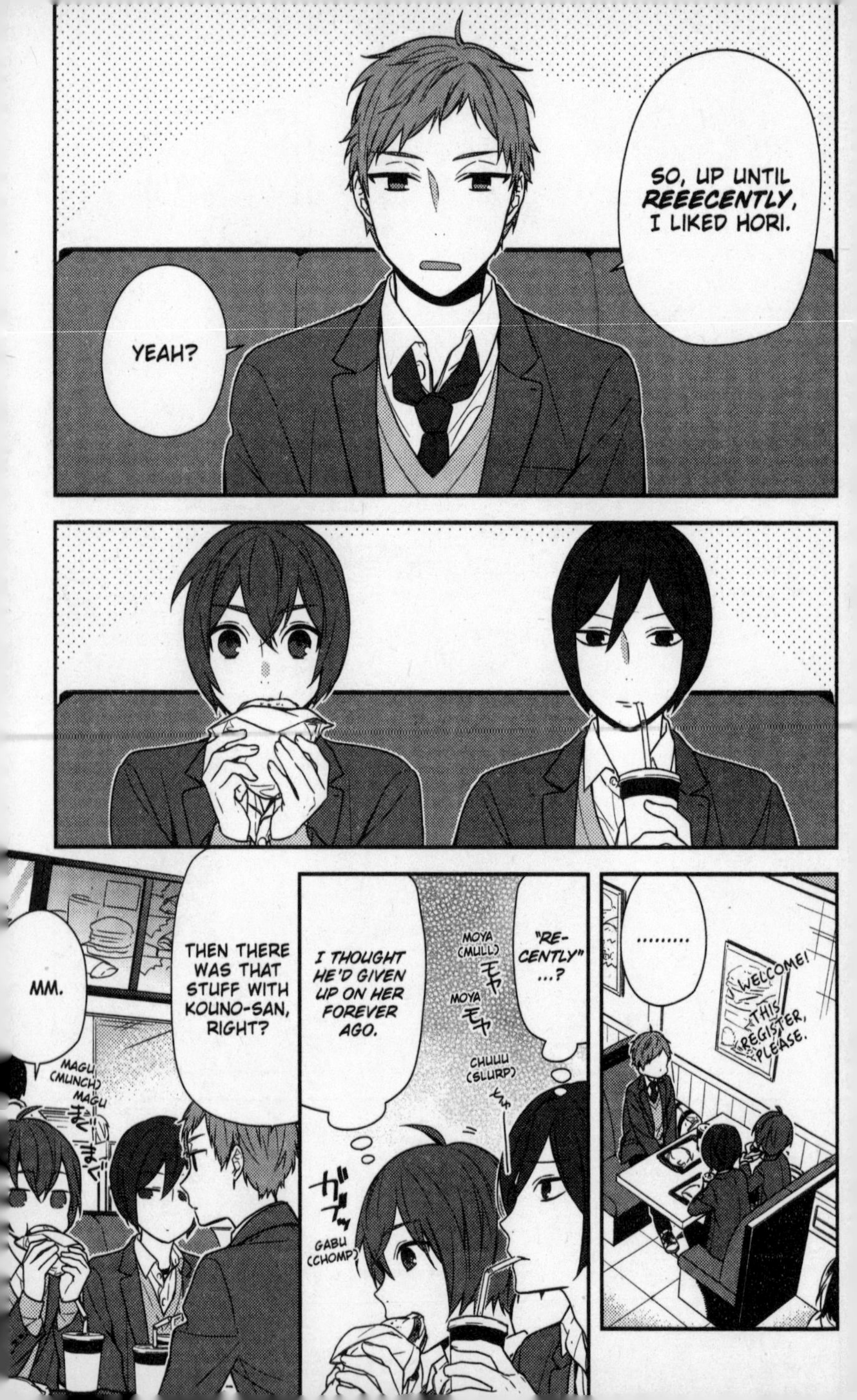
SO, UP UNTIL REEECENTLY, I LIKED HORI.
YEAH?
WELCOME! THIS REGISTER, PLEASE.
.........
"RE-CENTLY" ...?
MOYA (MULL) モヤ
MOYA モヤ
CHUUU (SLURP)
I THOUGHT HE'D GIVEN UP ON HER FOREVER AGO.
ガブッ GABU (CHOMP)
THEN THERE WAS THAT STUFF WITH KOUNO-SAN, RIGHT?
MM.
MAGU (MUNCH) MAGU まぐ まぐ

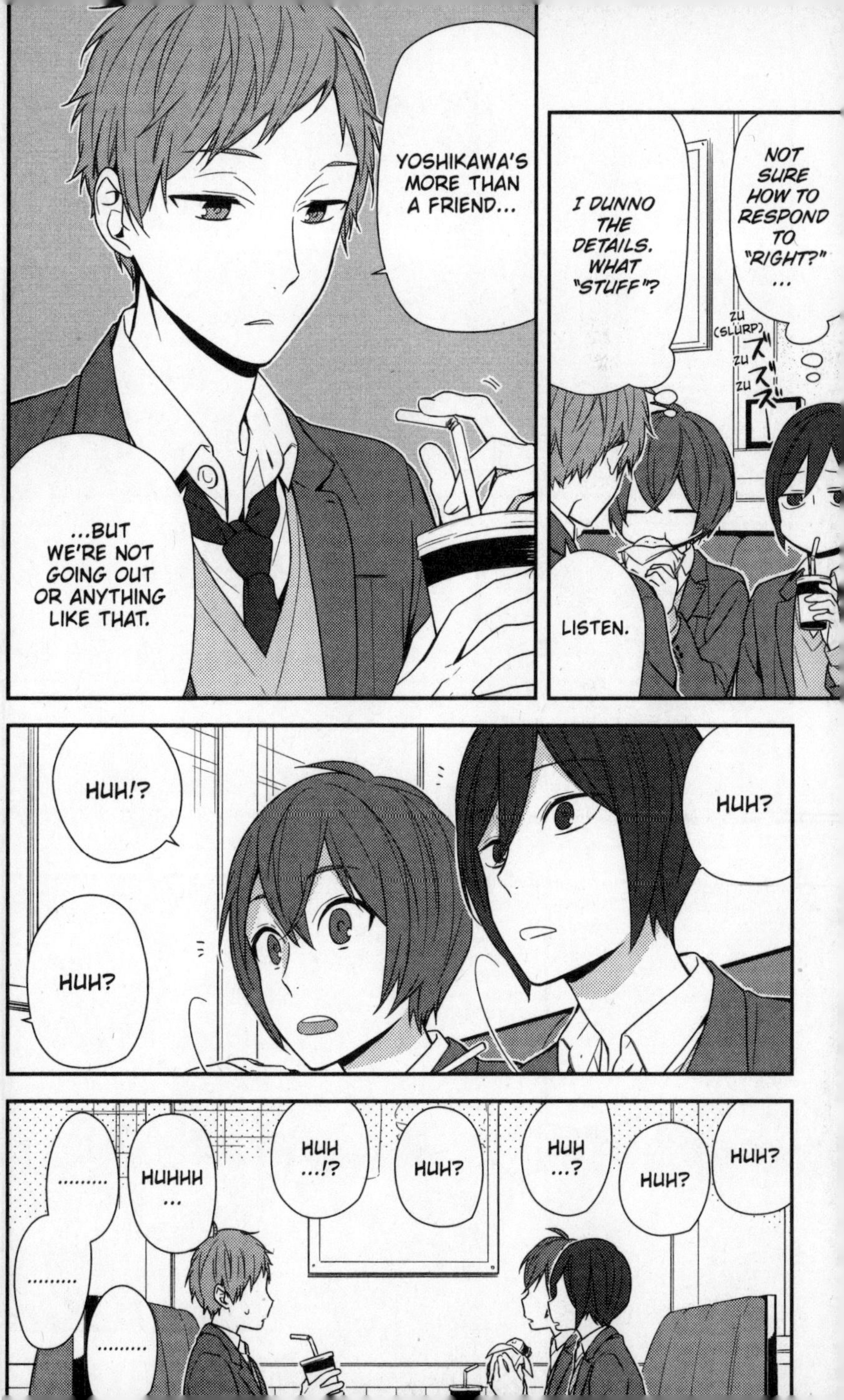
NOT SURE HOW TO RESPOND TO "RIGHT?" ...
ZU (SLURP) ZU ZU
I DUNNO THE DETAILS. WHAT "STUFF"?
LISTEN.
YOSHIKAWA'S MORE THAN A FRIEND...
...BUT WE'RE NOT GOING OUT OR ANYTHING LIKE THAT.
HUH?
HUH!?
HUH?
HUH?
HUH?
HUH ...?
HUH?
HUH ...!?
HUHHH ...
.........
.........
.........

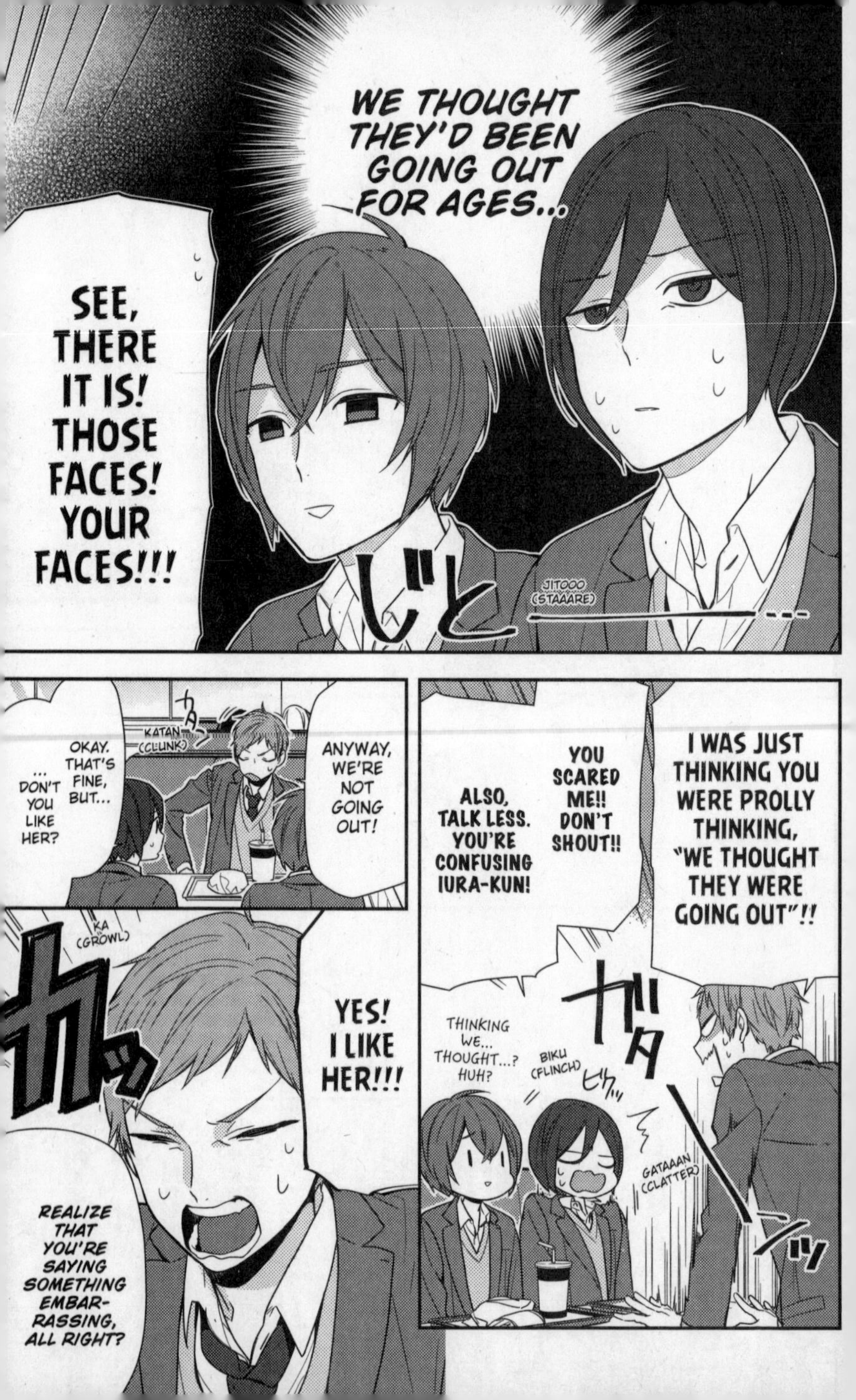
WE THOUGHT THEY'D BEEN GOING OUT FOR AGES...
SEE, THERE IT IS! THOSE FACES! YOUR FACES!!!
JITOOO (STAAARE)
I WAS JUST THINKING YOU WERE PROLLY THINKING, "WE THOUGHT THEY WERE GOING OUT"!!
YOU SCARED ME!! DON'T SHOUT!!
ALSO, TALK LESS. YOU'RE CONFUSING IURA-KUN!
GATAAAN (CLATTER)
BIKU (FLINCH)
THINKING WE... THOUGHT...? HUH?
ANYWAY, WE'RE NOT GOING OUT!
KATAN (CLUNK)
OKAY. THAT'S FINE, BUT...
... DON'T YOU LIKE HER?
KA (GROWL)
YES! I LIKE HER!!!
REALIZE THAT YOU'RE SAYING SOMETHING EMBARRASSING, ALL RIGHT?

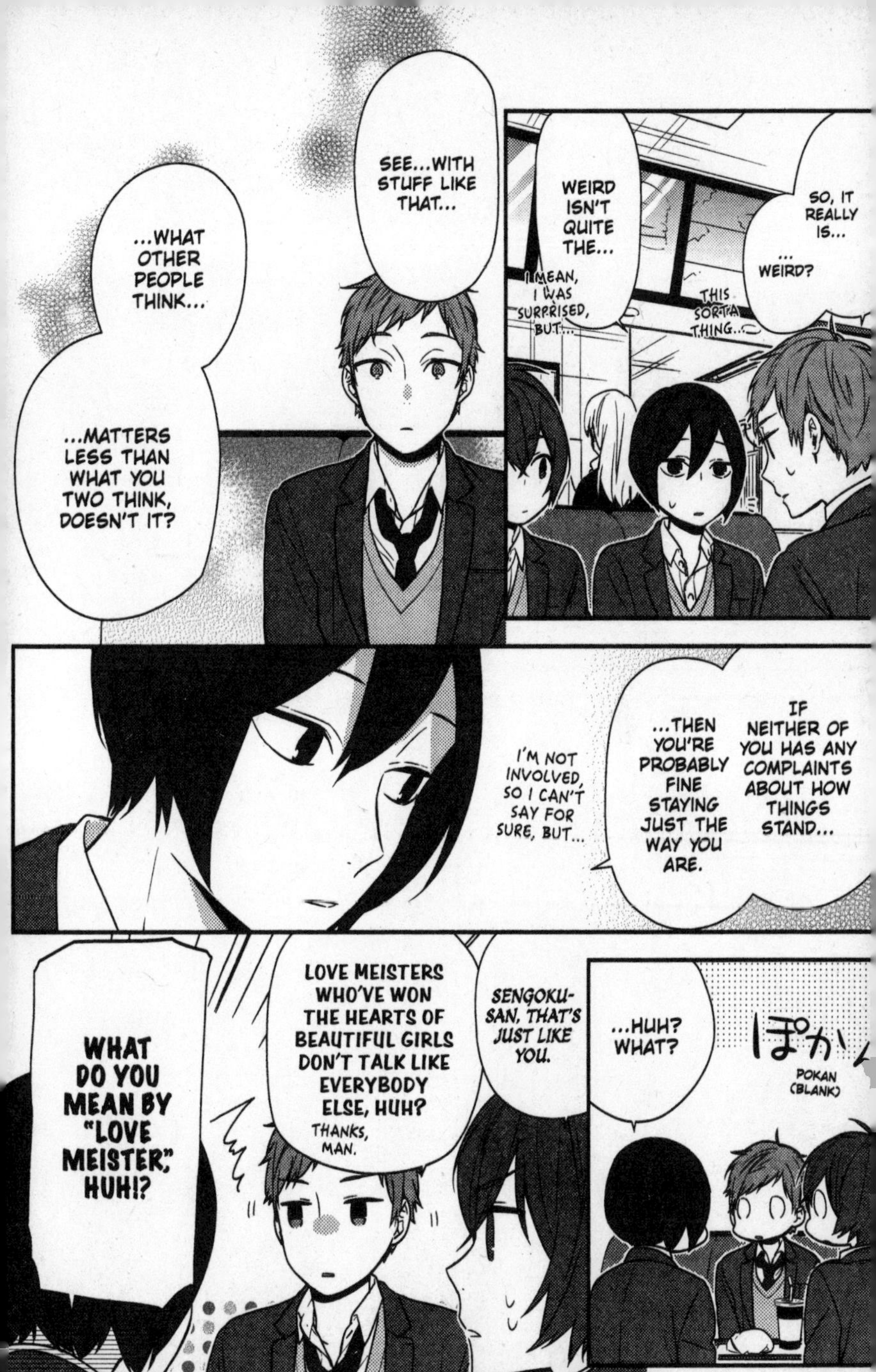
SO, IT REALLY IS... ...WEIRD?
THIS SORTA THING...
WEIRD ISN'T QUITE THE...
I MEAN, I WAS SURPRISED, BUT...
SEE...WITH STUFF LIKE THAT...
...WHAT OTHER PEOPLE THINK...
...MATTERS LESS THAN WHAT YOU TWO THINK, DOESN'T IT?
IF NEITHER OF YOU HAS ANY COMPLAINTS ABOUT HOW THINGS STAND...
...THEN YOU'RE PROBABLY FINE STAYING JUST THE WAY YOU ARE.
I'M NOT INVOLVED, SO I CAN'T SAY FOR SURE, BUT...
ぽかん
POKAN (BLANK)
...HUH? WHAT?
SENGOKU-SAN, THAT'S JUST LIKE YOU.
LOVE MEISTERS WHO'VE WON THE HEARTS OF BEAUTIFUL GIRLS DON'T TALK LIKE EVERYBODY ELSE, HUH?
THANKS, MAN.
WHAT DO YOU MEAN BY "LOVE MEISTER," HUH!?

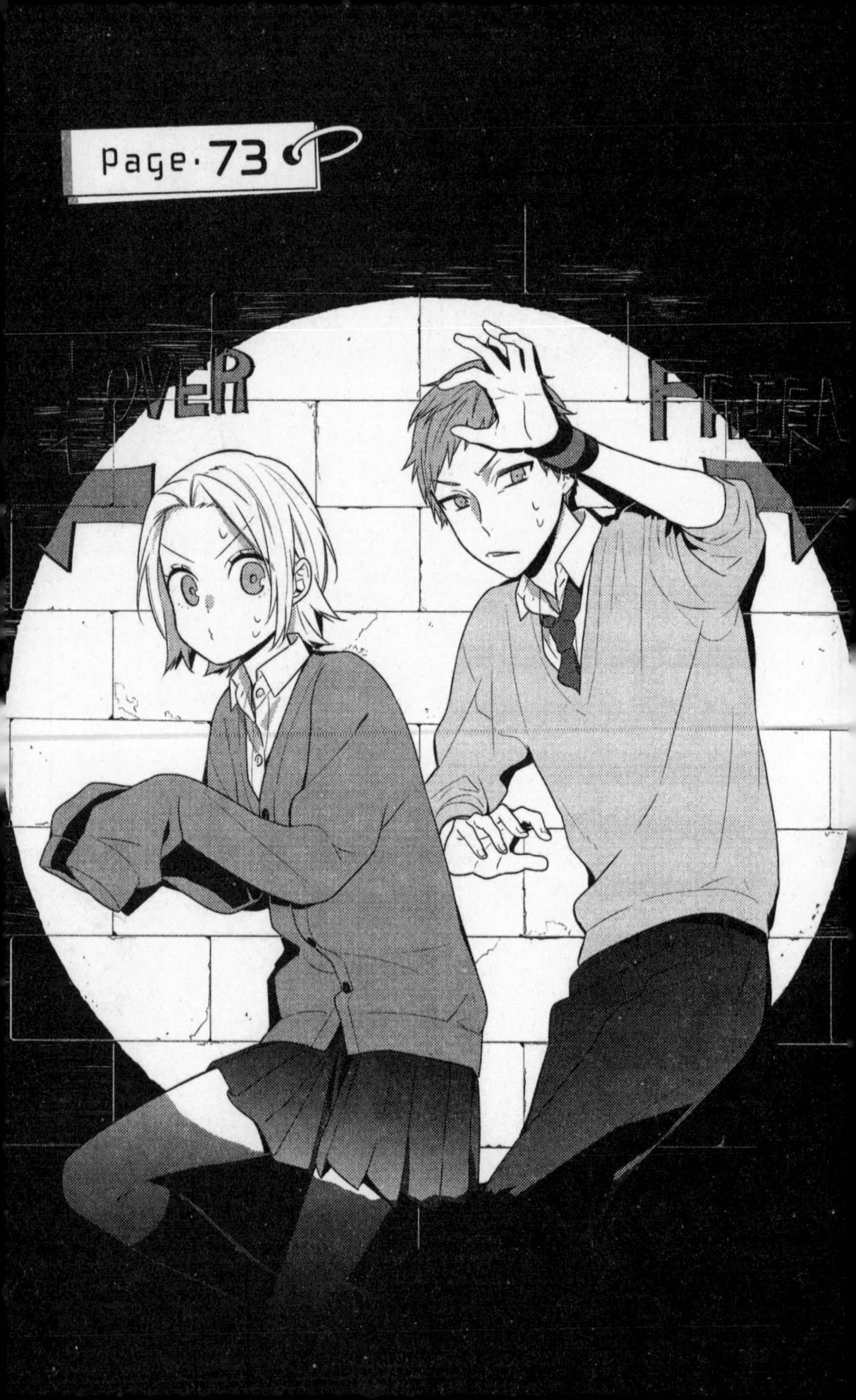
Page·73

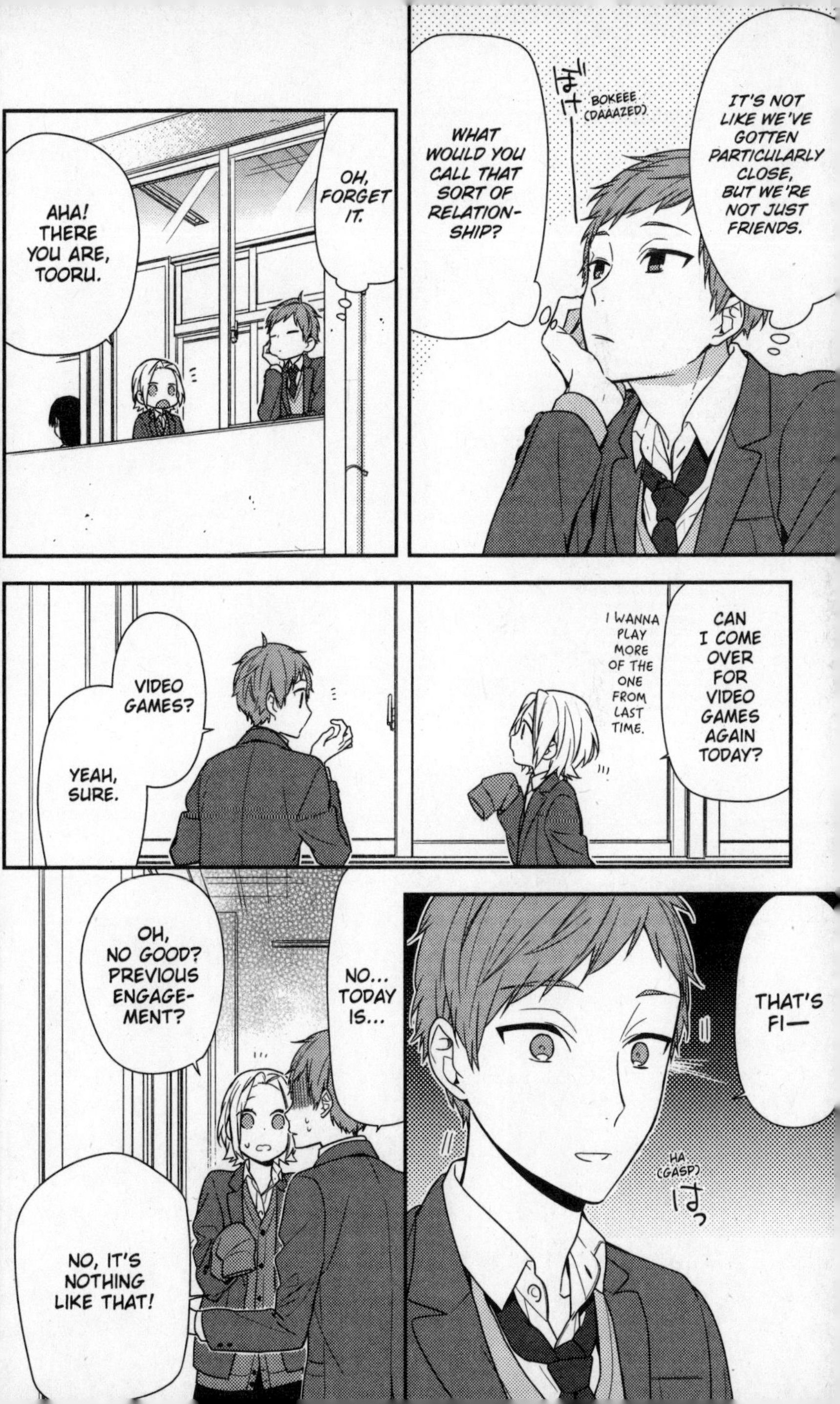
IT'S NOT LIKE WE'VE GOTTEN PARTICULARLY CLOSE, BUT WE'RE NOT JUST FRIENDS.
BOKEEE (DAAAZED)
WHAT WOULD YOU CALL THAT SORT OF RELATION-SHIP?
OH, FORGET IT.
AHA! THERE YOU ARE, TOORU.
CAN I COME OVER FOR VIDEO GAMES AGAIN TODAY?
I WANNA PLAY MORE OF THE ONE FROM LAST TIME.
VIDEO GAMES?
YEAH, SURE.
THAT'S FI—
HA (GASP)
NO... TODAY IS...
OH, NO GOOD? PREVIOUS ENGAGE-MENT?
NO, IT'S NOTHING LIKE THAT!

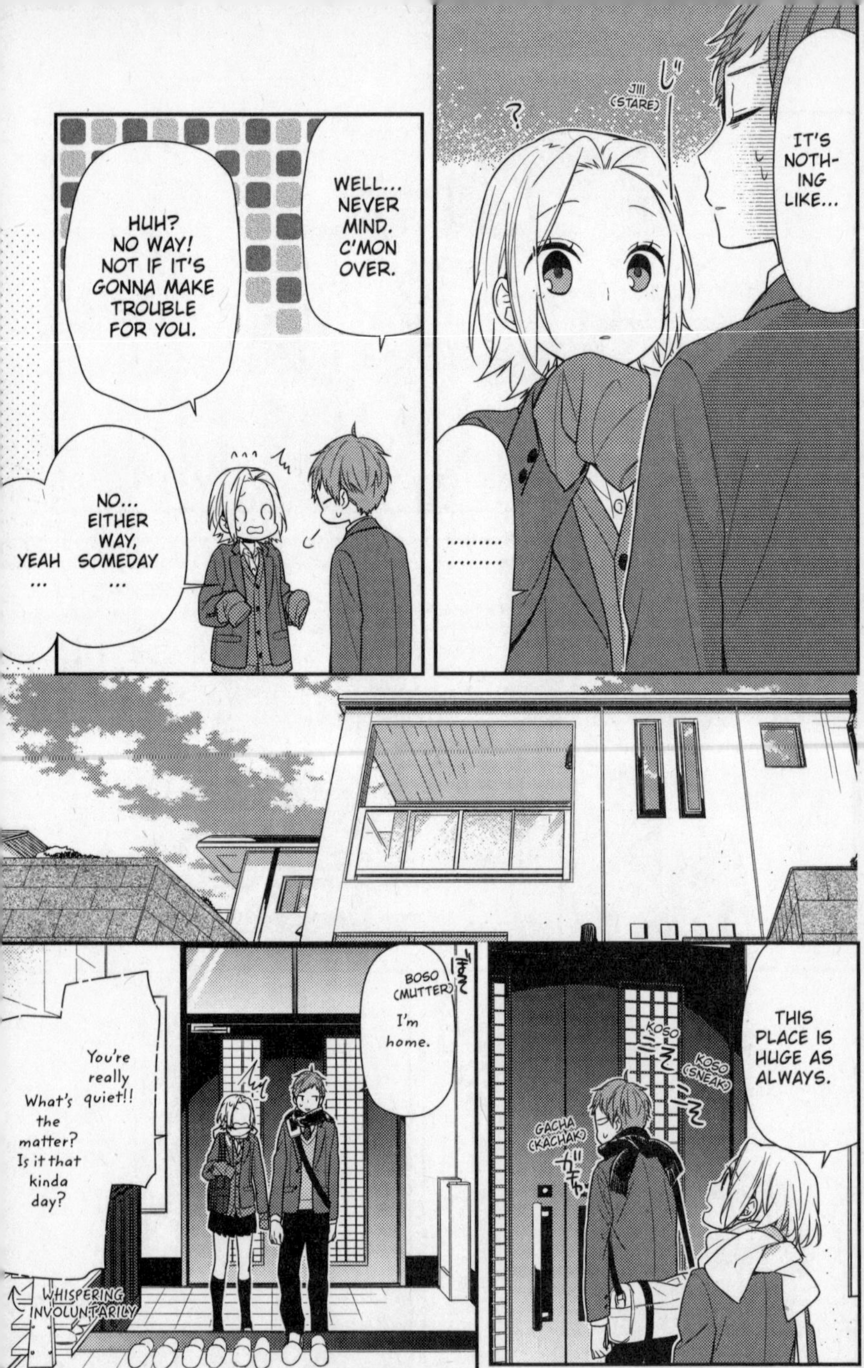
JIII (STARE)
IT'S NOTHING LIKE...
.........
.........
WELL... NEVER MIND. C'MON OVER.
HUH? NO WAY! NOT IF IT'S GONNA MAKE TROUBLE FOR YOU.
NO... EITHER WAY, SOMEDAY...
YEAH...
THIS PLACE IS HUGE AS ALWAYS.
KOSO
KOSO (SNEAK)
GACHA (KACHAK)
BOSO (MUTTER)
I'm home.
You're really quiet!!
What's the matter? Is it that kinda day?
WHISPERING INVOLUNTARILY

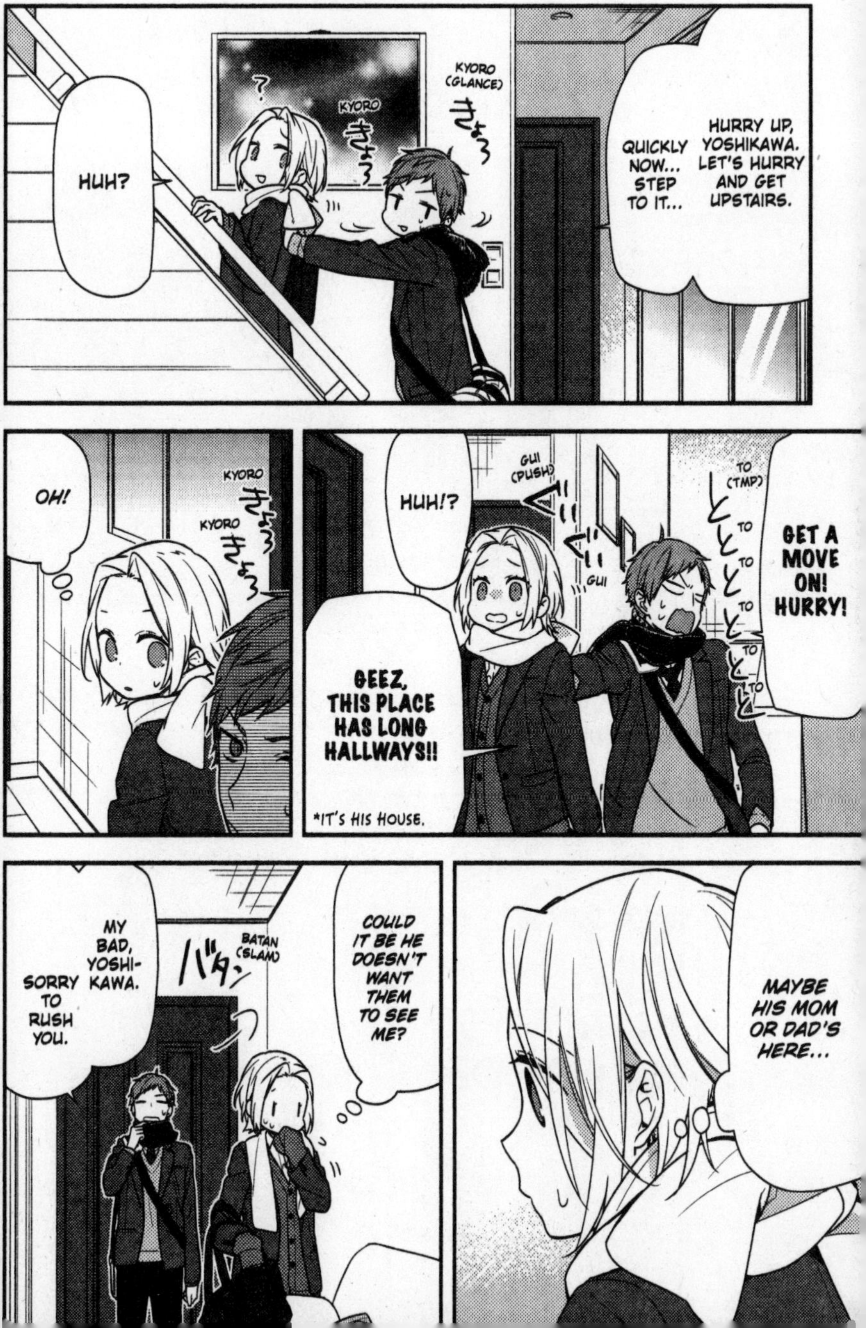
HURRY UP, YOSHIKAWA. LET'S HURRY AND GET UPSTAIRS.
QUICKLY NOW... STEP TO IT...
KYORO (GLANCE)
きょろ
KYORO
きょろ
?
HUH?
GET A MOVE ON! HURRY!
TO (TMP)
とととととと
TO
TO
TO
TO
TO
GUI (PUSH)
ぐい
ぐい
GUI
HUH!?
GEEZ, THIS PLACE HAS LONG HALLWAYS!!
*IT'S HIS HOUSE.
KYORO
きょろ
KYORO
きょろ
OH!
MAYBE HIS MOM OR DAD'S HERE...
COULD IT BE HE DOESN'T WANT THEM TO SEE ME?
BATAN (SLAM)
バタン
MY BAD, YOSHIKAWA.
SORRY TO RUSH YOU.

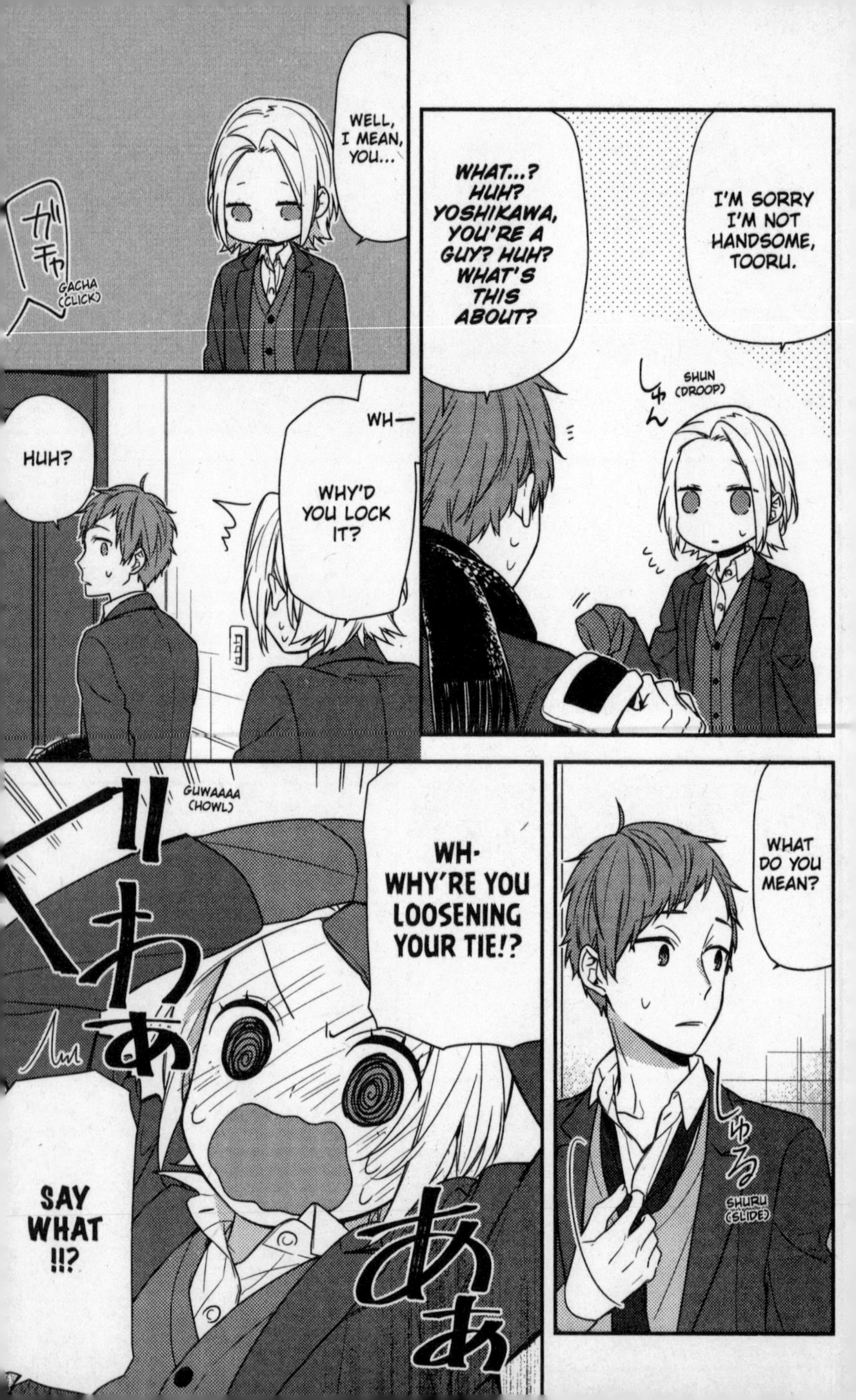

WELL, I MEAN, YOU...
ガチャ
GACHA (CLICK)
WH—
WHY'D YOU LOCK IT?
HUH?
I'M SORRY I'M NOT HANDSOME, TOORU.
WHAT...? HUH? YOSHIKAWA, YOU'RE A GUY? HUH? WHAT'S THIS ABOUT?
しゅん
SHUN (DROOP)
WHAT DO YOU MEAN?
しゅる
SHURU (SLIDE)
WH- WHY'RE YOU LOOSENING YOUR TIE!?
GUWAAA (HOWL)
SAY WHAT !!?

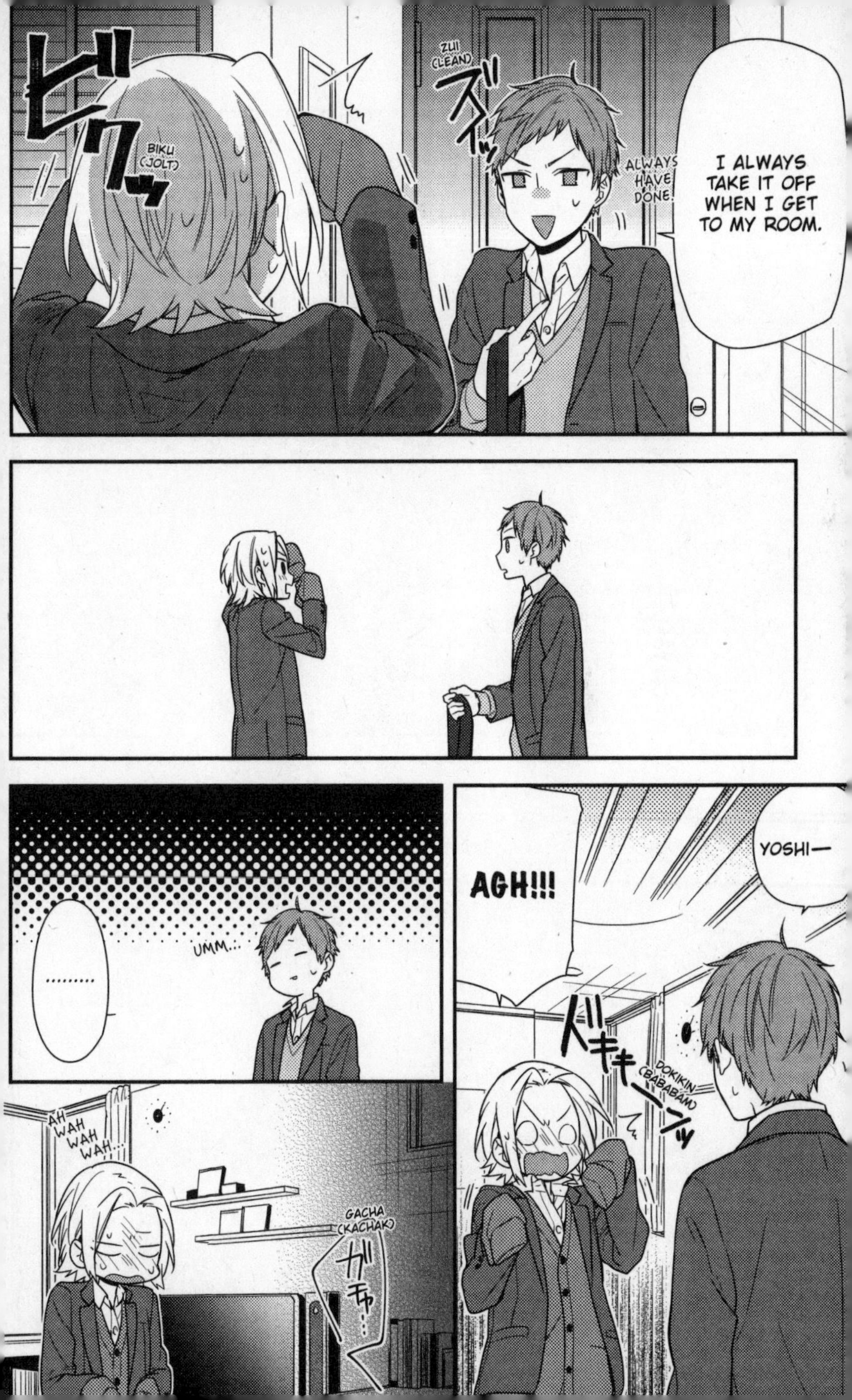
I ALWAYS TAKE IT OFF WHEN I GET TO MY ROOM.
ALWAYS HAVE DONE!
ZUI (LEAN)
BIKU (JOLT)
YOSHI—
AGH!!!
DOKIKIN (BABABAM)
..........
UMM...
GACHA (KACHAK)
AH WAH WAH WAH...

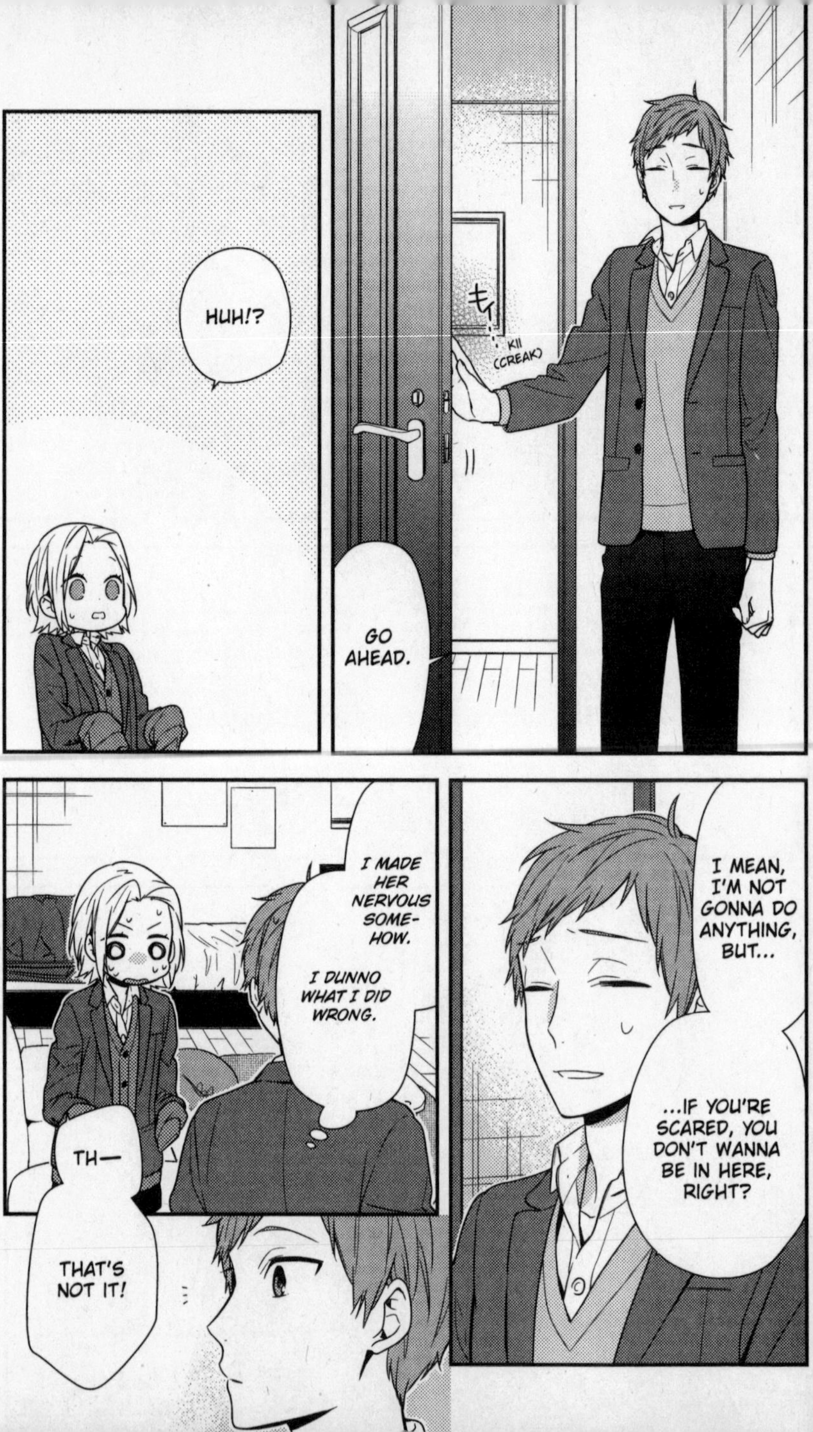
KII (CREAK)
GO AHEAD.
HUH!?
I MEAN, I'M NOT GONNA DO ANYTHING, BUT...
...IF YOU'RE SCARED, YOU DON'T WANNA BE IN HERE, RIGHT?
I MADE HER NERVOUS SOME-HOW.
I DUNNO WHAT I DID WRONG.
TH—
THAT'S NOT IT!

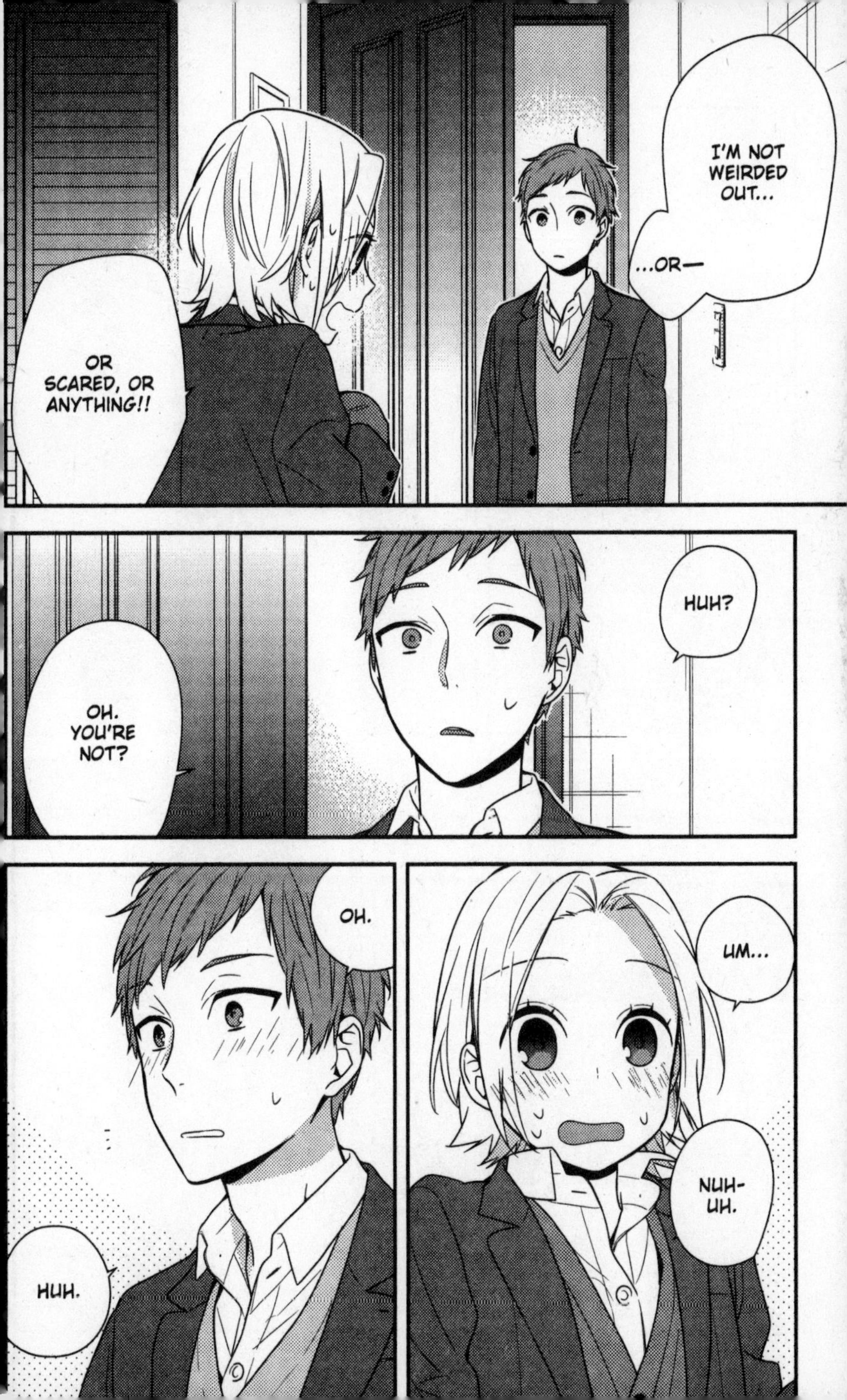
I'M NOT WEIRDED OUT...
...OR—
OR SCARED, OR ANYTHING!!
HUH?
OH. YOU'RE NOT?
UM...
NUH-UH.
OH.
HUH.

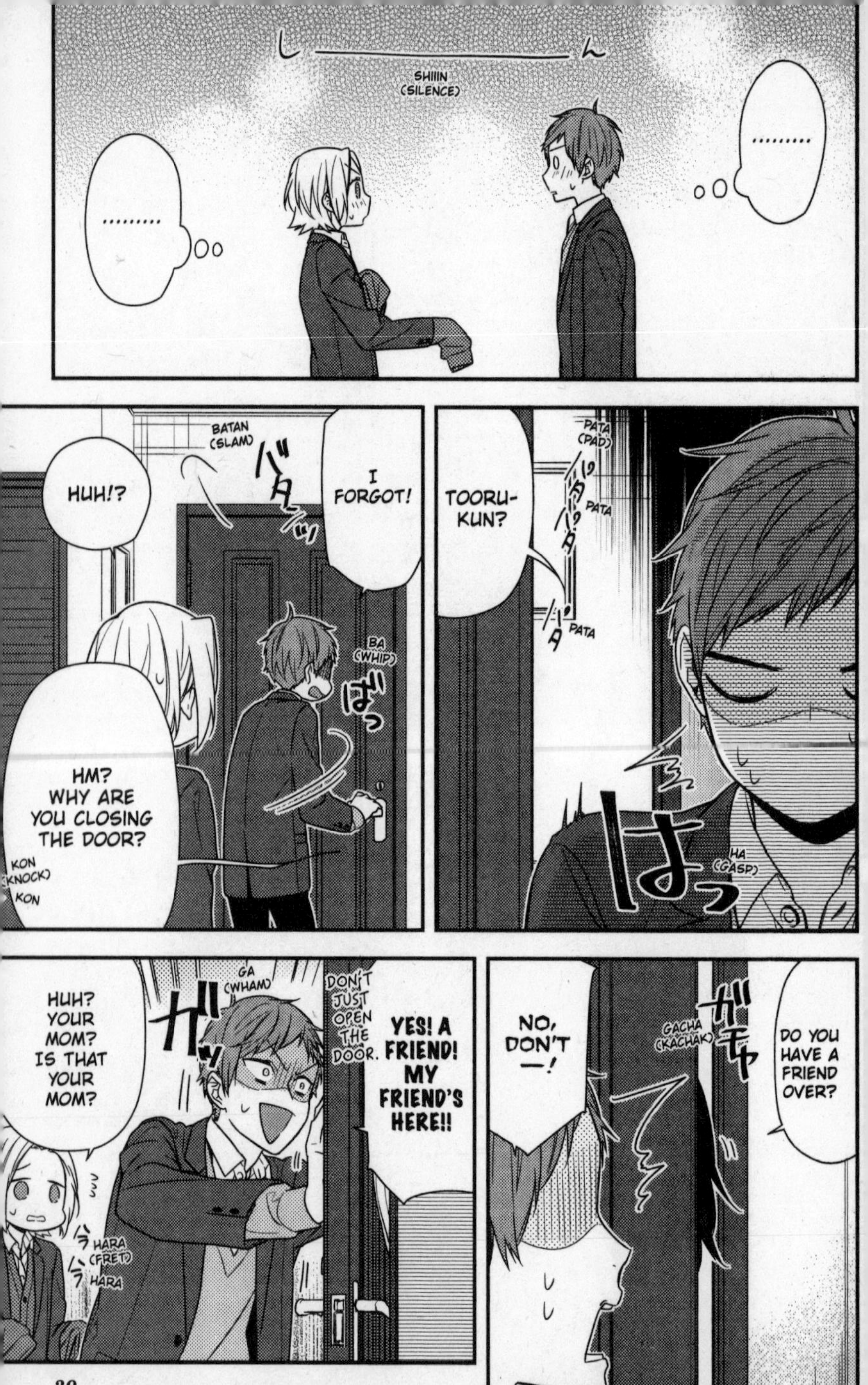
SHIIIN (SILENCE)
.........
.........
TOORU-KUN?
PATA (PAD) PATA PATA
HA (GASP)
I FORGOT!
BATAN (SLAM)
HUH!?
BA (WHIP)
HM? WHY ARE YOU CLOSING THE DOOR?
KON (KNOCK) KON
DO YOU HAVE A FRIEND OVER?
GACHA (KACHAK)
NO, DON'T—!
YES! A FRIEND! MY FRIEND'S HERE!!
DON'T JUST OPEN THE DOOR.
GA (WHAM)
HUH? YOUR MOM? IS THAT YOUR MOM?
HARA (FRET) HARA

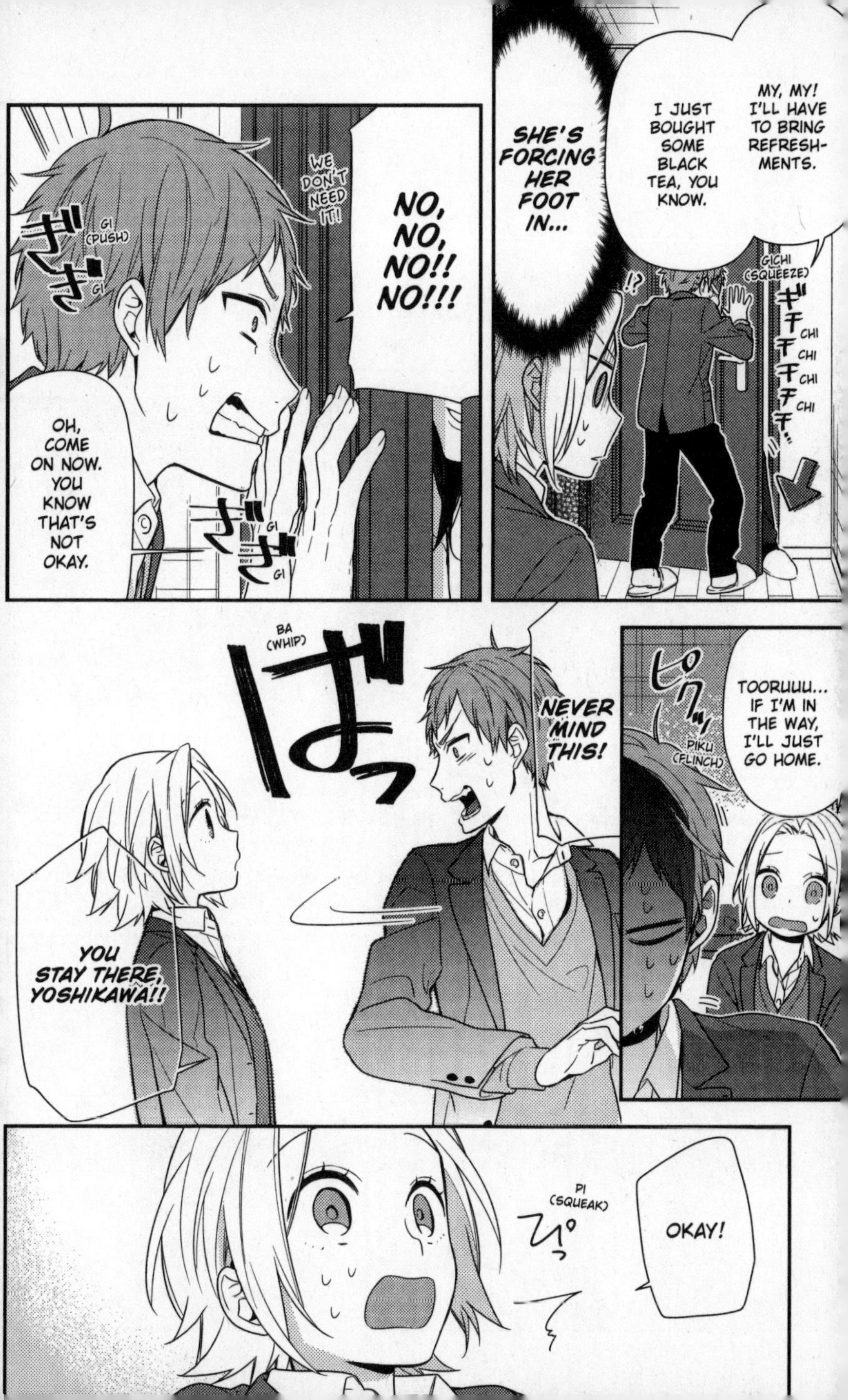
MY, MY! I'LL HAVE TO BRING REFRESHMENTS.
I JUST BOUGHT SOME BLACK TEA, YOU KNOW.
SHE'S FORCING HER FOOT IN...
!?
GICHI (SQUEEZE)
CHI CHI CHI CHI
NO, NO, NO!! NO!!!
WE DON'T NEED IT!
GI (PUSH) GI
OH, COME ON NOW. YOU KNOW THAT'S NOT OKAY.
GI GI
TOORUUU... IF I'M IN THE WAY, I'LL JUST GO HOME.
PIKU (FLINCH)
NEVER MIND THIS!
BA (WHIP)
YOU STAY THERE, YOSHIKAWA!!
OKAY!
PI (SQUEAK)

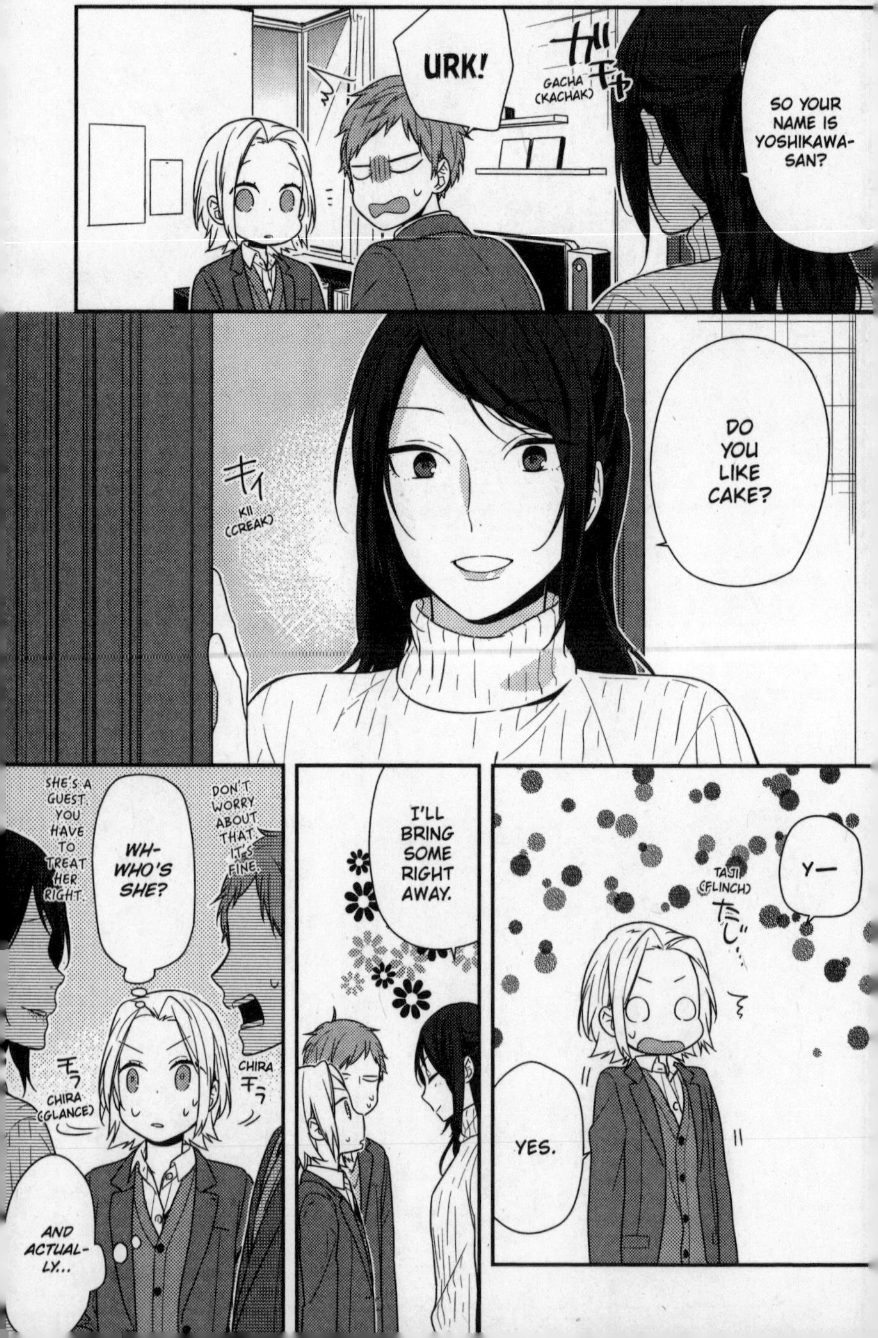
SO YOUR NAME IS YOSHIKAWA-SAN?
GACHA (KACHAK)
URK!
DO YOU LIKE CAKE?
KII (CREAK)
Y—
TAJI (FLINCH)
YES.
I'LL BRING SOME RIGHT AWAY.
DON'T WORRY ABOUT THAT. IT'S FINE.
WH-WHO'S SHE?
SHE'S A GUEST. YOU HAVE TO TREAT HER RIGHT.
CHIRA
CHIRA (GLANCE)
AND ACTUAL-LY...

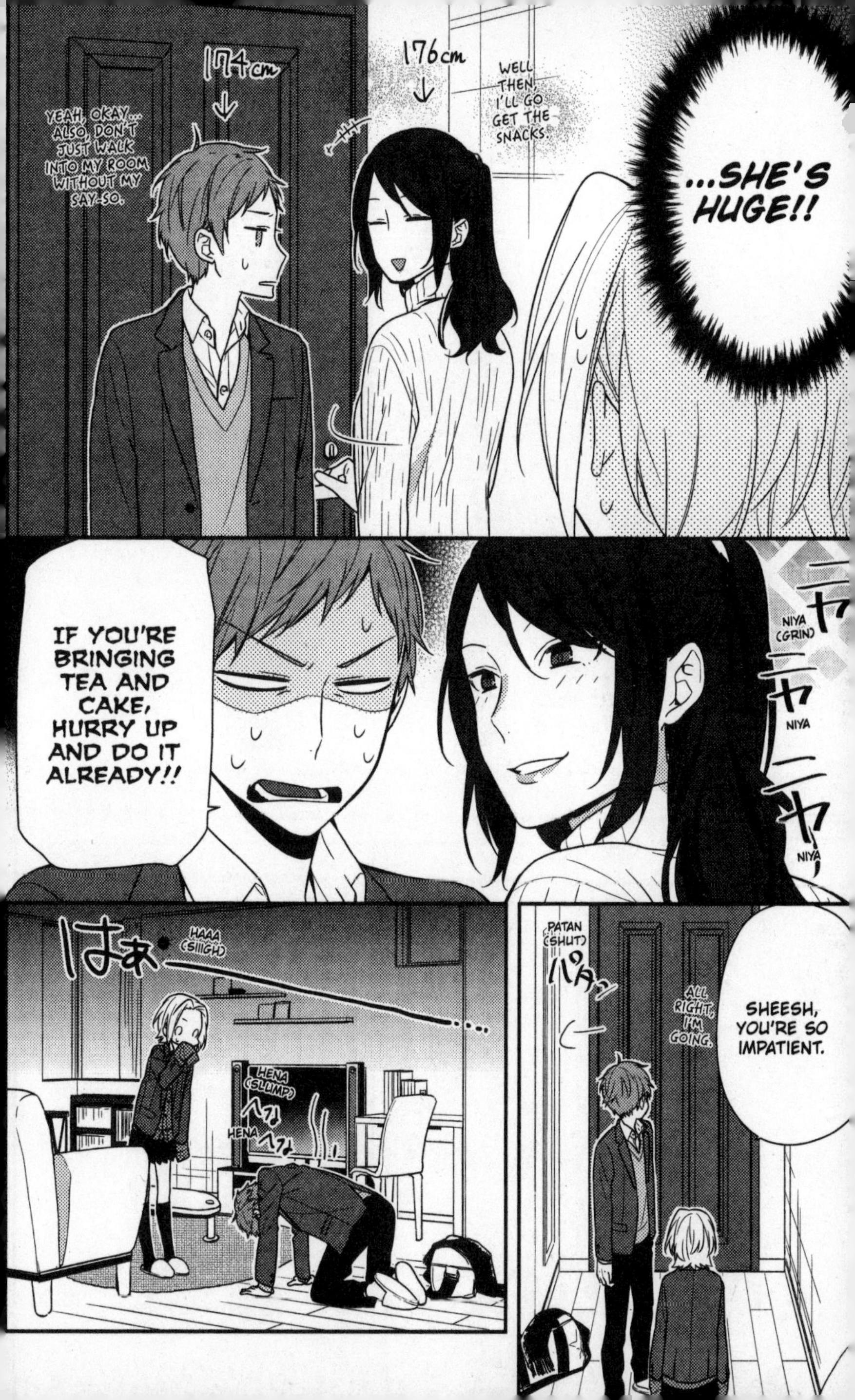

...SHE'S HUGE!!
WELL THEN, I'LL GO GET THE SNACKS.
176cm
174cm
YEAH, OKAY... ALSO, DON'T JUST WALK INTO MY ROOM WITHOUT MY SAY-SO.
ニヤ
NIYA (GRIN)
ニヤ
NIYA
ニヤ
NIYA
IF YOU'RE BRINGING TEA AND CAKE, HURRY UP AND DO IT ALREADY!!
SHEESH, YOU'RE SO IMPATIENT.
ALL RIGHT, I'M GOING.
パタン
PATAN (SHUT)
はぁ
HAAA (SIIIGH)
へな
HENA (SLUMP)
へな
HENA

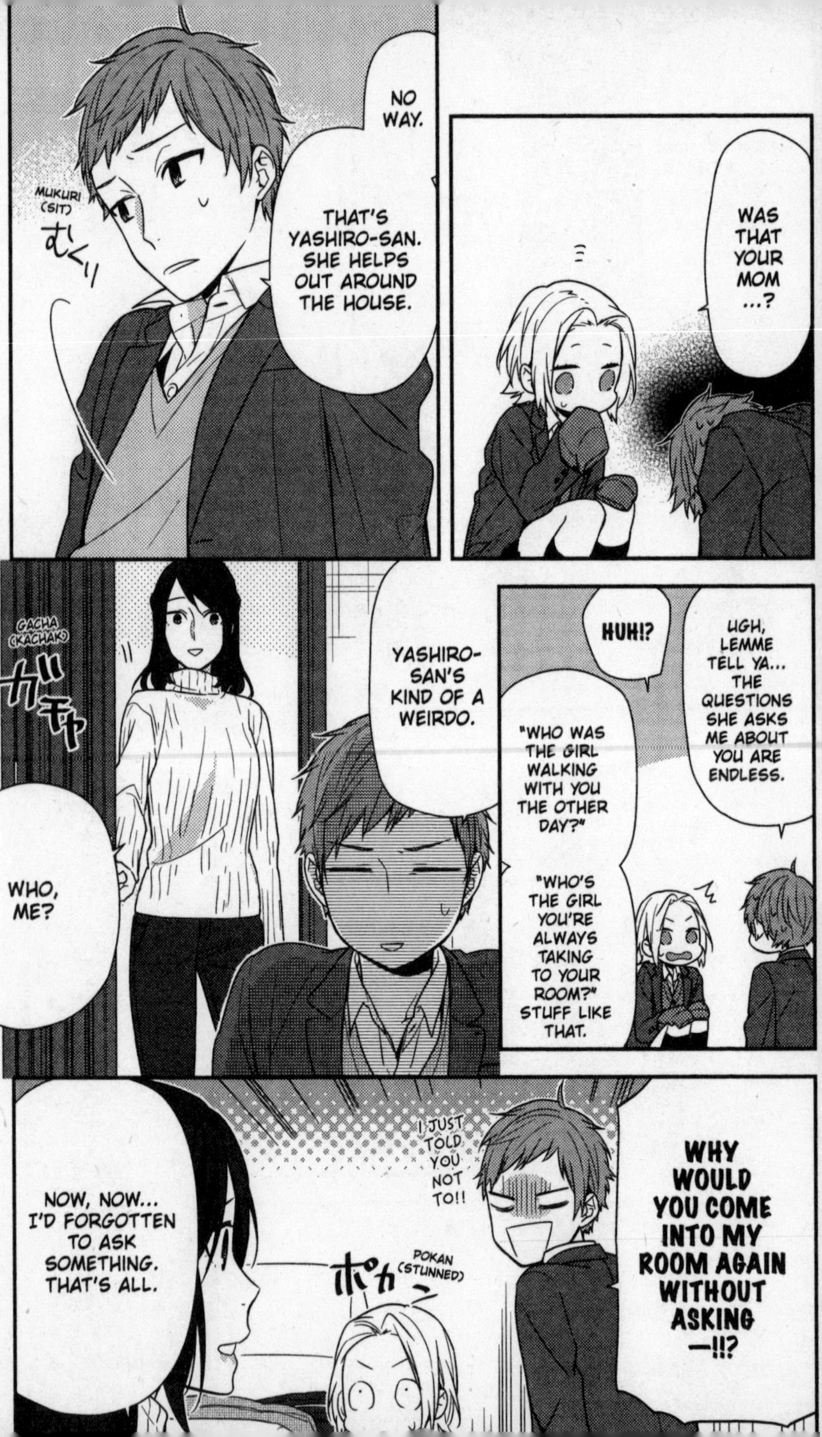
WAS THAT YOUR MOM ...?
NO WAY.
THAT'S YASHIRO-SAN. SHE HELPS OUT AROUND THE HOUSE.
MUKURI (SIT)
むくり
UGH, LEMME TELL YA... THE QUESTIONS SHE ASKS ME ABOUT YOU ARE ENDLESS.
HUH!?
"WHO WAS THE GIRL WALKING WITH YOU THE OTHER DAY?"
"WHO'S THE GIRL YOU'RE ALWAYS TAKING TO YOUR ROOM?" STUFF LIKE THAT.
YASHIRO-SAN'S KIND OF A WEIRDO.
GACHA (KACHAK)
ガチャ
WHO, ME?
WHY WOULD YOU COME INTO MY ROOM AGAIN WITHOUT ASKING—!!?
I JUST TOLD YOU NOT TO!!
POKAN (STUNNED)
ポカー
NOW, NOW... I'D FORGOTTEN TO ASK SOMETHING. THAT'S ALL.

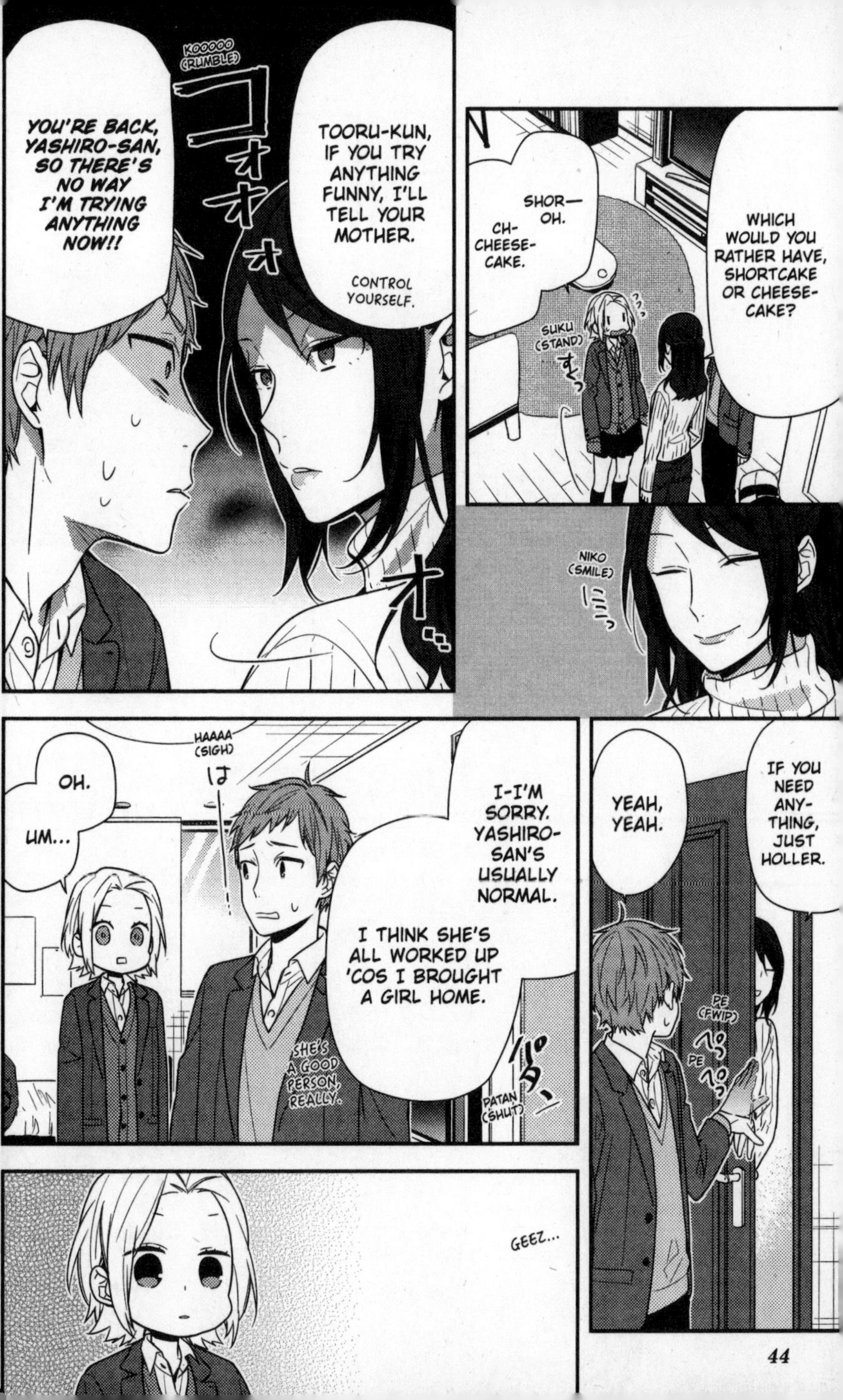
WHICH WOULD YOU RATHER HAVE, SHORTCAKE OR CHEESE-CAKE?
SHOR— OH.
CH-CHEESE-CAKE.
SUKU (STAND)
NIKO (SMILE)
TOORU-KUN, IF YOU TRY ANYTHING FUNNY, I'LL TELL YOUR MOTHER.
KOOOOO (RUMBLE)
CONTROL YOURSELF.
YOU'RE BACK, YASHIRO-SAN, SO THERE'S NO WAY I'M TRYING ANYTHING NOW!!
IF YOU NEED ANY-THING, JUST HOLLER.
YEAH, YEAH.
PE (FWIP) PE
HAAAA (SIGH)
OH.
UM...
I-I'M SORRY. YASHIRO-SAN'S USUALLY NORMAL.
I THINK SHE'S ALL WORKED UP 'COS I BROUGHT A GIRL HOME.
SHE'S A GOOD PERSON, REALLY.
PATAN (SHUT)
GEEZ...

YOU'RE BACK, YASHIRO-SAN, SO THERE'S NO WAY I'M TRYING ANYTHING NOW!!

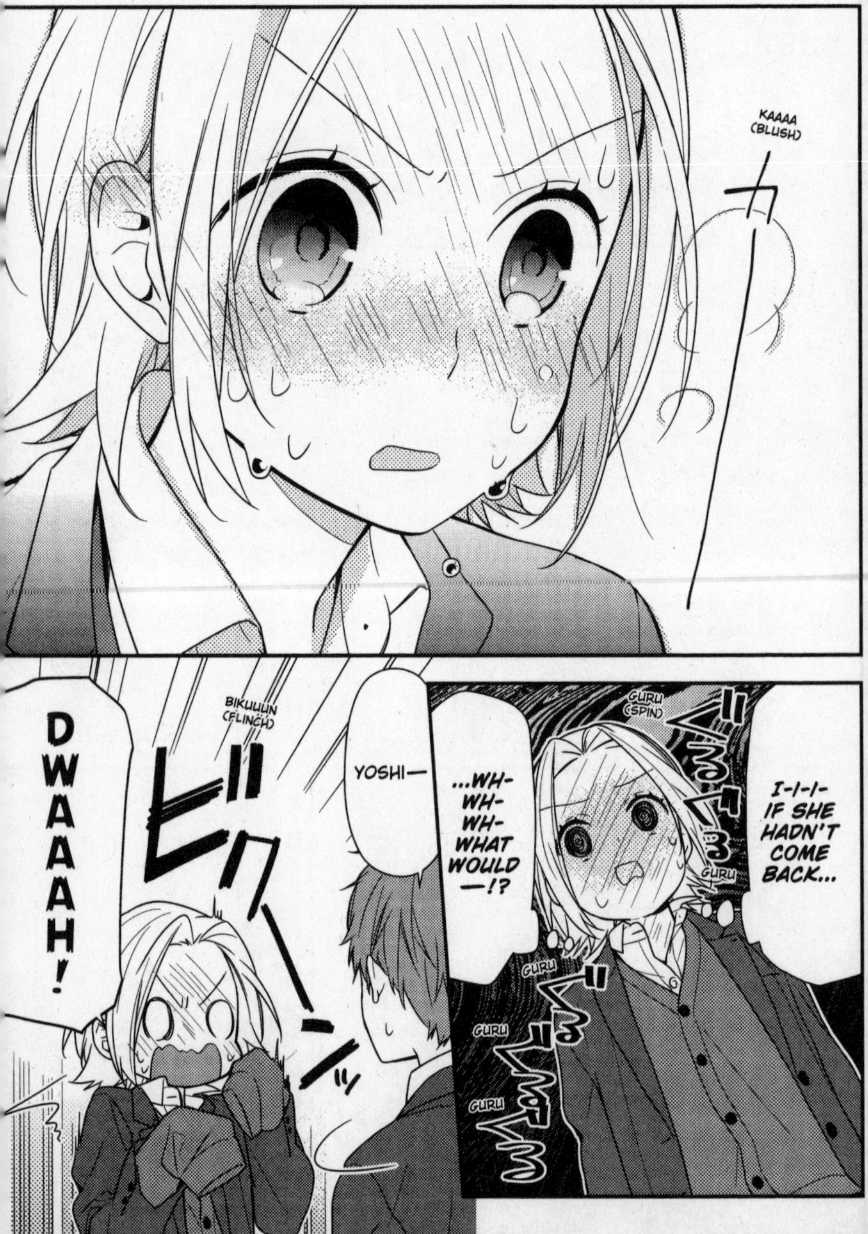
KAAAA (BLUSH)
I-I-I- IF SHE HADN'T COME BACK...
GURU (SPIN)
GURU
GURU
GURU
GURU
...WH-WH-WH-WHAT WOULD—!?
YOSHI—
BIKUUUN (FLINCH)
DWAAAAH!

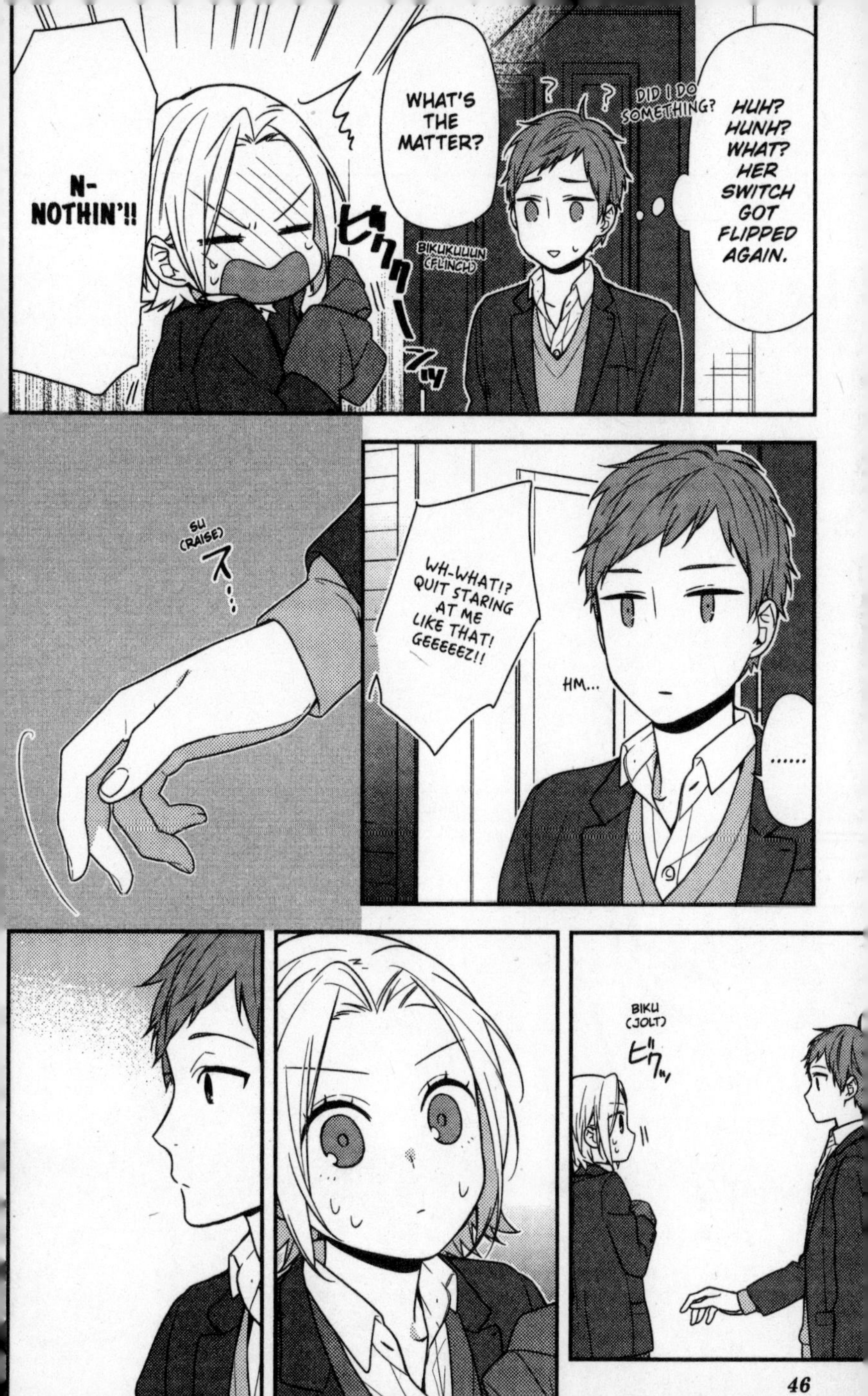
HUH? HUNH? WHAT? HER SWITCH GOT FLIPPED AGAIN.
DID I DO SOMETHING?
WHAT'S THE MATTER?
BIKUKUUUN (FLINCH)
N-NOTHIN'!!
WH-WHAT!? QUIT STARING AT ME LIKE THAT! GEEEEEZ!!
HM...
......
SU (RAISE)
BIKU (JOLT)

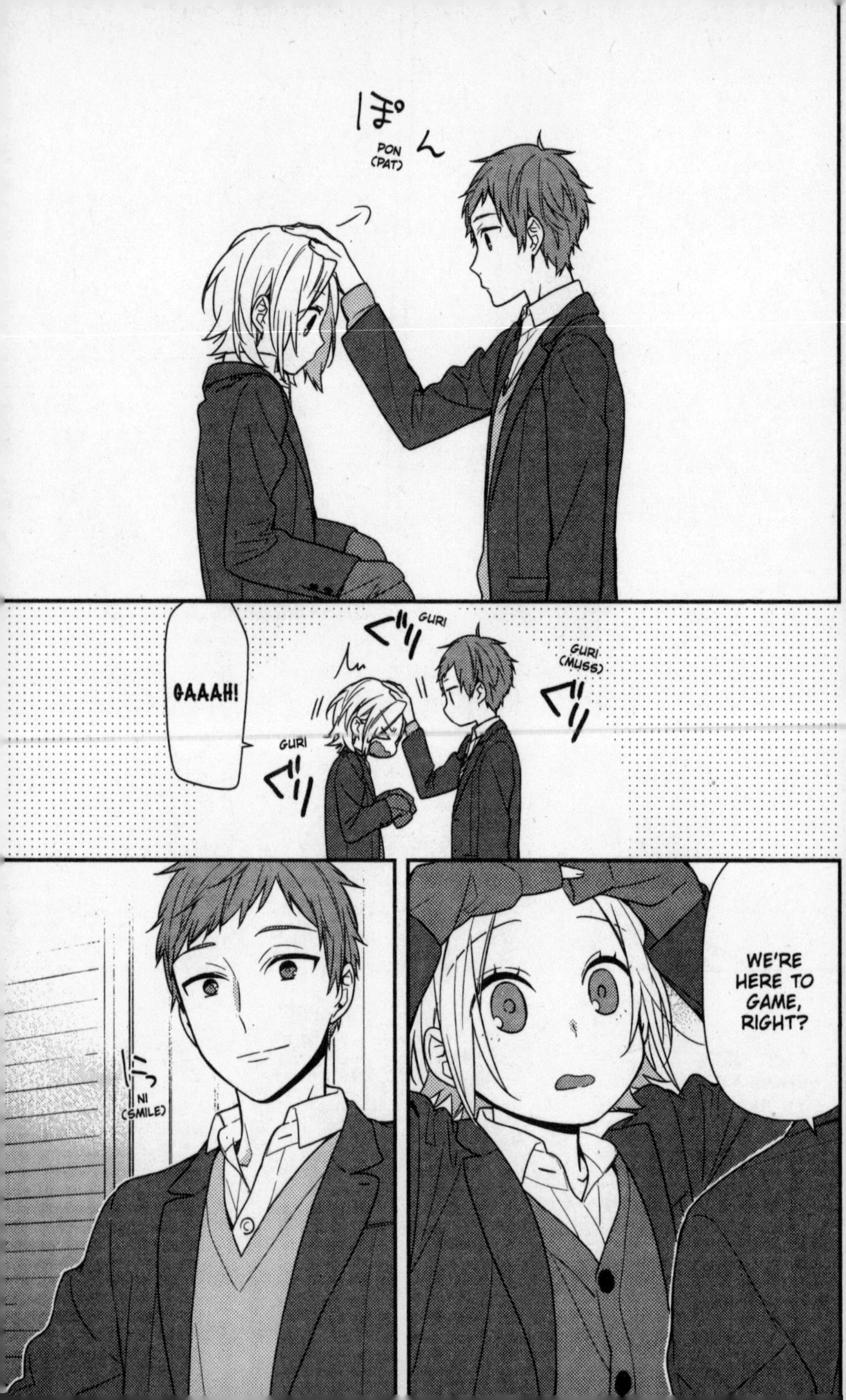
ぽん
PON
(PAT)
ぐり
GURI
(MUSS)
ぐり
GURI
GAAAH!
ぐり
GURI
WE'RE HERE TO GAME, RIGHT?
にっ
NI
(SMILE)

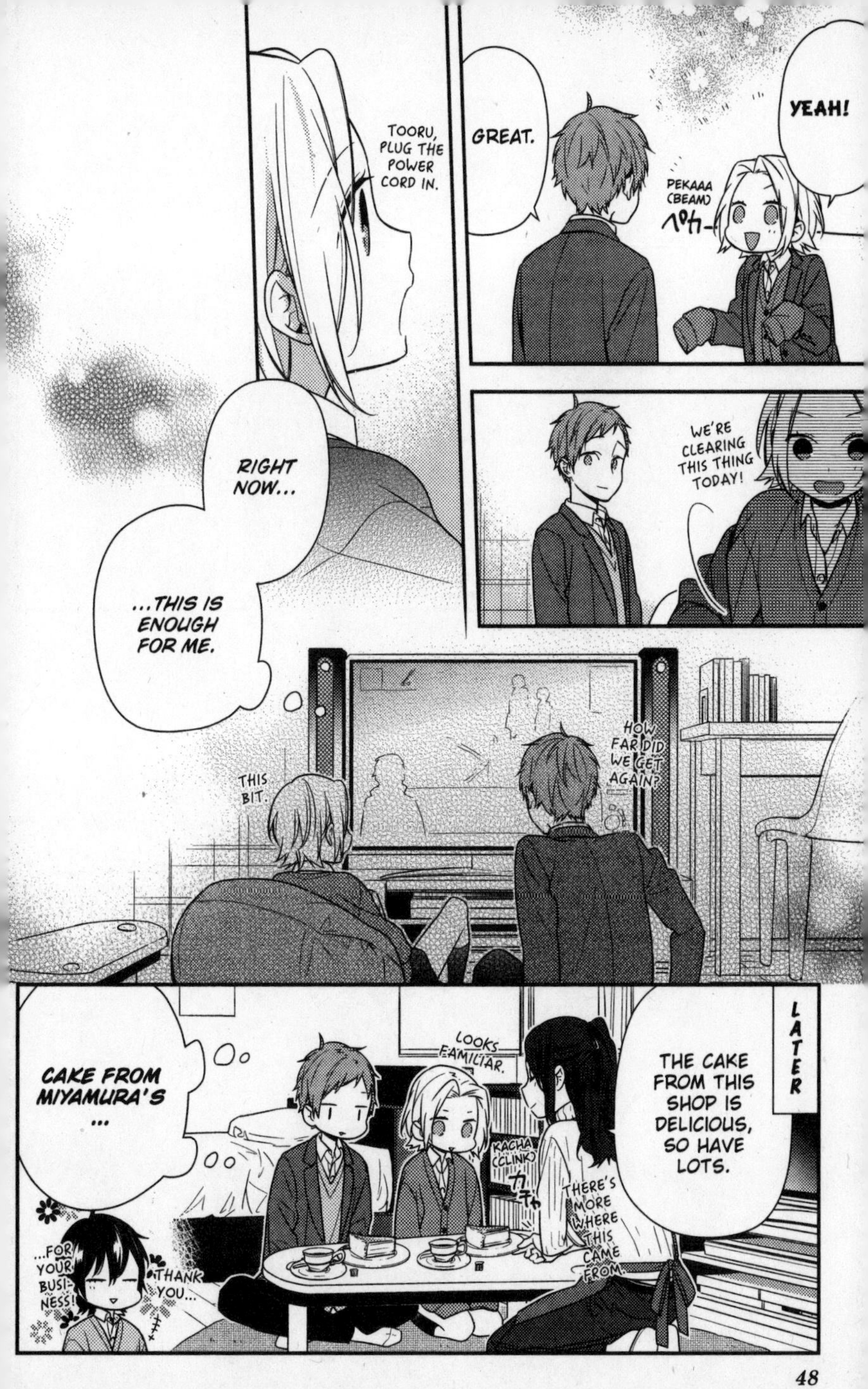
YEAH!
PEKAAA (BEAM)
GREAT.
WE'RE CLEARING THIS THING TODAY!
TOORU, PLUG THE POWER CORD IN.
RIGHT NOW...
...THIS IS ENOUGH FOR ME.
HOW FAR DID WE GET AGAIN?
THIS BIT.
LATER
THE CAKE FROM THIS SHOP IS DELICIOUS, SO HAVE LOTS.
THERE'S MORE WHERE THIS CAME FROM.
KACHA (CLINK)
LOOKS FAMILIAR.
CAKE FROM MIYAMURA'S...
THANK YOU...
...FOR YOUR BUSINESS!

HORIMIYA

HORIMIYA

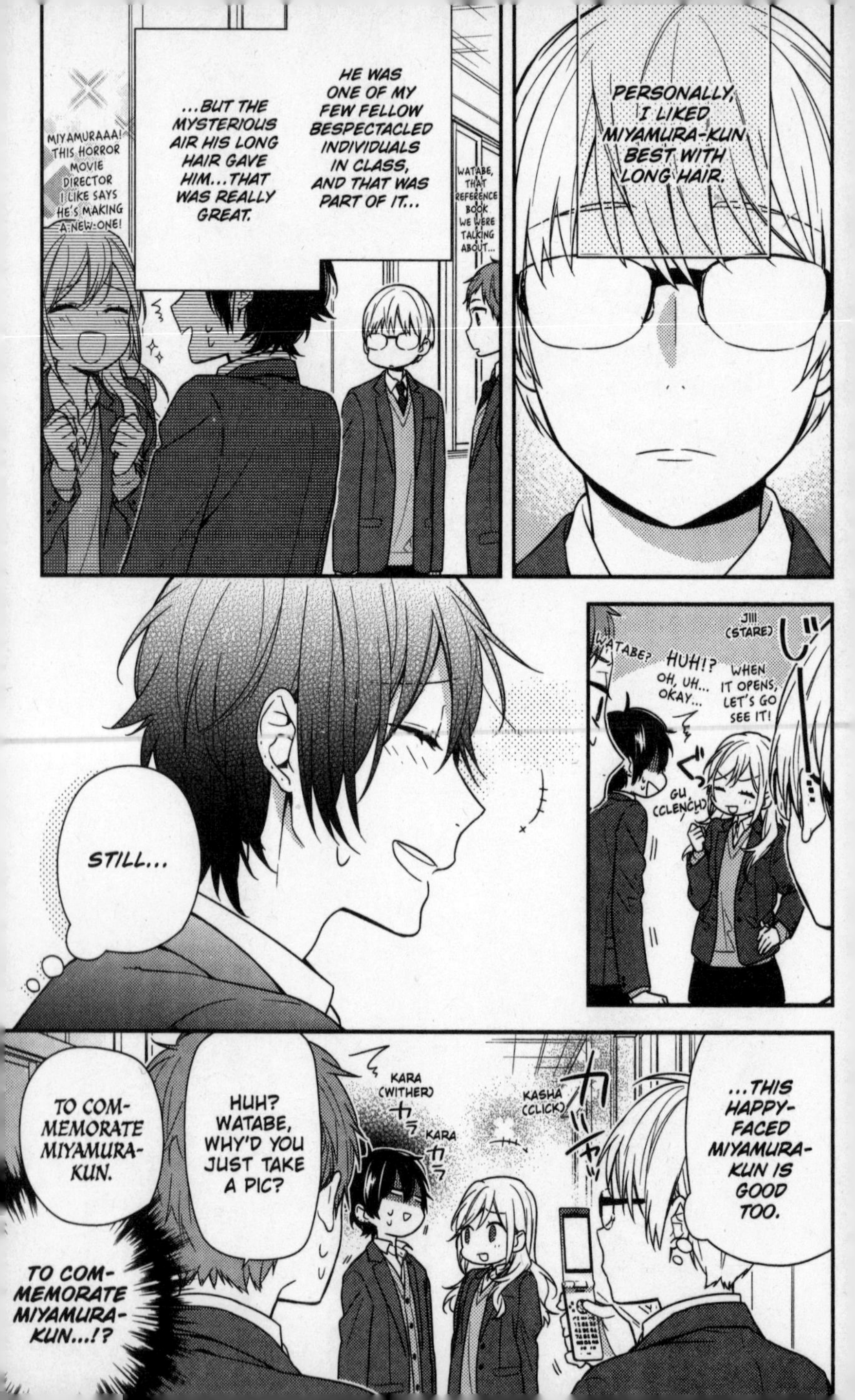
PERSONALLY, I LIKED MIYAMURA-KUN BEST WITH LONG HAIR.
WATABE, THAT REFERENCE BOOK WE WERE TALKING ABOUT...
HE WAS ONE OF MY FEW FELLOW BESPECTACLED INDIVIDUALS IN CLASS, AND THAT WAS PART OF IT...
...BUT THE MYSTERIOUS AIR HIS LONG HAIR GAVE HIM...THAT WAS REALLY GREAT.
MIYAMURAAA! THIS HORROR MOVIE DIRECTOR I LIKE SAYS HE'S MAKING A NEW ONE!
JIII (STARE)
WHEN IT OPENS, LET'S GO SEE IT!
HUH!? OH, UH... OKAY...
WATABE?
GU (CLENCH)
STILL...
...THIS HAPPY-FACED MIYAMURA-KUN IS GOOD TOO.
KASHA (CLICK)
KARA (WITHER)
KARA
HUH? WATABE, WHY'D YOU JUST TAKE A PIC?
TO COM-MEMORATE MIYAMURA-KUN.
TO COM-MEMORATE MIYAMURA-KUN...!?

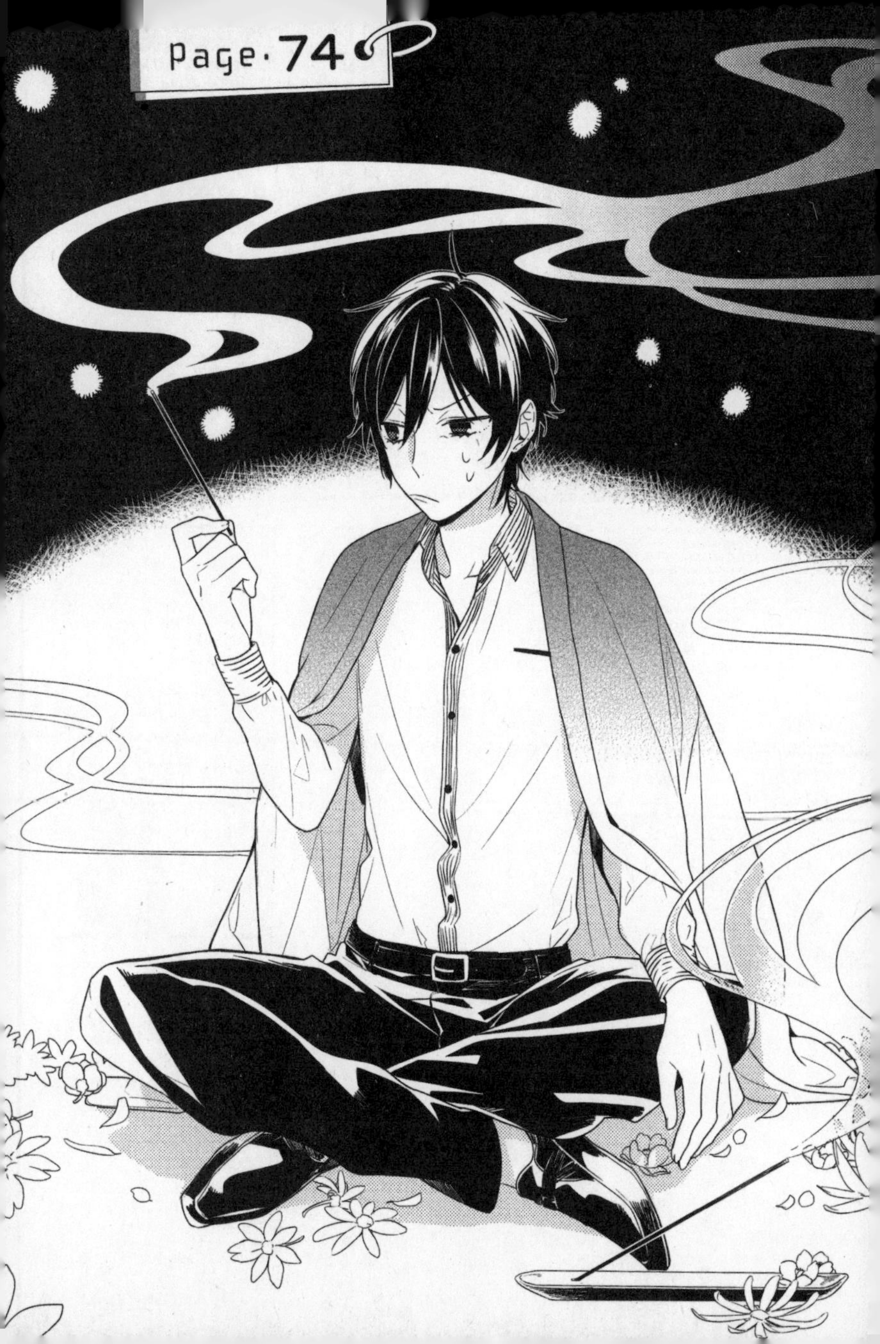
Page. 74

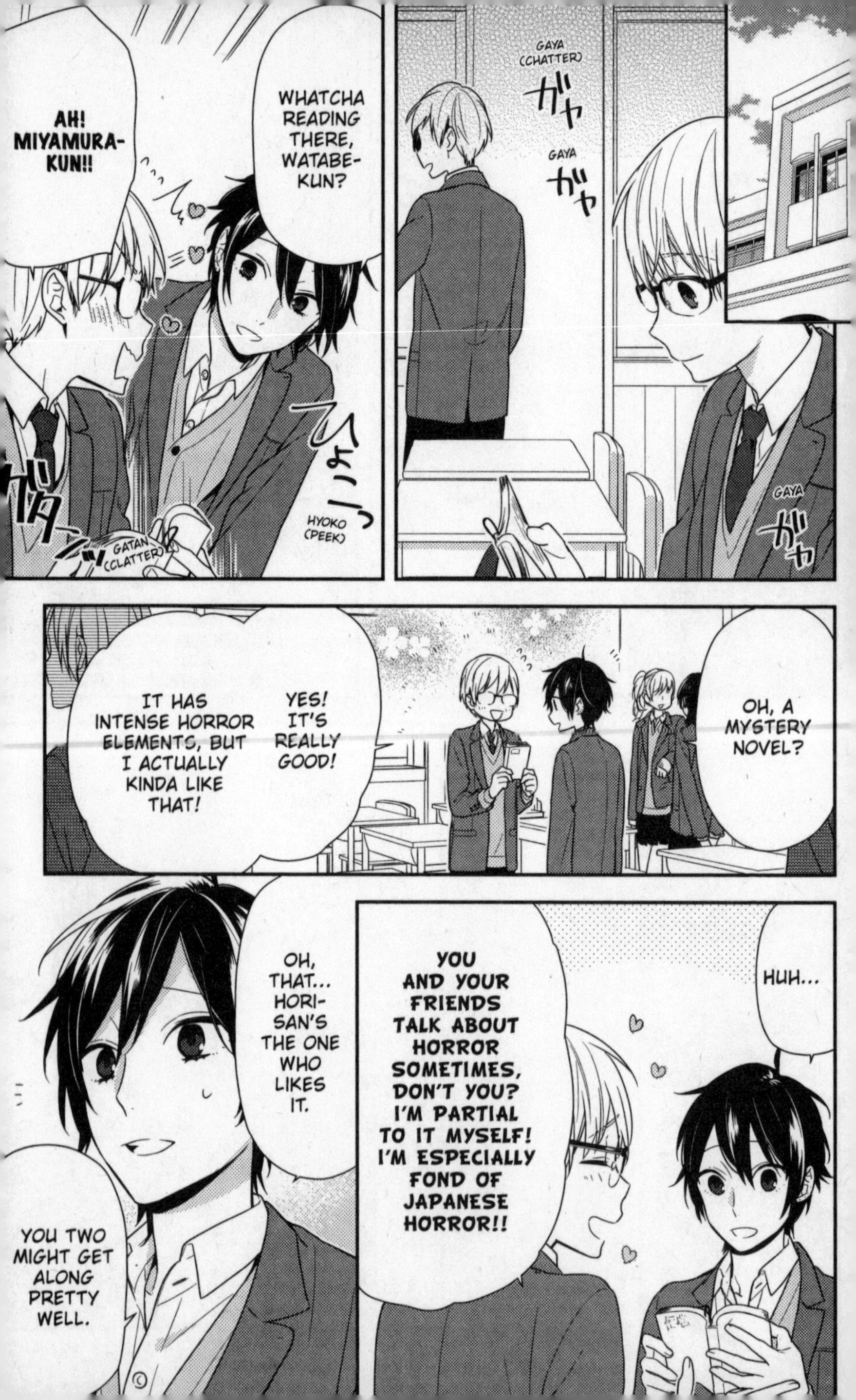
GAYA (CHATTER)
ガヤ
GAYA
ガヤ
GAYA
ガヤ
WHATCHA READING THERE, WATABE-KUN?
AH! MIYAMURA-KUN!!
HYOKO (PEEK)
GATAN (CLATTER)
OH, A MYSTERY NOVEL?
YES! IT'S REALLY GOOD!
IT HAS INTENSE HORROR ELEMENTS, BUT I ACTUALLY KINDA LIKE THAT!
HUH...
YOU AND YOUR FRIENDS TALK ABOUT HORROR SOMETIMES, DON'T YOU? I'M PARTIAL TO IT MYSELF! I'M ESPECIALLY FOND OF JAPANESE HORROR!!
OH, THAT... HORI-SAN'S THE ONE WHO LIKES IT.
YOU TWO MIGHT GET ALONG PRETTY WELL.

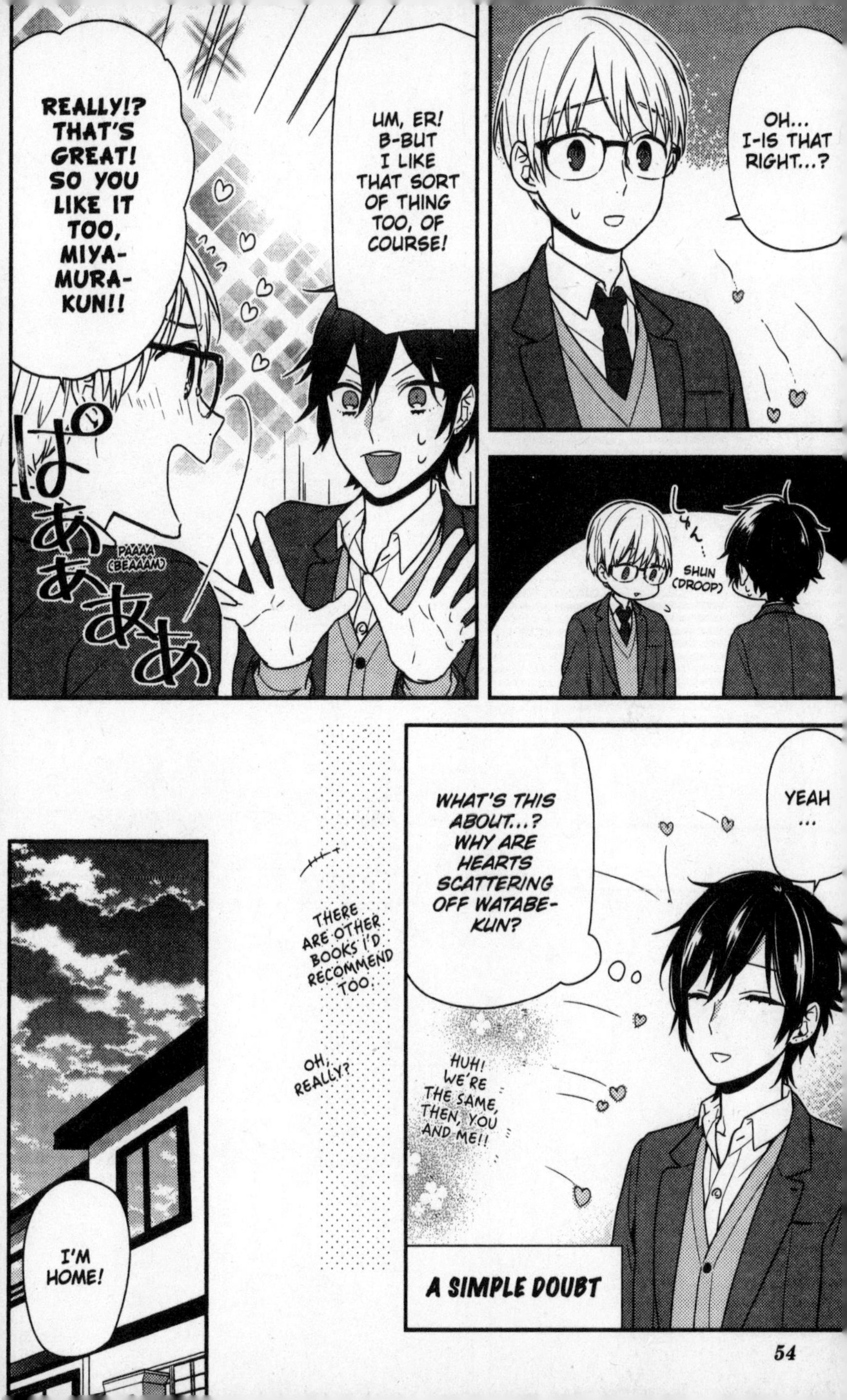
OH... I-IS THAT RIGHT...?
しゅん
SHUN (DROOP)
UM, ER! B-BUT I LIKE THAT SORT OF THING TOO, OF COURSE!
REALLY!? THAT'S GREAT! SO YOU LIKE IT TOO, MIYAMURA-KUN!!
ぱあああ
PAAAA (BEAAAM)
YEAH...
WHAT'S THIS ABOUT...? WHY ARE HEARTS SCATTERING OFF WATABE-KUN?
HUH! WE'RE THE SAME, THEN, YOU AND ME!!
A SIMPLE DOUBT
THERE ARE OTHER BOOKS I'D RECOMMEND TOO.
OH, REALLY?
I'M HOME!

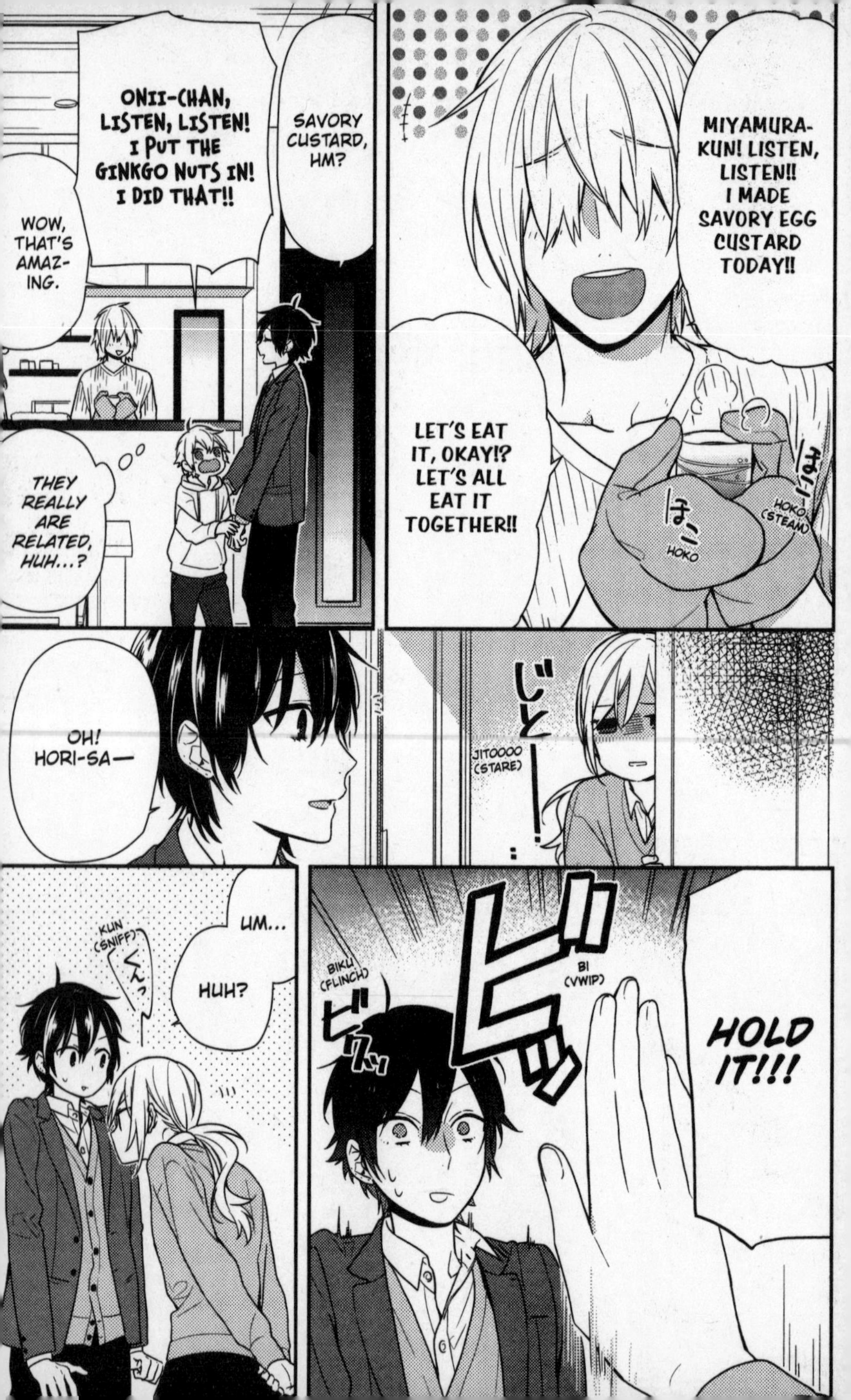
MIYAMURA-KUN! LISTEN, LISTEN!! I MADE SAVORY EGG CUSTARD TODAY!!
LET'S EAT IT, OKAY!? LET'S ALL EAT IT TOGETHER!!
ほこ
HOKO (STEAM)
ほこ
HOKO
SAVORY CUSTARD, HM?
ONII-CHAN, LISTEN, LISTEN! I PUT THE GINKGO NUTS IN! I DID THAT!!
WOW, THAT'S AMAZ-ING.
THEY REALLY ARE RELATED, HUH...?
じとー
JITOOOO (STARE)
OH! HORI-SA—
HOLD IT!!!
ビッ
BI (VWIP)
ビクッ
BIKU (FLINCH)
UM...
HUH?
くんっ
KUN (SNIFF)

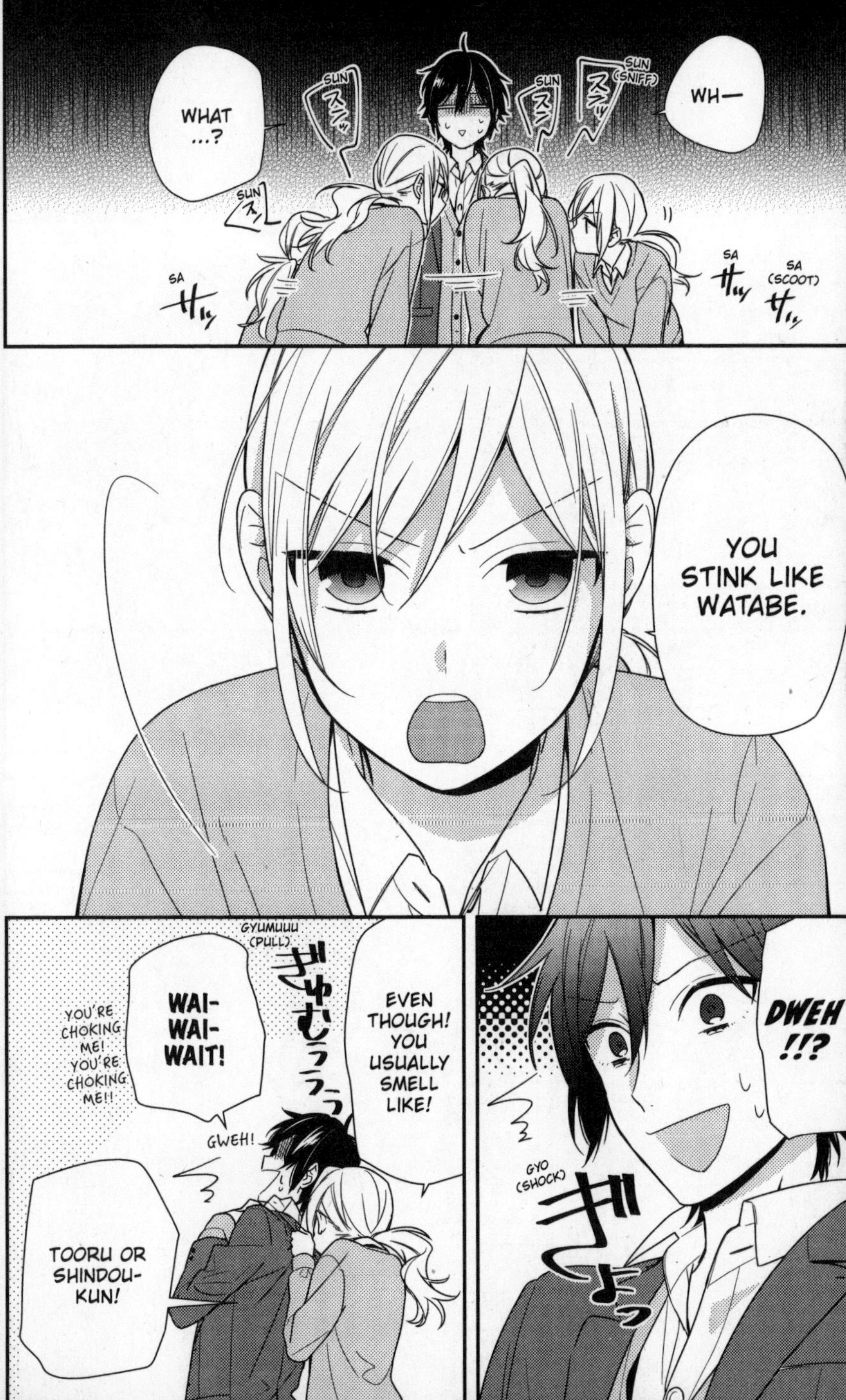
WH—
SUN (SNIFF)
SUN
SUN
WHAT ...?
SUN
SA (SCOOT)
SA
SA
YOU STINK LIKE WATABE.
DWEH !!?
GYO (SHOCK)
EVEN THOUGH! YOU USUALLY SMELL LIKE!
GYUMUUU (PULL)
WAI-WAI-WAIT!
YOU'RE CHOKING ME! YOU'RE CHOKING ME!!
GWEH!
TOORU OR SHINDOU-KUN!

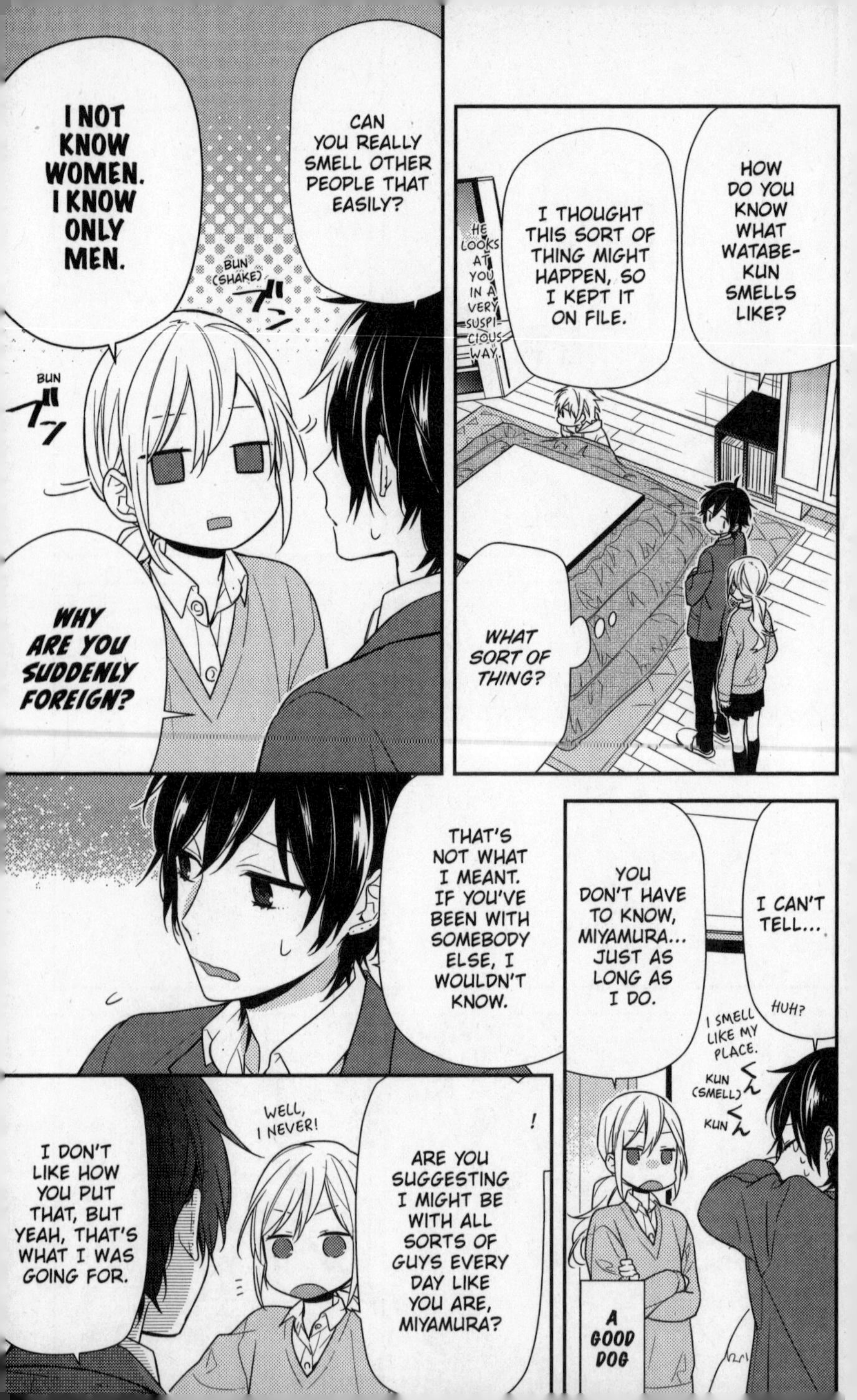
HOW DO YOU KNOW WHAT WATABE-KUN SMELLS LIKE?
I THOUGHT THIS SORT OF THING MIGHT HAPPEN, SO I KEPT IT ON FILE.
HE LOOKS AT YOU IN A VERY SUSPICIOUS WAY.
WHAT SORT OF THING?
CAN YOU REALLY SMELL OTHER PEOPLE THAT EASILY?
I NOT KNOW WOMEN. I KNOW ONLY MEN.
BUN (SHAKE)
BUN
WHY ARE YOU SUDDENLY FOREIGN?
I CAN'T TELL...
YOU DON'T HAVE TO KNOW, MIYAMURA... JUST AS LONG AS I DO.
HUH?
I SMELL LIKE MY PLACE.
KUN (SMELL)
KUN
A GOOD DOG
THAT'S NOT WHAT I MEANT. IF YOU'VE BEEN WITH SOMEBODY ELSE, I WOULDN'T KNOW.
!
ARE YOU SUGGESTING I MIGHT BE WITH ALL SORTS OF GUYS EVERY DAY LIKE YOU ARE, MIYAMURA?
WELL, I NEVER!
I DON'T LIKE HOW YOU PUT THAT, BUT YEAH, THAT'S WHAT I WAS GOING FOR.

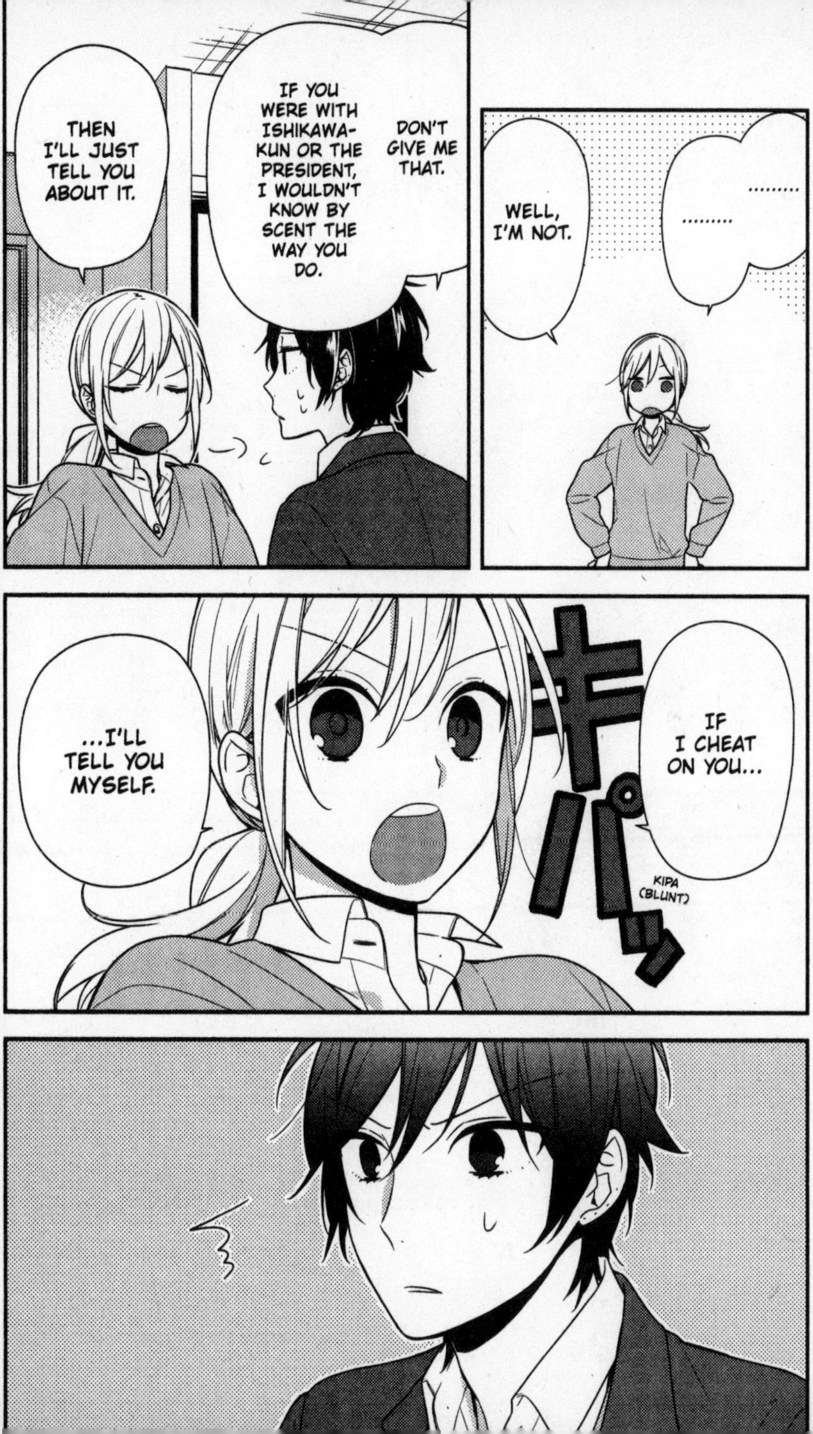
.........
.........
WELL, I'M NOT.
DON'T GIVE ME THAT.
IF YOU WERE WITH ISHIKAWA-KUN OR THE PRESIDENT, I WOULDN'T KNOW BY SCENT THE WAY YOU DO.
THEN I'LL JUST TELL YOU ABOUT IT.
IF I CHEAT ON YOU...
KIPA (BLUNT)
...I'LL TELL YOU MYSELF.

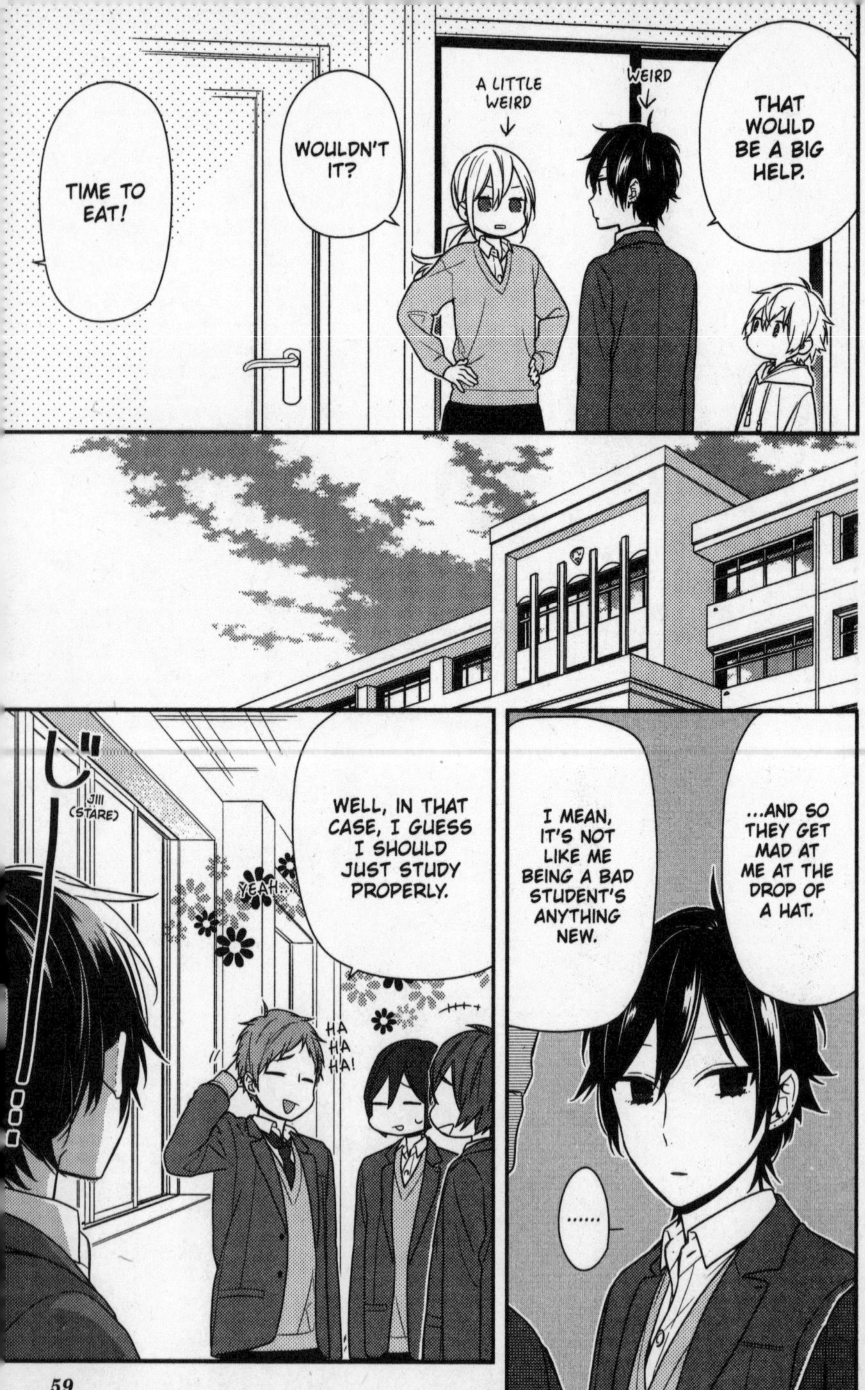
THAT WOULD BE A BIG HELP.
WEIRD
A LITTLE WEIRD
WOULDN'T IT?
TIME TO EAT!
...AND SO THEY GET MAD AT ME AT THE DROP OF A HAT.
I MEAN, IT'S NOT LIKE ME BEING A BAD STUDENT'S ANYTHING NEW.
......
WELL, IN THAT CASE, I GUESS I SHOULD JUST STUDY PROPERLY.
HA HA HA!
YEAH...
JIII (STARE)

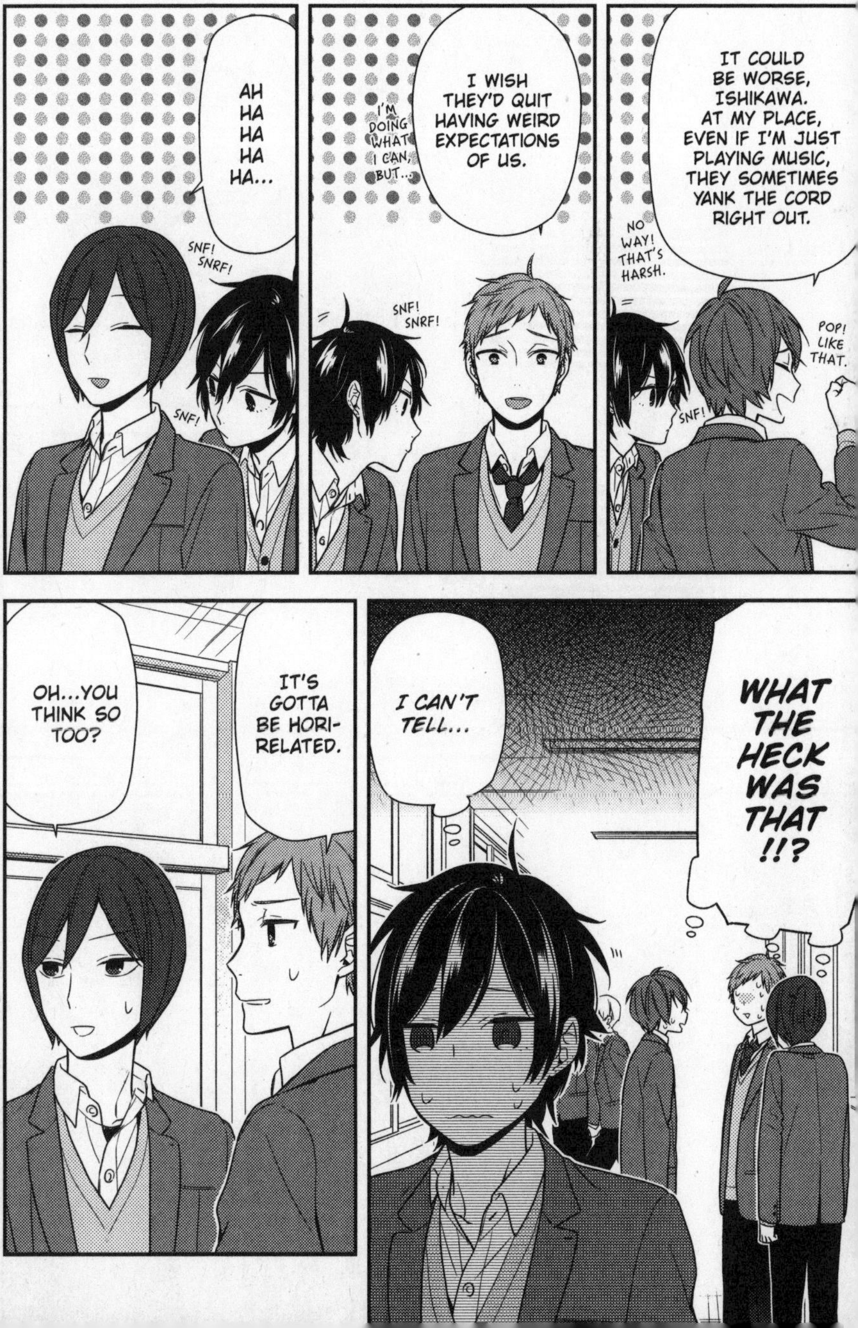
IT COULD BE WORSE, ISHIKAWA. AT MY PLACE, EVEN IF I'M JUST PLAYING MUSIC, THEY SOMETIMES YANK THE CORD RIGHT OUT.
NO WAY! THAT'S HARSH.
POP! LIKE THAT.
SNF!
I WISH THEY'D QUIT HAVING WEIRD EXPECTATIONS OF US.
I'M DOING WHAT I CAN, BUT...
SNF! SNRF!
AH HA HA HA HA...
SNF! SNRF!
SNF!
WHAT THE HECK WAS THAT!!?
I CAN'T TELL...
IT'S GOTTA BE HORI-RELATED.
OH...YOU THINK SO TOO?

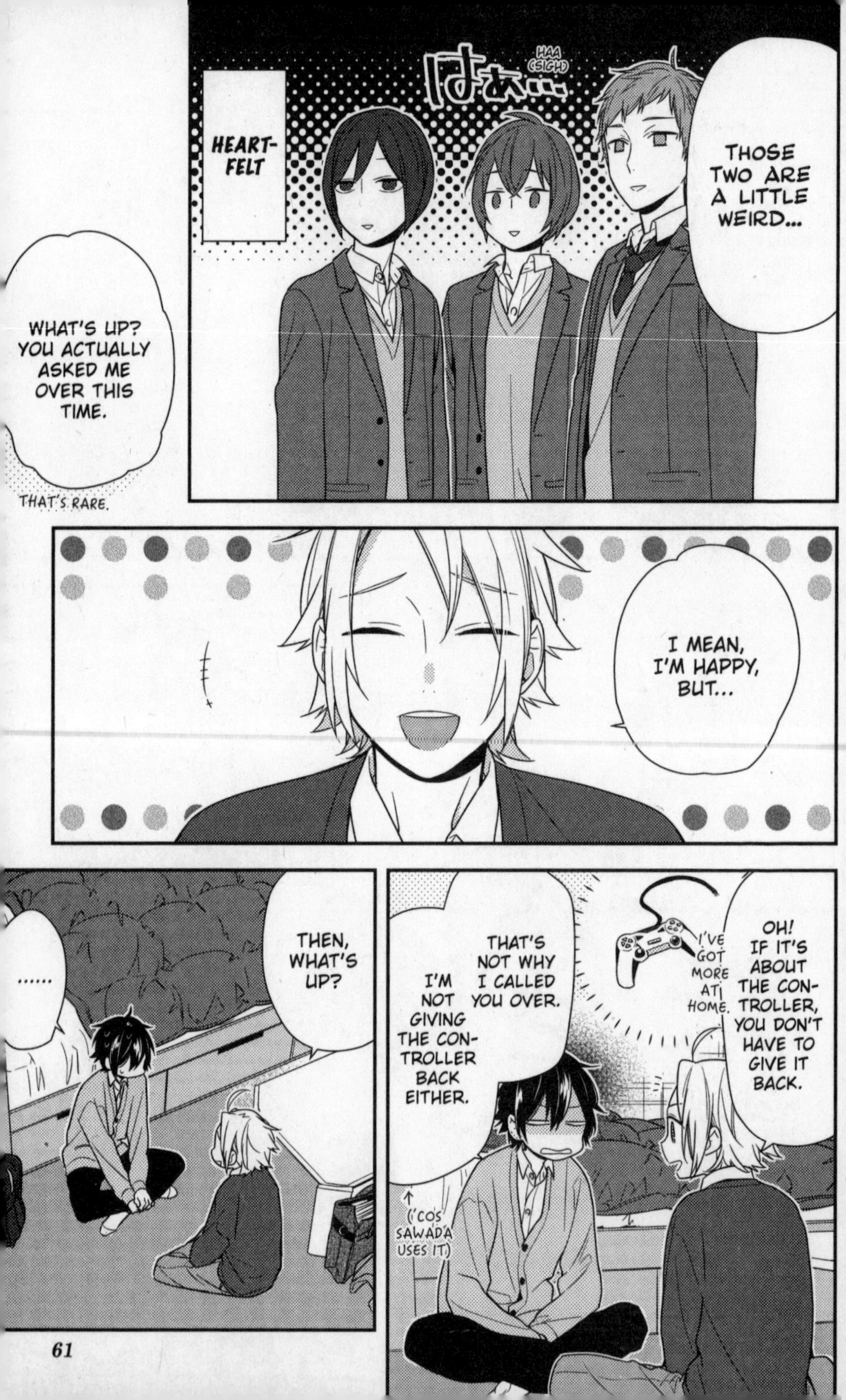
THOSE TWO ARE A LITTLE WEIRD...
HAA (SIGH)
はあ…
HEART-FELT
WHAT'S UP? YOU ACTUALLY ASKED ME OVER THIS TIME.
THAT'S RARE.
I MEAN, I'M HAPPY, BUT...
OH! IF IT'S ABOUT THE CON-TROLLER, YOU DON'T HAVE TO GIVE IT BACK.
I'VE GOT MORE AT HOME.
THAT'S NOT WHY I CALLED YOU OVER.
I'M NOT GIVING THE CON-TROLLER BACK EITHER.
('COS SAWADA USES IT)
THEN, WHAT'S UP?
......

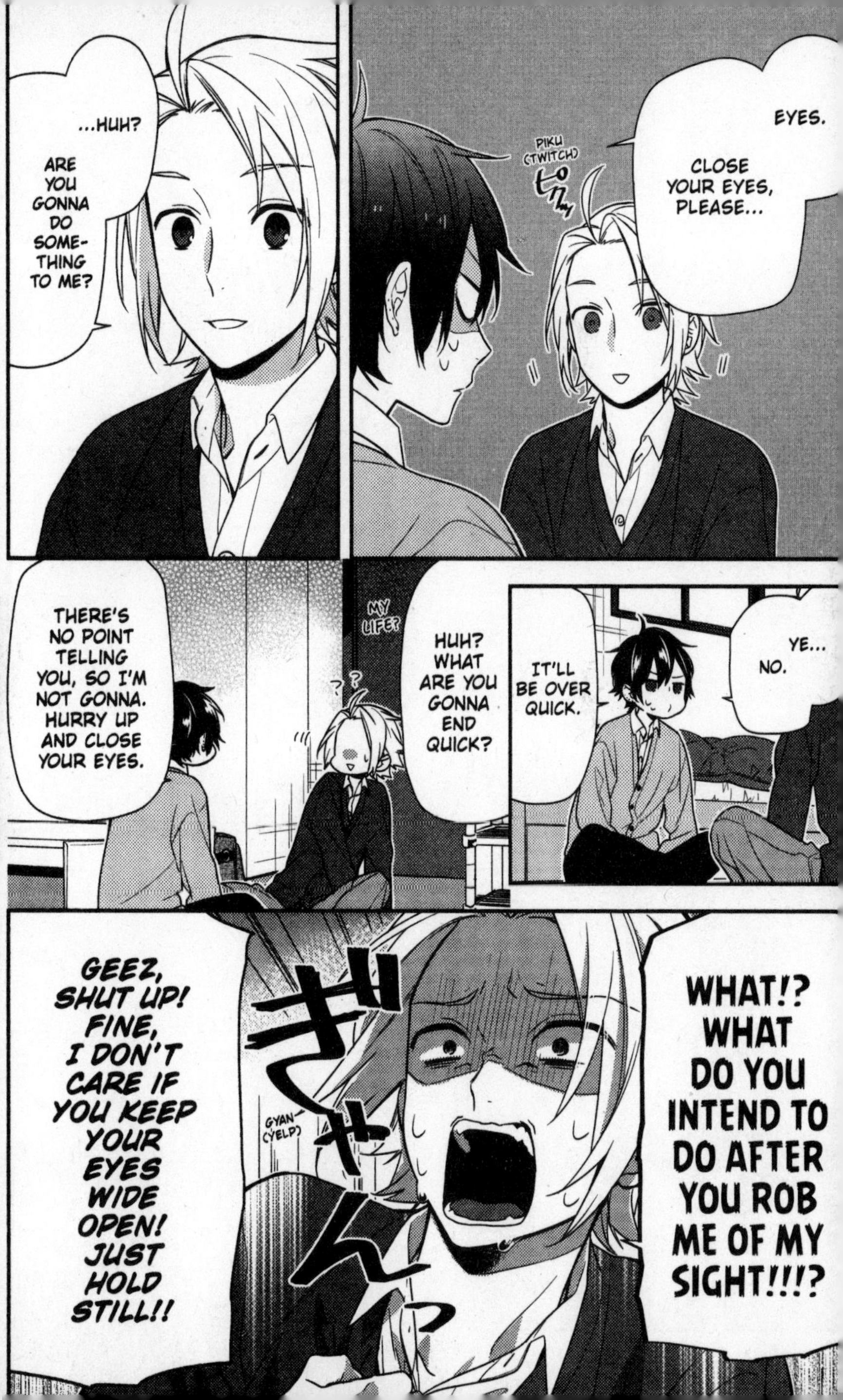
EYES.
CLOSE YOUR EYES, PLEASE...
PIKU (TWITCH)
...HUH?
ARE YOU GONNA DO SOMETHING TO ME?
YE... NO.
IT'LL BE OVER QUICK.
HUH? WHAT ARE YOU GONNA END QUICK?
MY LIFE?
THERE'S NO POINT TELLING YOU, SO I'M NOT GONNA. HURRY UP AND CLOSE YOUR EYES.
WHAT!? WHAT DO YOU INTEND TO DO AFTER YOU ROB ME OF MY SIGHT!!!?
GYAN (YELP)
GEEZ, SHUT UP! FINE, I DON'T CARE IF YOU KEEP YOUR EYES WIDE OPEN! JUST HOLD STILL!!

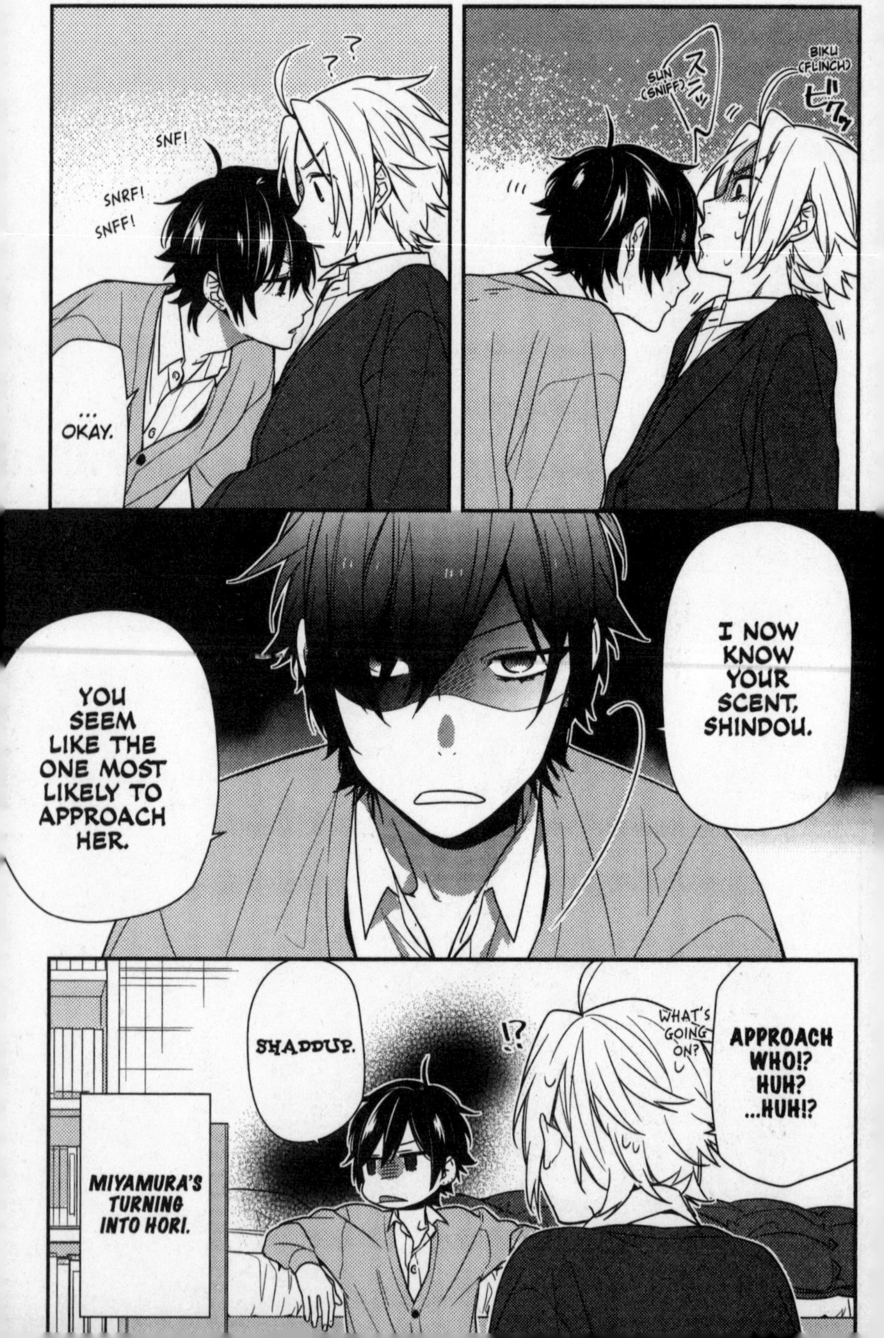
BIKU (FLINCH)
SUN (SNIFF)
SNF!
SNRF!
SNFF!
...OKAY.
I NOW KNOW YOUR SCENT, SHINDOU.
YOU SEEM LIKE THE ONE MOST LIKELY TO APPROACH HER.
APPROACH WHO!? HUH? ...HUH!?
WHAT'S GOING ON?
!?
SHADDUP.
MIYAMURA'S TURNING INTO HORI.

HORIMIYA

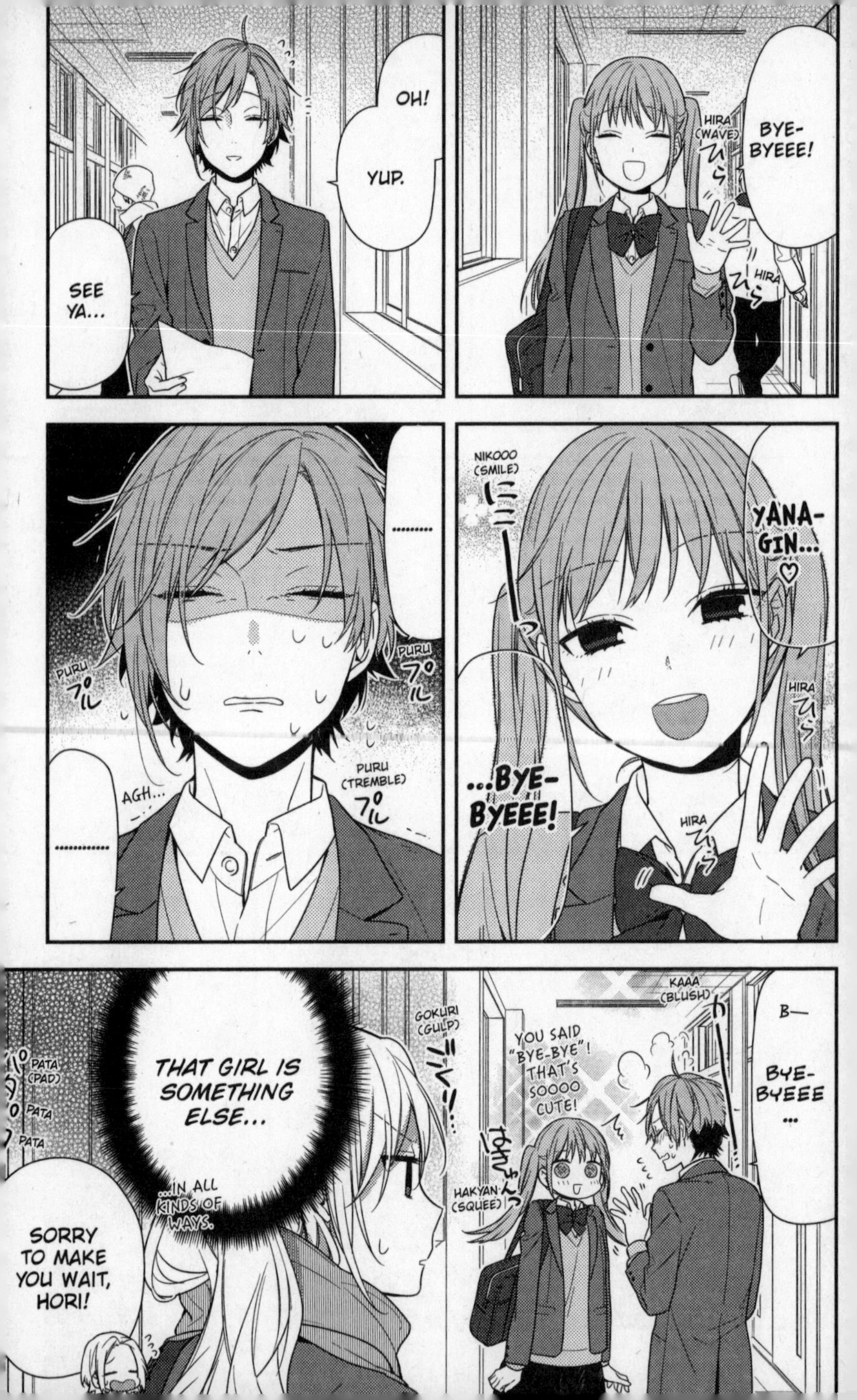
HIRA (WAVE)
BYE-BYEEE!
HIRA
OH!
YUP.
SEE YA...
NIKOOO (SMILE)
YANA-GIN... ♡
HIRA
...BYE-BYEEE!
HIRA
..........
PURU
PURU
PURU (TREMBLE)
AGH...
............
KAAA (BLUSH)
B—
BYE-BYEEE ...
YOU SAID "BYE-BYE"! THAT'S SOOOO CUTE!
HAKYAN (SQUEE)
GOKURI (GULP)
THAT GIRL IS SOMETHING ELSE...
...IN ALL KINDS OF WAYS.
PATA (PAD)
PATA
PATA
SORRY TO MAKE YOU WAIT, HORI!

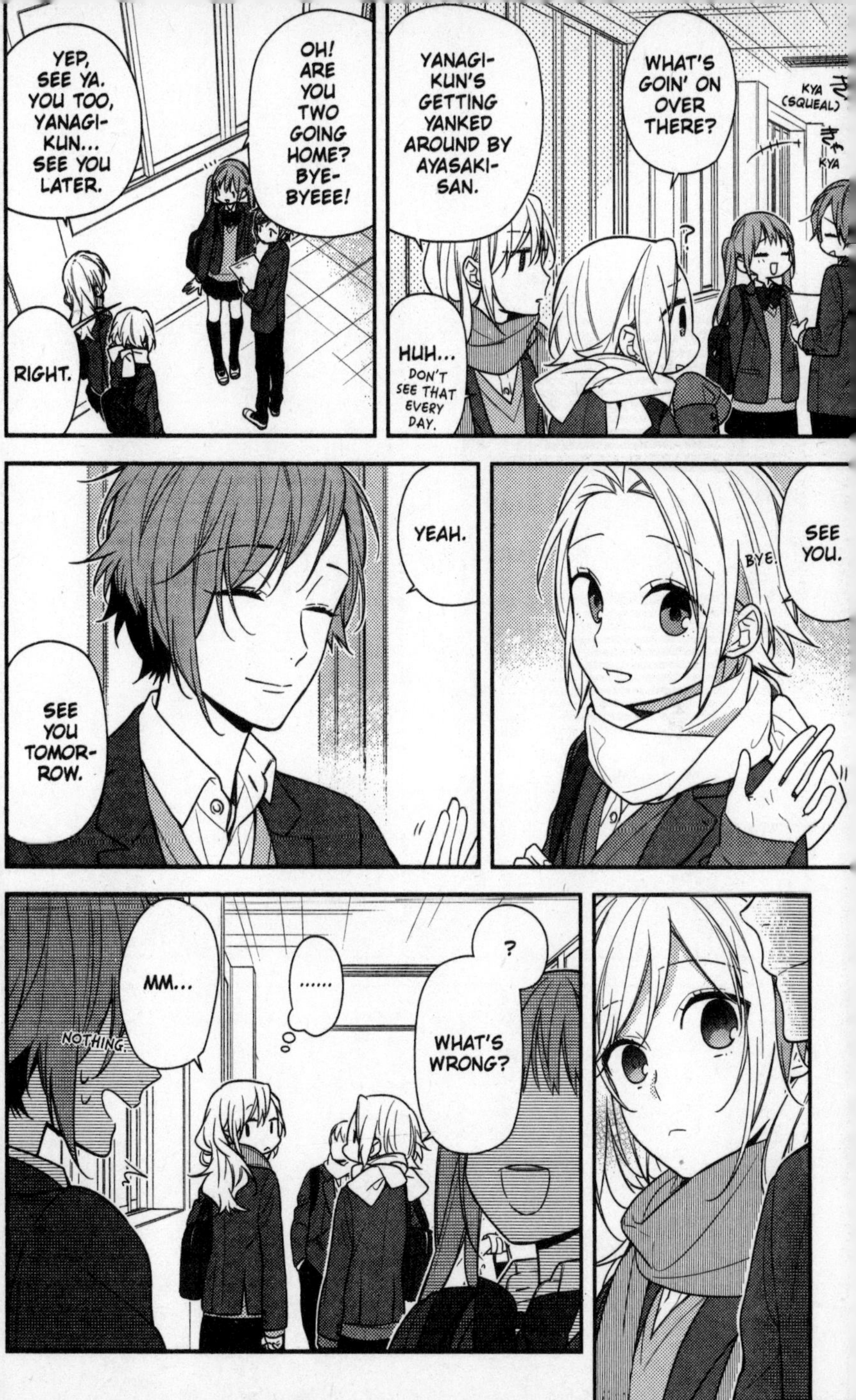
KYA (SQUEAL)
KYA
WHAT'S GOIN' ON OVER THERE?
YANAGI-KUN'S GETTING YANKED AROUND BY AYASAKI-SAN.
HUH... DON'T SEE THAT EVERY DAY.
OH! ARE YOU TWO GOING HOME? BYE-BYEEE!
YEP, SEE YA. YOU TOO, YANAGI-KUN... SEE YOU LATER.
RIGHT.
SEE YOU.
BYE.
YEAH.
SEE YOU TOMORROW.
? WHAT'S WRONG?
......
MM...
NOTHING.

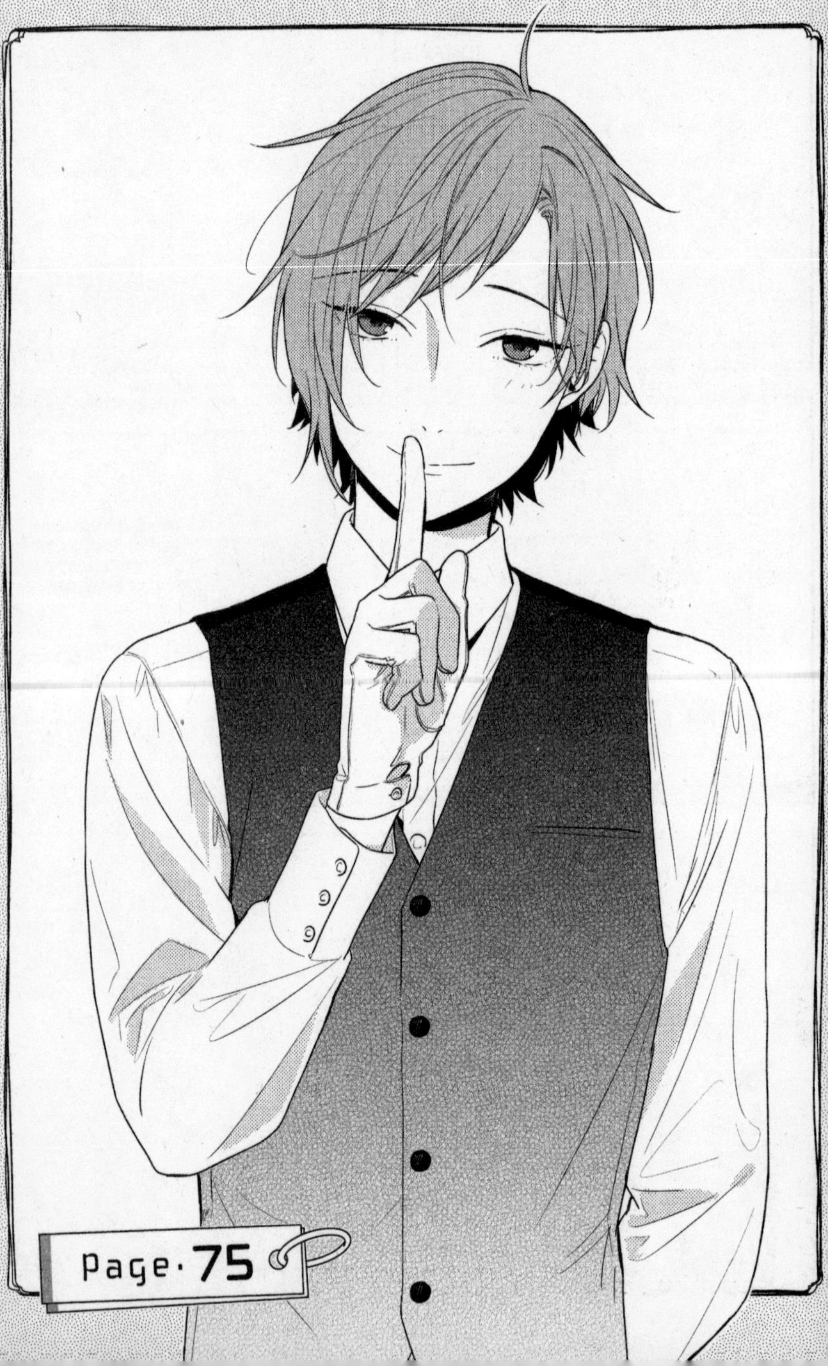
Page·75

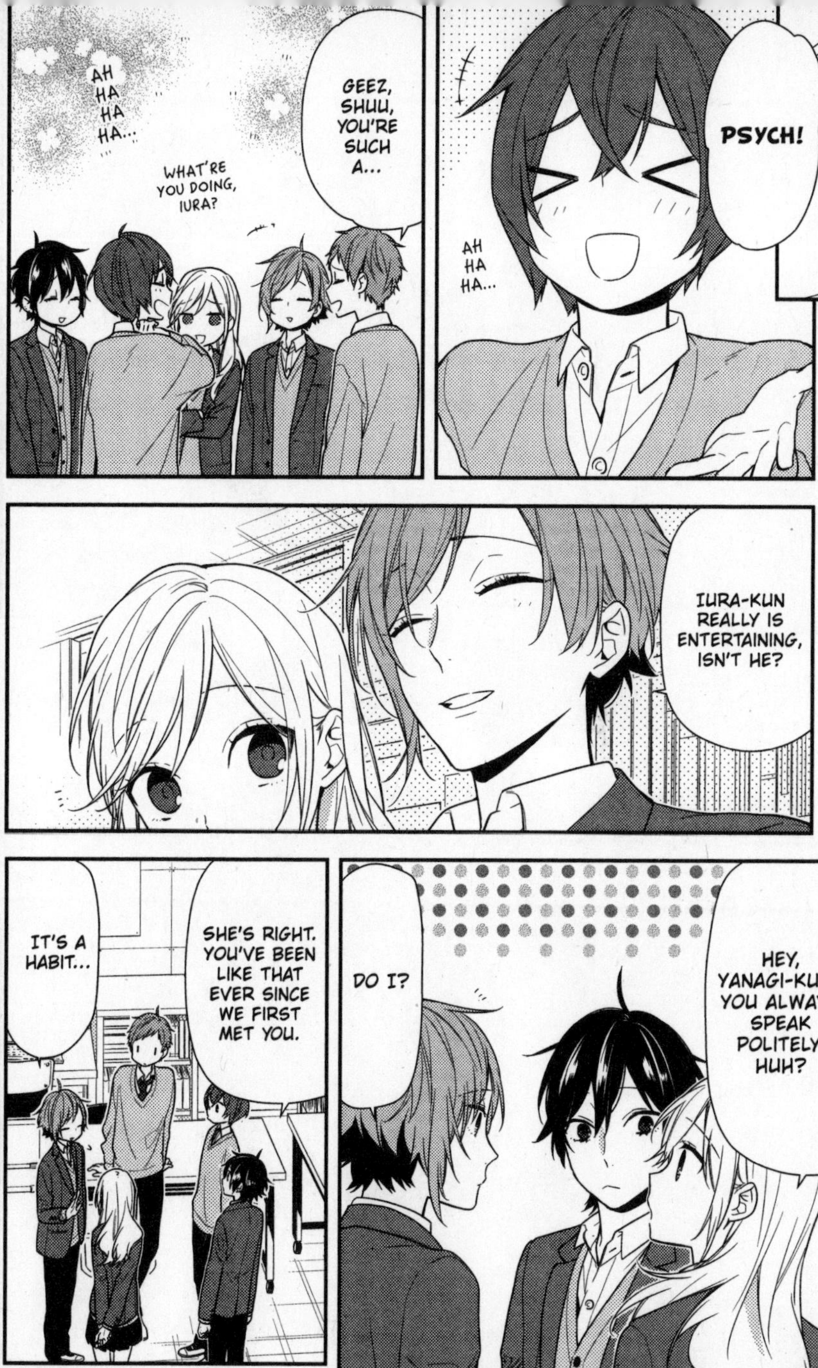
PSYCH!
AH HA HA...
GEEZ, SHUU, YOU'RE SUCH A...
AH HA HA HA...
WHAT'RE YOU DOING, IURA?
IURA-KUN REALLY IS ENTERTAINING, ISN'T HE?
HEY, YANAGI-KUN? YOU ALWAYS SPEAK POLITELY, HUH?
DO I?
SHE'S RIGHT. YOU'VE BEEN LIKE THAT EVER SINCE WE FIRST MET YOU.
IT'S A HABIT...

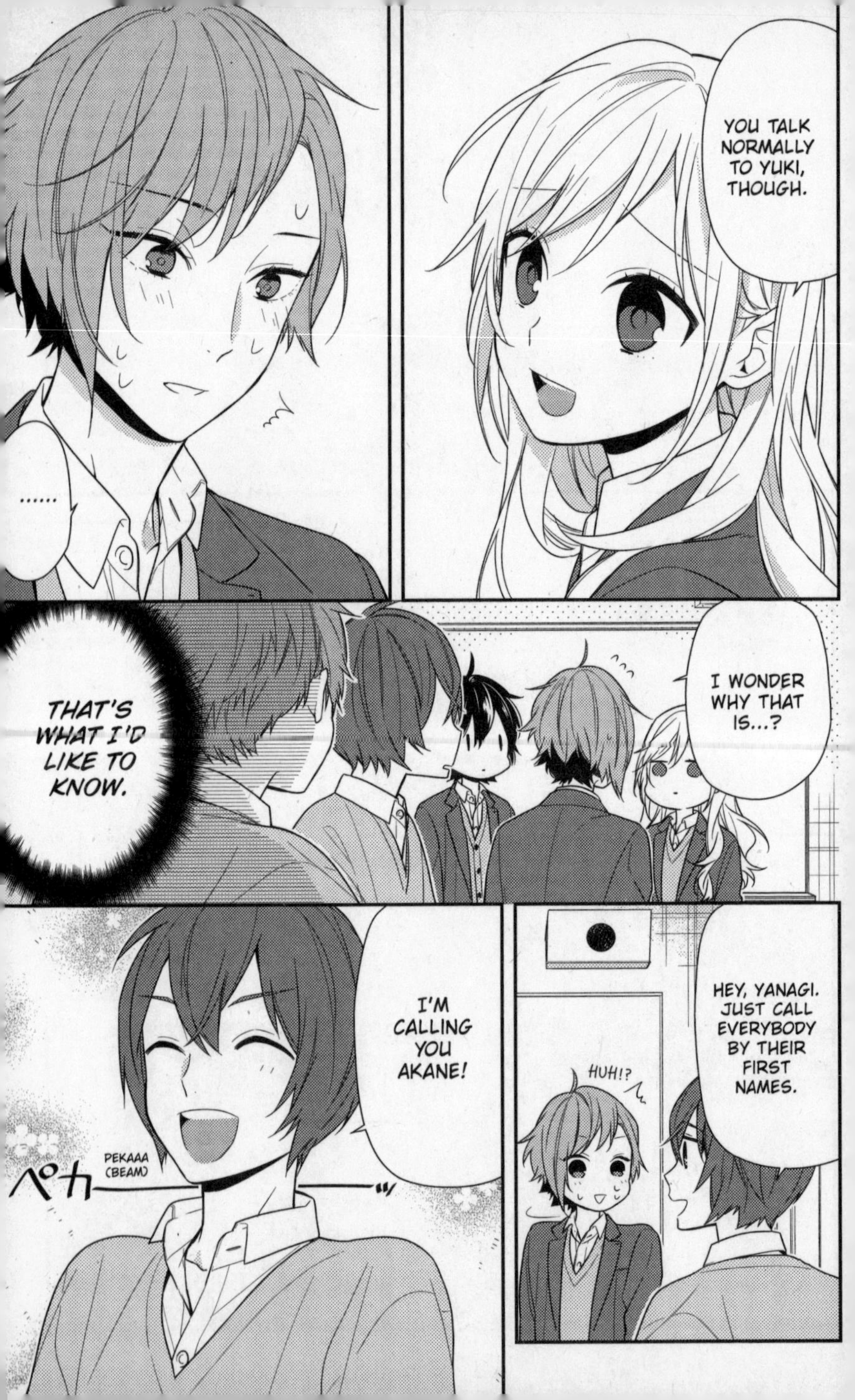
YOU TALK NORMALLY TO YUKI, THOUGH.
......
I WONDER WHY THAT IS...?
THAT'S WHAT I'D LIKE TO KNOW.
HEY, YANAGI. JUST CALL EVERYBODY BY THEIR FIRST NAMES.
HUH!?
I'M CALLING YOU AKANE!
ペカ
PEKAAA (BEAM)

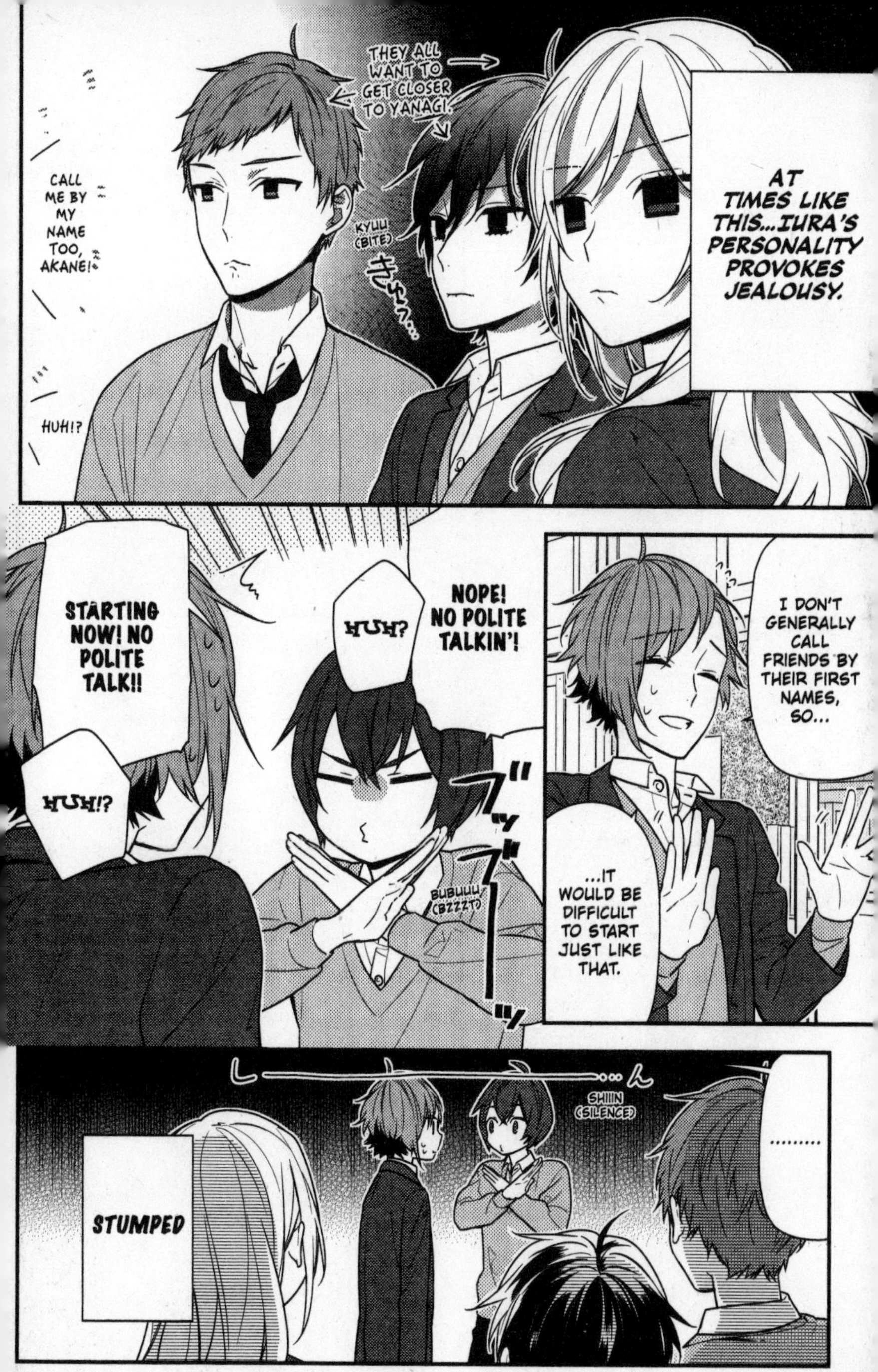
AT TIMES LIKE THIS...IURA'S PERSONALITY PROVOKES JEALOUSY.
THEY ALL WANT TO GET CLOSER TO YANAGI.
KYUU (BITE)
CALL ME BY MY NAME TOO, AKANE!
HUH!?
I DON'T GENERALLY CALL FRIENDS BY THEIR FIRST NAMES, SO...
...IT WOULD BE DIFFICULT TO START JUST LIKE THAT.
NOPE! NO POLITE TALKIN'!
HUH?
BUBUUU (BZZZT)
STARTING NOW! NO POLITE TALK!!
HUH!?
.........
SHIIIN (SILENCE)
STUMPED

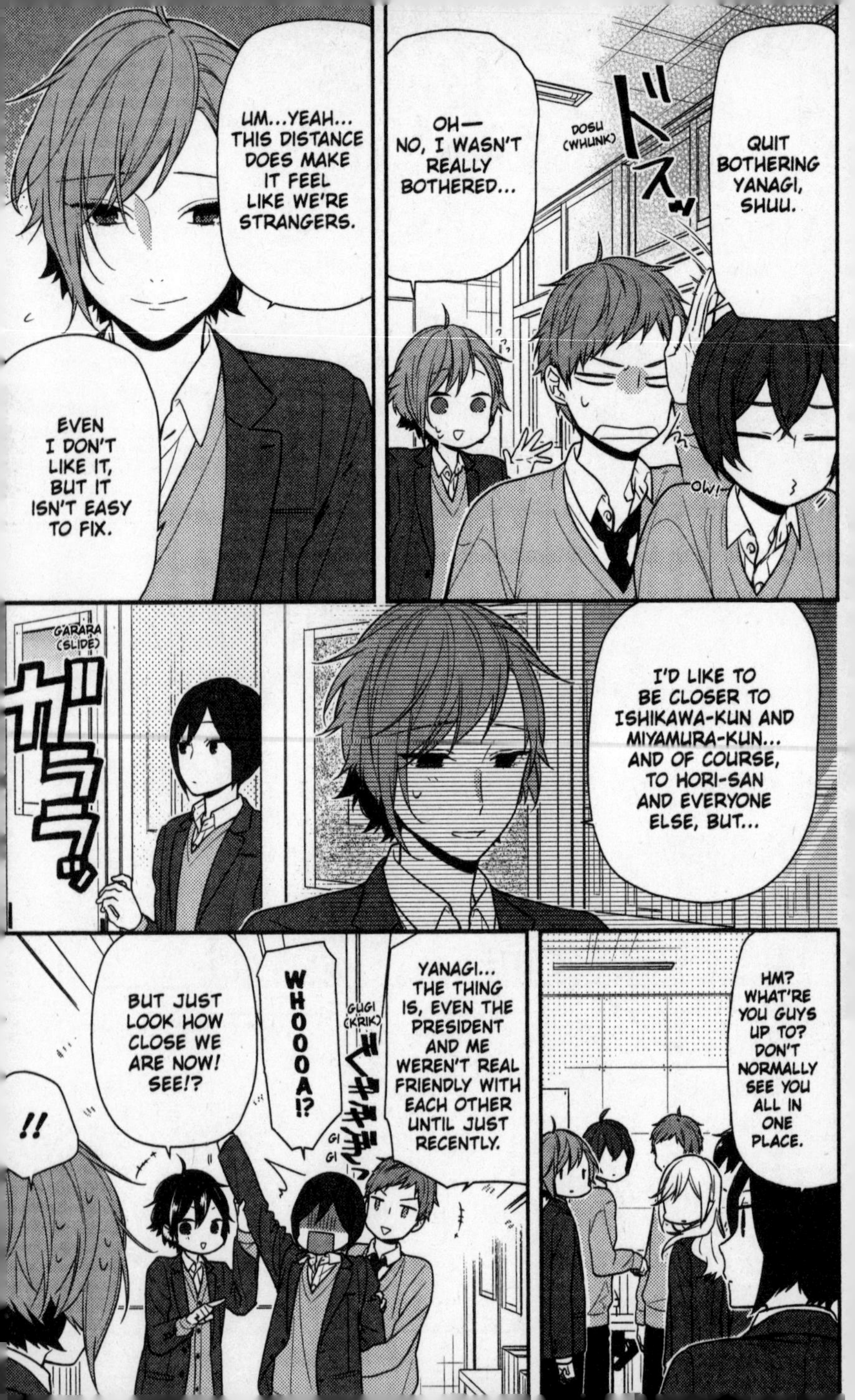
QUIT BOTHERING YANAGI, SHUU.
DOSU (WHUNK)
OW
OH— NO, I WASN'T REALLY BOTHERED...
UM...YEAH... THIS DISTANCE DOES MAKE IT FEEL LIKE WE'RE STRANGERS.
EVEN I DON'T LIKE IT, BUT IT ISN'T EASY TO FIX.
I'D LIKE TO BE CLOSER TO ISHIKAWA-KUN AND MIYAMURA-KUN... AND OF COURSE, TO HORI-SAN AND EVERYONE ELSE, BUT...
GARARA (SLIDE)
HM? WHAT'RE YOU GUYS UP TO? DON'T NORMALLY SEE YOU ALL IN ONE PLACE.
YANAGI... THE THING IS, EVEN THE PRESIDENT AND ME WEREN'T REAL FRIENDLY WITH EACH OTHER UNTIL JUST RECENTLY.
GUGI (KRIK)
GI GI
WHOOOA!?
BUT JUST LOOK HOW CLOSE WE ARE NOW! SEE!?
!!

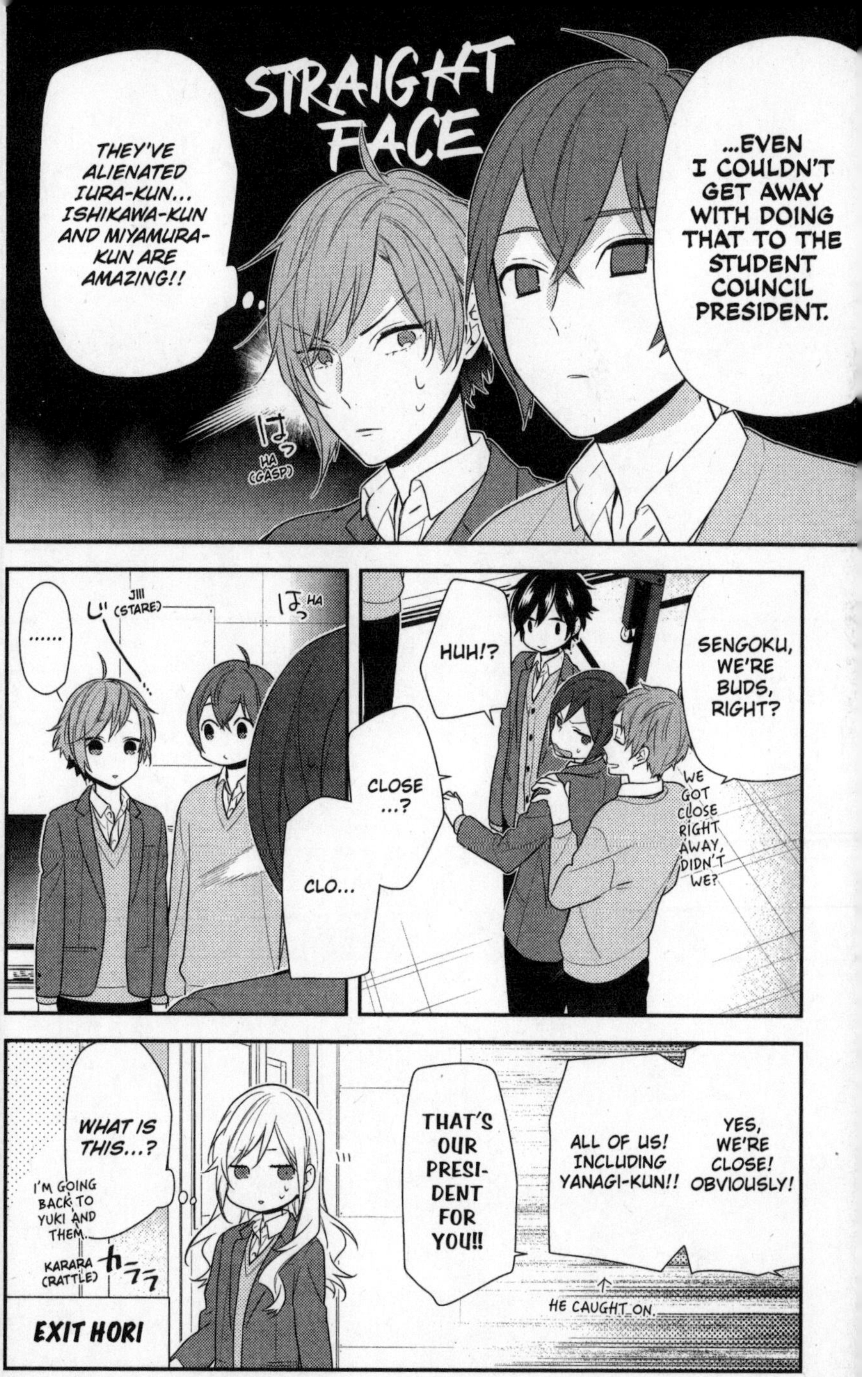

...EVEN I COULDN'T GET AWAY WITH DOING THAT TO THE STUDENT COUNCIL PRESIDENT.
STRAIGHT FACE
THEY'VE ALIENATED IURA-KUN... ISHIKAWA-KUN AND MIYAMURA-KUN ARE AMAZING!!
はっ HA (GASP)
SENGOKU, WE'RE BUDS, RIGHT?
WE GOT CLOSE RIGHT AWAY, DIDN'T WE?
HUH!?
CLOSE ...?
CLO...
はっ HA
じー JIII (STARE)
......
YES, WE'RE CLOSE! OBVIOUSLY!
ALL OF US! INCLUDING YANAGI-KUN!!
HE CAUGHT ON.
THAT'S OUR PRESI-DENT FOR YOU!!
WHAT IS THIS...?
I'M GOING BACK TO YUKI AND THEM.
KARARA (RATTLE) カラララ
EXIT HORI

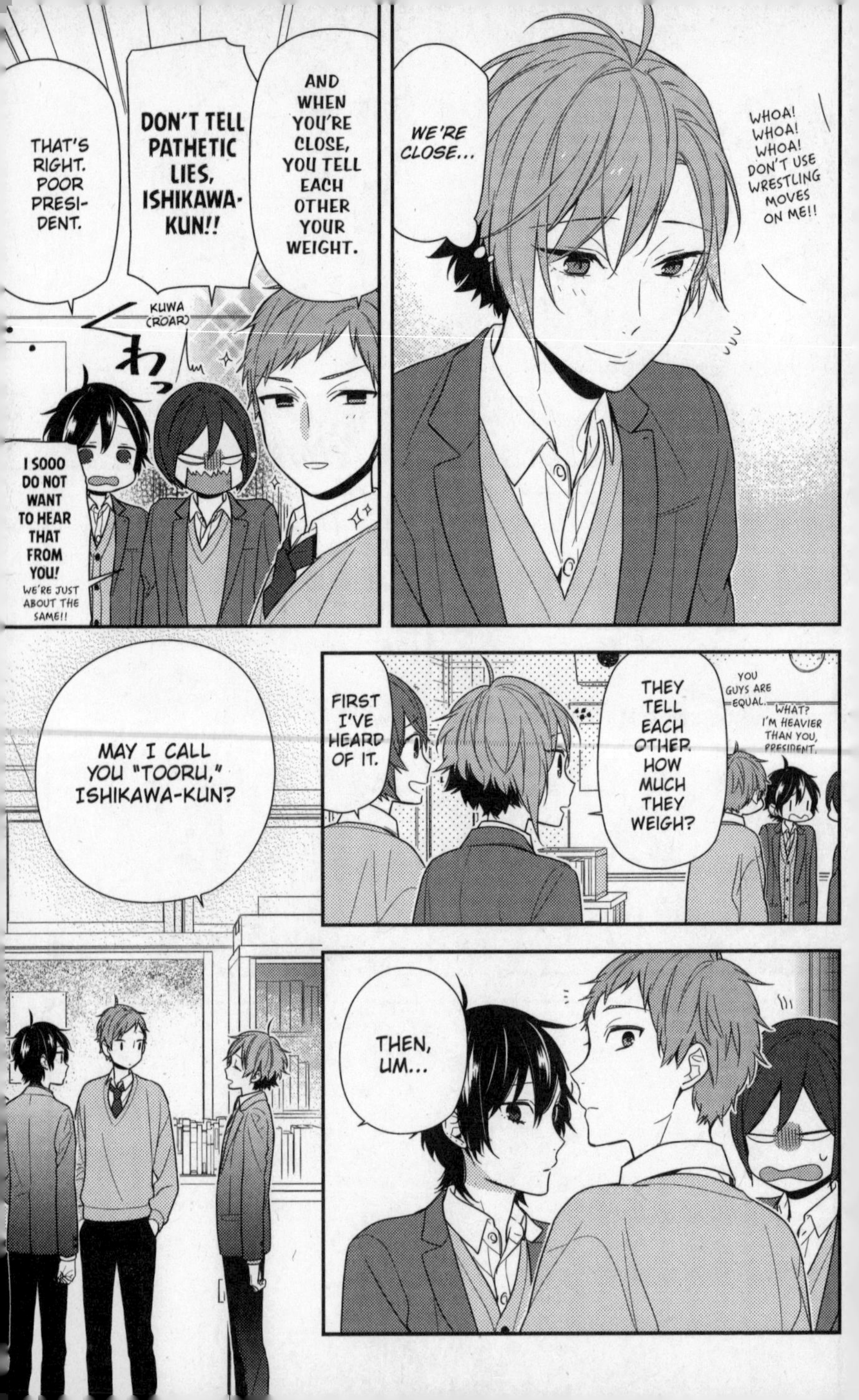
WHOA! WHOA! WHOA! DON'T USE WRESTLING MOVES ON ME!!
WE'RE CLOSE...
AND WHEN YOU'RE CLOSE, YOU TELL EACH OTHER YOUR WEIGHT.
DON'T TELL PATHETIC LIES, ISHIKAWA-KUN!!
THAT'S RIGHT. POOR PRESIDENT.
KUWA (ROAR)
I SOOO DO NOT WANT TO HEAR THAT FROM YOU!
WE'RE JUST ABOUT THE SAME!!
YOU GUYS ARE EQUAL.
WHAT? I'M HEAVIER THAN YOU, PRESIDENT.
THEY TELL EACH OTHER HOW MUCH THEY WEIGH?
FIRST I'VE HEARD OF IT.
THEN, UM...
MAY I CALL YOU "TOORU," ISHIKAWA-KUN?

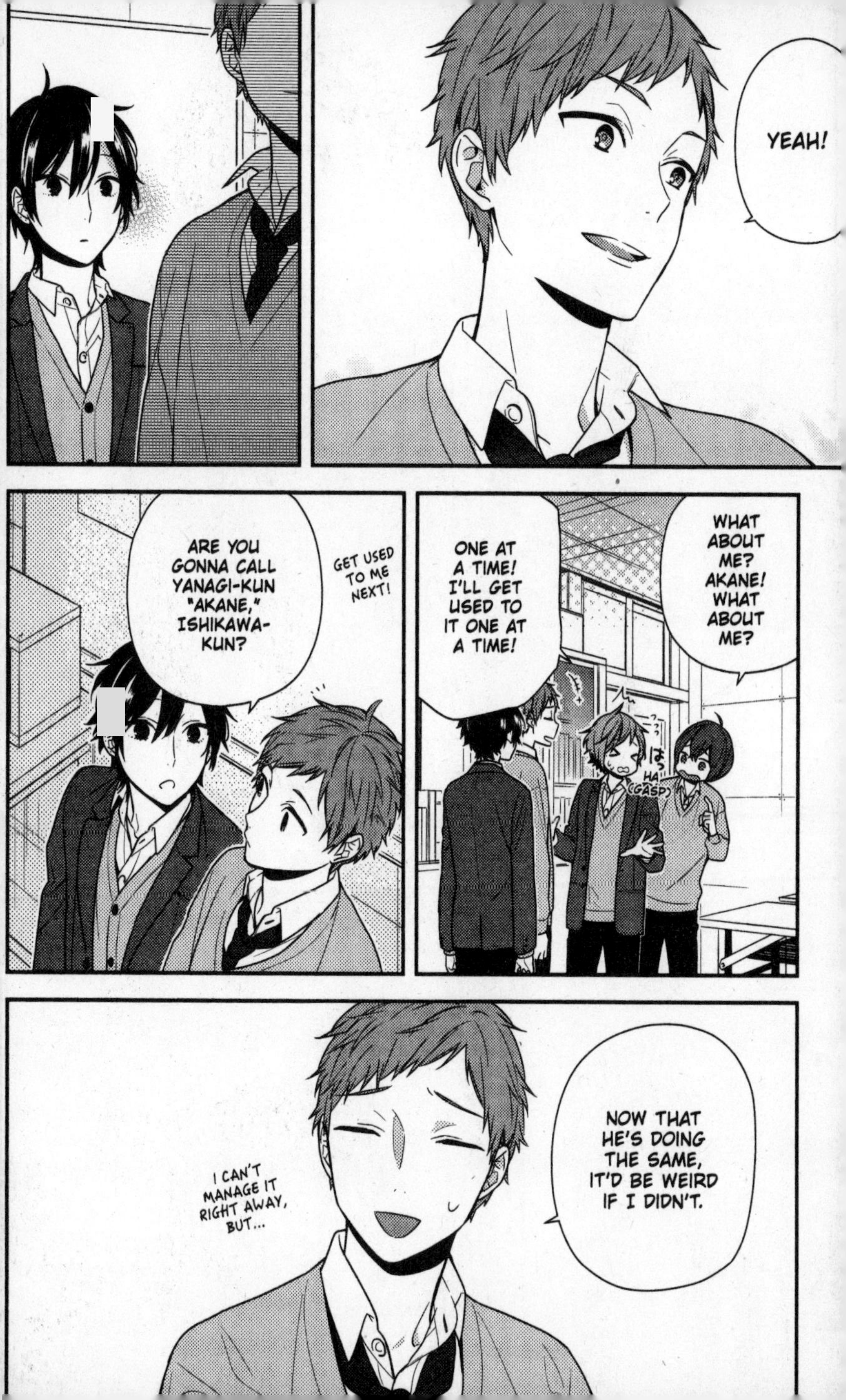
YEAH!
WHAT ABOUT ME? AKANE! WHAT ABOUT ME?
ONE AT A TIME! I'LL GET USED TO IT ONE AT A TIME!
はっ
HA (GASP)
GET USED TO ME NEXT!
ARE YOU GONNA CALL YANAGI-KUN "AKANE," ISHIKAWA-KUN?
NOW THAT HE'S DOING THE SAME, IT'D BE WEIRD IF I DIDN'T.
I CAN'T MANAGE IT RIGHT AWAY, BUT...

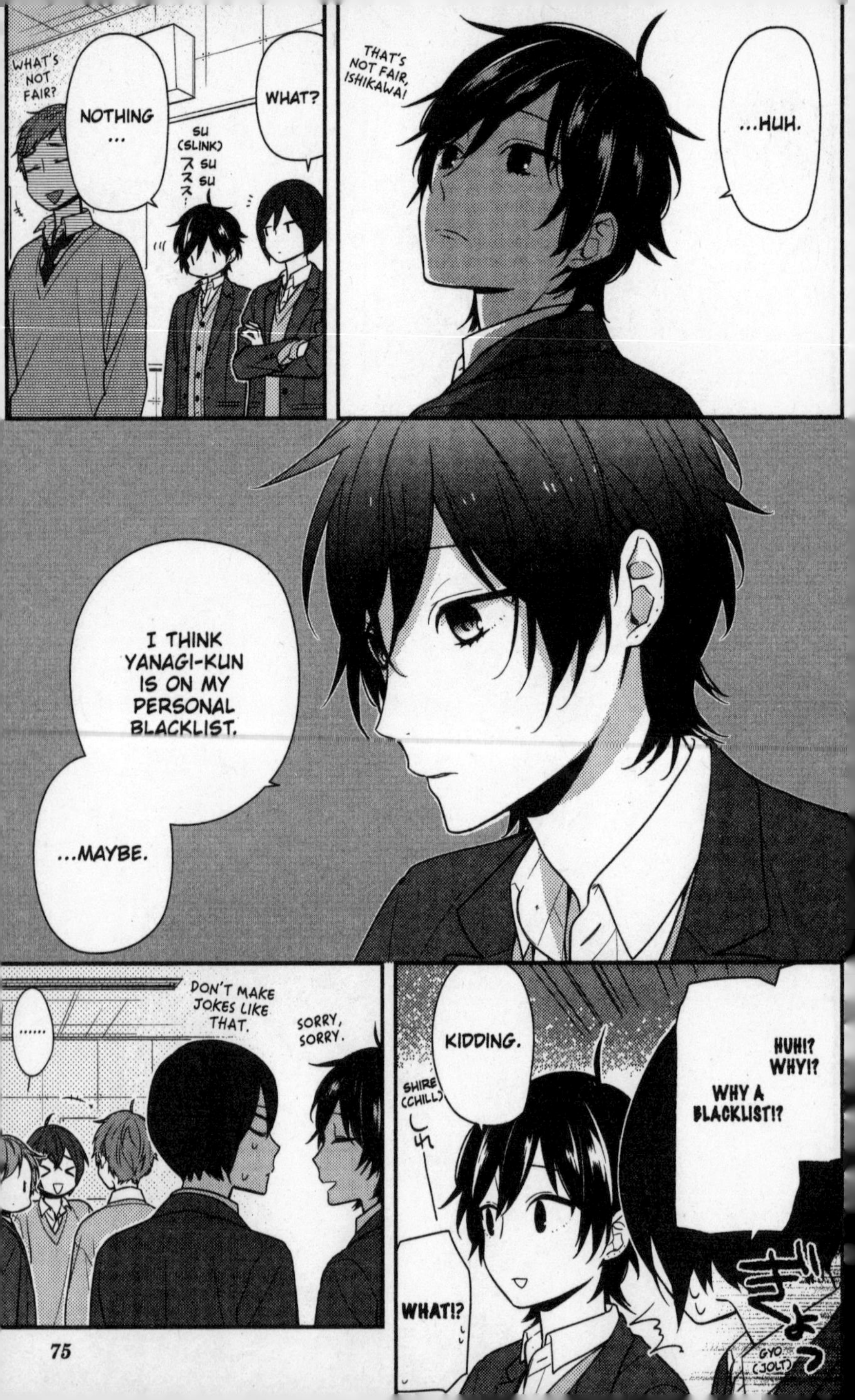
...HUH.
THAT'S NOT FAIR, ISHIKAWA!
WHAT?
NOTHING...
WHAT'S NOT FAIR?
SU (SLINK) SU SU
ススス…
I THINK YANAGI-KUN IS ON MY PERSONAL BLACKLIST.
...MAYBE.
HUH!? WHY!?
WHY A BLACKLIST!?
KIDDING.
SHIRE (CHILL)
GYO (JOLT)
WHAT!?
SORRY, SORRY.
DON'T MAKE JOKES LIKE THAT.
......

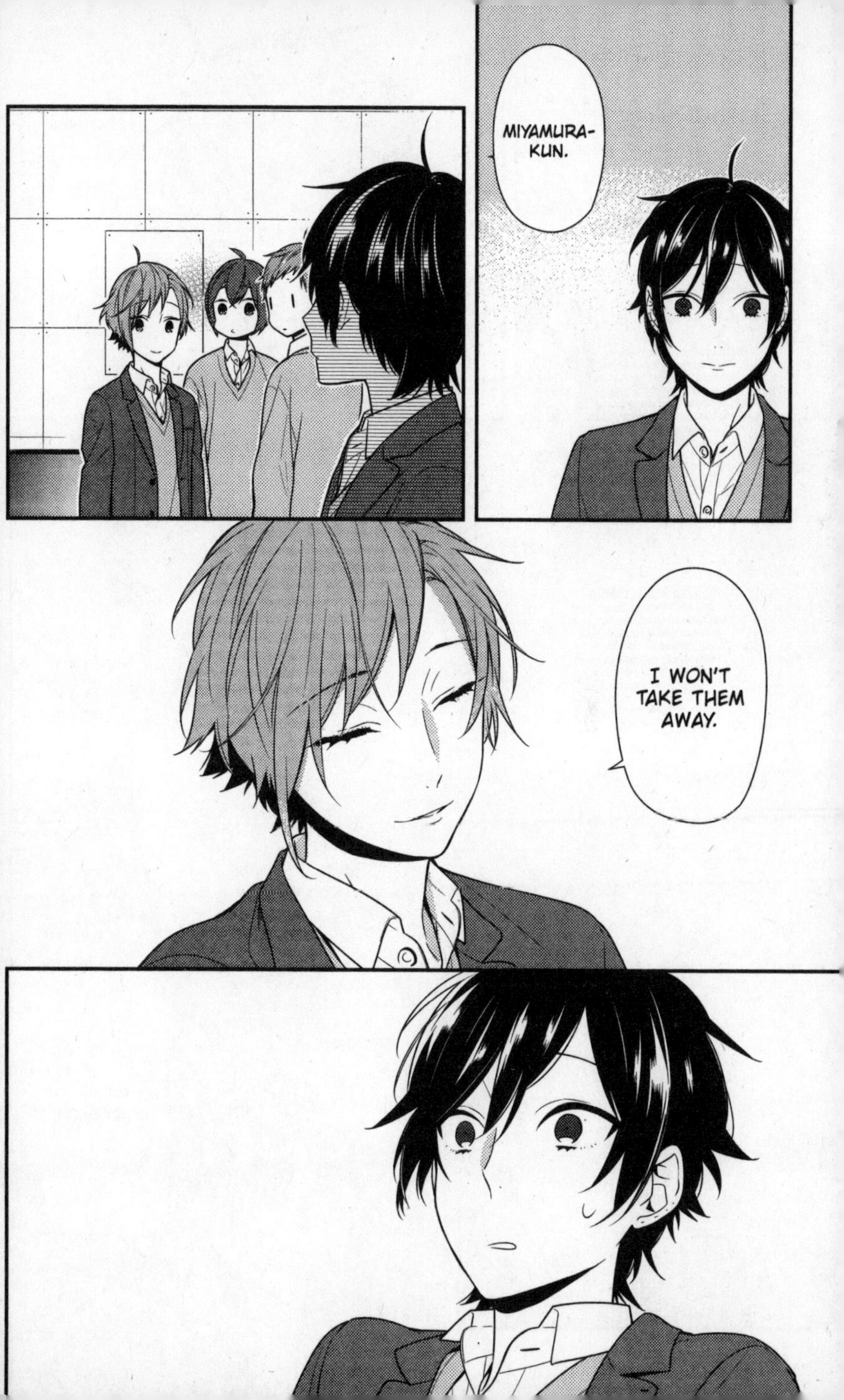
MIYAMURA-KUN.
I WON'T TAKE THEM AWAY.

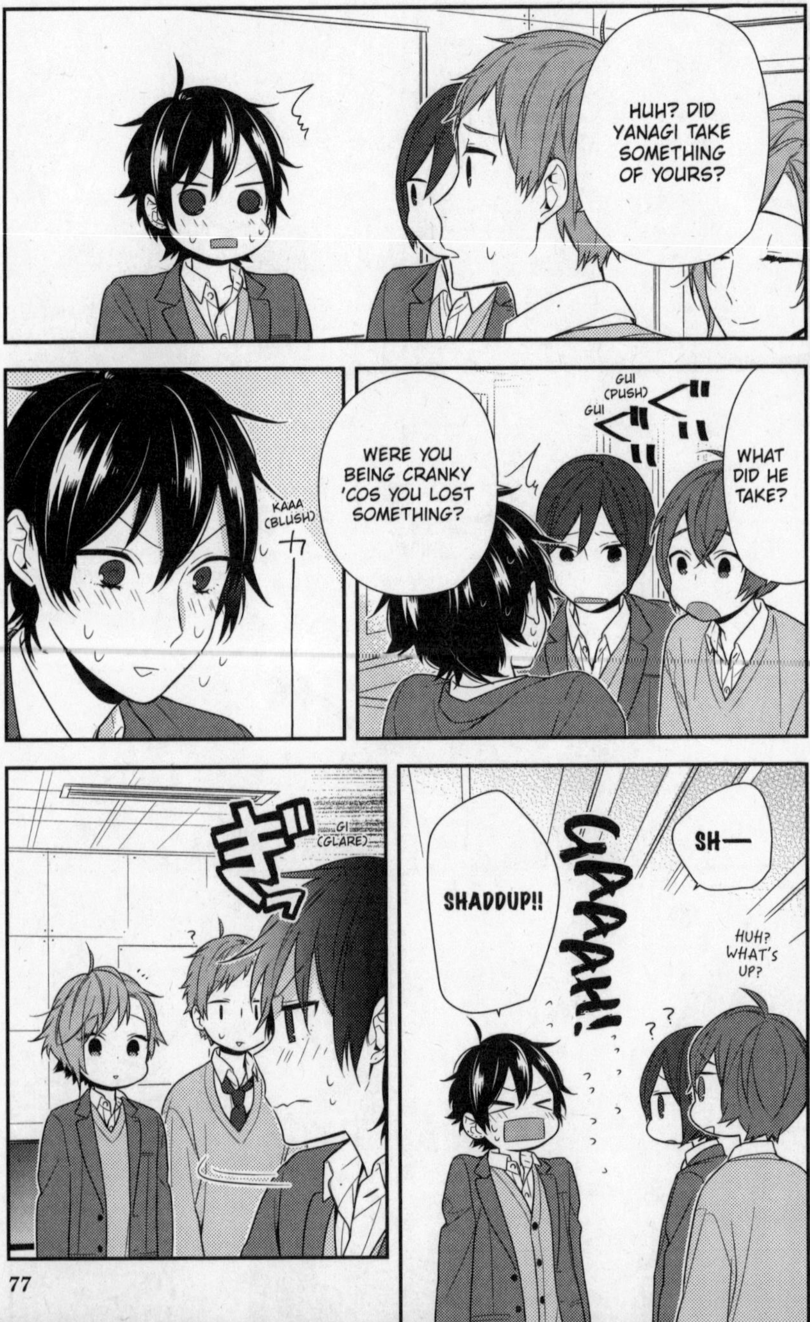
HUH? DID YANAGI TAKE SOMETHING OF YOURS?
WHAT DID HE TAKE?
GUI (PUSH)
GUI
WERE YOU BEING CRANKY 'COS YOU LOST SOMETHING?
KAAA (BLUSH)
SH—
HUH? WHAT'S UP?
GAAAAH!
SHADDUP!!
GI (GLARE)

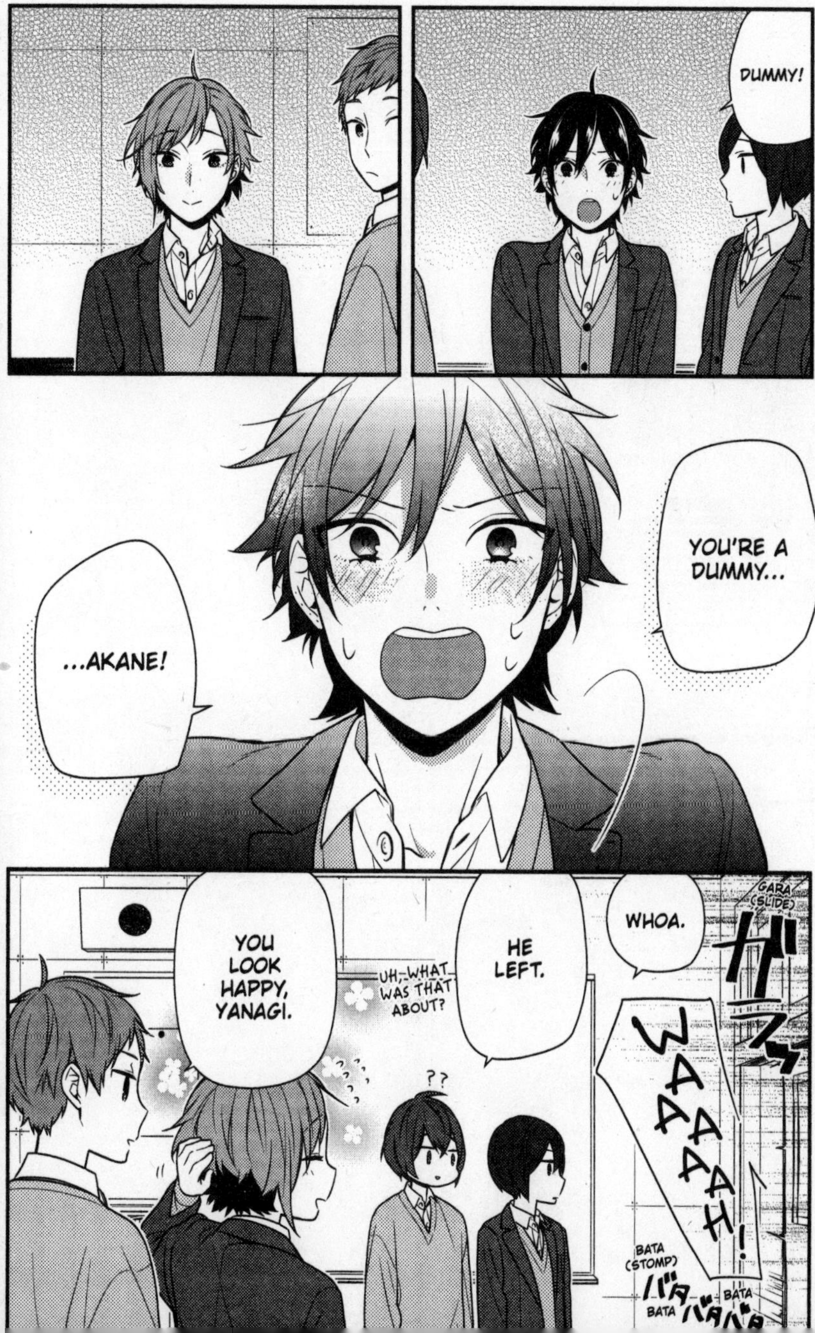
DUMMY!
YOU'RE A DUMMY...
...AKANE!
GARA (SLIDE)
WAAAAH!
BATA (STOMP)
BATA
BATA
WHOA.
HE LEFT.
UH, WHAT WAS THAT ABOUT?
YOU LOOK HAPPY, YANAGI.

HORIMIYA

HORIMIYA

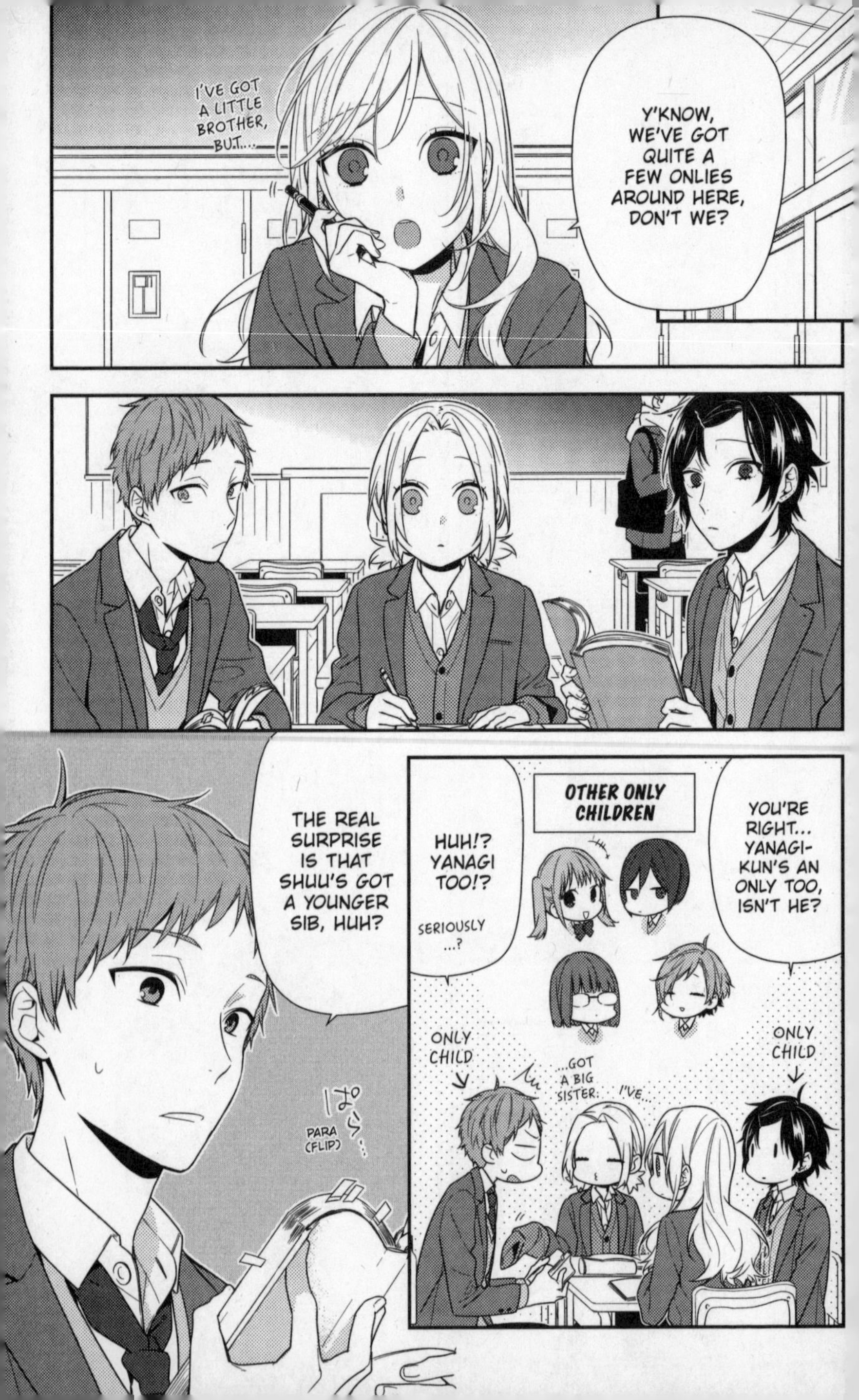
Y'KNOW, WE'VE GOT QUITE A FEW ONLIES AROUND HERE, DON'T WE?
I'VE GOT A LITTLE BROTHER, BUT....
OTHER ONLY CHILDREN
YOU'RE RIGHT... YANAGI-KUN'S AN ONLY TOO, ISN'T HE?
HUH!? YANAGI TOO!?
SERIOUSLY ...?
ONLY CHILD
I'VE...
...GOT A BIG SISTER.
ONLY CHILD
THE REAL SURPRISE IS THAT SHUU'S GOT A YOUNGER SIB, HUH?
ぱら…
PARA (FLIP)

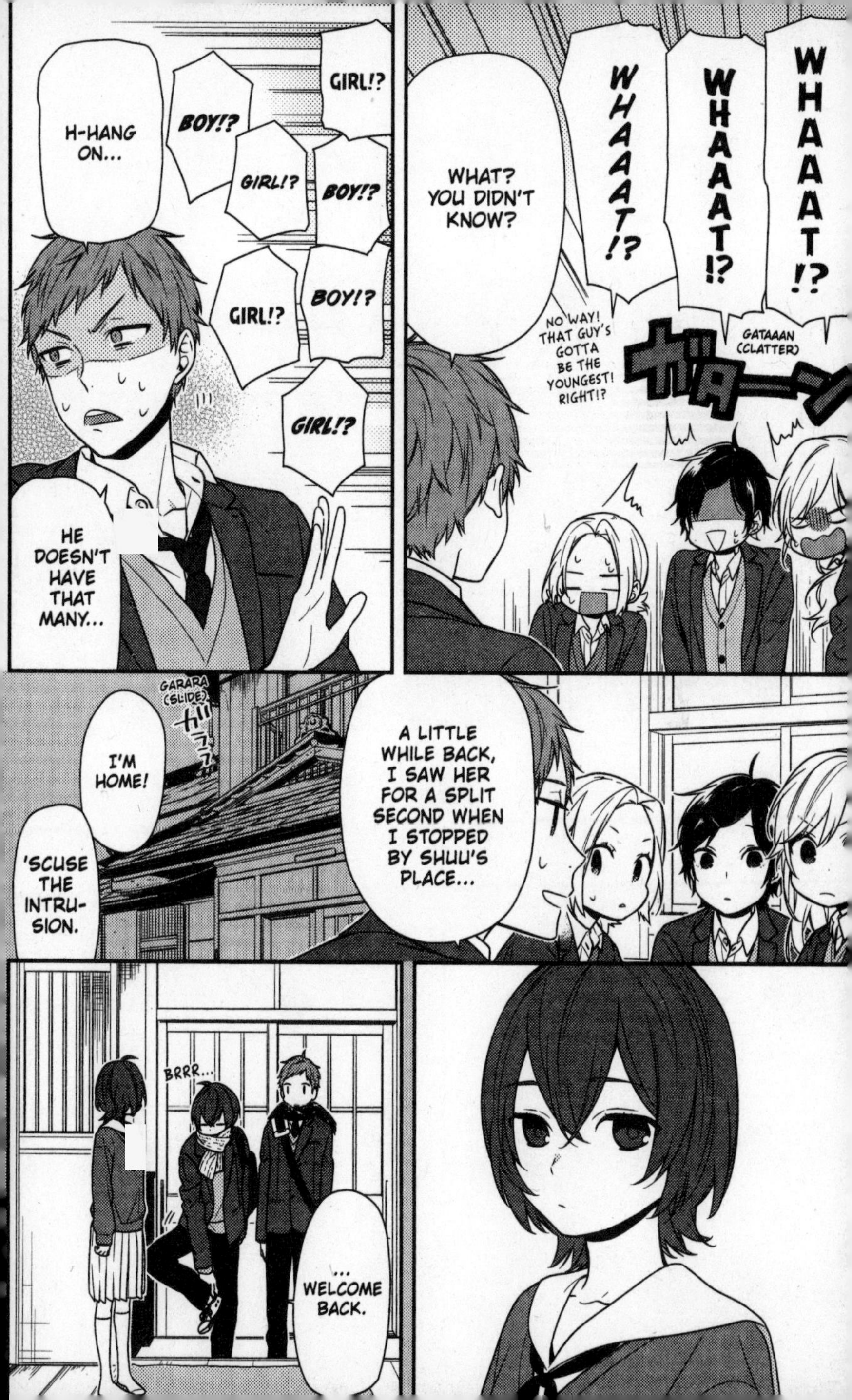
WHAAAT!?
WHAAAT!?
WHAAAT!?
GATAAAN (CLATTER)
WHAT? YOU DIDN'T KNOW?
NO WAY! THAT GUY'S GOTTA BE THE YOUNGEST! RIGHT!?
GIRL!?
BOY!?
BOY!?
GIRL!?
H-HANG ON...
BOY!?
GIRL!?
GIRL!?
HE DOESN'T HAVE THAT MANY...
A LITTLE WHILE BACK, I SAW HER FOR A SPLIT SECOND WHEN I STOPPED BY SHUU'S PLACE...
GARARA (SLIDE)
I'M HOME!
'SCUSE THE INTRUSION.
BRRR...
...WELCOME BACK.

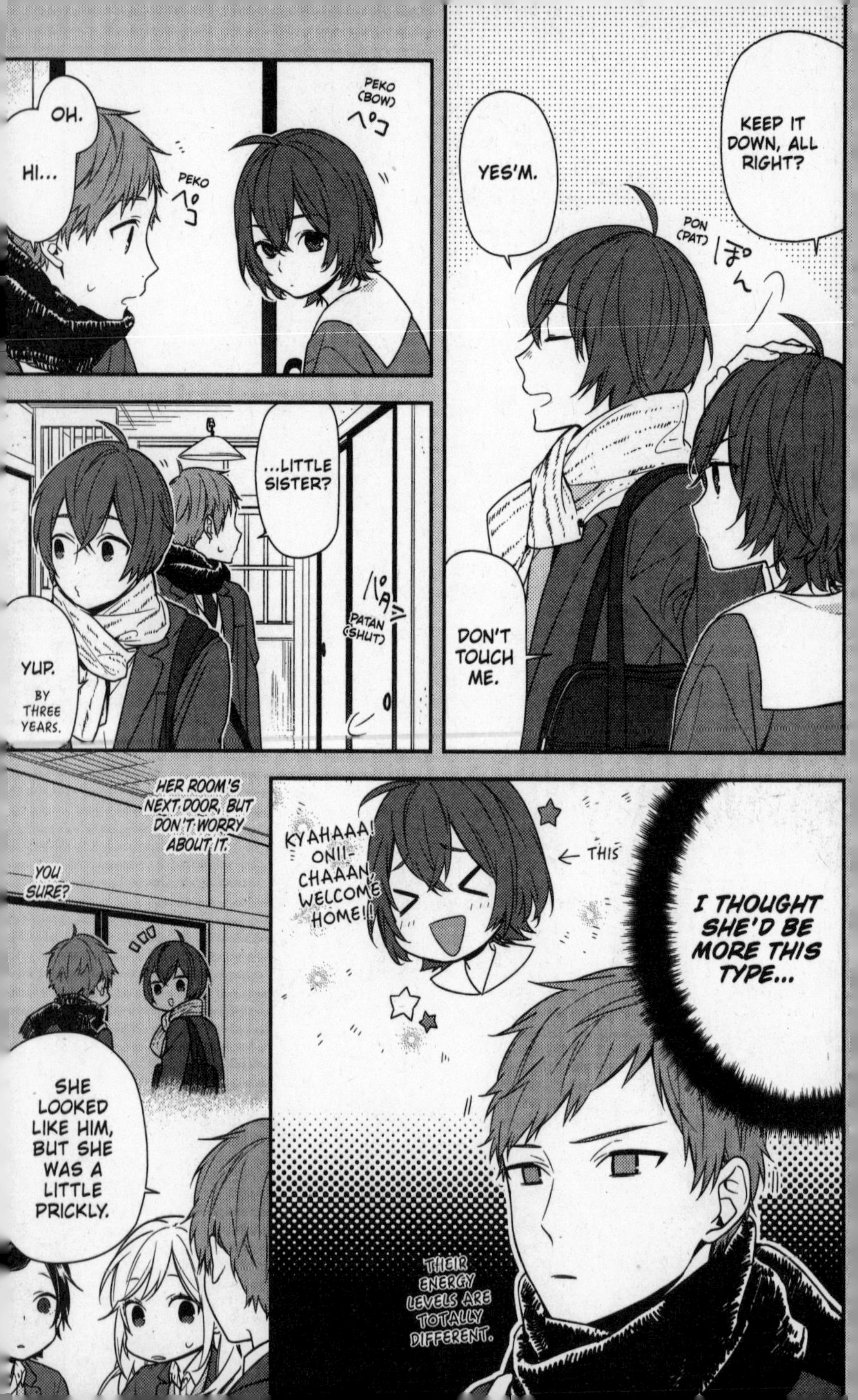
KEEP IT DOWN, ALL RIGHT?
PON (PAT) ぽん
YES'M.
DON'T TOUCH ME.
PEKO (BOW) ペコ
PEKO ペコ
OH.
HI...
...LITTLE SISTER?
パタン PATAN (SHUT)
YUP.
BY THREE YEARS.
I THOUGHT SHE'D BE MORE THIS TYPE...
← THIS
KYAHAAA! ONII-CHAAAN, WELCOME HOME!!
THEIR ENERGY LEVELS ARE TOTALLY DIFFERENT.
HER ROOM'S NEXT DOOR, BUT DON'T WORRY ABOUT IT.
YOU SURE?
SHE LOOKED LIKE HIM, BUT SHE WAS A LITTLE PRICKLY.

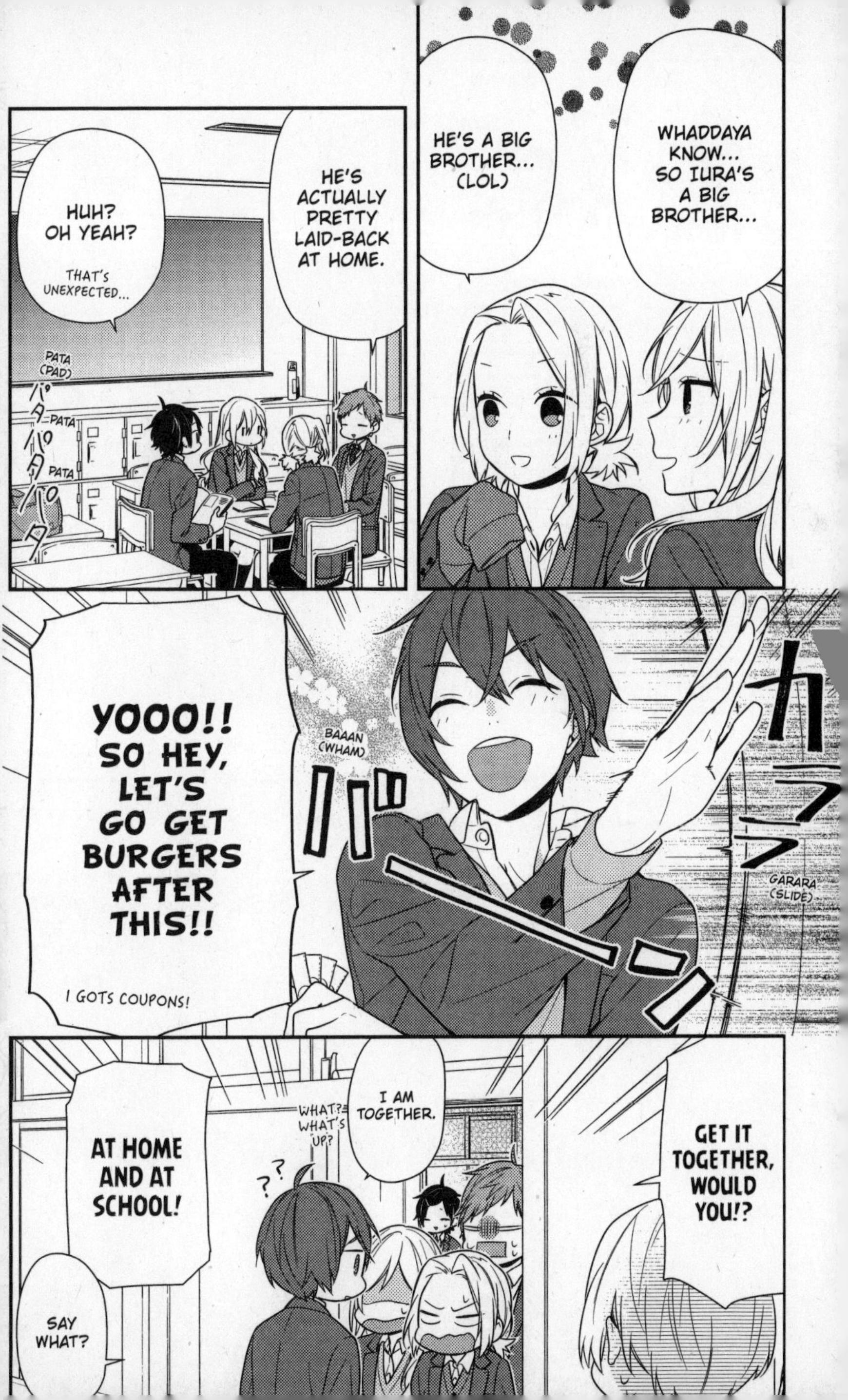
WHADDAYA KNOW... SO IURA'S A BIG BROTHER...
HE'S A BIG BROTHER... (LOL)
HE'S ACTUALLY PRETTY LAID-BACK AT HOME.
HUH? OH YEAH?
THAT'S UNEXPECTED...
PATA (PAD)
PATA
PATA
GARARA (SLIDE)
BAAAN (WHAM)
YOOO!! SO HEY, LET'S GO GET BURGERS AFTER THIS!!
I GOTS COUPONS!
GET IT TOGETHER, WOULD YOU!?
I AM TOGETHER.
WHAT?= WHAT'S UP?
AT HOME AND AT SCHOOL!
SAY WHAT?

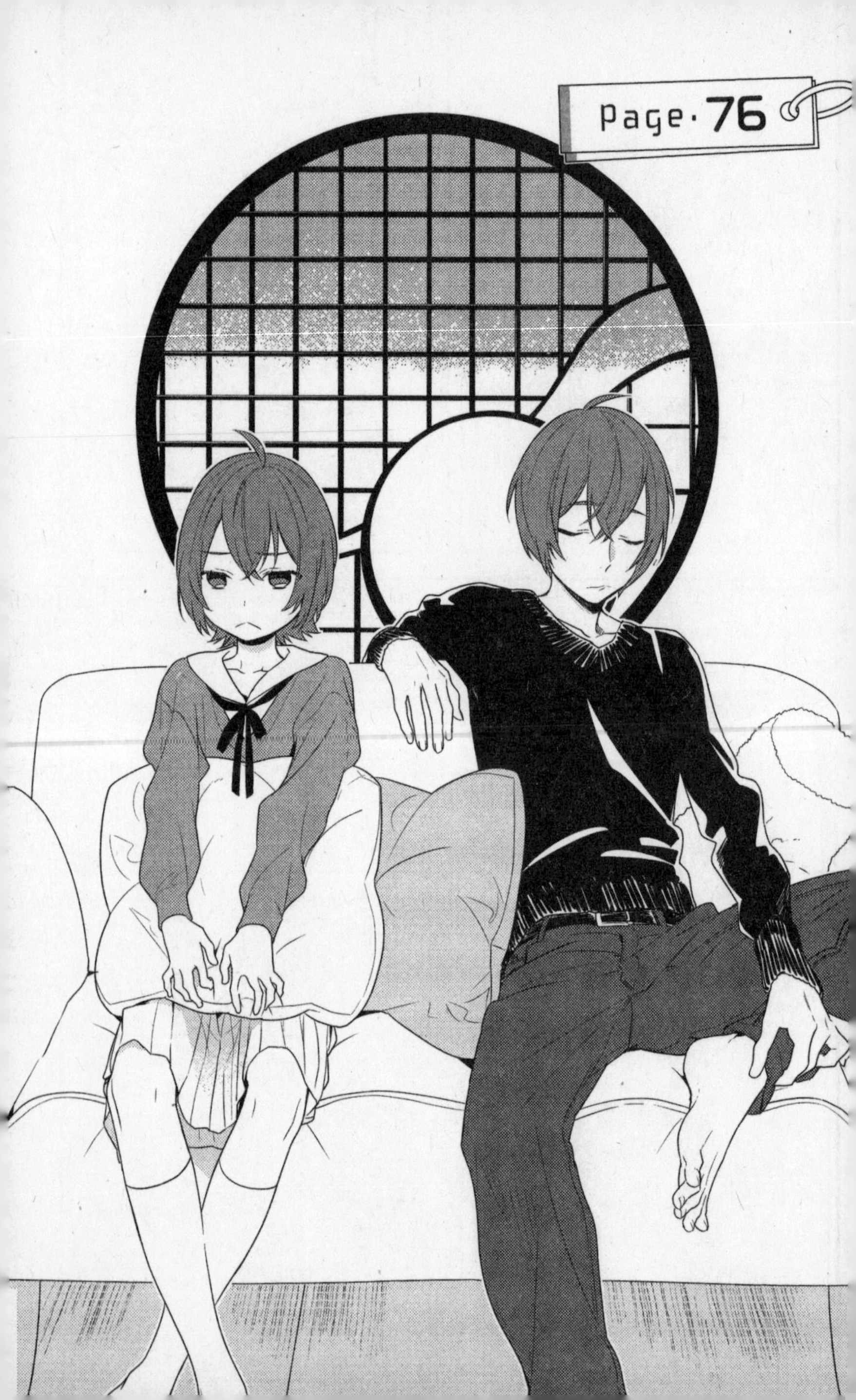
Page. 76

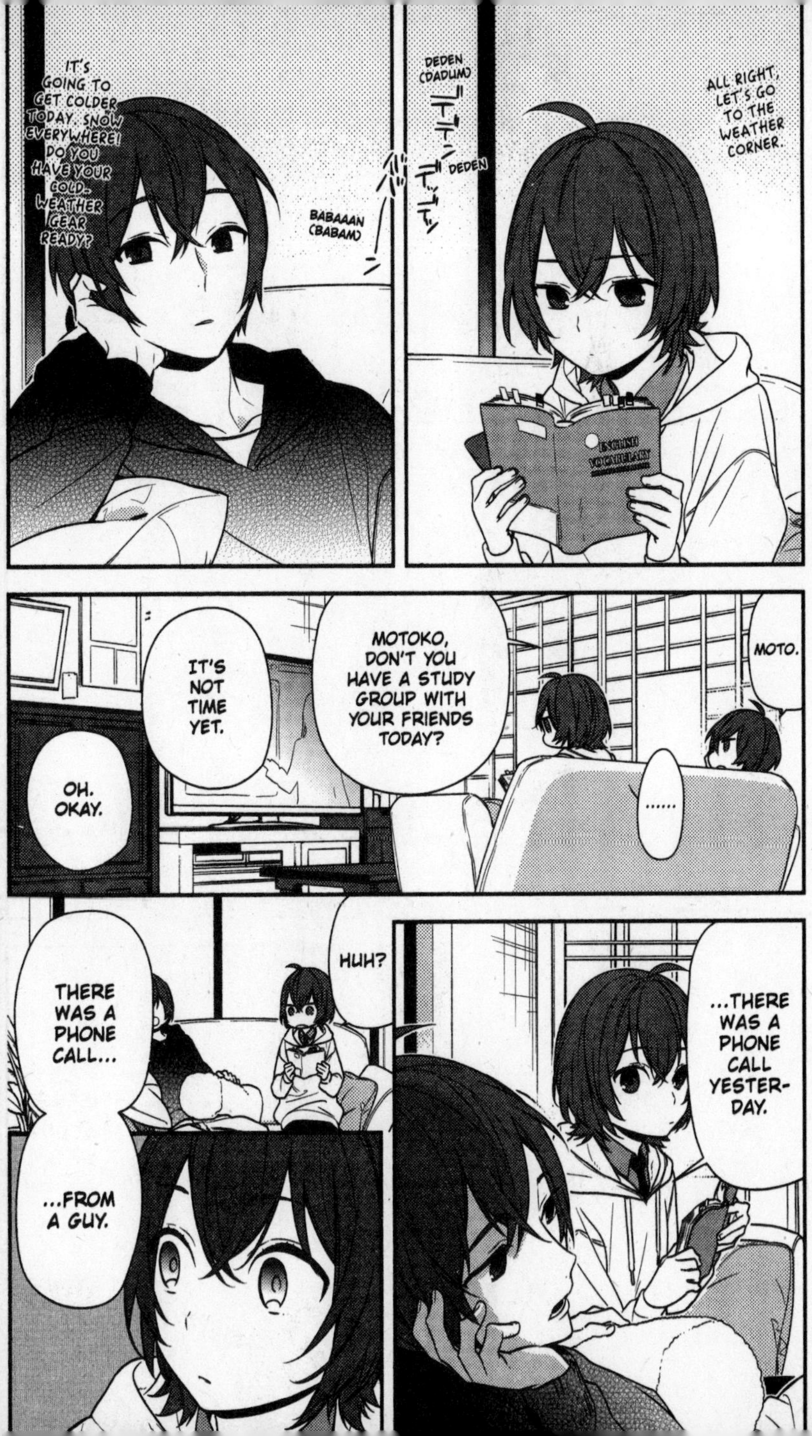
ALL RIGHT, LET'S GO TO THE WEATHER CORNER.
DEDEN (DADUM)
DEDEN
BABAAAN (BABAM)
IT'S GOING TO GET COLDER TODAY. SNOW EVERYWHERE! DO YOU HAVE YOUR COLD-WEATHER GEAR READY?
MOTO.
......
MOTOKO, DON'T YOU HAVE A STUDY GROUP WITH YOUR FRIENDS TODAY?
IT'S NOT TIME YET.
OH. OKAY.
...THERE WAS A PHONE CALL YESTERDAY.
HUH?
THERE WAS A PHONE CALL...
...FROM A GUY.

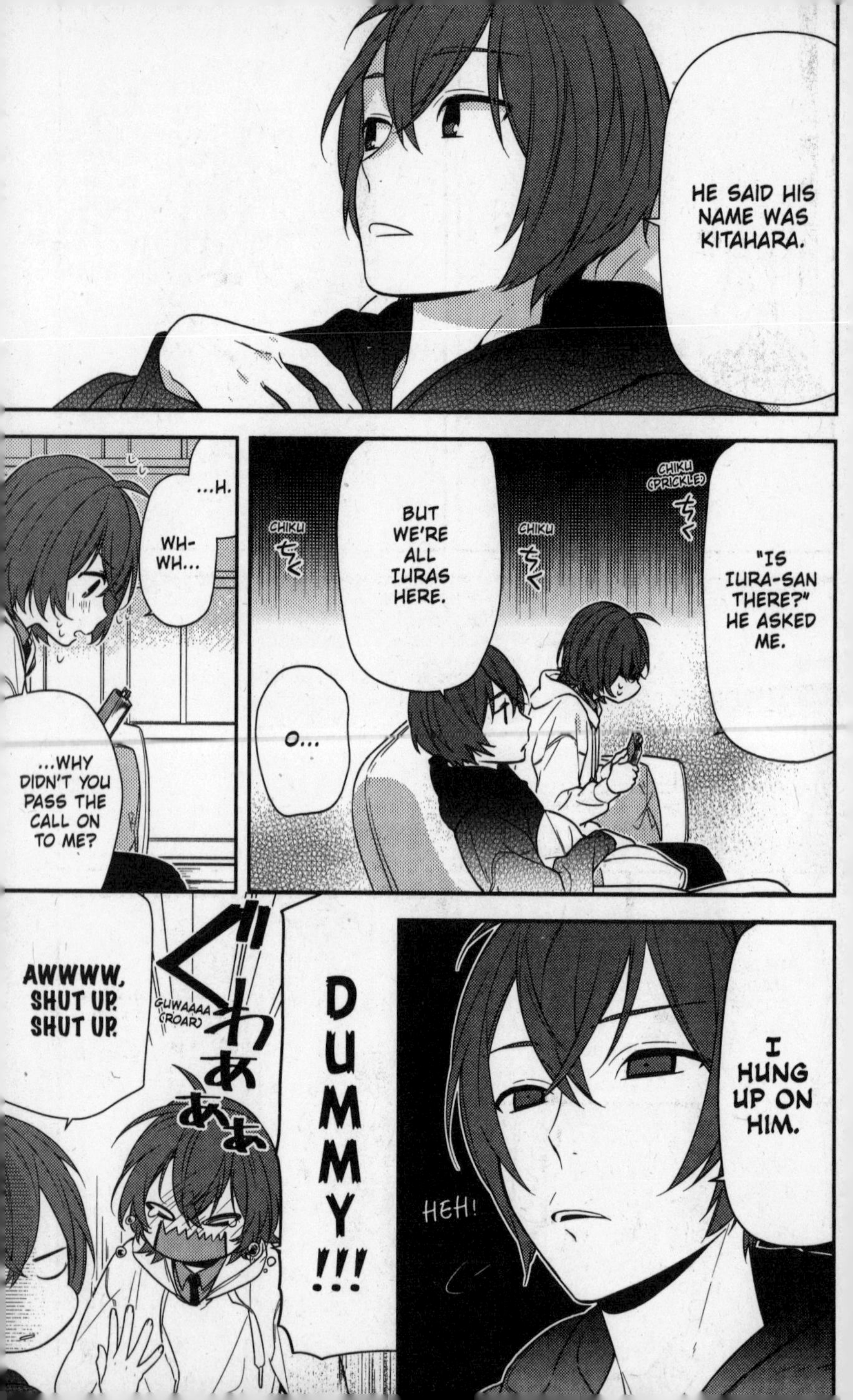
HE SAID HIS NAME WAS KITAHARA.
CHIKU (PRICKLE) ちく
"IS IURA-SAN THERE?" HE ASKED ME.
CHIKU ちく
BUT WE'RE ALL IURAS HERE.
CHIKU ちく
O...
...H.
WH- WH...
...WHY DIDN'T YOU PASS THE CALL ON TO ME?
I HUNG UP ON HIM.
HEH!
DUMMY!!!
GUWAAAA (ROAR) ぐわぁぁ
AWWWW, SHUT UP. SHUT UP.

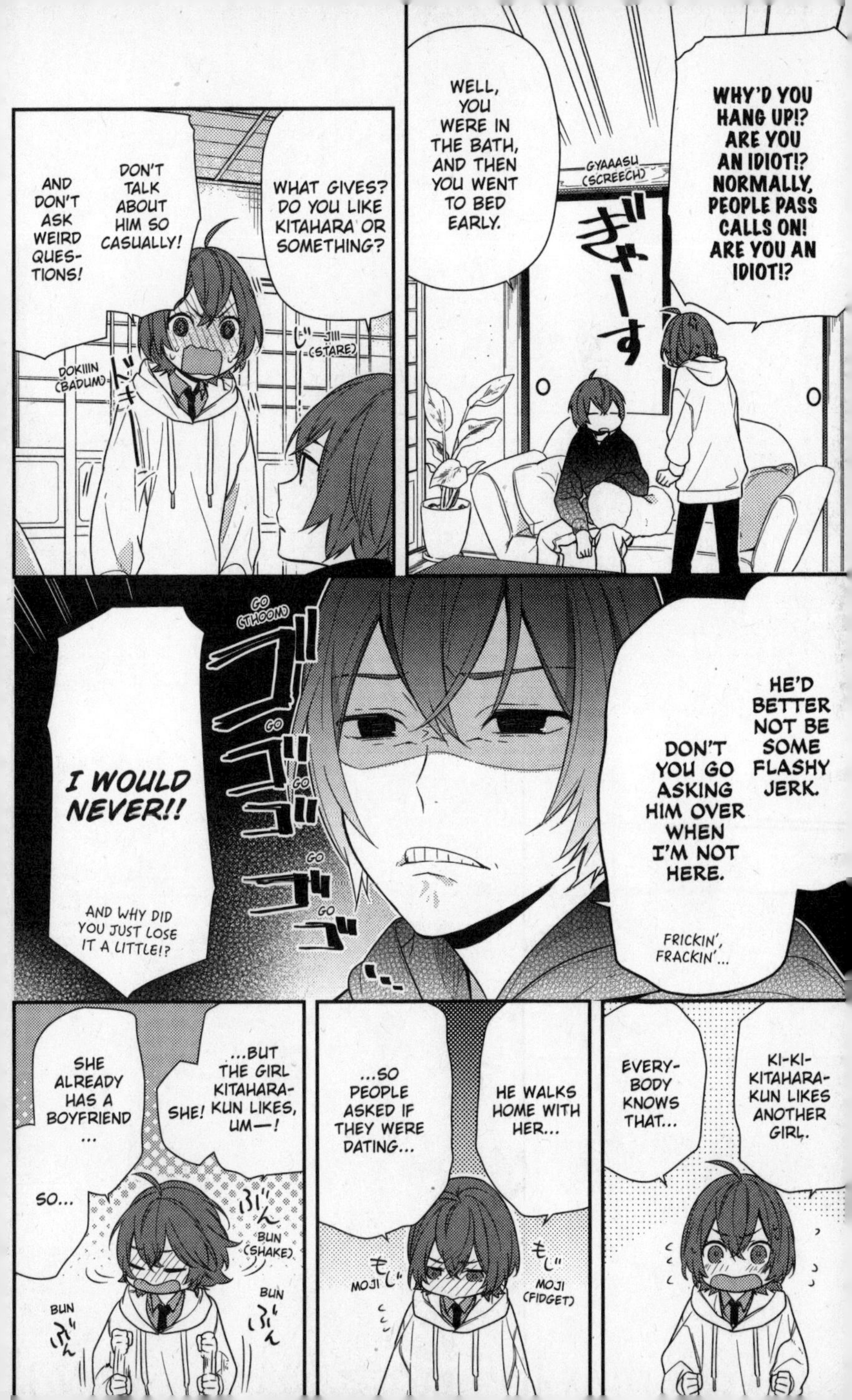
WHY'D YOU HANG UP!? ARE YOU AN IDIOT!? NORMALLY, PEOPLE PASS CALLS ON! ARE YOU AN IDIOT!?
GYAAASU (SCREECH)
WELL, YOU WERE IN THE BATH, AND THEN YOU WENT TO BED EARLY.
WHAT GIVES? DO YOU LIKE KITAHARA OR SOMETHING?
JIII (STARE)
DON'T TALK ABOUT HIM SO CASUALLY!
AND DON'T ASK WEIRD QUES-TIONS!
DOKIIIN (BADUM)
HE'D BETTER NOT BE SOME FLASHY JERK.
DON'T YOU GO ASKING HIM OVER WHEN I'M NOT HERE.
FRICKIN', FRACKIN'...
GO (THOOM)
GO
GO
GO
GO
I WOULD NEVER!!
AND WHY DID YOU JUST LOSE IT A LITTLE!?
KI-KI-KITAHARA-KUN LIKES ANOTHER GIRL.
EVERY-BODY KNOWS THAT...
HE WALKS HOME WITH HER...
...SO PEOPLE ASKED IF THEY WERE DATING...
MOJI (FIDGET)
MOJI
...BUT THE GIRL KITAHARA-KUN LIKES, UM—!
SHE!
SHE ALREADY HAS A BOYFRIEND...
BUN (SHAKE)
BUN
BUN
SO...

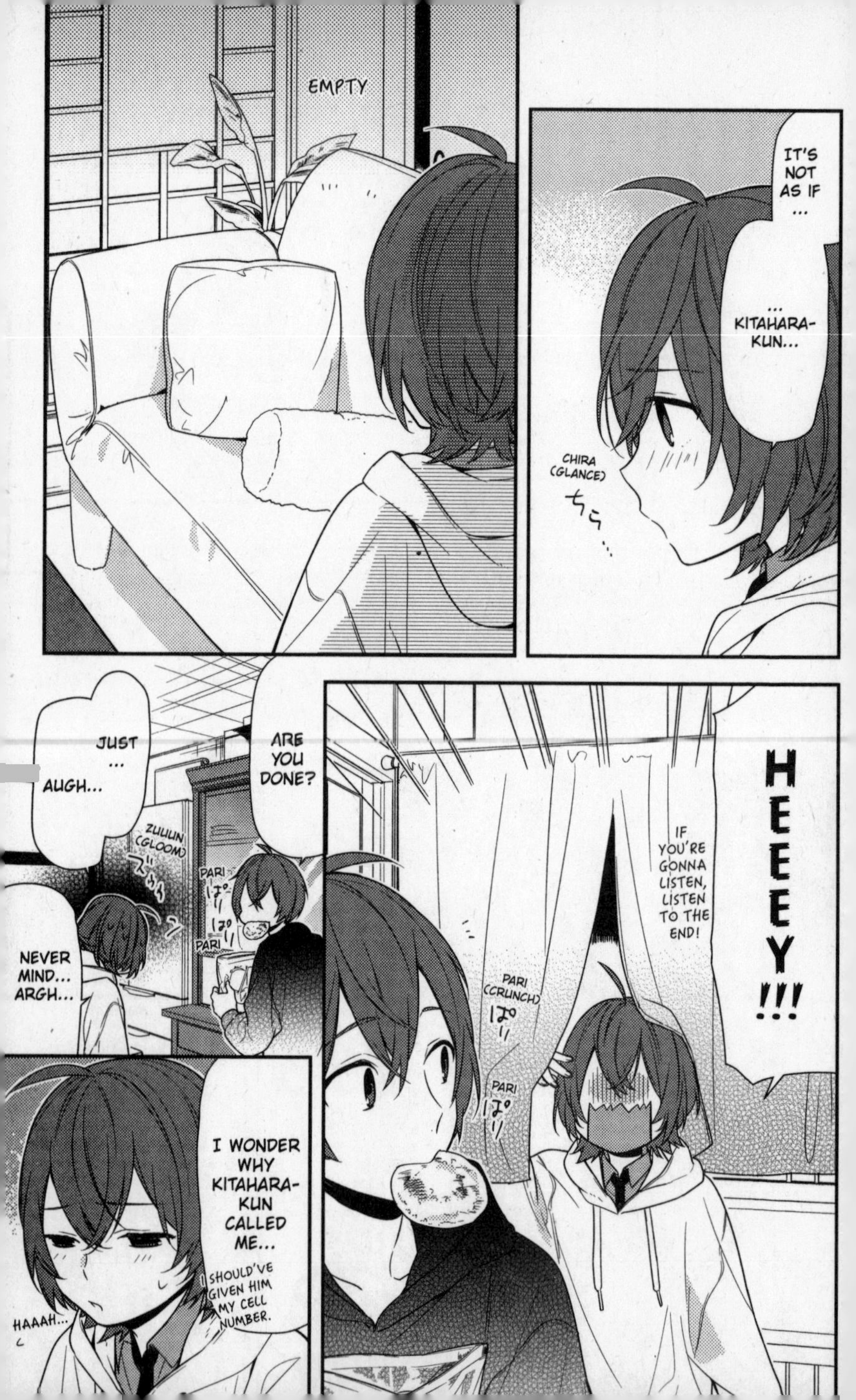
IT'S NOT AS IF ...
... KITAHARA-KUN...
CHIRA (GLANCE)
EMPTY
HEEEY!!!
IF YOU'RE GONNA LISTEN, LISTEN TO THE END!
PARI (CRUNCH)
PARI
ARE YOU DONE?
JUST ... AUGH...
ZUUUN (GLOOM)
PARI
PARI
NEVER MIND... ARGH...
I WONDER WHY KITAHARA-KUN CALLED ME...
I SHOULD'VE GIVEN HIM MY CELL NUMBER.
HAAAH...

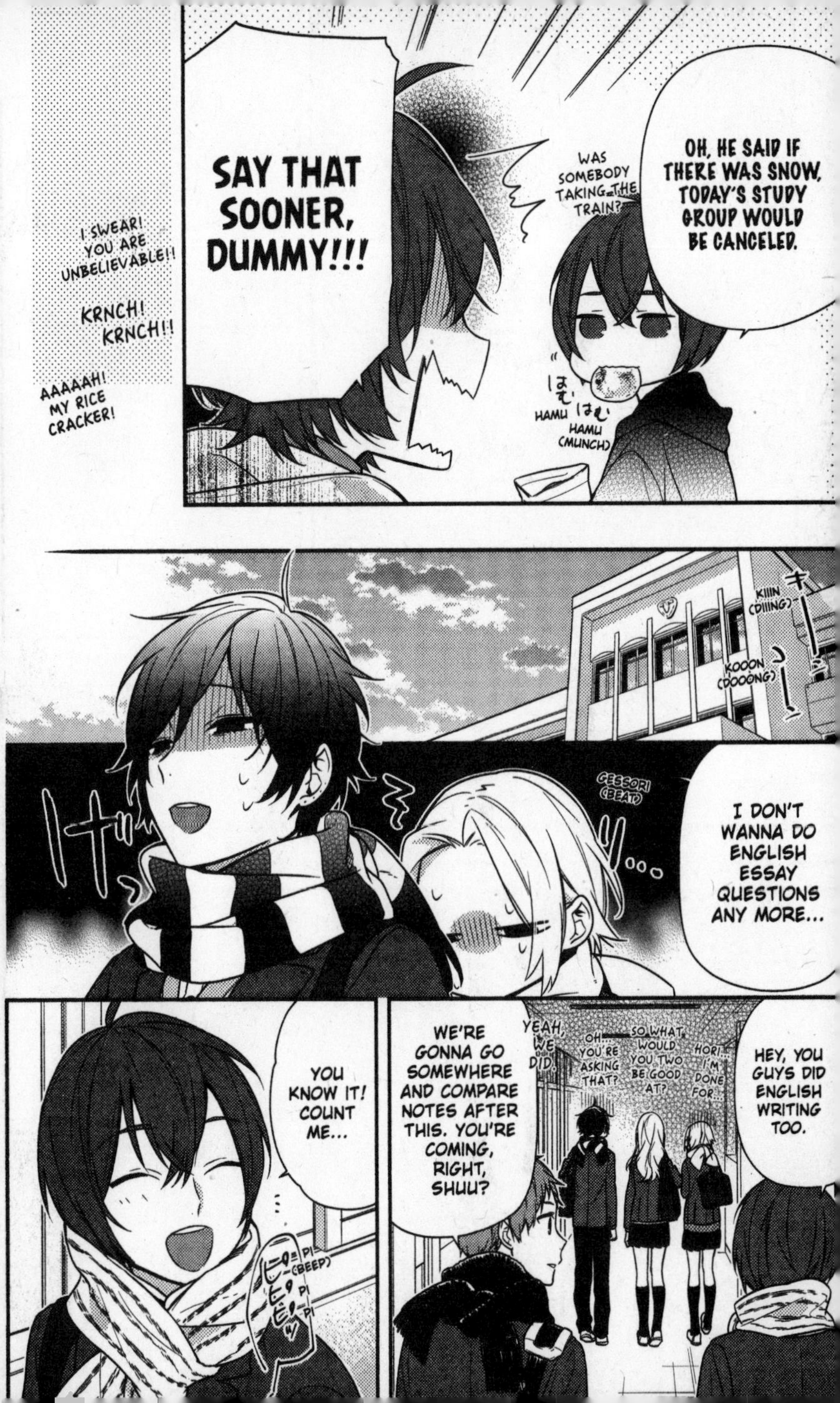
OH, HE SAID IF THERE WAS SNOW, TODAY'S STUDY GROUP WOULD BE CANCELED.
WAS SOMEBODY TAKING THE TRAIN?
HAMU HAMU (MUNCH)
SAY THAT SOONER, DUMMY!!!
I SWEAR! YOU ARE UNBELIEVABLE!!
KRNCH! KRNCH!!
AAAAAH! MY RICE CRACKER!
KIIN (DIIING)
KOOON (DOOONG)
I DON'T WANNA DO ENGLISH ESSAY QUESTIONS ANY MORE...
GESSORI (BEAT)
HEY, YOU GUYS DID ENGLISH WRITING TOO.
HORI... I'M DONE FOR...
SO WHAT WOULD YOU TWO BE GOOD AT?
OH... YOU'RE ASKING THAT?
YEAH, WE DID.
WE'RE GONNA GO SOMEWHERE AND COMPARE NOTES AFTER THIS. YOU'RE COMING, RIGHT, SHUU?
YOU KNOW IT! COUNT ME...
PI (BEEP) PI PI

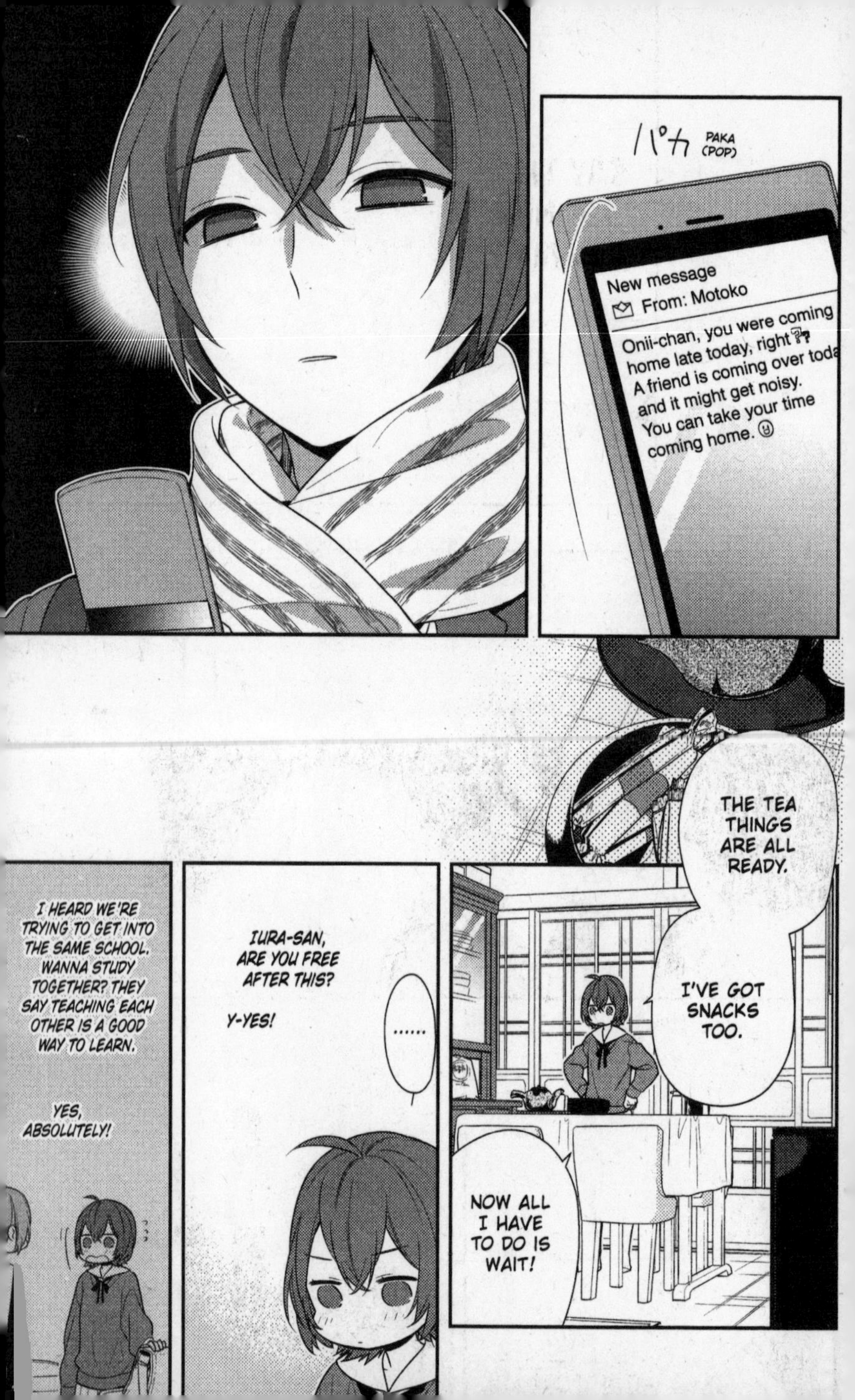

パカ
PAKA (POP)
New message
From: Motoko
Onii-chan, you were coming home late today, right?? A friend is coming over toda and it might get noisy. You can take your time coming home.
THE TEA THINGS ARE ALL READY.
I'VE GOT SNACKS TOO.
NOW ALL I HAVE TO DO IS WAIT!
IURA-SAN, ARE YOU FREE AFTER THIS?
Y-YES!
......
I HEARD WE'RE TRYING TO GET INTO THE SAME SCHOOL. WANNA STUDY TOGETHER? THEY SAY TEACHING EACH OTHER IS A GOOD WAY TO LEARN.
YES, ABSOLUTELY!

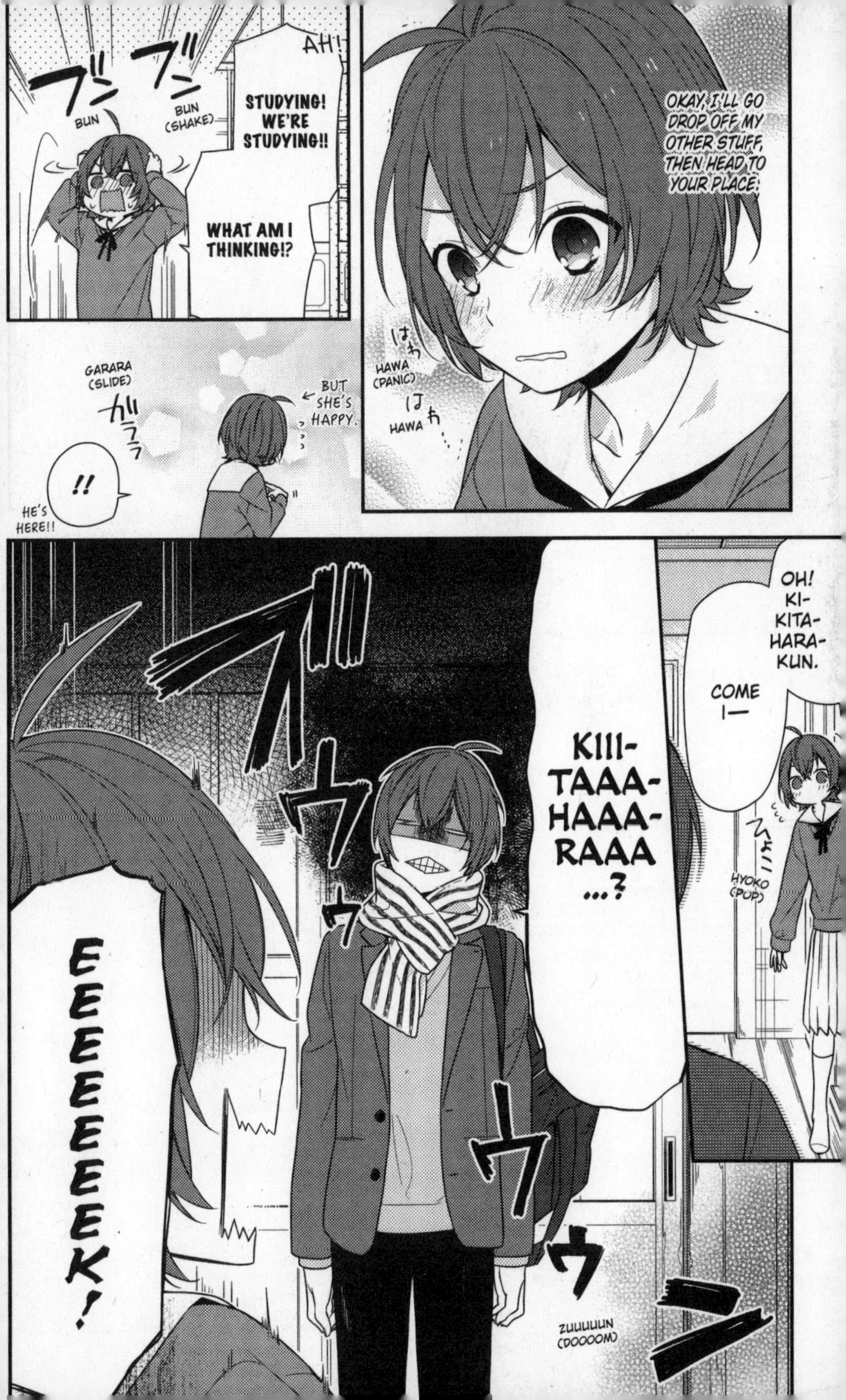
OKAY, I'LL GO DROP OFF MY OTHER STUFF, THEN HEAD TO YOUR PLACE.
HAWA (PANIC)
HAWA
AH!
STUDYING! WE'RE STUDYING!!
BUN
BUN (SHAKE)
WHAT AM I THINKING!?
BUT SHE'S HAPPY.
GARARA (SLIDE)
!!
HE'S HERE!!
OH! KI-KITA-HARA-KUN.
COME I—
HYOKO (POP)
KIII-TAAA-HAAA-RAAA...?
EEEEEEEEEK!
ZUUUUUN (DOOOOM)

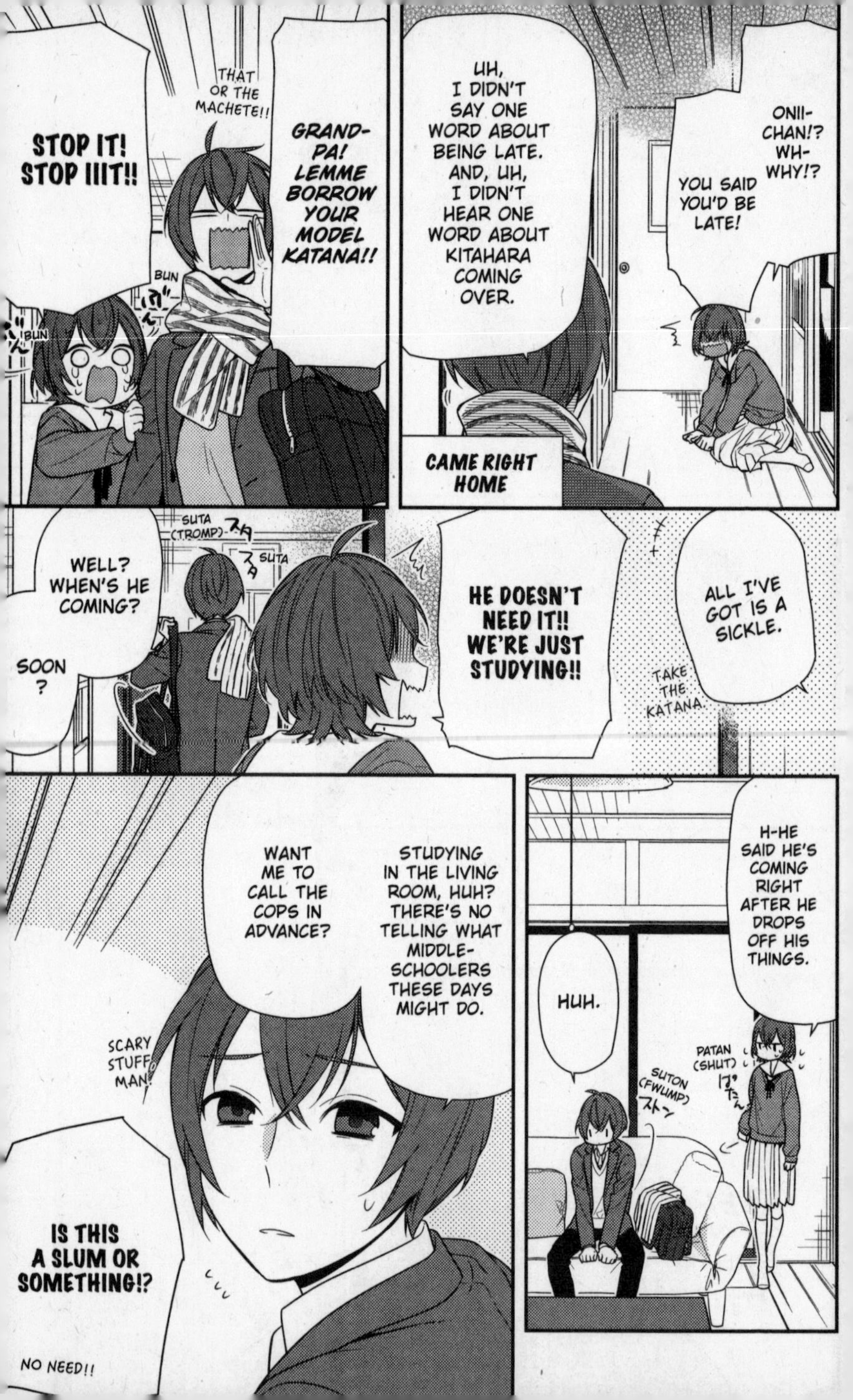
ONII-CHAN!? WH-WHY!?
YOU SAID YOU'D BE LATE!
UH, I DIDN'T SAY ONE WORD ABOUT BEING LATE. AND, UH, I DIDN'T HEAR ONE WORD ABOUT KITAHARA COMING OVER.
CAME RIGHT HOME
GRAND-PA! LEMME BORROW YOUR MODEL KATANA!!
THAT OR THE MACHETE!!
STOP IT! STOP IIIT!!
BUN
BUN
ALL I'VE GOT IS A SICKLE.
TAKE THE KATANA.
HE DOESN'T NEED IT!! WE'RE JUST STUDYING!!
SUTA (TROMP)
SUTA
WELL? WHEN'S HE COMING?
SOON?
H-HE SAID HE'S COMING RIGHT AFTER HE DROPS OFF HIS THINGS.
PATAN (SHUT)
HUH.
SUTON (FWUMP)
STUDYING IN THE LIVING ROOM, HUH? THERE'S NO TELLING WHAT MIDDLE-SCHOOLERS THESE DAYS MIGHT DO.
WANT ME TO CALL THE COPS IN ADVANCE?
SCARY STUFF MAN
IS THIS A SLUM OR SOMETHING!?
NO NEED!!

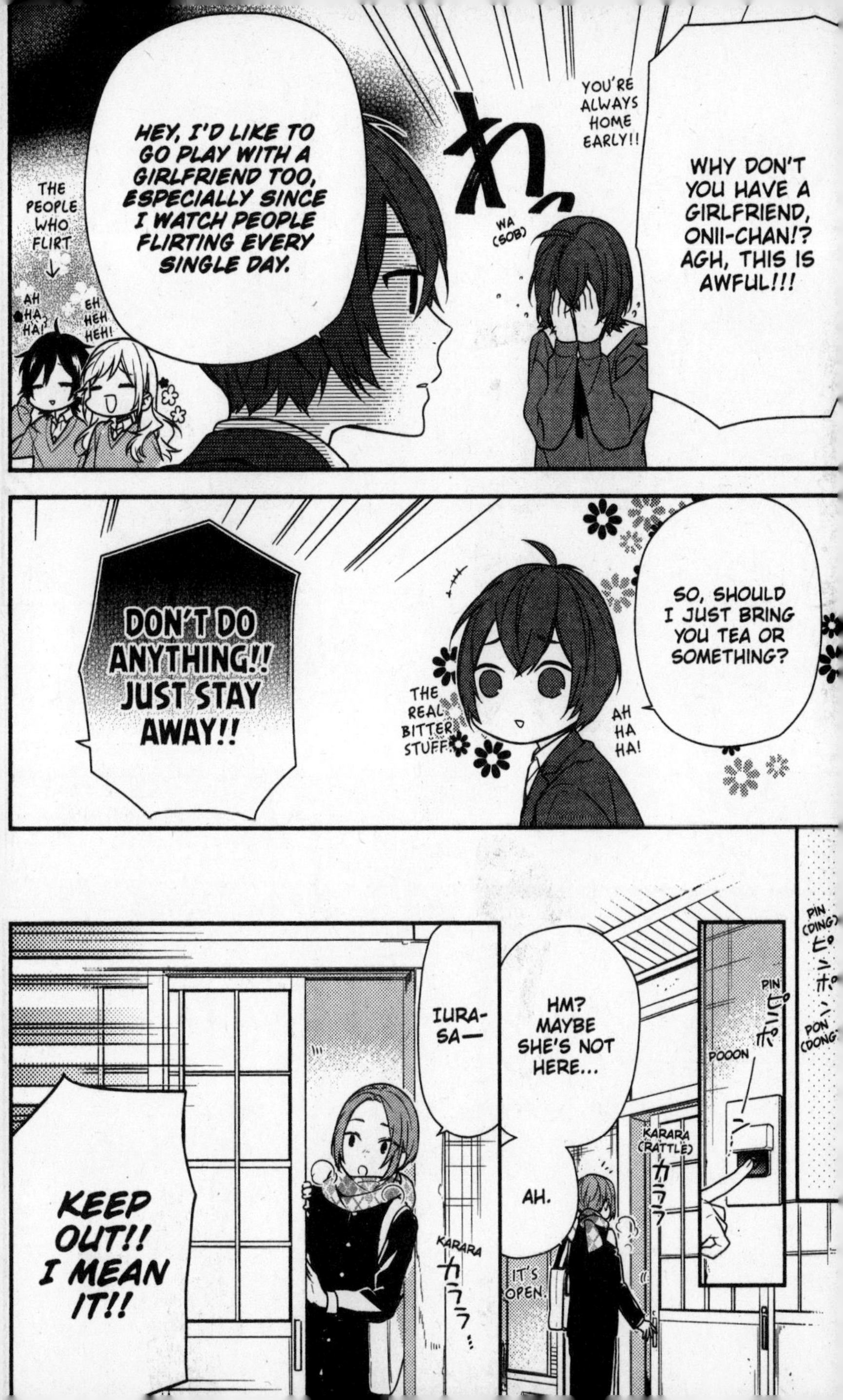
WHY DON'T YOU HAVE A GIRLFRIEND, ONII-CHAN!? AGH, THIS IS AWFUL!!!
YOU'RE ALWAYS HOME EARLY!!
WA (SOB)
HEY, I'D LIKE TO GO PLAY WITH A GIRLFRIEND TOO, ESPECIALLY SINCE I WATCH PEOPLE FLIRTING EVERY SINGLE DAY.
THE PEOPLE WHO FLIRT
EH HEH HEH!
AH HA HA!
SO, SHOULD I JUST BRING YOU TEA OR SOMETHING?
AH HA HA!
THE REAL BITTER STUFF
DON'T DO ANYTHING!! JUST STAY AWAY!!
PIN (DING)
PON (DONG)
PIN
POOON
KARARA (RATTLE)
HM? MAYBE SHE'S NOT HERE...
AH.
IT'S OPEN.
IURA-SA—
KARARA
KEEP OUT!! I MEAN IT!!

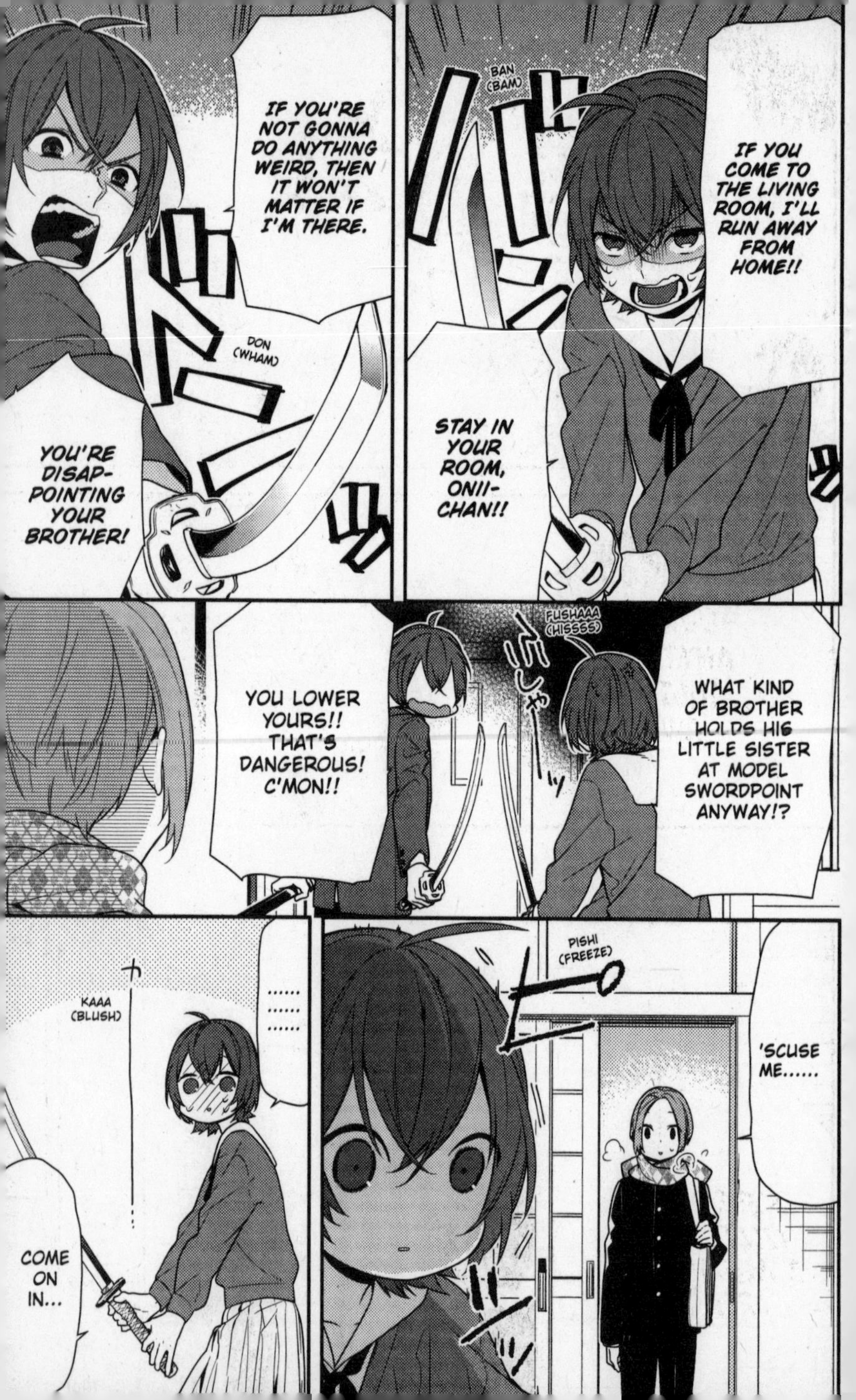
BAN (BAM)
IF YOU COME TO THE LIVING ROOM, I'LL RUN AWAY FROM HOME!!
STAY IN YOUR ROOM, ONII-CHAN!!
IF YOU'RE NOT GONNA DO ANYTHING WEIRD, THEN IT WON'T MATTER IF I'M THERE.
DON (WHAM)
YOU'RE DISAP-POINTING YOUR BROTHER!
FUSHAAA (HISSSS)
WHAT KIND OF BROTHER HOLDS HIS LITTLE SISTER AT MODEL SWORDPOINT ANYWAY!?
YOU LOWER YOURS!! THAT'S DANGEROUS! C'MON!!
PISHI (FREEZE)
'SCUSE ME......
..................
KAAA (BLUSH)
COME ON IN...

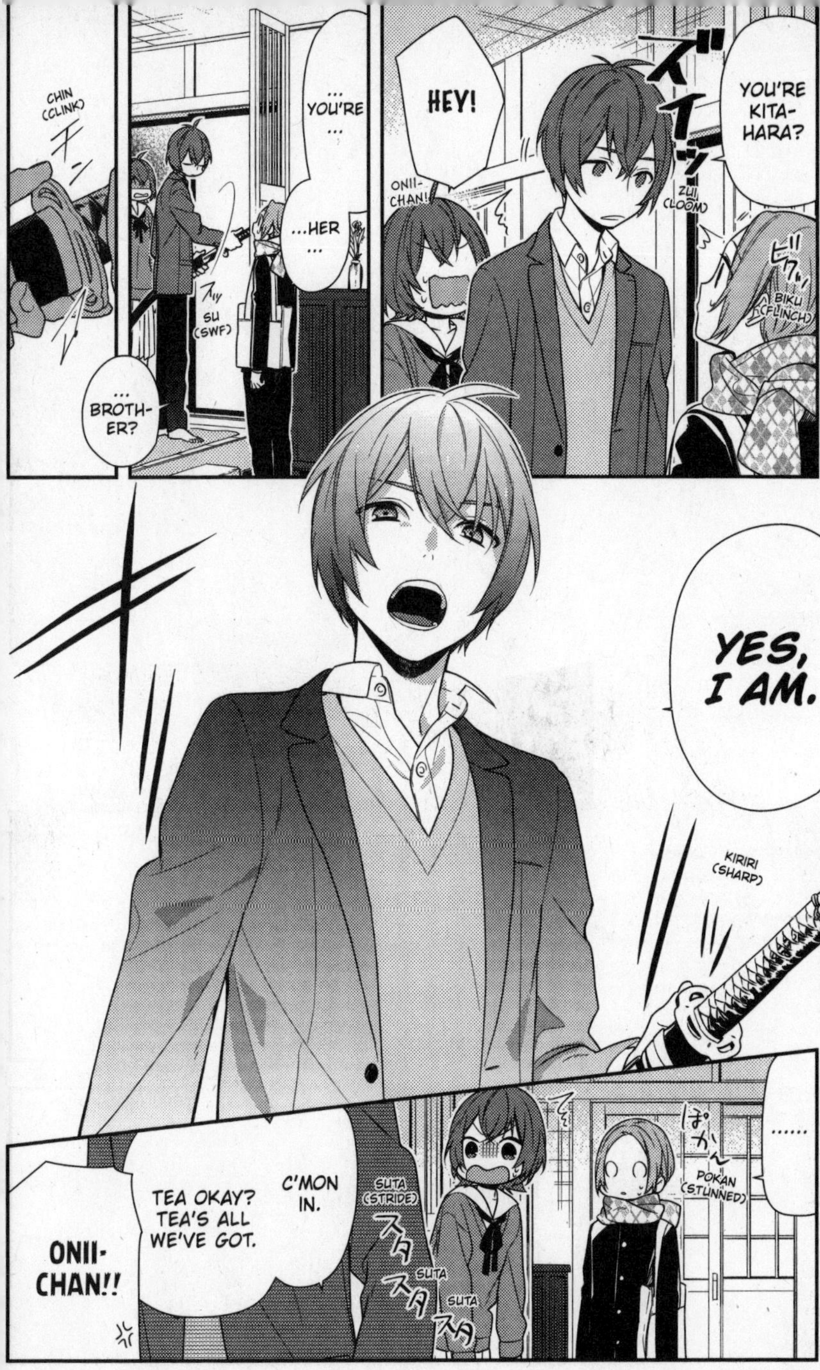
YOU'RE KITA-HARA?
ZUI (LOOM)
BIKU (FLINCH)
HEY!
ONII-CHAN!
... YOU'RE ...
...HER ...
SU (SWF)
CHIN (CLINK)
... BROTH-ER?
YES, I AM.
KIRIRI (SHARP)
......
POKAN (STUNNED)
SUTA (STRIDE)
SUTA
SUTA
C'MON IN.
TEA OKAY? TEA'S ALL WE'VE GOT.
ONII-CHAN!!

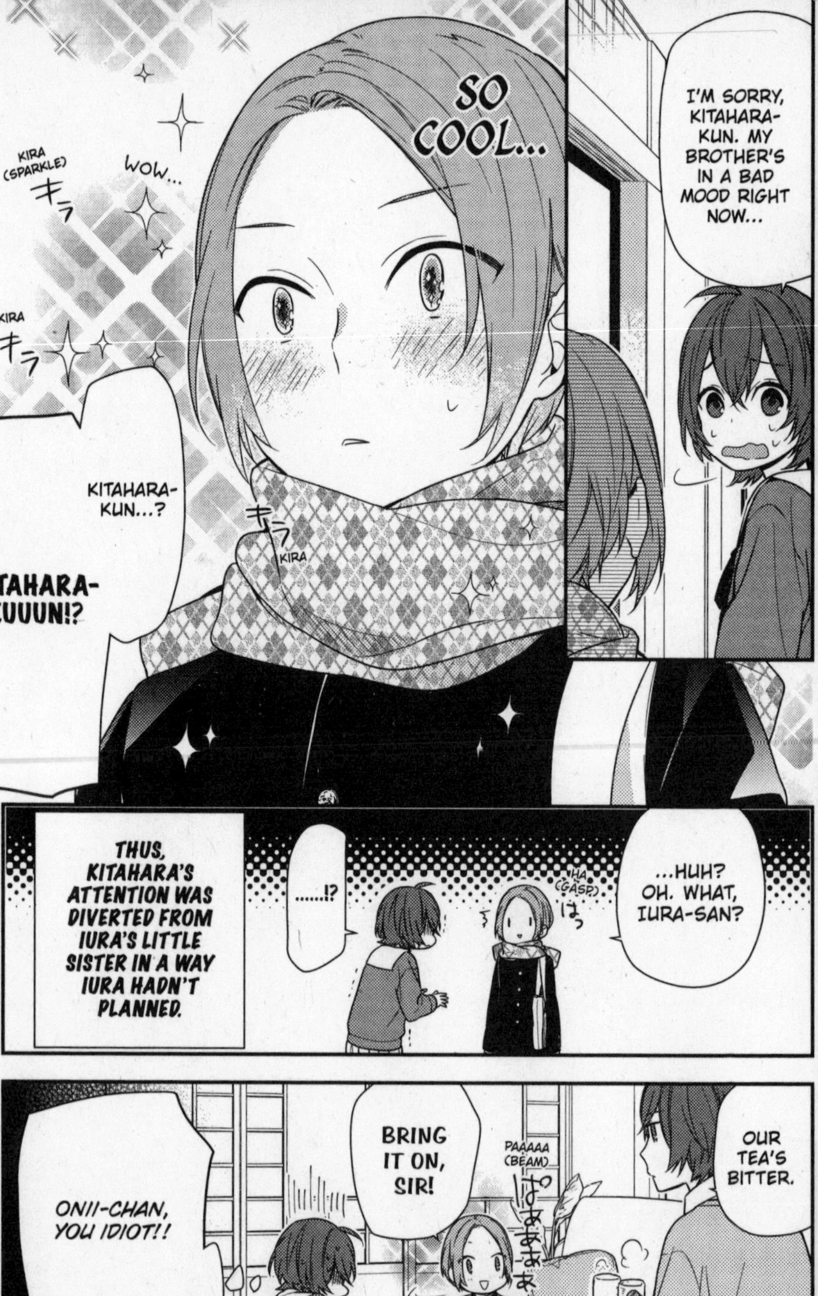
I'M SORRY, KITAHARA-KUN. MY BROTHER'S IN A BAD MOOD RIGHT NOW...
SO COOL...
WOW...
KIRA (SPARKLE)
キラ
KIRA
キラ
KITAHARA-KUN...?
キラ
KIRA
KITAHARA-KUUUN!?
...HUH? OH. WHAT, IURA-SAN?
HA (GASP)
はっ
......!?
THUS, KITAHARA'S ATTENTION WAS DIVERTED FROM IURA'S LITTLE SISTER IN A WAY IURA HADN'T PLANNED.
OUR TEA'S BITTER.
PAAAAA (BEAM)
ぱあああ
BRING IT ON, SIR!
ONII-CHAN, YOU IDIOT!!

HORIMIYA

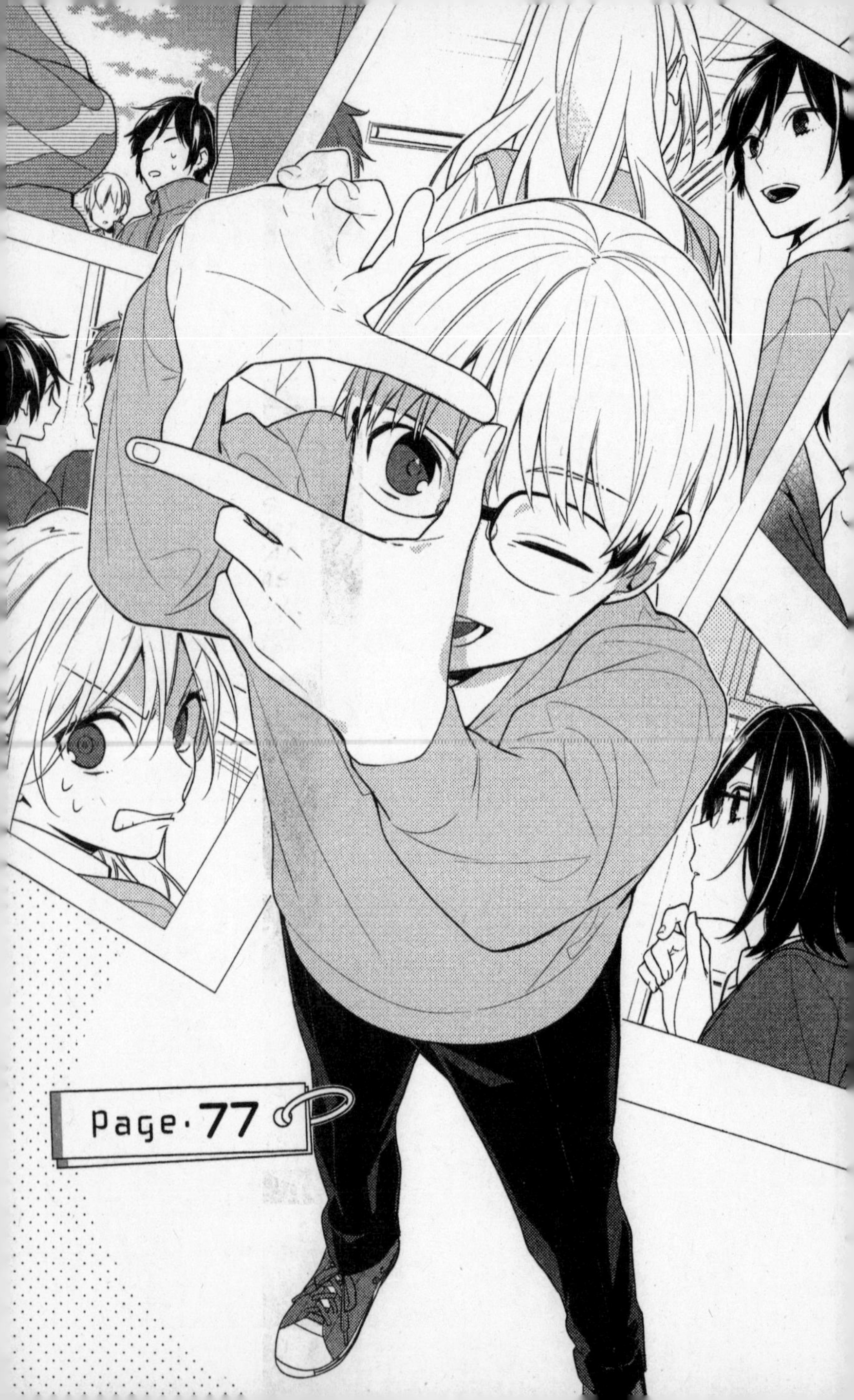
page·77

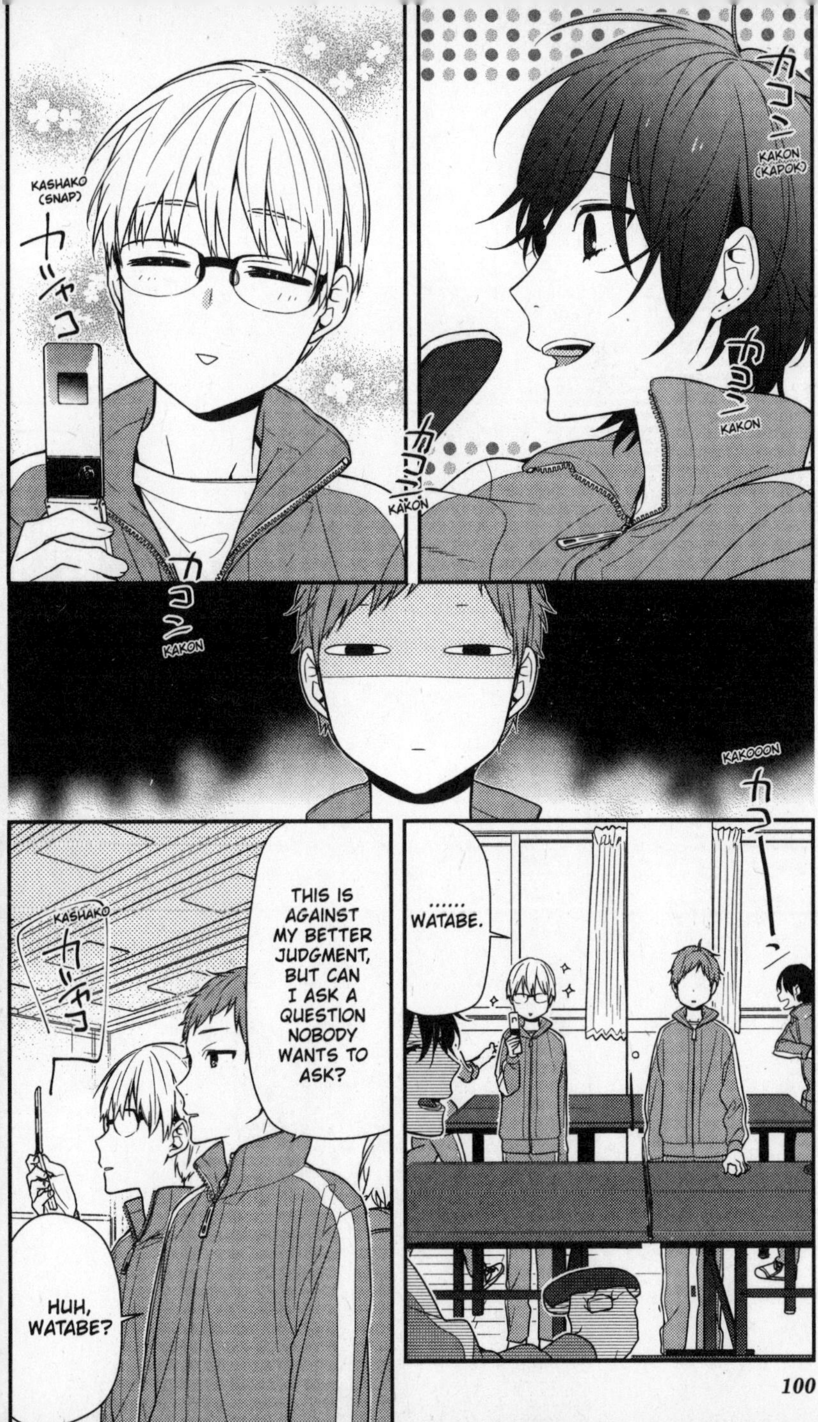
KAKON (KAPOK)
KAKON
KAKON
KASHAKO (SNAP)
KAKON
KAKOOON
......WATABE.
THIS IS AGAINST MY BETTER JUDGMENT, BUT CAN I ASK A QUESTION NOBODY WANTS TO ASK?
KASHAKO
HUH, WATABE?

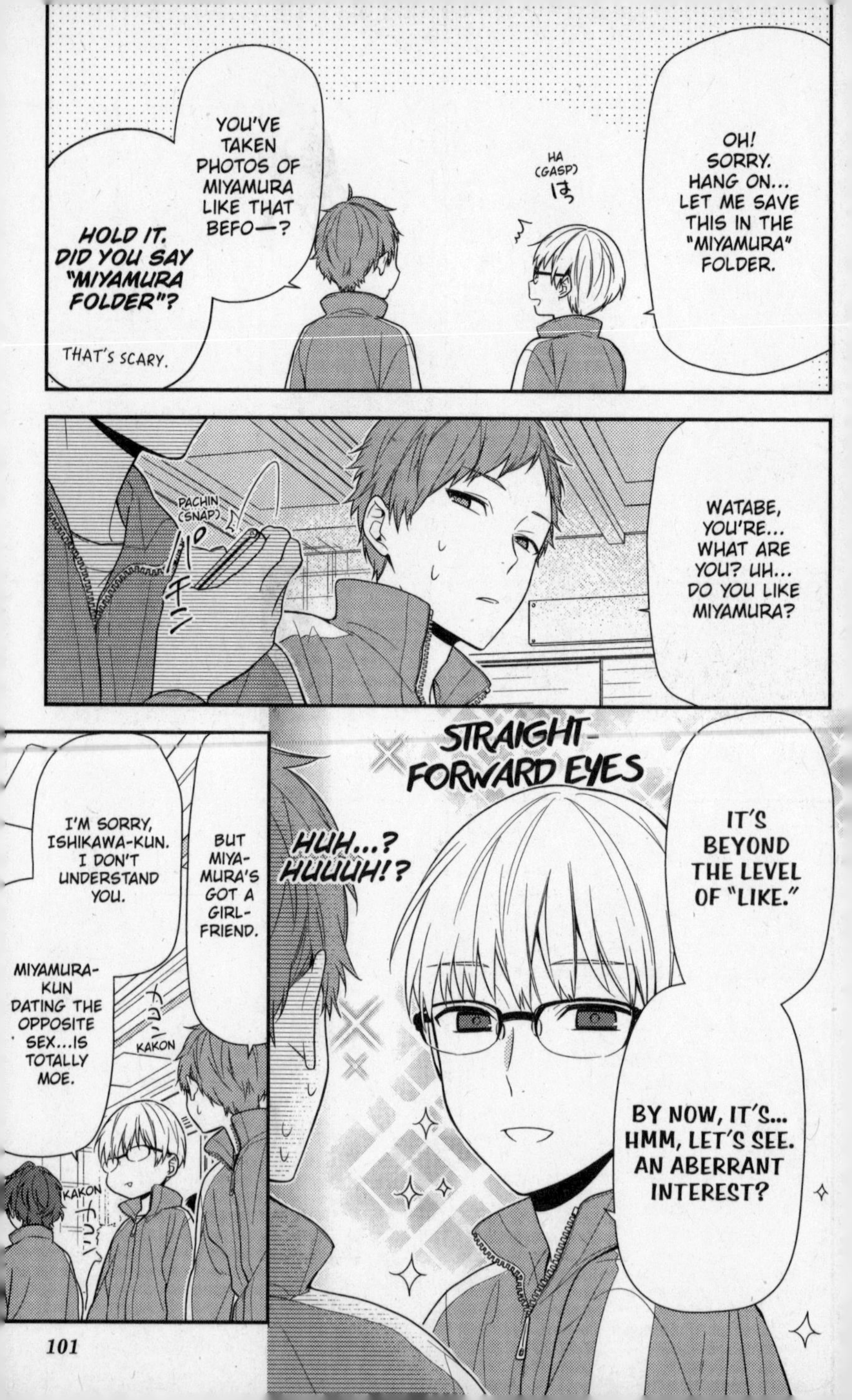
OH! SORRY. HANG ON... LET ME SAVE THIS IN THE "MIYAMURA" FOLDER.
HA (GASP) はっ
YOU'VE TAKEN PHOTOS OF MIYAMURA LIKE THAT BEFO—?
HOLD IT. DID YOU SAY "MIYAMURA FOLDER"?
THAT'S SCARY.
WATABE, YOU'RE... WHAT ARE YOU? UH... DO YOU LIKE MIYAMURA?
PACHIN (SNAP)
STRAIGHT-FORWARD EYES
IT'S BEYOND THE LEVEL OF "LIKE."
BY NOW, IT'S... HMM, LET'S SEE. AN ABERRANT INTEREST?
HUH...? HUUUH!?
BUT MIYA-MURA'S GOT A GIRL-FRIEND.
I'M SORRY, ISHIKAWA-KUN. I DON'T UNDERSTAND YOU.
MIYAMURA-KUN DATING THE OPPOSITE SEX...IS TOTALLY MOE.
KAKON
KAKON

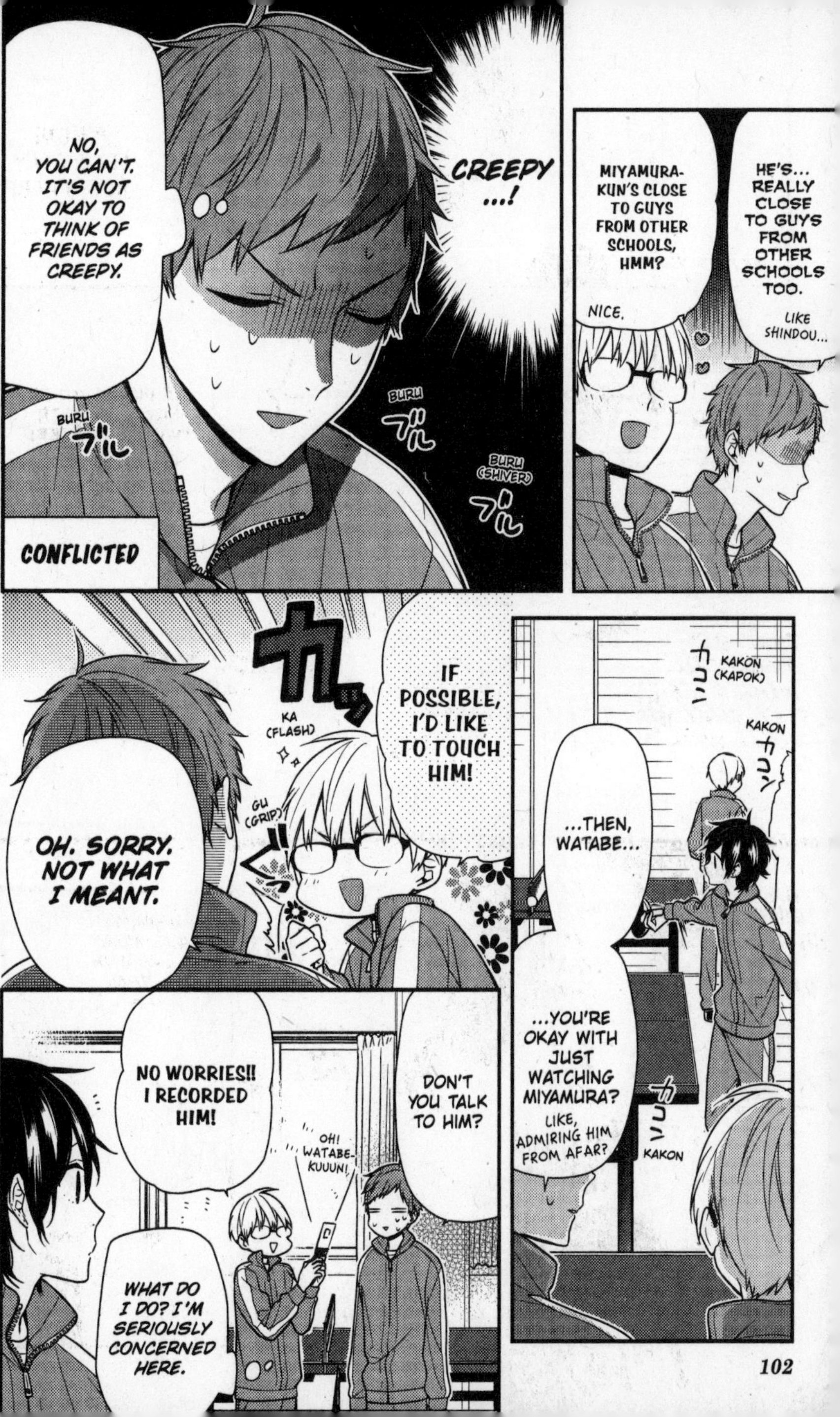
HE'S... REALLY CLOSE TO GUYS FROM OTHER SCHOOLS TOO.
LIKE SHINDOU...
MIYAMURA-KUN'S CLOSE TO GUYS FROM OTHER SCHOOLS, HMM?
NICE.
CREEPY ...!
BURU
BURU (SHIVER)
BURU
NO, YOU CAN'T. IT'S NOT OKAY TO THINK OF FRIENDS AS CREEPY.
CONFLICTED
KAKON (KAPOK)
KAKON
...THEN, WATABE...
...YOU'RE OKAY WITH JUST WATCHING MIYAMURA?
LIKE, ADMIRING HIM FROM AFAR?
KAKON
IF POSSIBLE, I'D LIKE TO TOUCH HIM!
KA (FLASH)
GU (GRIP)
OH. SORRY. NOT WHAT I MEANT.
DON'T YOU TALK TO HIM?
NO WORRIES!! I RECORDED HIM!
OH! WATABE-KUUUN!
WHAT DO I DO? I'M SERIOUSLY CONCERNED HERE.

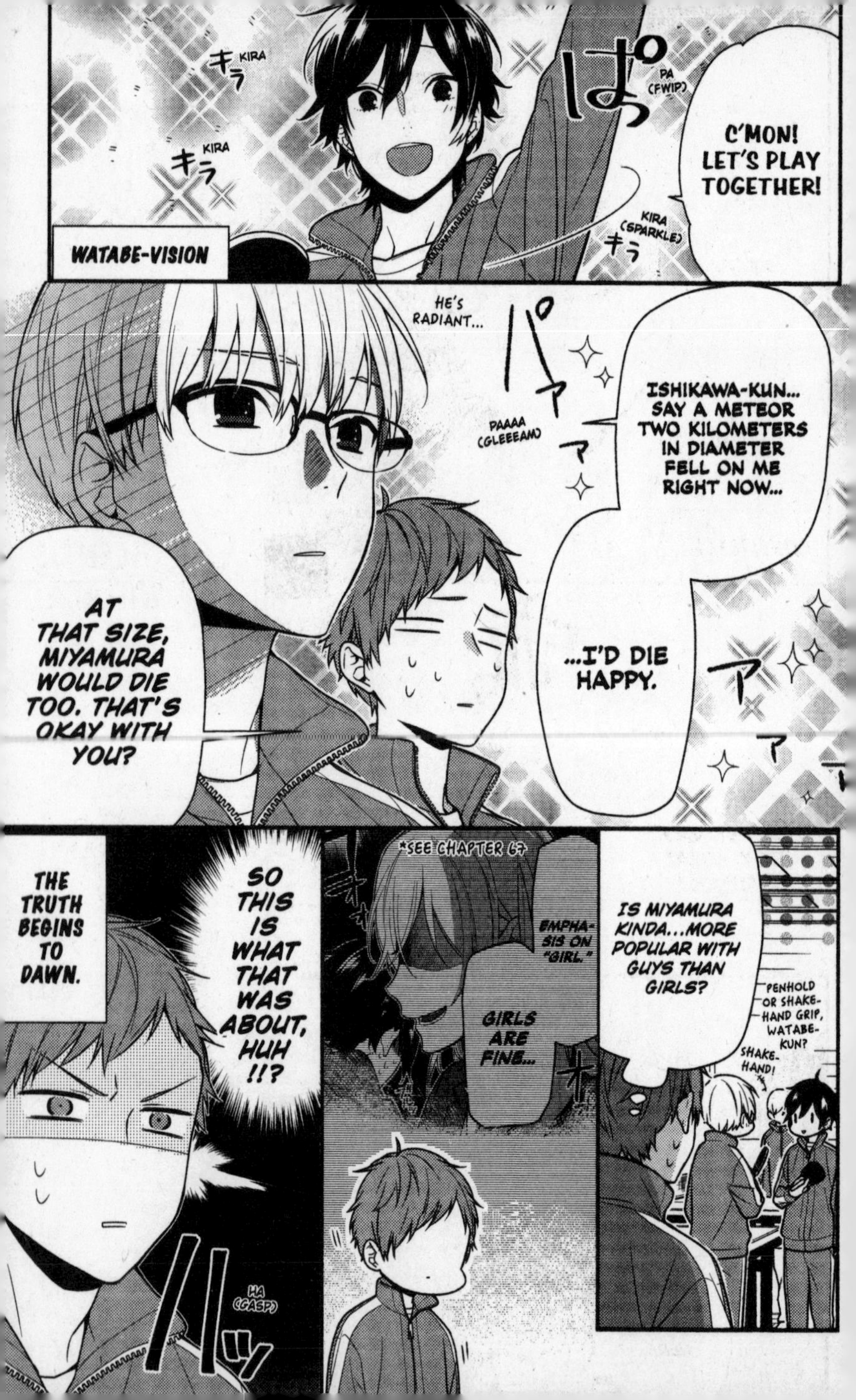
PA (FWIP)
C'MON! LET'S PLAY TOGETHER!
KIRA (SPARKLE)
KIRA
KIRA
WATABE-VISION
ISHIKAWA-KUN... SAY A METEOR TWO KILOMETERS IN DIAMETER FELL ON ME RIGHT NOW...
...I'D DIE HAPPY.
PAAAA (GLEEEAM)
HE'S RADIANT...
AT THAT SIZE, MIYAMURA WOULD DIE TOO. THAT'S OKAY WITH YOU?
IS MIYAMURA KINDA...MORE POPULAR WITH GUYS THAN GIRLS?
PENHOLD OR SHAKE-HAND GRIP, WATABE-KUN?
SHAKE-HAND!
*SEE CHAPTER 67
EMPHA-SIS ON "GIRL."
GIRLS ARE FINE...
SO THIS IS WHAT THAT WAS ABOUT, HUH!!?
THE TRUTH BEGINS TO DAWN.
HA (GASP)

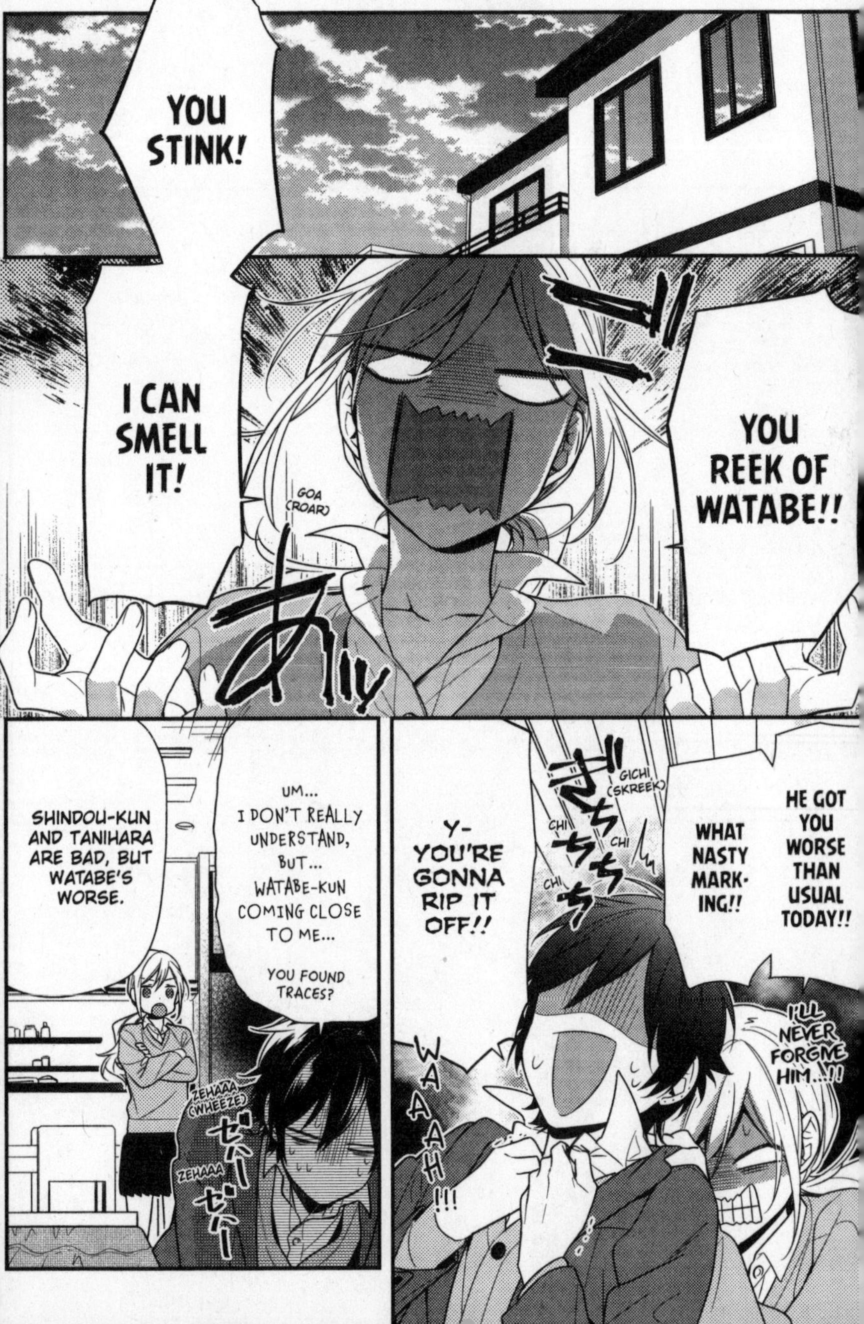
YOU STINK!
YOU REEK OF WATABE!!
I CAN SMELL IT!
GOA (ROAR)
HE GOT YOU WORSE THAN USUAL TODAY!!
WHAT NASTY MARK-ING!!
GICHI (SKREEK)
CHI
CHI
CHI
Y- YOU'RE GONNA RIP IT OFF!!
I'LL NEVER FORGIVE HIM...!!
WAAAAH!!!
UM... I DON'T REALLY UNDERSTAND, BUT... WATABE-KUN COMING CLOSE TO ME...
YOU FOUND TRACES?
SHINDOU-KUN AND TANIHARA ARE BAD, BUT WATABE'S WORSE.
ZEHAAA (WHEEZE)
ZEHAAA

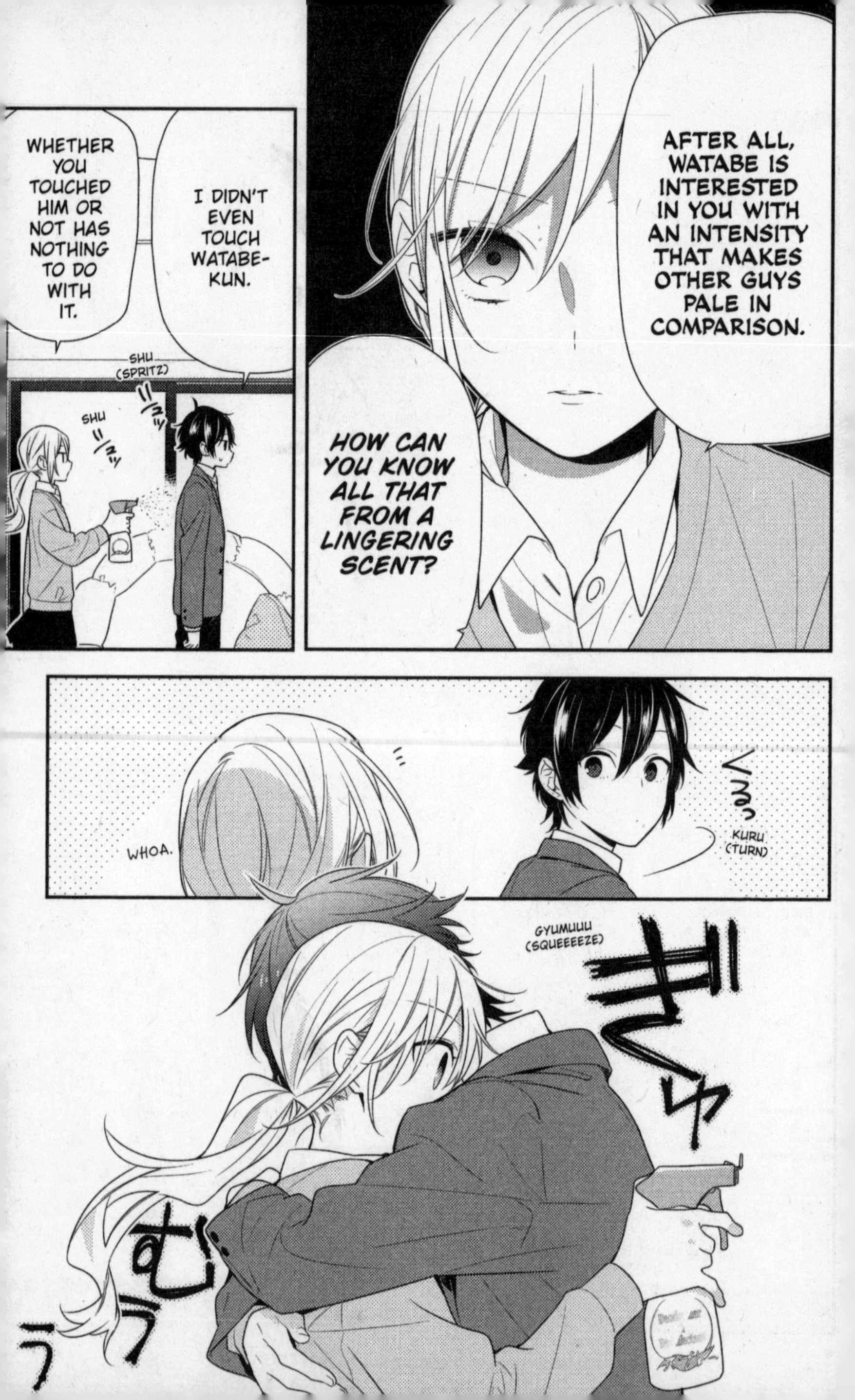
AFTER ALL, WATABE IS INTERESTED IN YOU WITH AN INTENSITY THAT MAKES OTHER GUYS PALE IN COMPARISON.
HOW CAN YOU KNOW ALL THAT FROM A LINGERING SCENT?
I DIDN'T EVEN TOUCH WATABE-KUN.
WHETHER YOU TOUCHED HIM OR NOT HAS NOTHING TO DO WITH IT.
SHU (SPRITZ)
SHU
KURU (TURN)
WHOA.
GYUMUUU (SQUEEEEZE)

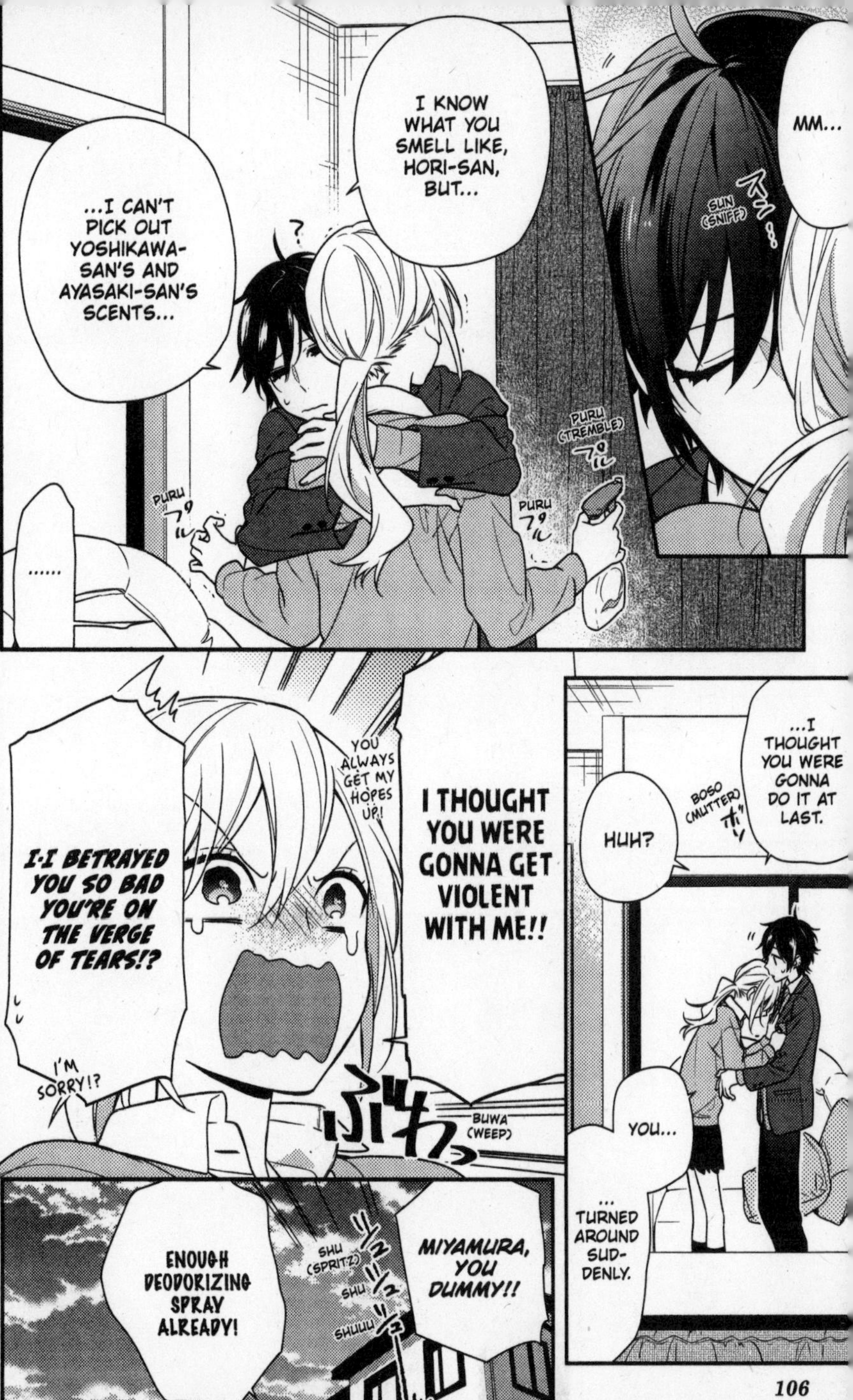
MM...
SUN (SNIFF)
I KNOW WHAT YOU SMELL LIKE, HORI-SAN, BUT...
...I CAN'T PICK OUT YOSHIKAWA-SAN'S AND AYASAKI-SAN'S SCENTS...
?
PURU (TREMBLE)
PURU
PURU
......
...I THOUGHT YOU WERE GONNA DO IT AT LAST.
BOSO (MUTTER)
HUH?
YOU...
...TURNED AROUND SUD-DENLY.
I THOUGHT YOU WERE GONNA GET VIOLENT WITH ME!!
YOU ALWAYS GET MY HOPES UP!
I-I BETRAYED YOU SO BAD YOU'RE ON THE VERGE OF TEARS!?
I'M SORRY!?
BUWA (WEEP)
MIYAMURA, YOU DUMMY!!
SHU (SPRITZ)
SHU
SHUUU
ENOUGH DEODORIZING SPRAY ALREADY!

HORIMIYA

HORIMIYA

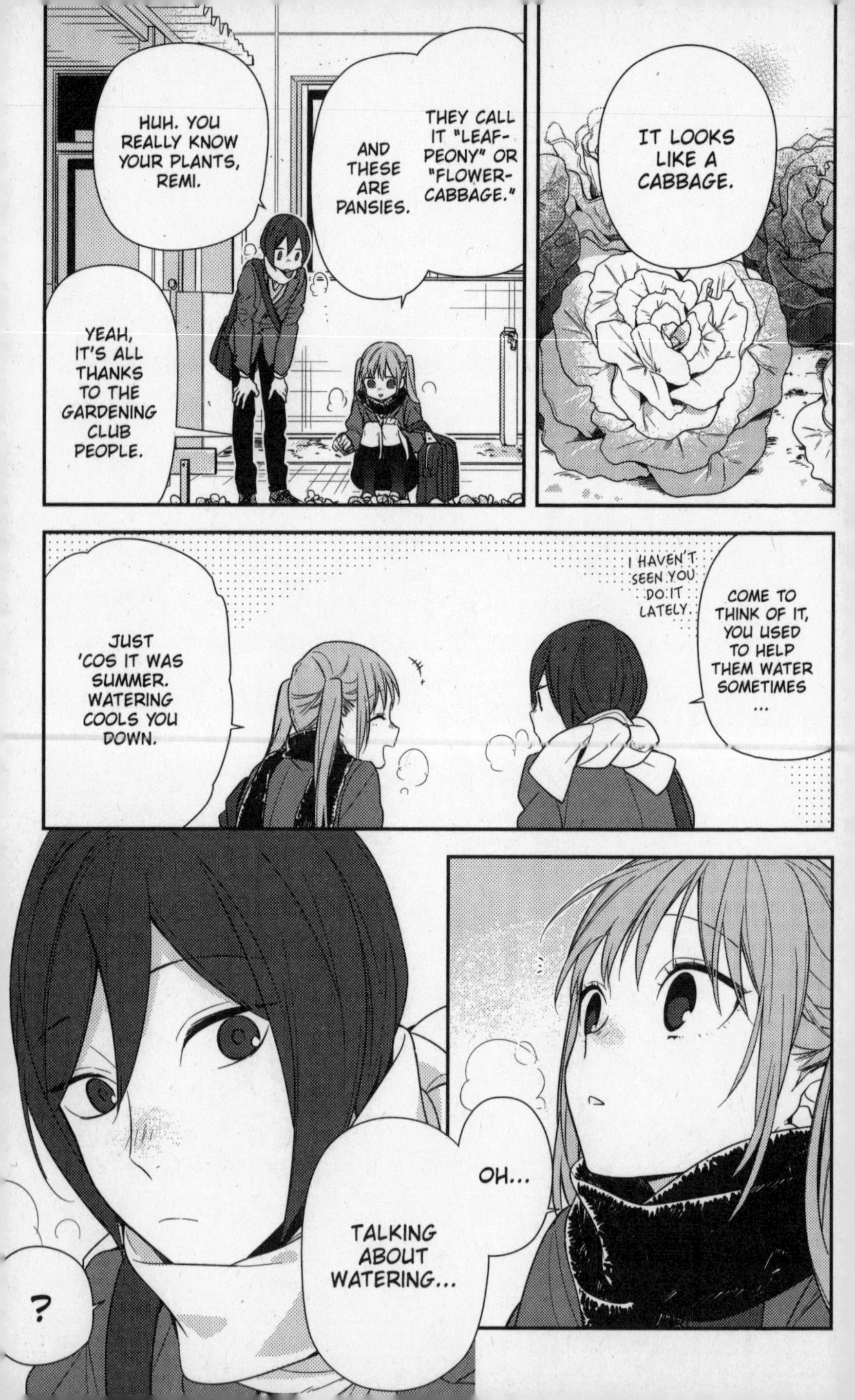
IT LOOKS LIKE A CABBAGE.
THEY CALL IT "LEAF-PEONY" OR "FLOWER-CABBAGE."
AND THESE ARE PANSIES.
HUH. YOU REALLY KNOW YOUR PLANTS, REMI.
YEAH, IT'S ALL THANKS TO THE GARDENING CLUB PEOPLE.
COME TO THINK OF IT, YOU USED TO HELP THEM WATER SOMETIMES ...
I HAVEN'T SEEN YOU DO IT LATELY.
JUST 'COS IT WAS SUMMER. WATERING COOLS YOU DOWN.
OH...
TALKING ABOUT WATERING...
?

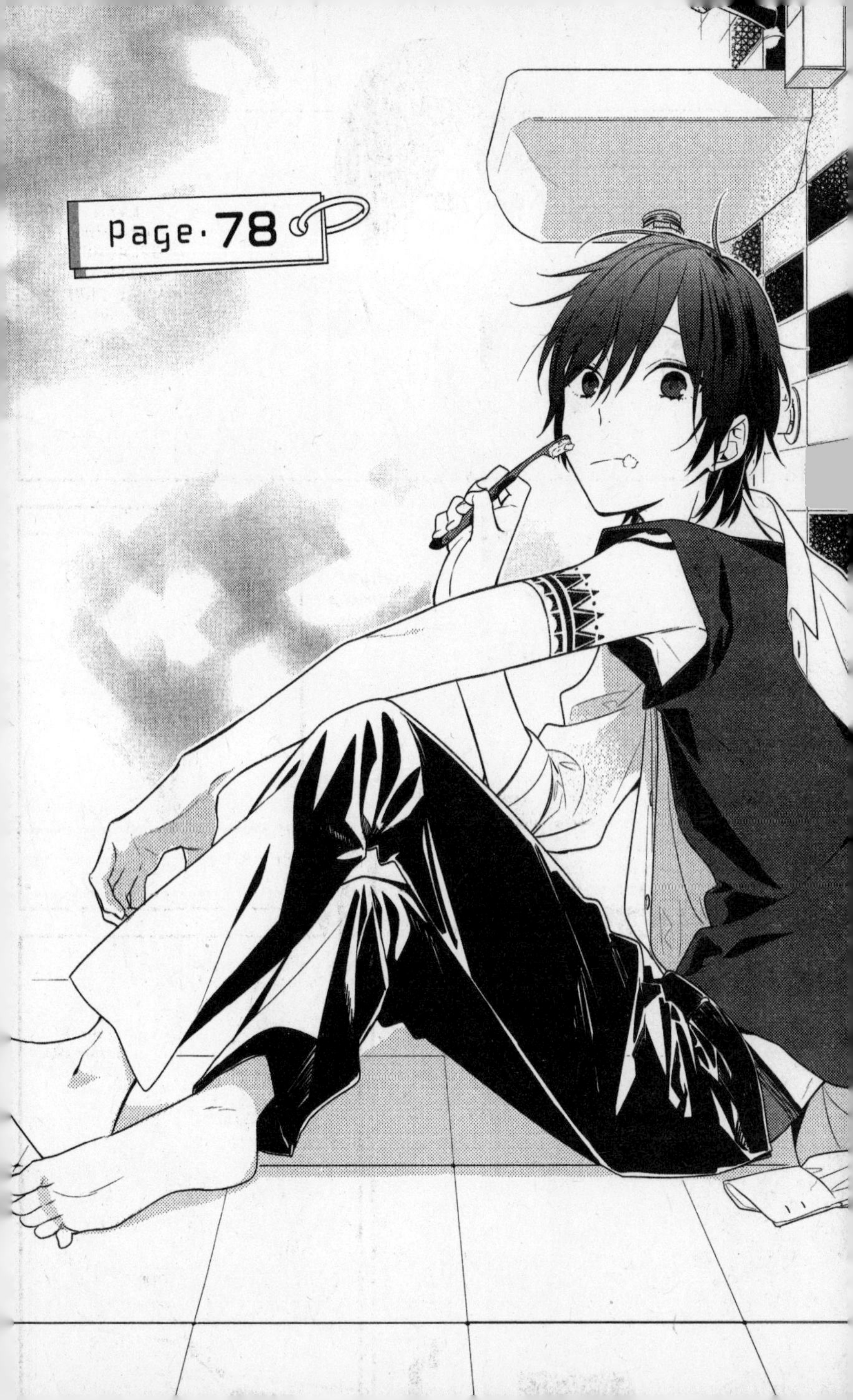
Page.78

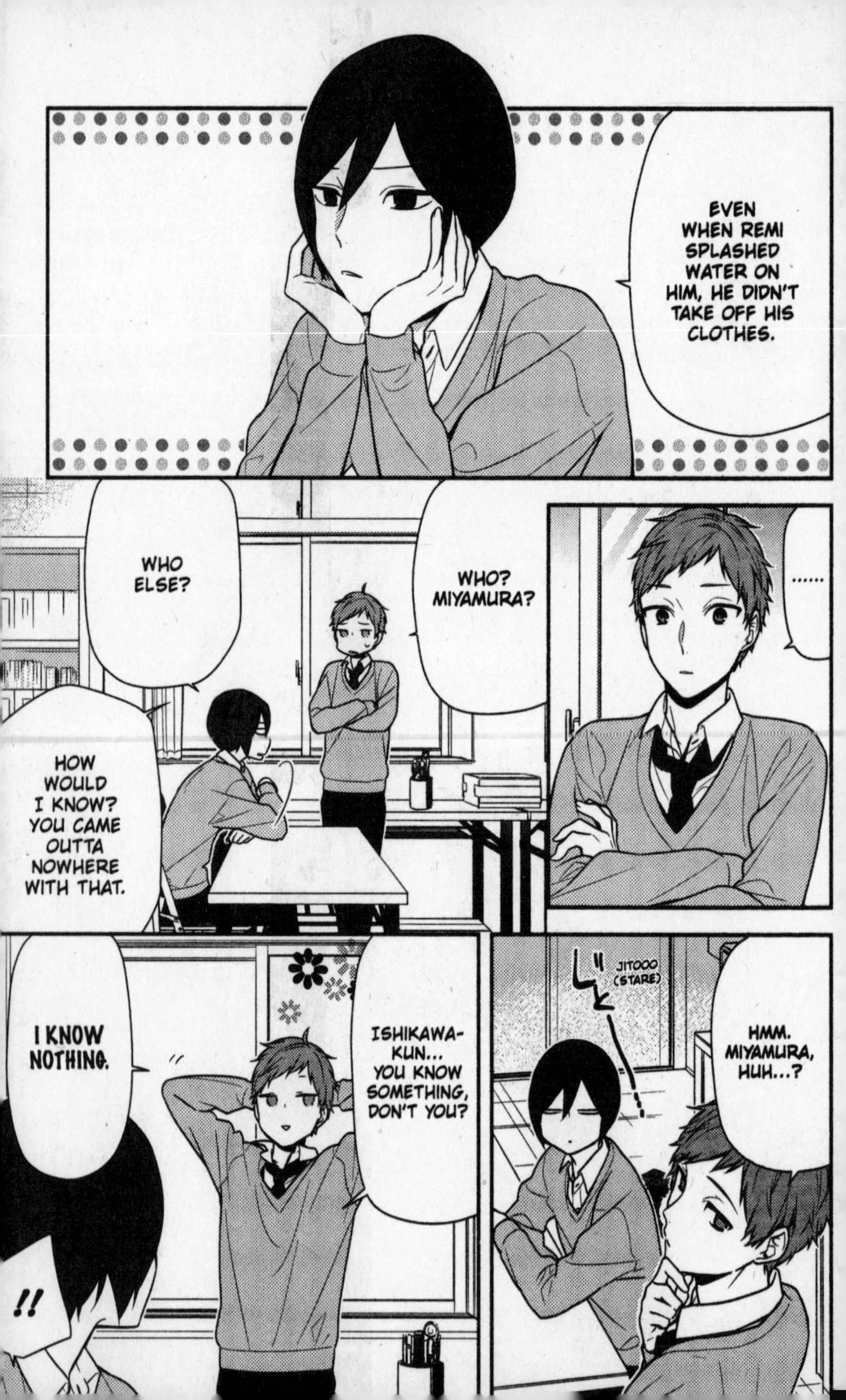
EVEN WHEN REMI SPLASHED WATER ON HIM, HE DIDN'T TAKE OFF HIS CLOTHES.
......
WHO? MIYAMURA?
WHO ELSE?
HOW WOULD I KNOW? YOU CAME OUTTA NOWHERE WITH THAT.
HMM. MIYAMURA, HUH...?
JITOOO (STARE)
ISHIKAWA-KUN... YOU KNOW SOMETHING, DON'T YOU?
I KNOW NOTHING.
!!

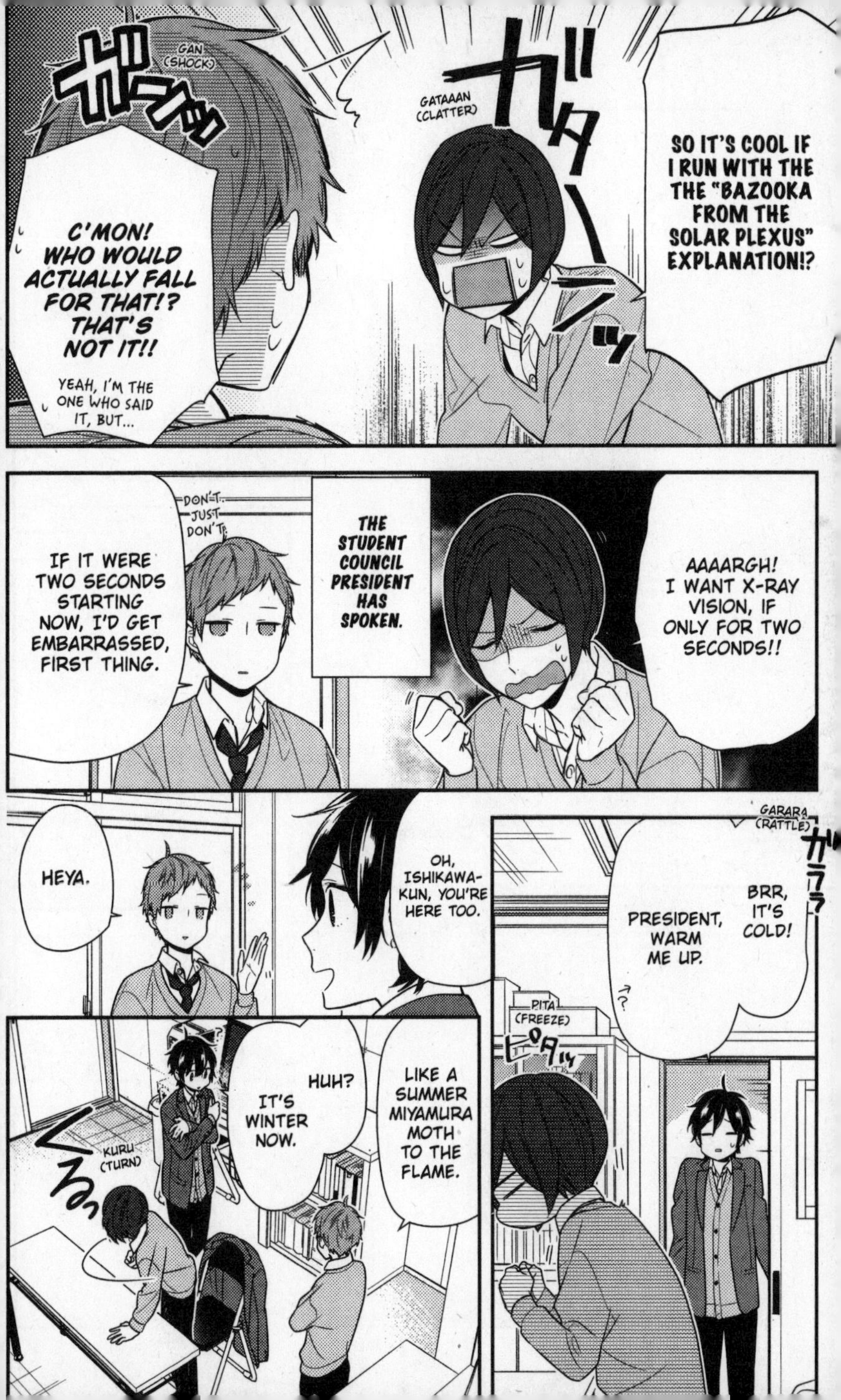

SO IT'S COOL IF I RUN WITH THE THE "BAZOOKA FROM THE SOLAR PLEXUS" EXPLANATION!?
GATAAAN (CLATTER)
GAN (SHOCK)
C'MON! WHO WOULD ACTUALLY FALL FOR THAT!? THAT'S NOT IT!!
YEAH, I'M THE ONE WHO SAID IT, BUT...
AAAARGH! I WANT X-RAY VISION, IF ONLY FOR TWO SECONDS!!
THE STUDENT COUNCIL PRESIDENT HAS SPOKEN.
IF IT WERE TWO SECONDS STARTING NOW, I'D GET EMBARRASSED, FIRST THING.
DON'T. JUST DON'T.
GARARA (RATTLE)
BRR, IT'S COLD!
PRESIDENT, WARM ME UP.
PITA (FREEZE)
OH, ISHIKAWA-KUN, YOU'RE HERE TOO.
HEYA.
LIKE A SUMMER MIYAMURA MOTH TO THE FLAME.
HUH?
IT'S WINTER NOW.
KURU (TURN)

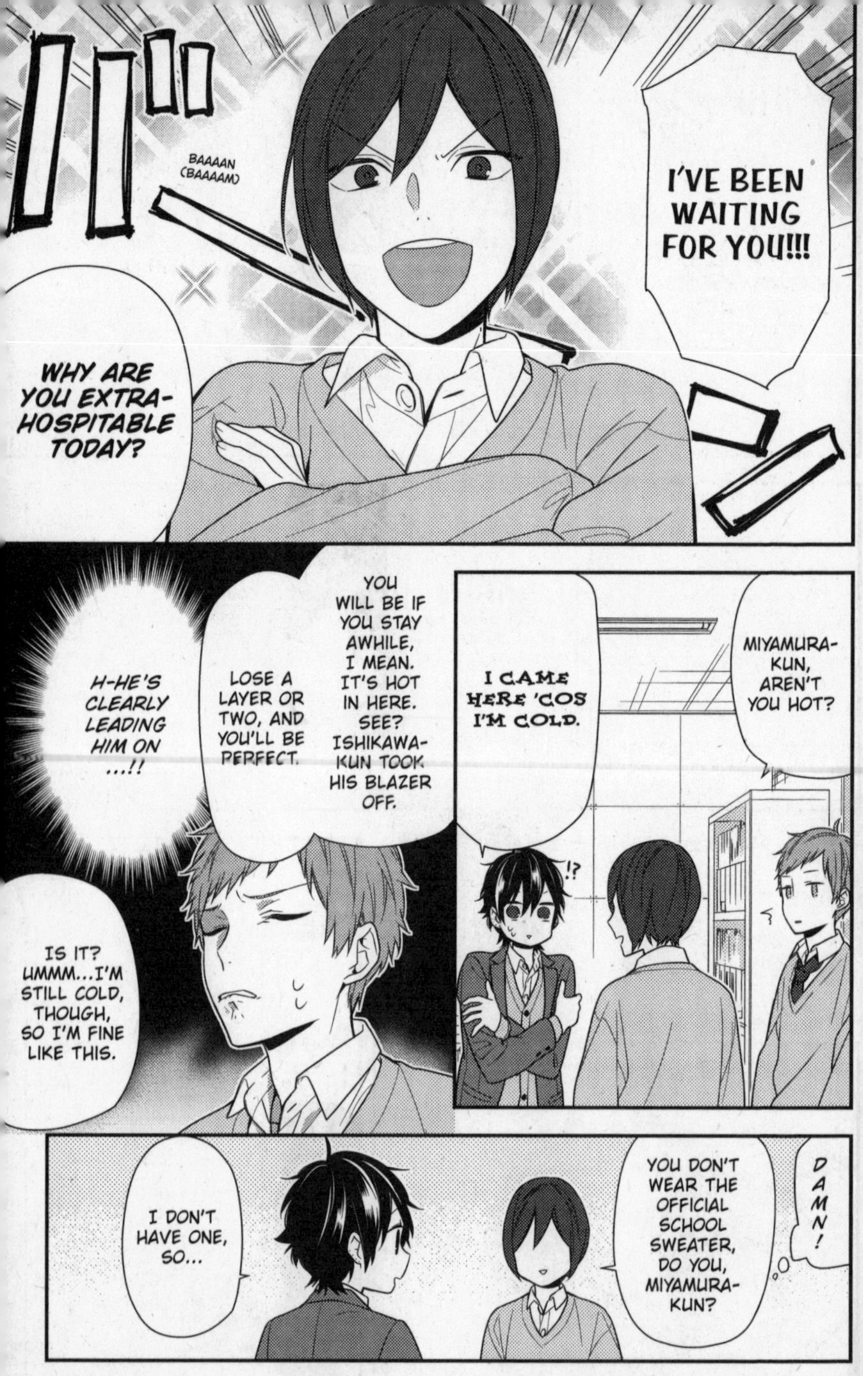
I'VE BEEN WAITING FOR YOU!!!
BAAAAN (BAAAAM)
WHY ARE YOU EXTRA-HOSPITABLE TODAY?
MIYAMURA-KUN, AREN'T YOU HOT?
I CAME HERE 'COS I'M COLD.
!?
YOU WILL BE IF YOU STAY AWHILE, I MEAN. IT'S HOT IN HERE. SEE? ISHIKAWA-KUN TOOK HIS BLAZER OFF.
LOSE A LAYER OR TWO, AND YOU'LL BE PERFECT.
H-HE'S CLEARLY LEADING HIM ON...!!
IS IT? UMMM...I'M STILL COLD, THOUGH, SO I'M FINE LIKE THIS.
DAMN!
YOU DON'T WEAR THE OFFICIAL SCHOOL SWEATER, DO YOU, MIYAMURA-KUN?
I DON'T HAVE ONE, SO...

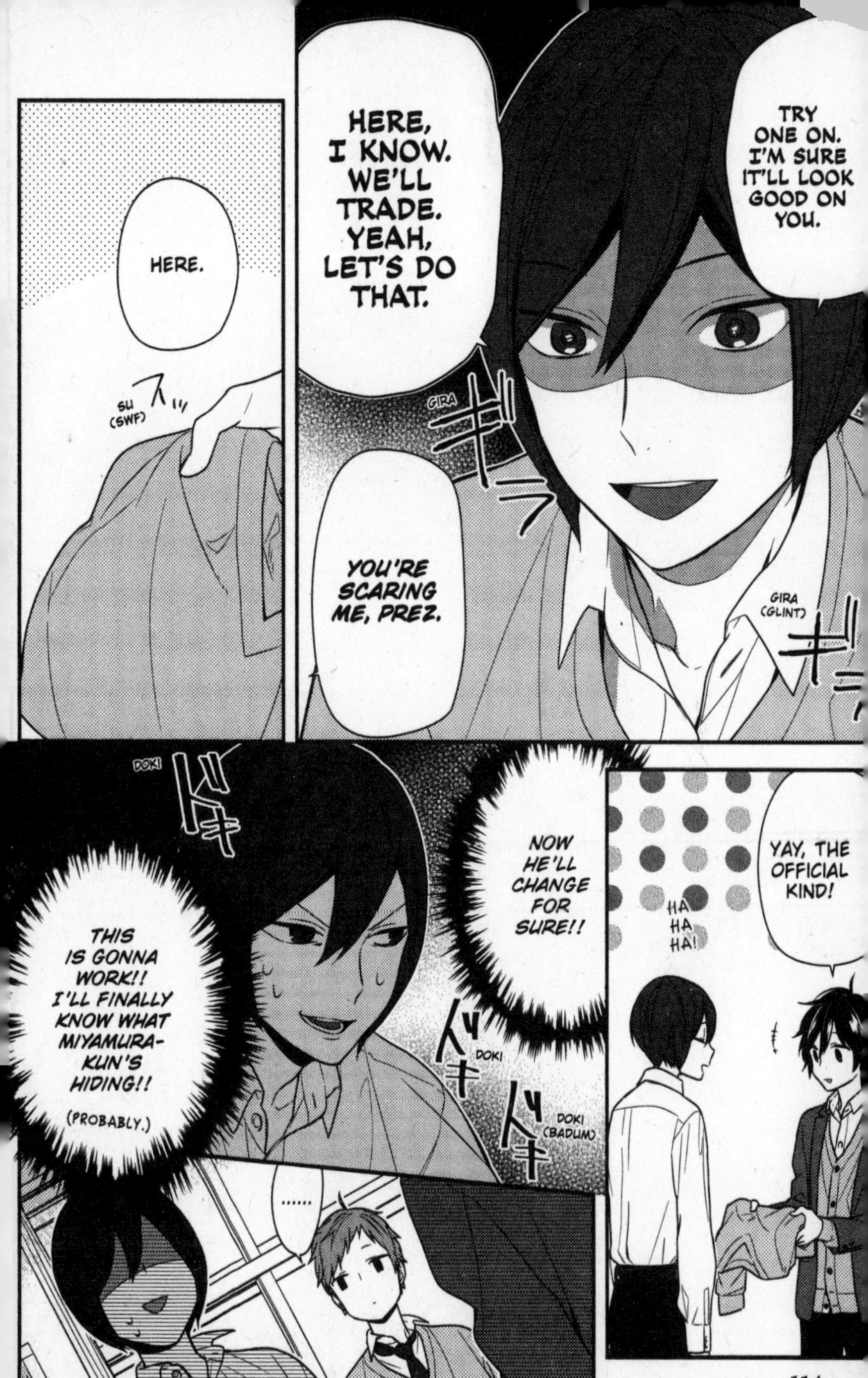
TRY ONE ON. I'M SURE IT'LL LOOK GOOD ON YOU.
HERE, I KNOW. WE'LL TRADE. YEAH, LET'S DO THAT.
GIRA
GIRA (GLINT)
YOU'RE SCARING ME, PREZ.
HERE.
SU (SWF)
YAY, THE OFFICIAL KIND!
HA HA HA!
DOKI
NOW HE'LL CHANGE FOR SURE!!
THIS IS GONNA WORK!! I'LL FINALLY KNOW WHAT MIYAMURA-KUN'S HIDING!!
(PROBABLY.)
DOKI
DOKI (BADUM)
......

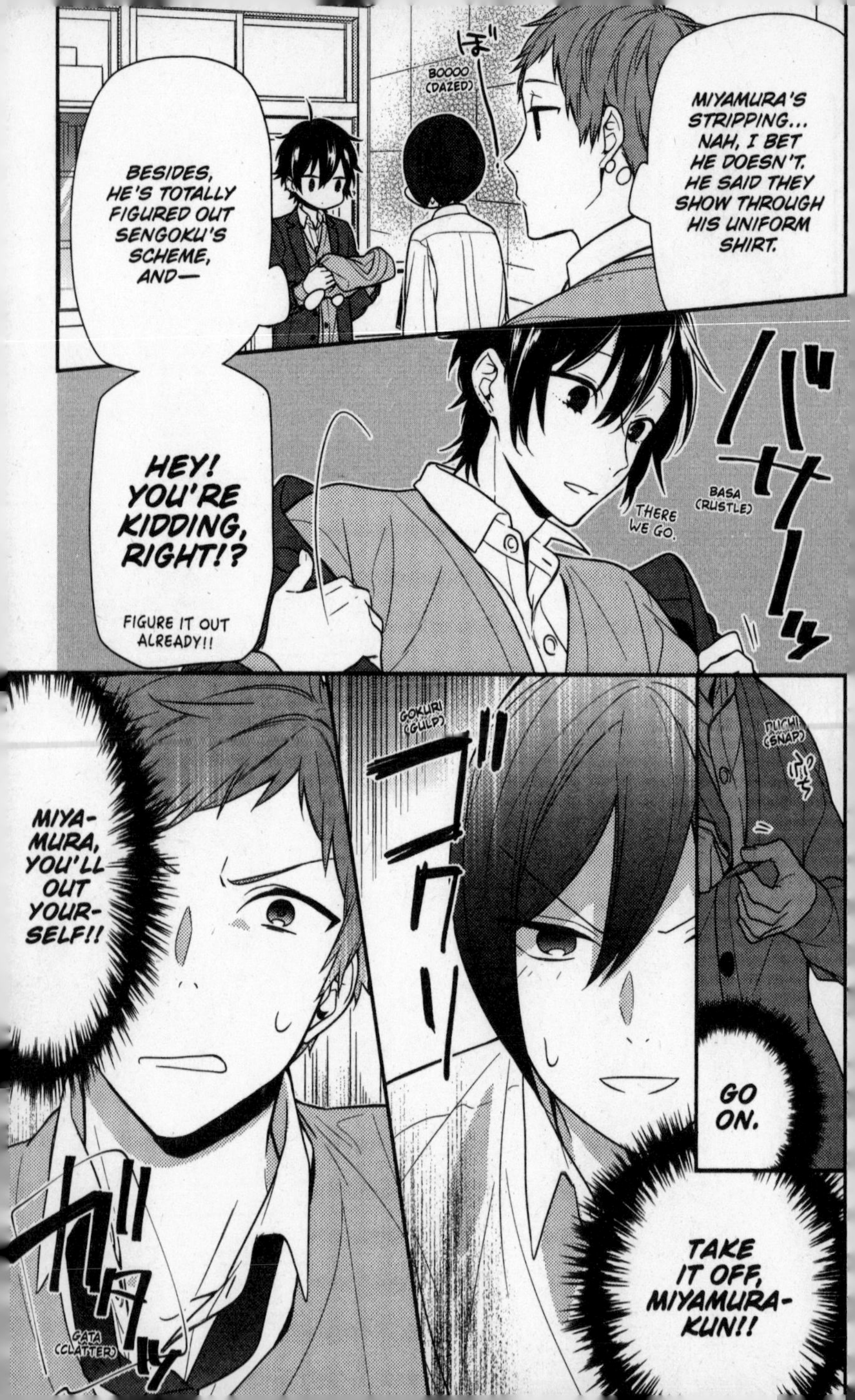
MIYAMURA'S STRIPPING... NAH, I BET HE DOESN'T. HE SAID THEY SHOW THROUGH HIS UNIFORM SHIRT.
ぼー
BOOOO (DAZED)
BESIDES, HE'S TOTALLY FIGURED OUT SENGOKU'S SCHEME, AND—
BASA (RUSTLE)
THERE WE GO.
HEY! YOU'RE KIDDING, RIGHT!?
FIGURE IT OUT ALREADY!!
PUCHI (SNAP)
GO ON.
TAKE IT OFF, MIYAMURA-KUN!!
GOKURI (GULP)
MIYA-MURA, YOU'LL OUT YOUR-SELF!!
GATA (CLATTER)

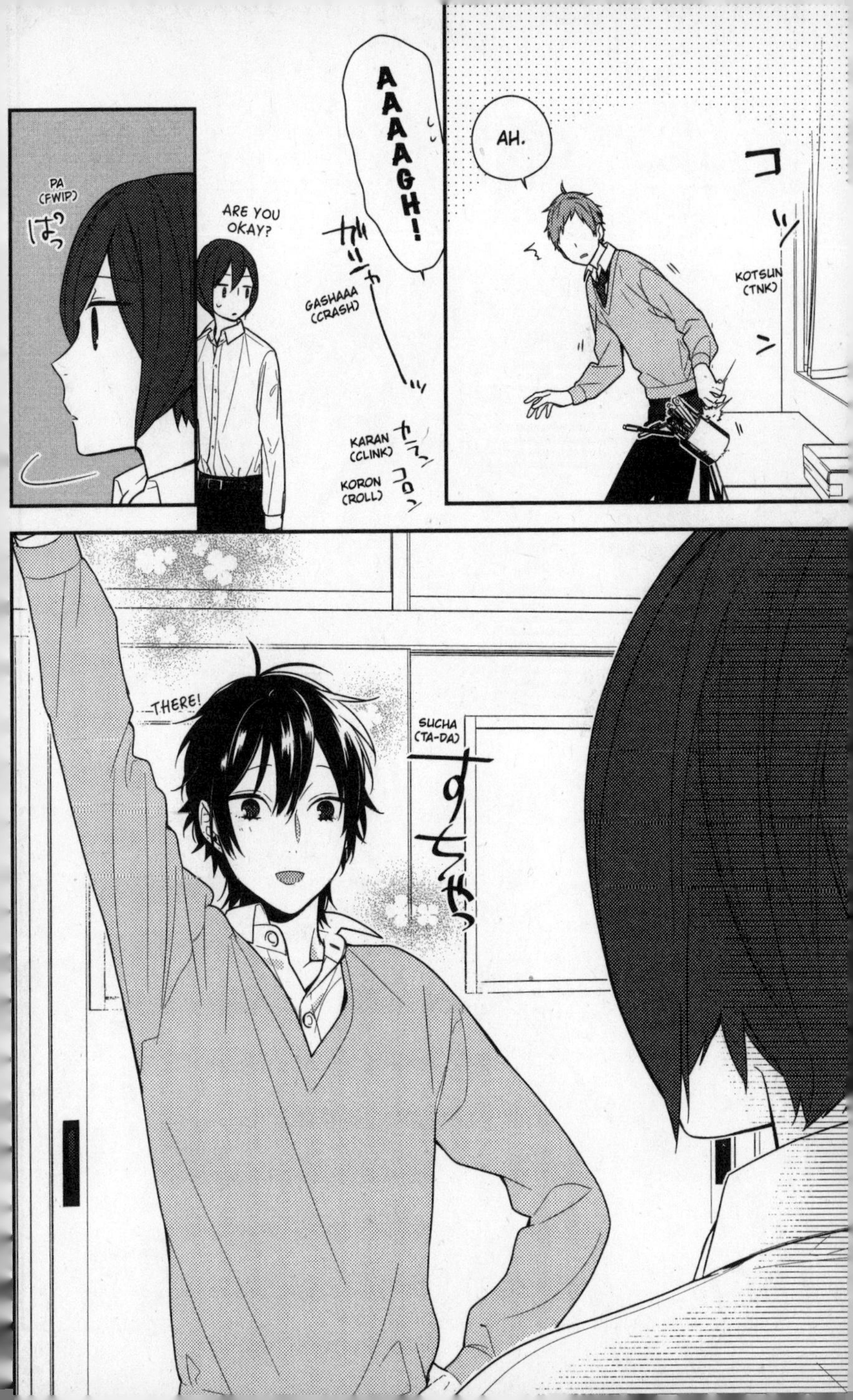

AH.
KOTSUN (TNK)
コツン
AAAAGH!
GASHAAA (CRASH)
ガシャーッ
KARAN (CLINK)
カラン
KORON (ROLL)
コロン
ARE YOU OKAY?
PA (FWIP)
ぱっ
SUCHA (TA-DA)
すちゃっ
...THERE!

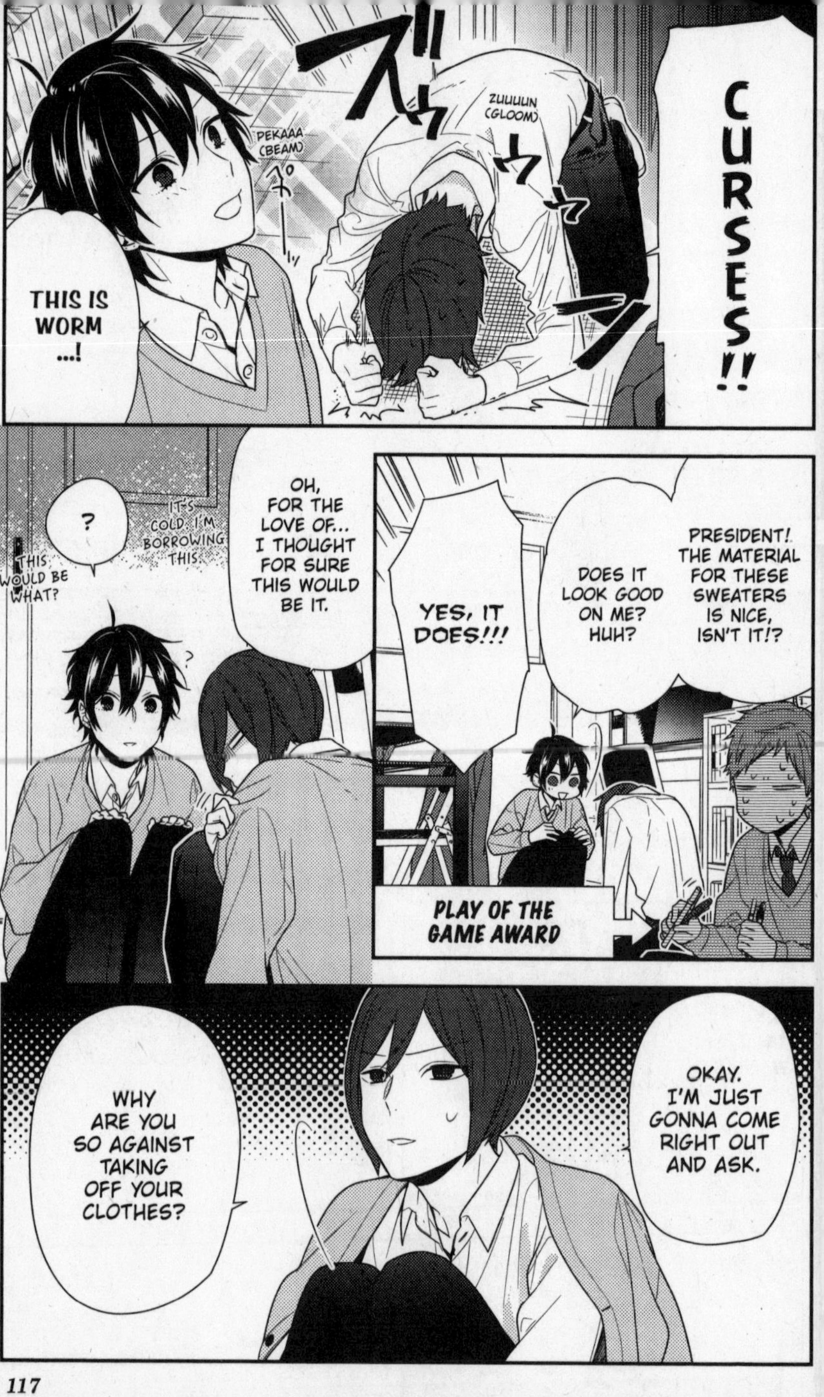
CURSES!!
ZUUUUN (GLOOM)
PEKAAA (BEAM)
THIS IS WORM ...!
PRESIDENT! THE MATERIAL FOR THESE SWEATERS IS NICE, ISN'T IT!?
DOES IT LOOK GOOD ON ME? HUH?
YES, IT DOES!!!
PLAY OF THE GAME AWARD
OH, FOR THE LOVE OF... I THOUGHT FOR SURE THIS WOULD BE IT.
IT'S COLD. I'M BORROWING THIS.
?
THIS WOULD BE WHAT?
?
OKAY. I'M JUST GONNA COME RIGHT OUT AND ASK.
WHY ARE YOU SO AGAINST TAKING OFF YOUR CLOTHES?

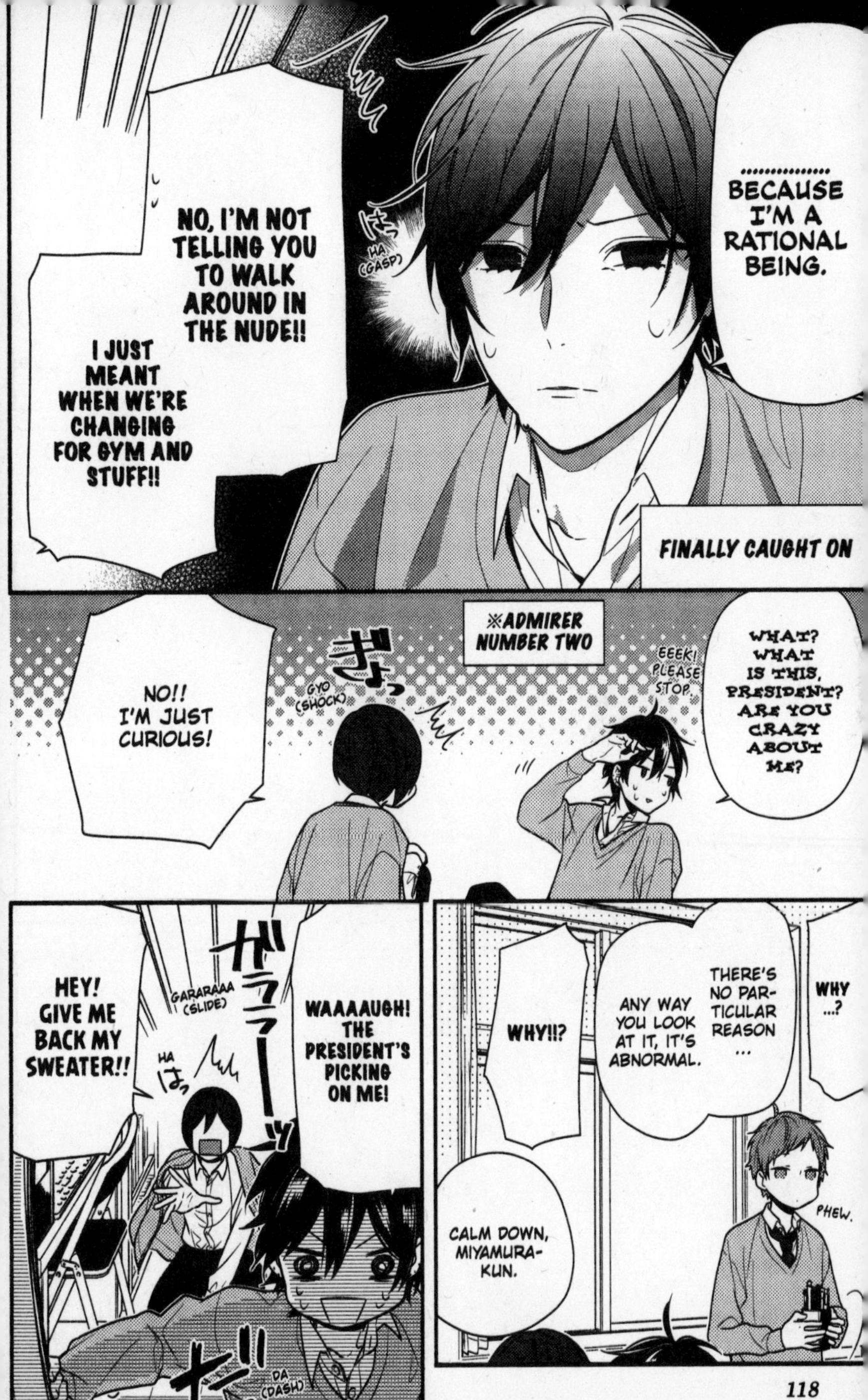

…………… BECAUSE I'M A RATIONAL BEING.
HA (GASP)
NO, I'M NOT TELLING YOU TO WALK AROUND IN THE NUDE!!
I JUST MEANT WHEN WE'RE CHANGING FOR GYM AND STUFF!!
FINALLY CAUGHT ON
WHAT? WHAT IS THIS, PRESIDENT? ARE YOU CRAZY ABOUT ME?
EEEK! PLEASE STOP.
※ADMIRER NUMBER TWO
GYO (SHOCK)
NO!! I'M JUST CURIOUS!
WHY …?
THERE'S NO PAR-TICULAR REASON …
ANY WAY YOU LOOK AT IT, IT'S ABNORMAL.
WHY!!?
PHEW.
CALM DOWN, MIYAMURA-KUN.
WAAAAUGH! THE PRESIDENT'S PICKING ON ME!
GARARAAA (SLIDE)
HA
HEY! GIVE ME BACK MY SWEATER!!
DA (DASH)

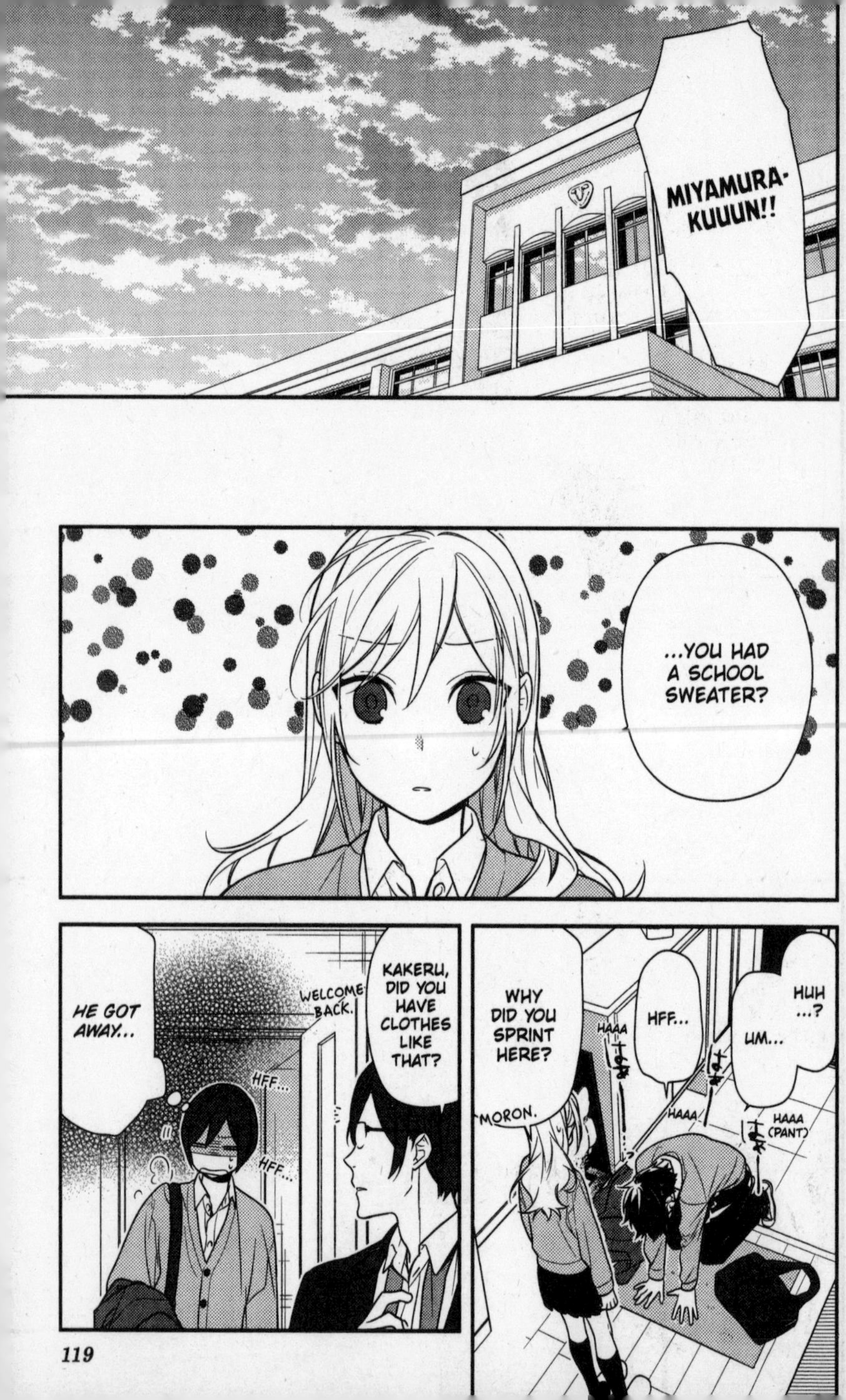
MIYAMURA-KUUUN!!
...YOU HAD A SCHOOL SWEATER?
HUH ...? UM...
HAAA (PANT)
HAAA
HFF...
HAAA
WHY DID YOU SPRINT HERE?
MORON.
KAKERU, DID YOU HAVE CLOTHES LIKE THAT?
WELCOME BACK.
HE GOT AWAY...
HFF...
HFF...

HORIMIYA

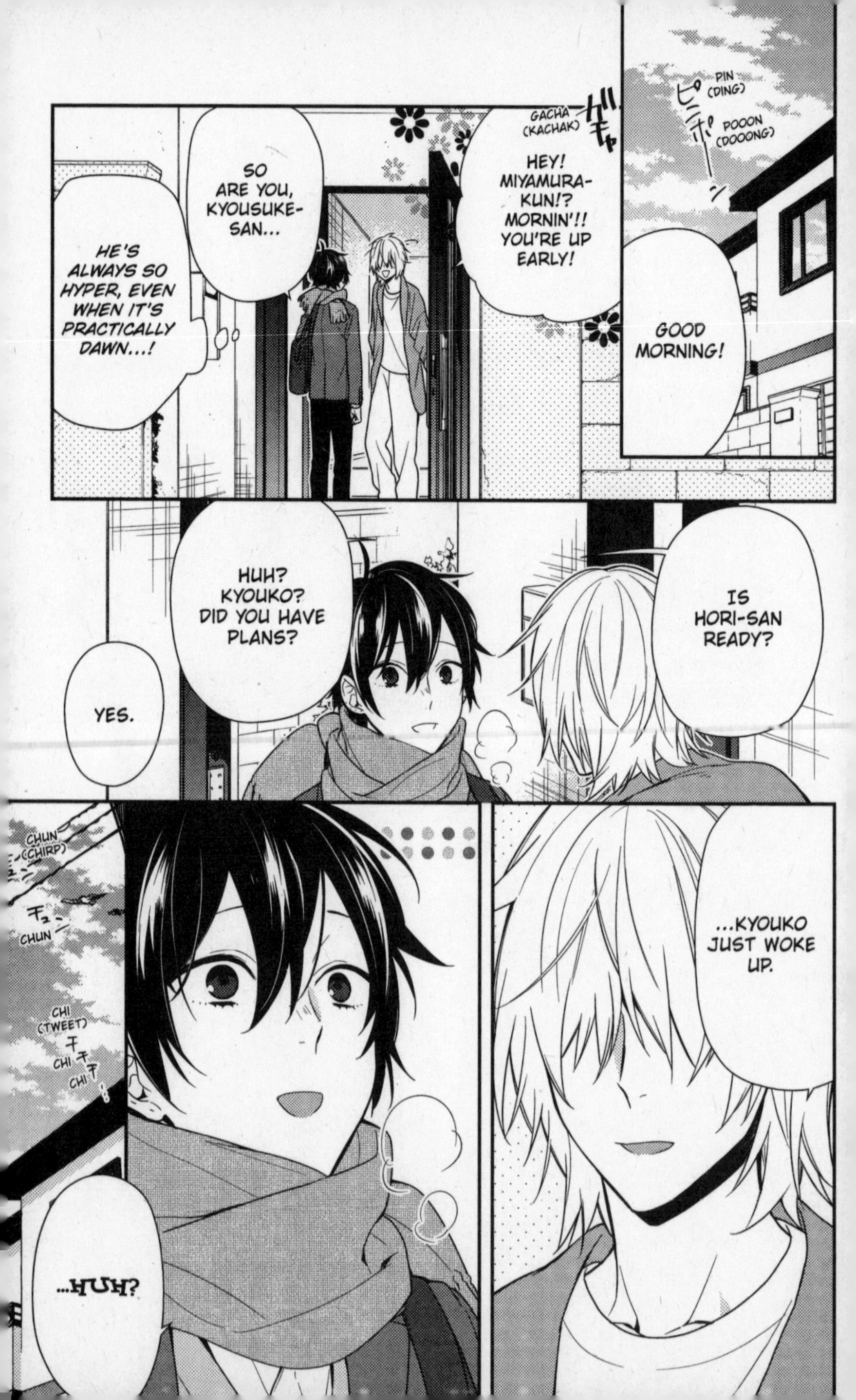
PIN (DING)
POOON (DOOONG)
GOOD MORNING!
GACHA (KACHAK)
HEY! MIYAMURA-KUN!? MORNIN'!! YOU'RE UP EARLY!
SO ARE YOU, KYOUSUKE-SAN...
HE'S ALWAYS SO HYPER, EVEN WHEN IT'S PRACTICALLY DAWN...!
IS HORI-SAN READY?
HUH? KYOUKO? DID YOU HAVE PLANS?
YES.
...KYOUKO JUST WOKE UP.
CHUN (CHIRP)
CHUN
CHI (TWEET)
CHI
CHI
...HUH?

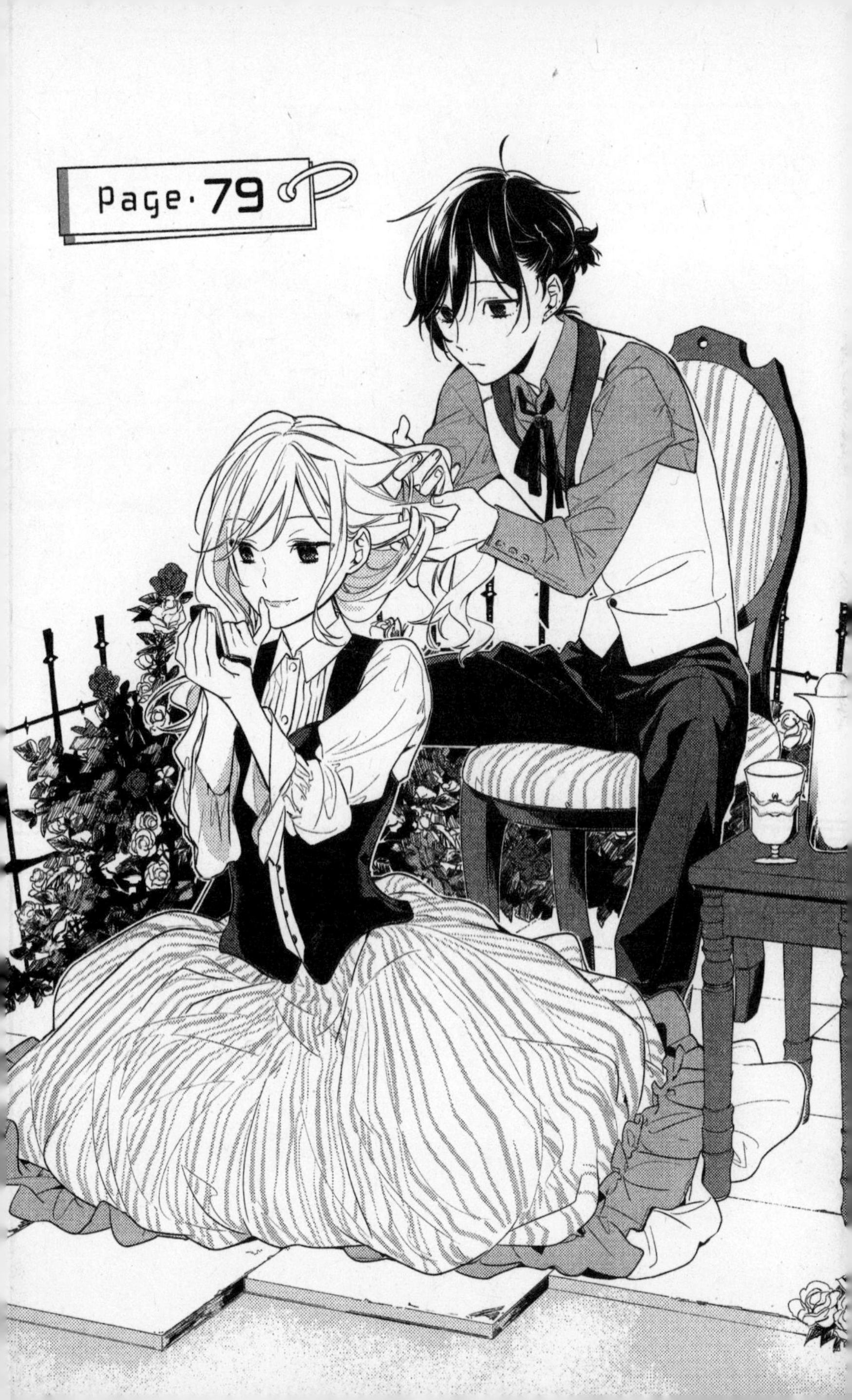
page·79

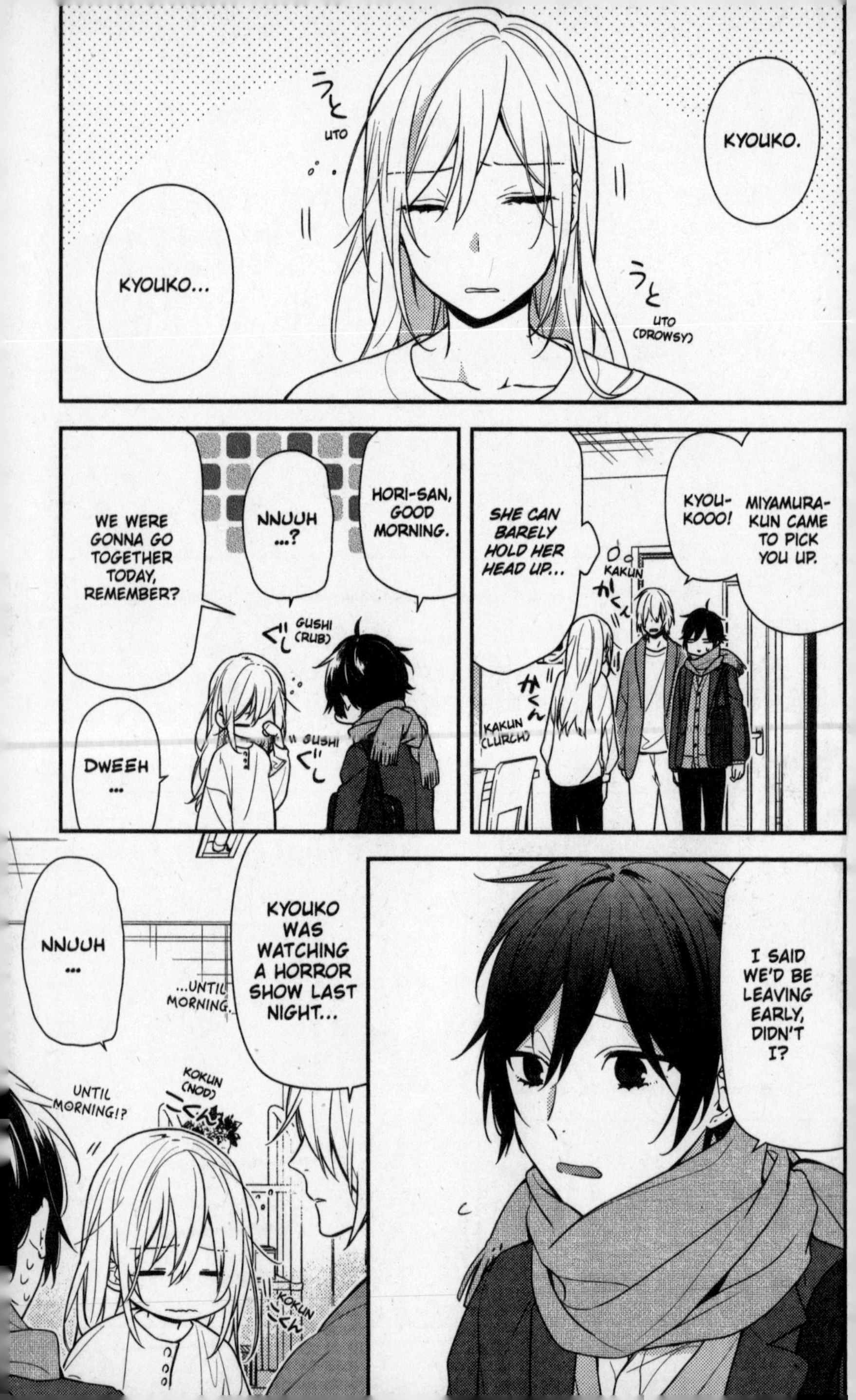
KYOUKO.
うと UTO
うと UTO (DROWSY)
KYOUKO...
KYOU-KOOO! MIYAMURA-KUN CAME TO PICK YOU UP.
SHE CAN BARELY HOLD HER HEAD UP...
かくん KAKUN
かくん KAKUN (LURCH)
HORI-SAN, GOOD MORNING.
NNUUH ...?
ぐし GUSHI (RUB)
WE WERE GONNA GO TOGETHER TODAY, REMEMBER?
ぐし GUSHI
DWEEH ...
I SAID WE'D BE LEAVING EARLY, DIDN'T I?
KYOUKO WAS WATCHING A HORROR SHOW LAST NIGHT...
...UNTIL MORNING.
NNUUH ...
こくん KOKUN (NOD)
UNTIL MORNING!?
こくん KOKUN

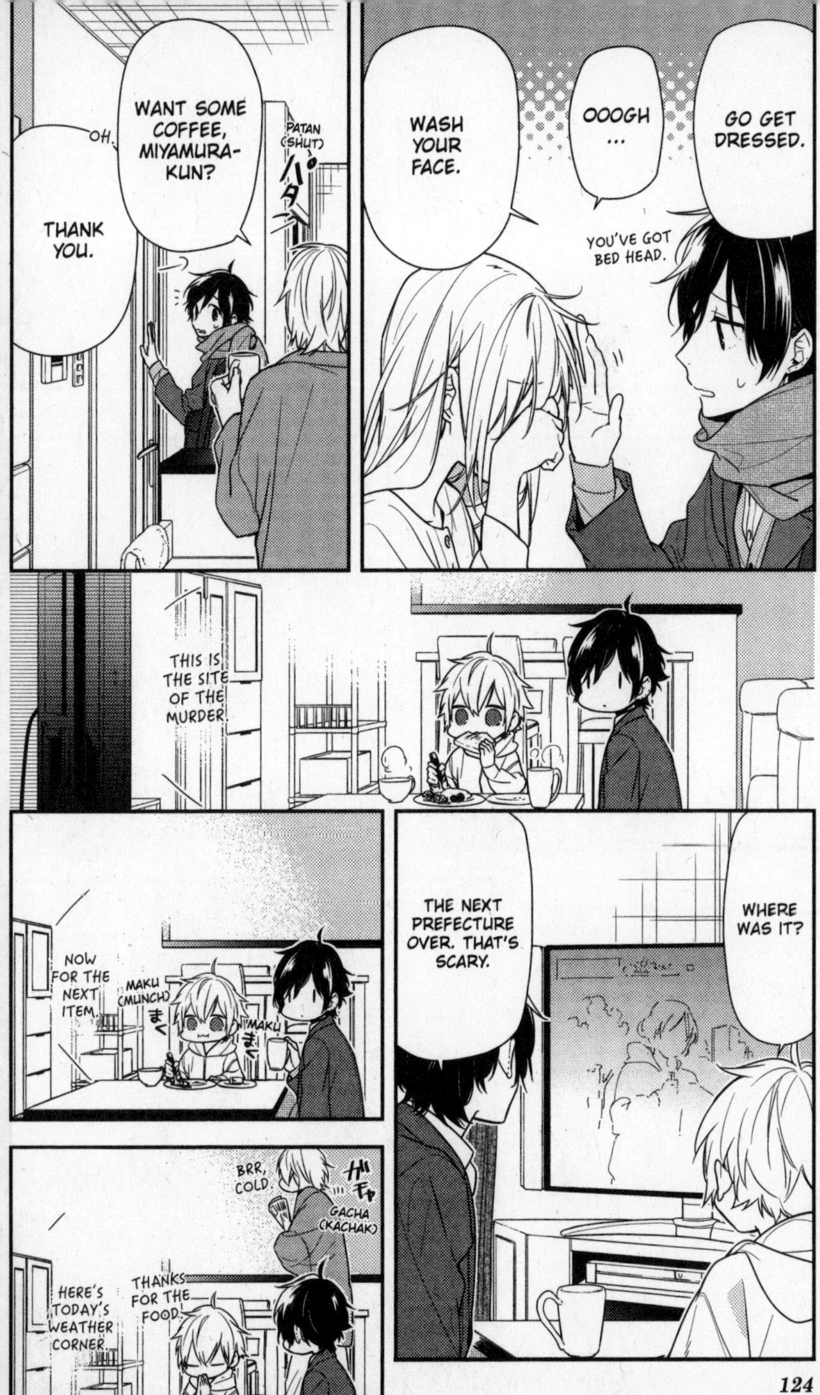
GO GET DRESSED.
OOOGH ...
YOU'VE GOT BED HEAD.
WASH YOUR FACE.
PATAN (SHUT)
パタ
WANT SOME COFFEE, MIYAMURA-KUN?
OH. THANK YOU.
THIS IS THE SITE OF THE MURDER.
WHERE WAS IT?
THE NEXT PREFECTURE OVER. THAT'S SCARY.
MAKU (MUNCH)
まく
MAKU
まく
NOW FOR THE NEXT ITEM.
BRR, COLD.
ガチャ
GACHA (KACHAK)
THANKS FOR THE FOOD.
HERE'S TODAY'S WEATHER CORNER.

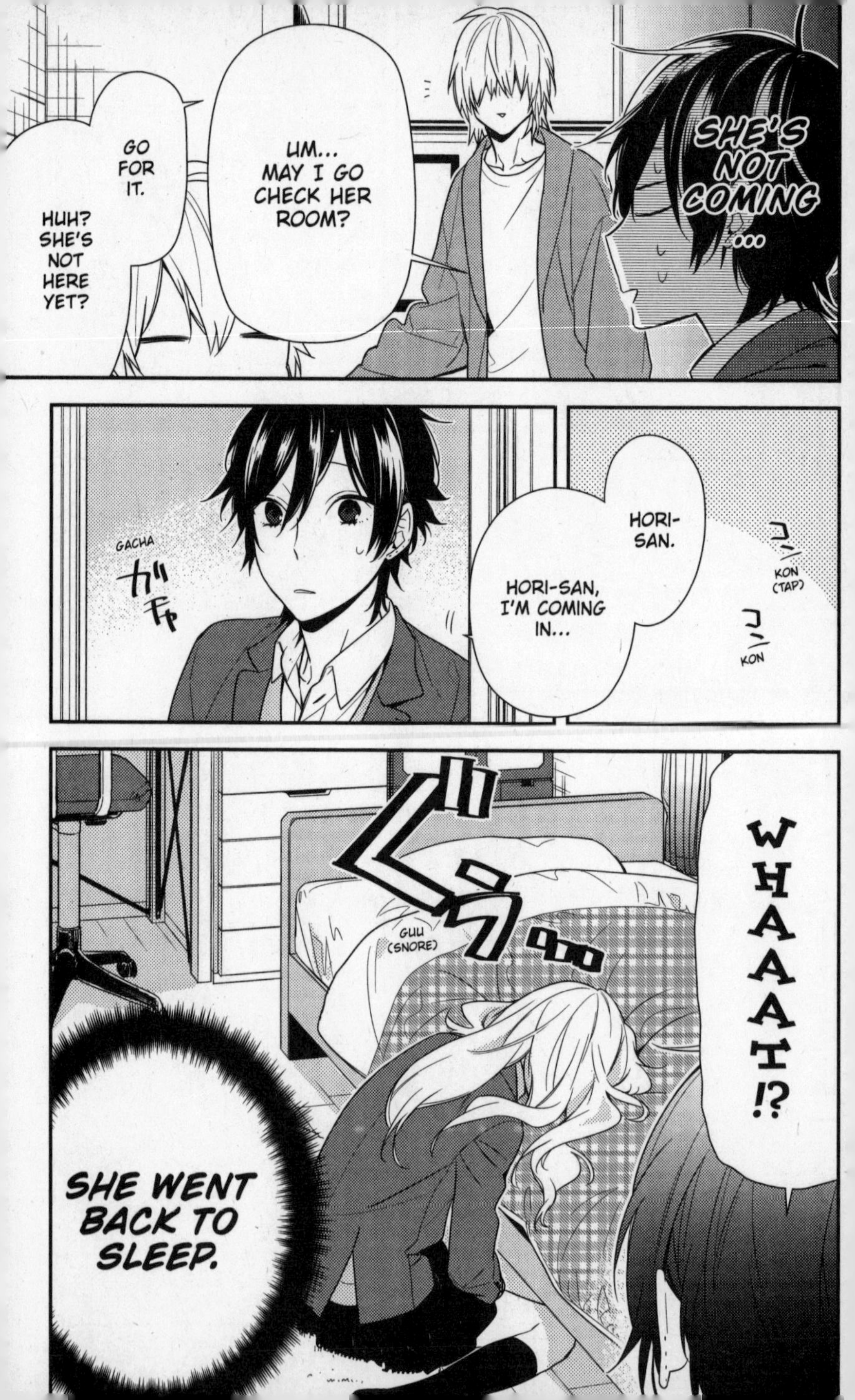
SHE'S NOT COMING...
UM... MAY I GO CHECK HER ROOM?
GO FOR IT.
HUH? SHE'S NOT HERE YET?
KON (TAP)
KON
HORI-SAN.
HORI-SAN, I'M COMING IN...
GACHA
WHAAAAT!?
GUU (SNORE)
SHE WENT BACK TO SLEEP.

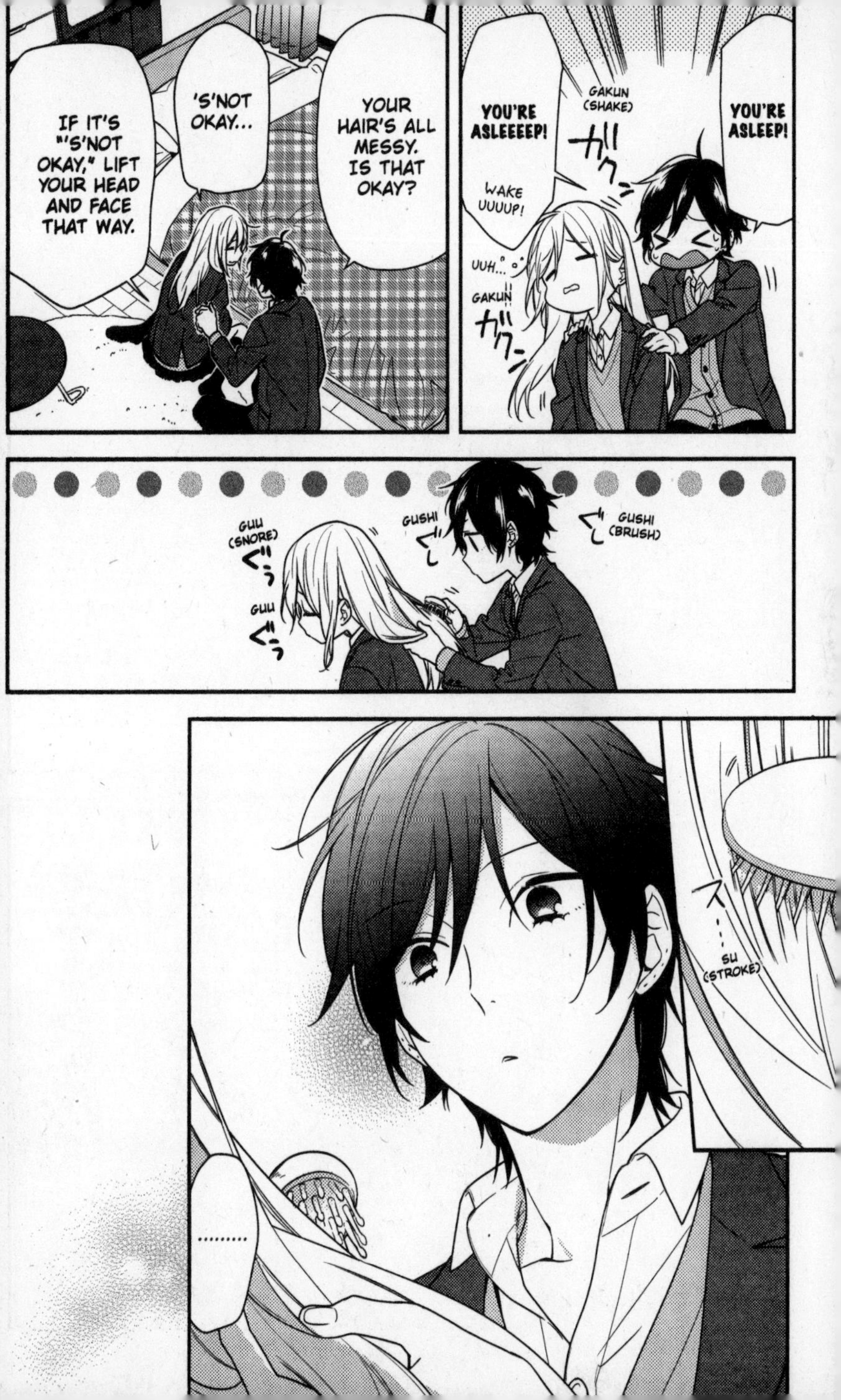
YOU'RE ASLEEP!
GAKUN (SHAKE)
YOU'RE ASLEEEEP!
WAKE UUUUP!
UUH...
GAKUN
YOUR HAIR'S ALL MESSY. IS THAT OKAY?
'S'NOT OKAY...
IF IT'S "S'NOT OKAY," LIFT YOUR HEAD AND FACE THAT WAY.
GUSHI (BRUSH)
GUSHI
GUU (SNORE)
GUU
SU (STROKE)
.........

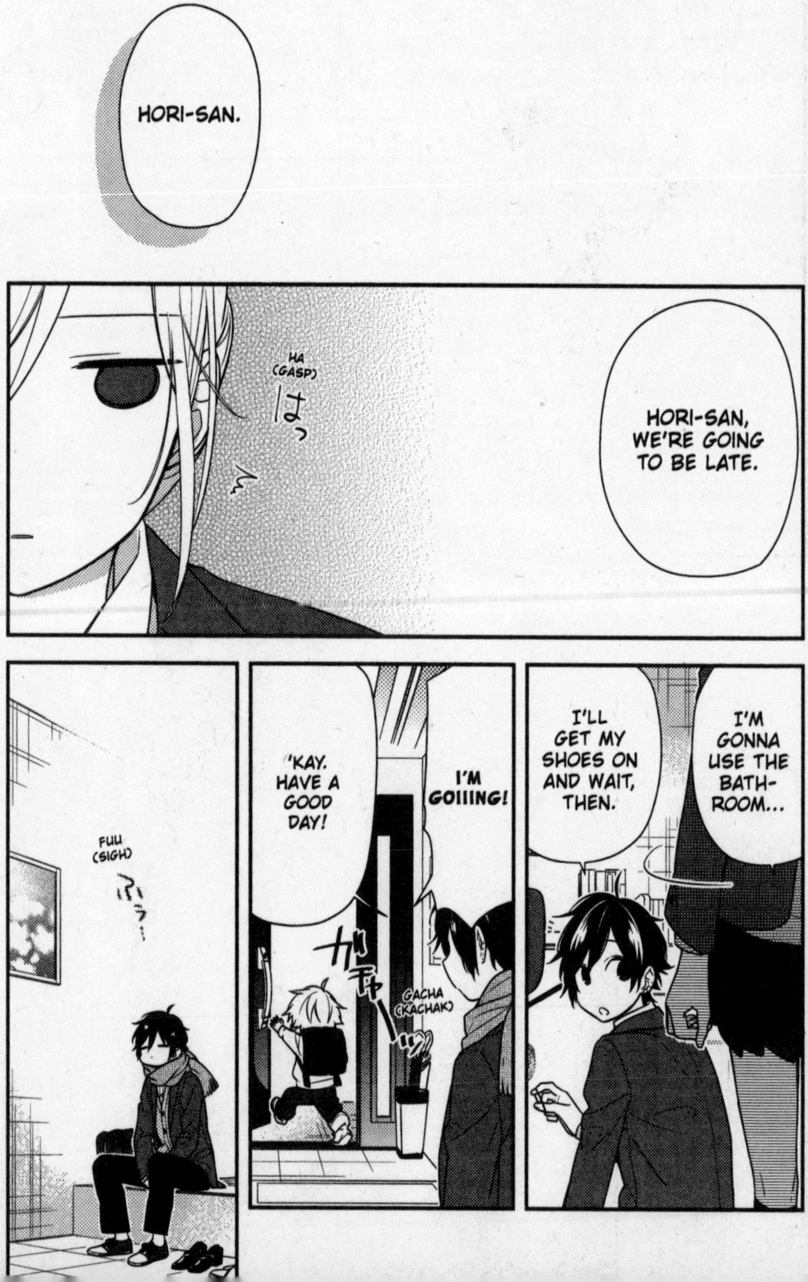
HORI-SAN.
HORI-SAN, WE'RE GOING TO BE LATE.
HA (GASP)
はっ
I'M GONNA USE THE BATH-ROOM...
I'LL GET MY SHOES ON AND WAIT, THEN.
I'M GOIIING!
'KAY. HAVE A GOOD DAY!
GACHA (KACHAK)
FUU (SIGH)

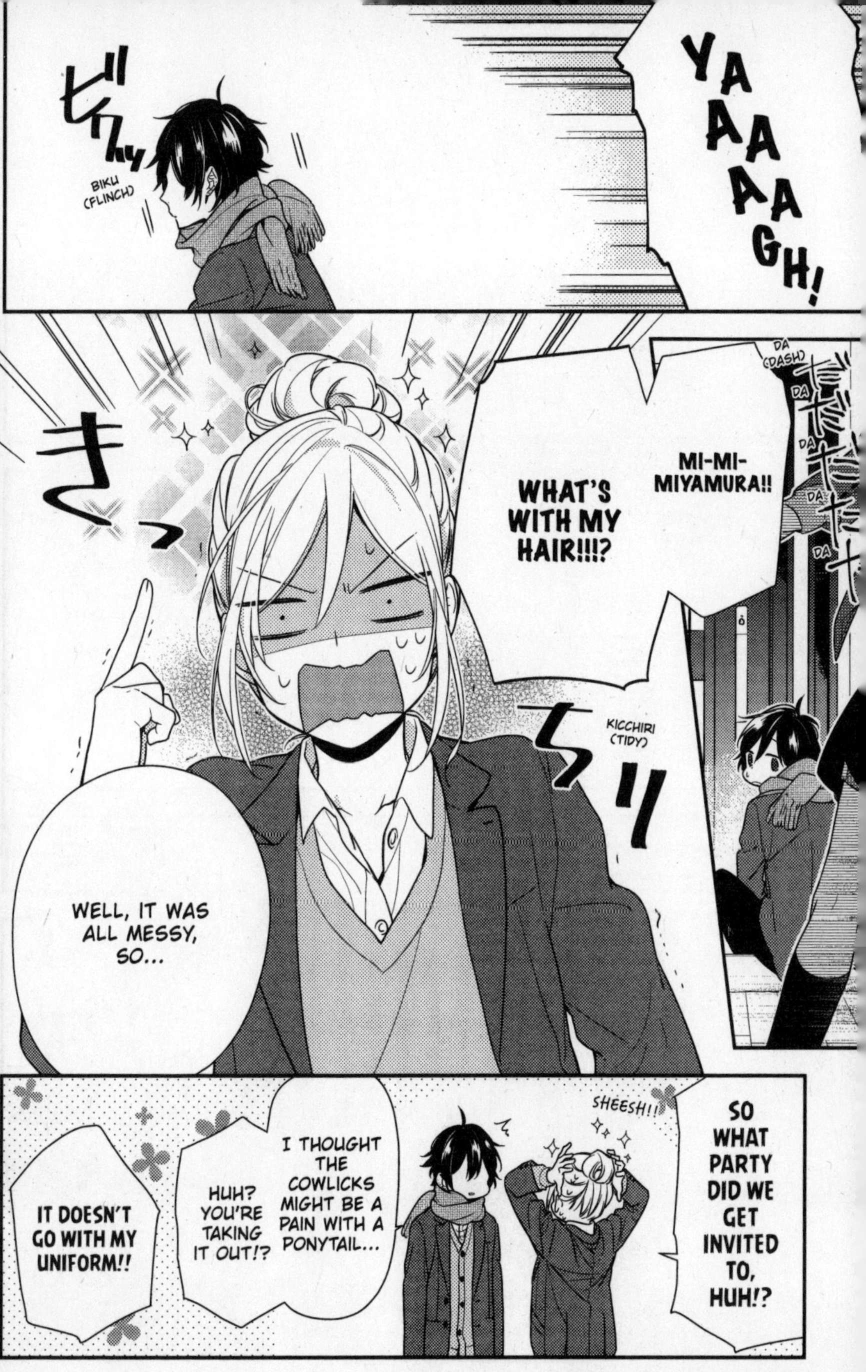
YAAAAAGH!
BIKU (FLINCH)
DA (DASH)
DA
DA
DA
DA
MI-MI-MIYAMURA!!
WHAT'S WITH MY HAIR!!!?
KICCHIRI (TIDY)
WELL, IT WAS ALL MESSY, SO...
SO WHAT PARTY DID WE GET INVITED TO, HUH!?
SHEESH!!
I THOUGHT THE COWLICKS MIGHT BE A PAIN WITH A PONYTAIL...
HUH? YOU'RE TAKING IT OUT!?
IT DOESN'T GO WITH MY UNIFORM!!

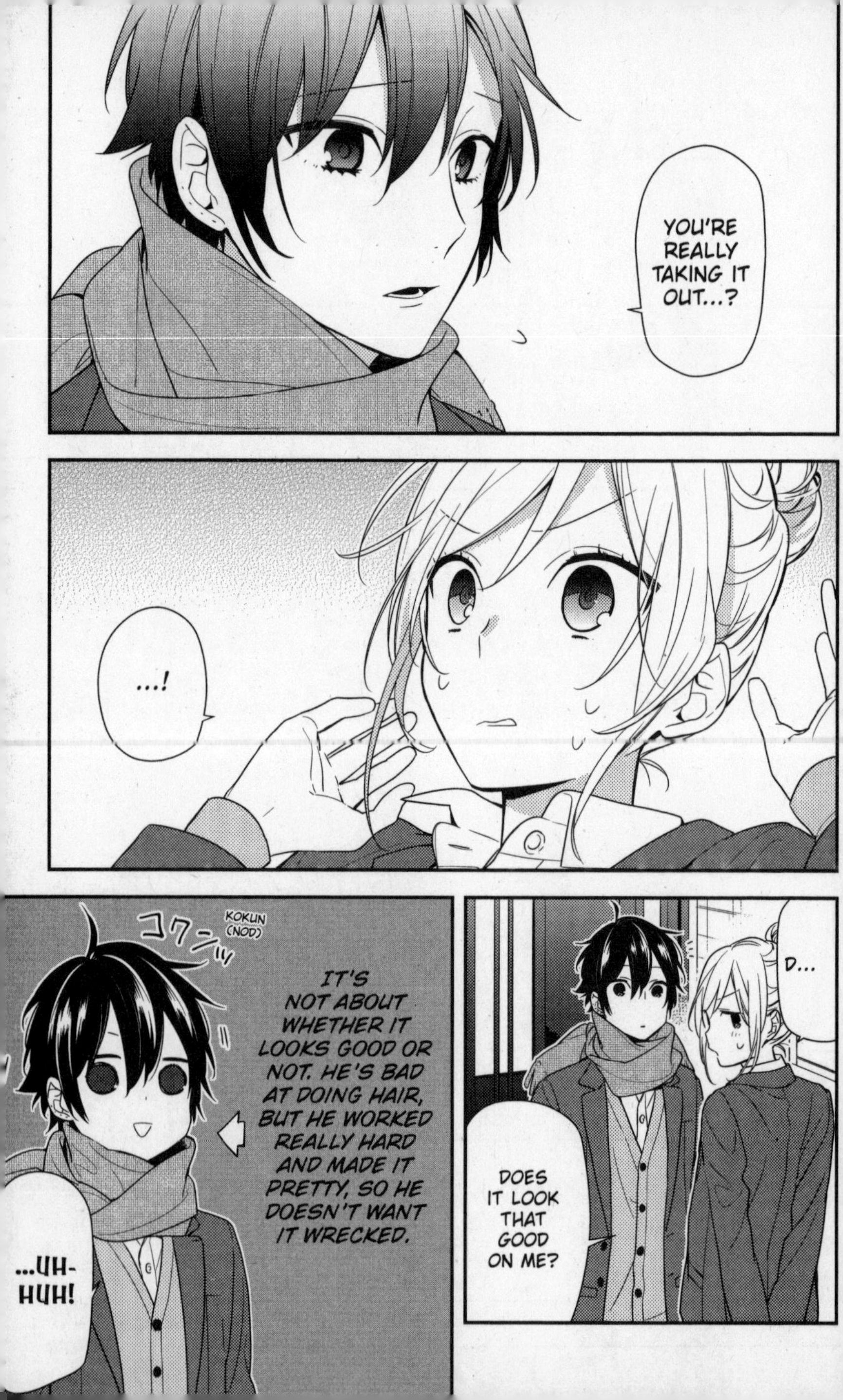
YOU'RE REALLY TAKING IT OUT...?
...!
D...
DOES IT LOOK THAT GOOD ON ME?
コクン
KOKUN (NOD)
IT'S NOT ABOUT WHETHER IT LOOKS GOOD OR NOT. HE'S BAD AT DOING HAIR, BUT HE WORKED REALLY HARD AND MADE IT PRETTY, SO HE DOESN'T WANT IT WRECKED.
...UH-HUH!

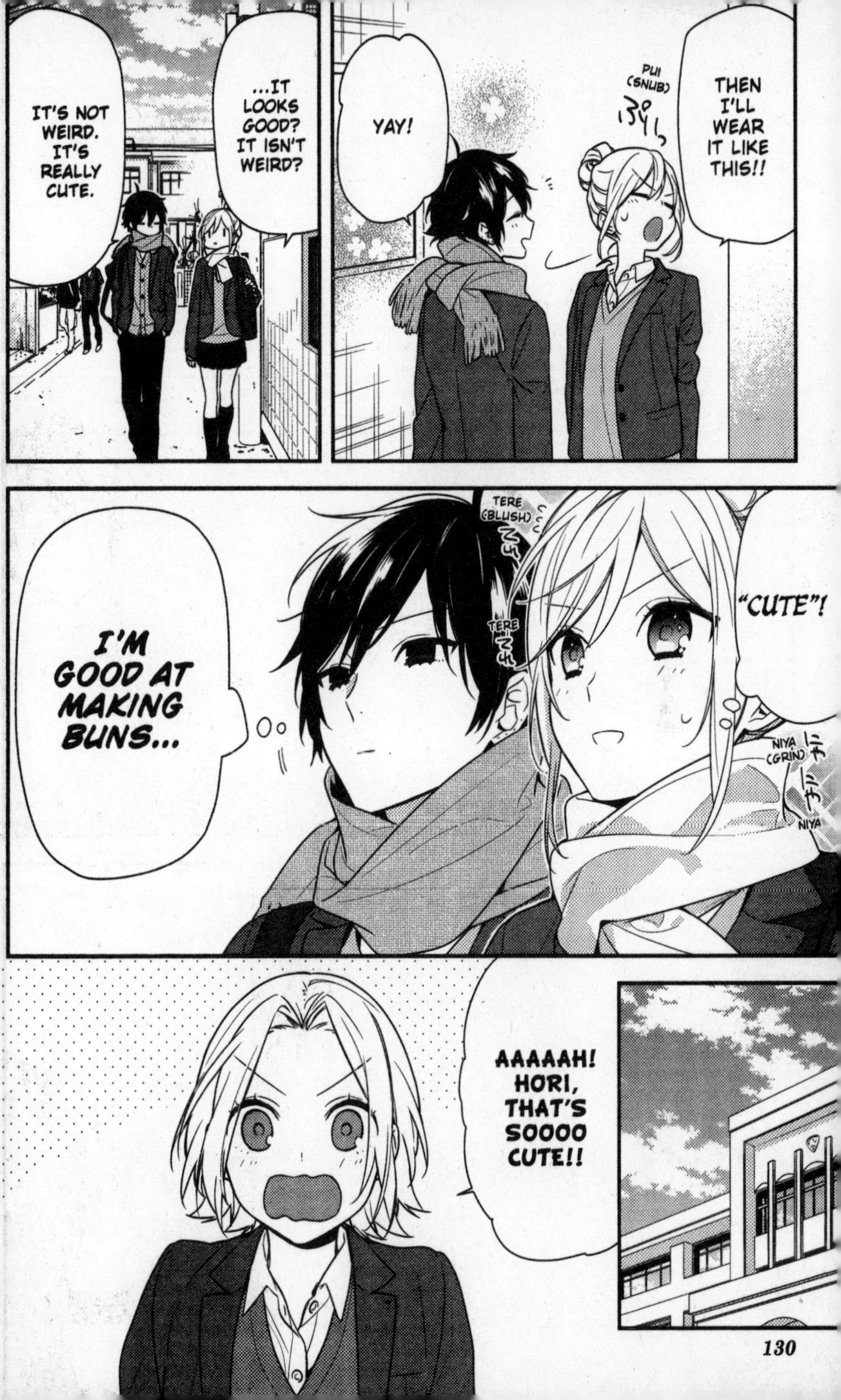
PUI (SNUB)
THEN I'LL WEAR IT LIKE THIS!!
YAY!
...IT LOOKS GOOD? IT ISN'T WEIRD?
IT'S NOT WEIRD. IT'S REALLY CUTE.
"CUTE"!
TERE (BLUSH)
TERE
NIYA (GRIN)
NIYA
I'M GOOD AT MAKING BUNS...
AAAAAH! HORI, THAT'S SOOOO CUTE!!

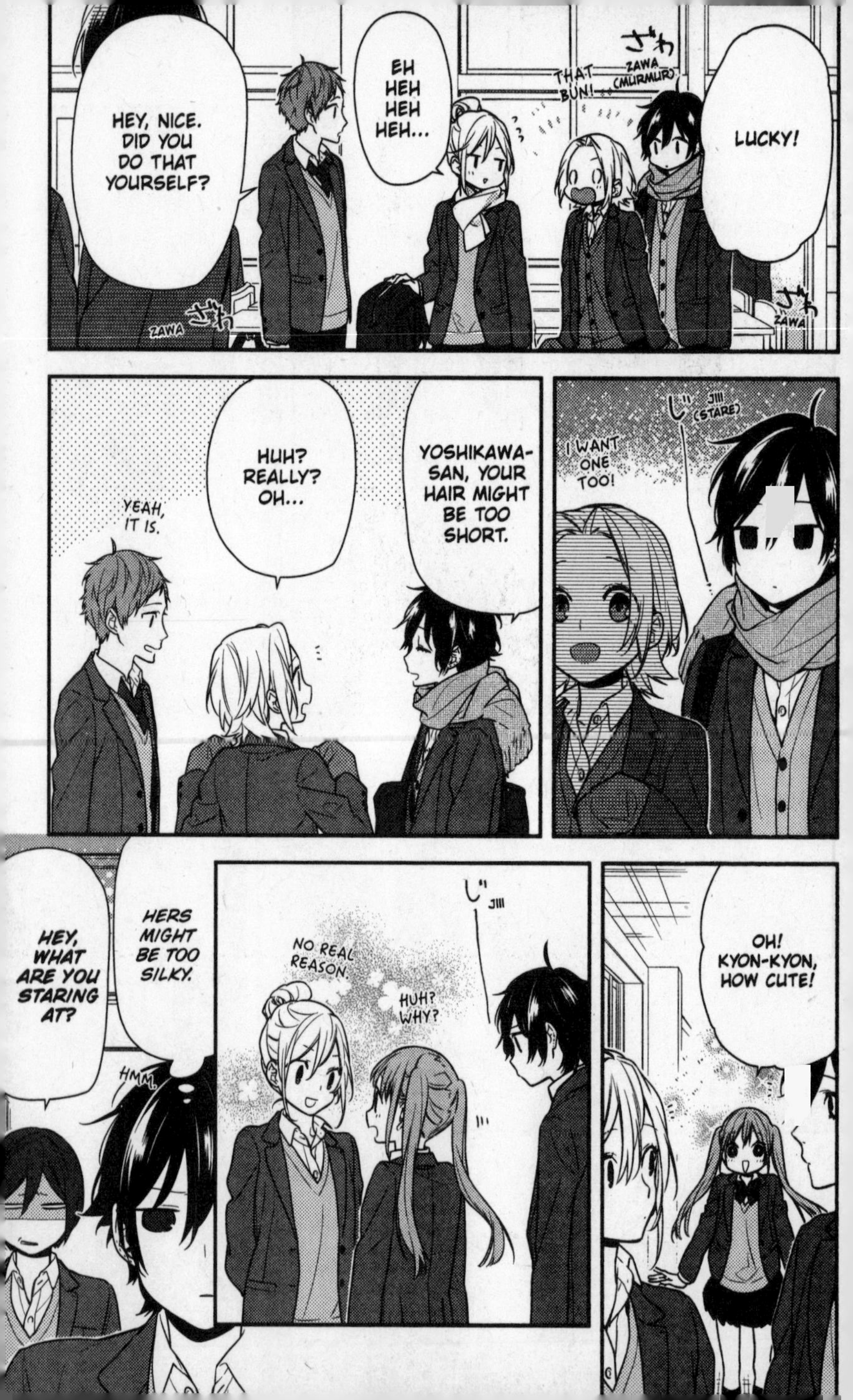
LUCKY!
ざわ
ZAWA (MURMUR)
THAT BUN!
EH HEH HEH HEH...
HEY, NICE. DID YOU DO THAT YOURSELF?
ざわ
ZAWA
ざわ
ZAWA
じ
JIII (STARE)
I WANT ONE TOO!
YOSHIKAWA-SAN, YOUR HAIR MIGHT BE TOO SHORT.
HUH? REALLY? OH...
YEAH, IT IS.
OH! KYON-KYON, HOW CUTE!
じ
JIII
HUH? WHY?
NO REAL REASON.
HERS MIGHT BE TOO SILKY.
HEY, WHAT ARE YOU STARING AT?
HMM.

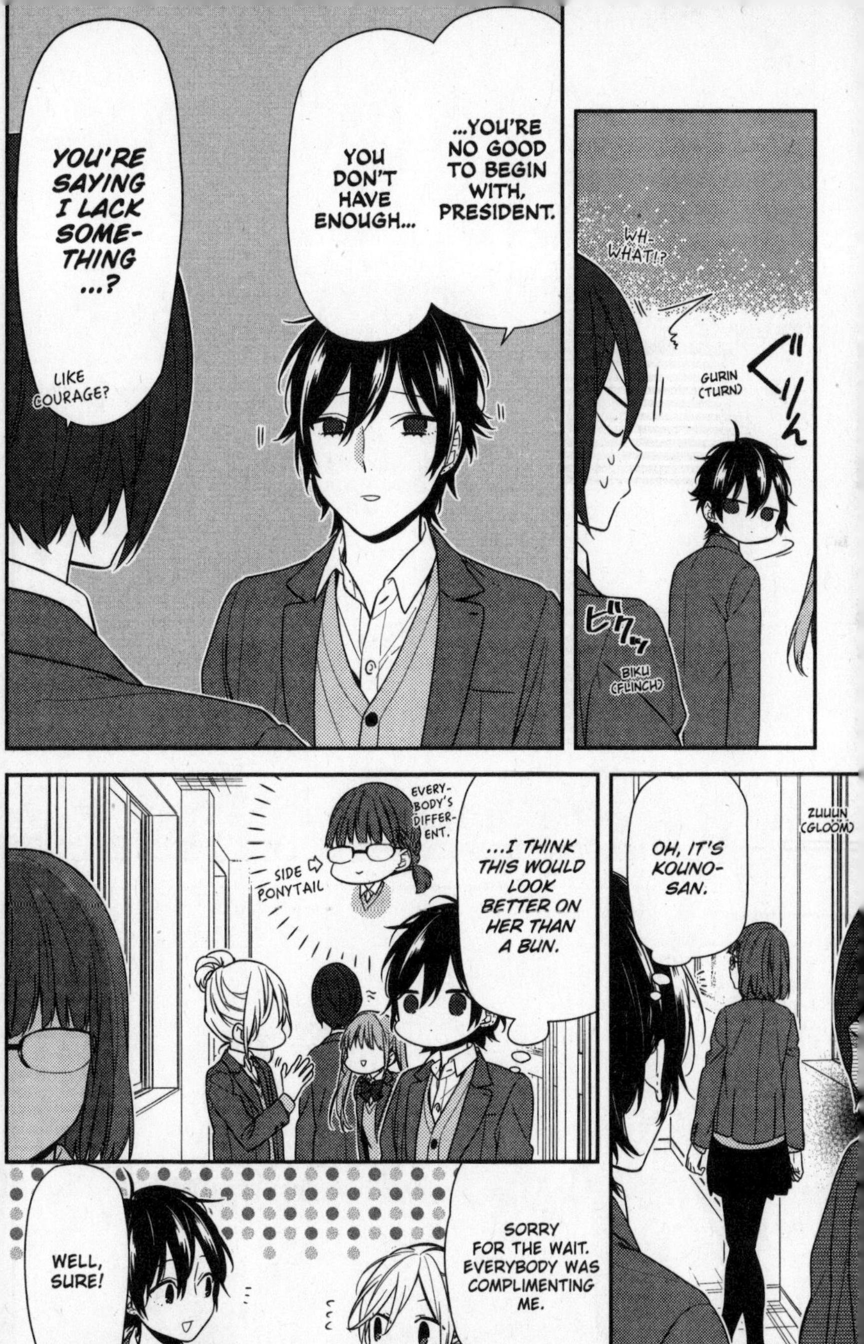
WH-WHAT!?
ぐりん
GURIN (TURN)
ビクッ
BIKU (FLINCH)
...YOU'RE NO GOOD TO BEGIN WITH, PRESIDENT.
YOU DON'T HAVE ENOUGH...
YOU'RE SAYING I LACK SOME-THING ...?
LIKE COURAGE?
ZUUUN (GLOOM)
OH, IT'S KOUNO-SAN.
...I THINK THIS WOULD LOOK BETTER ON HER THAN A BUN.
EVERY-BODY'S DIFFER-ENT.
SIDE PONYTAIL
SORRY FOR THE WAIT. EVERYBODY WAS COMPLIMENTING ME.
WELL, SURE!

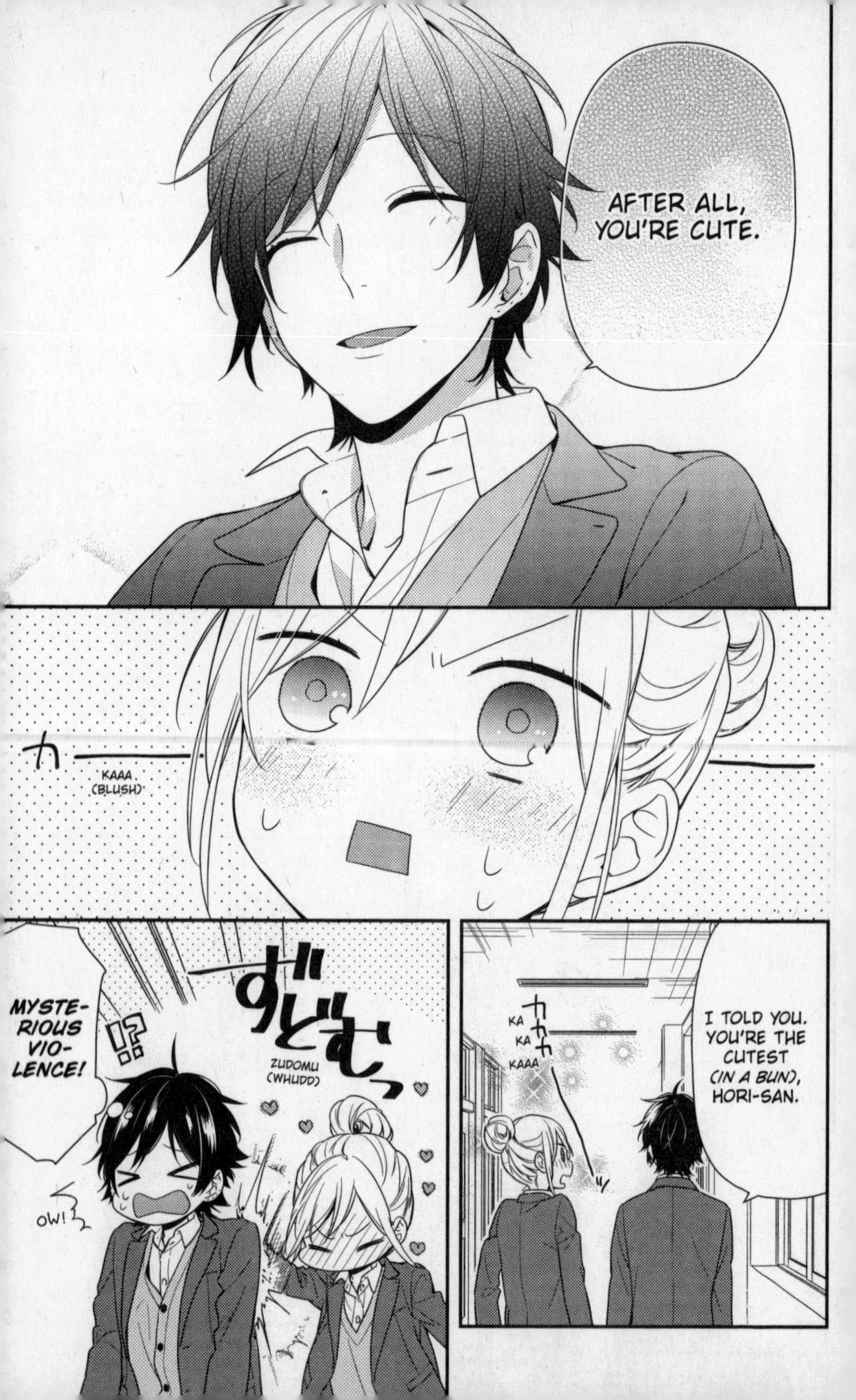
AFTER ALL, YOU'RE CUTE.
カー
KAAA (BLUSH)
I TOLD YOU. YOU'RE THE CUTEST (IN A BUN), HORI-SAN.
カカカ
KA KA KAAA
ずどむっ
ZUDOMU (WHUDD)
!?
MYSTE-RIOUS VIO-LENCE!
OW!

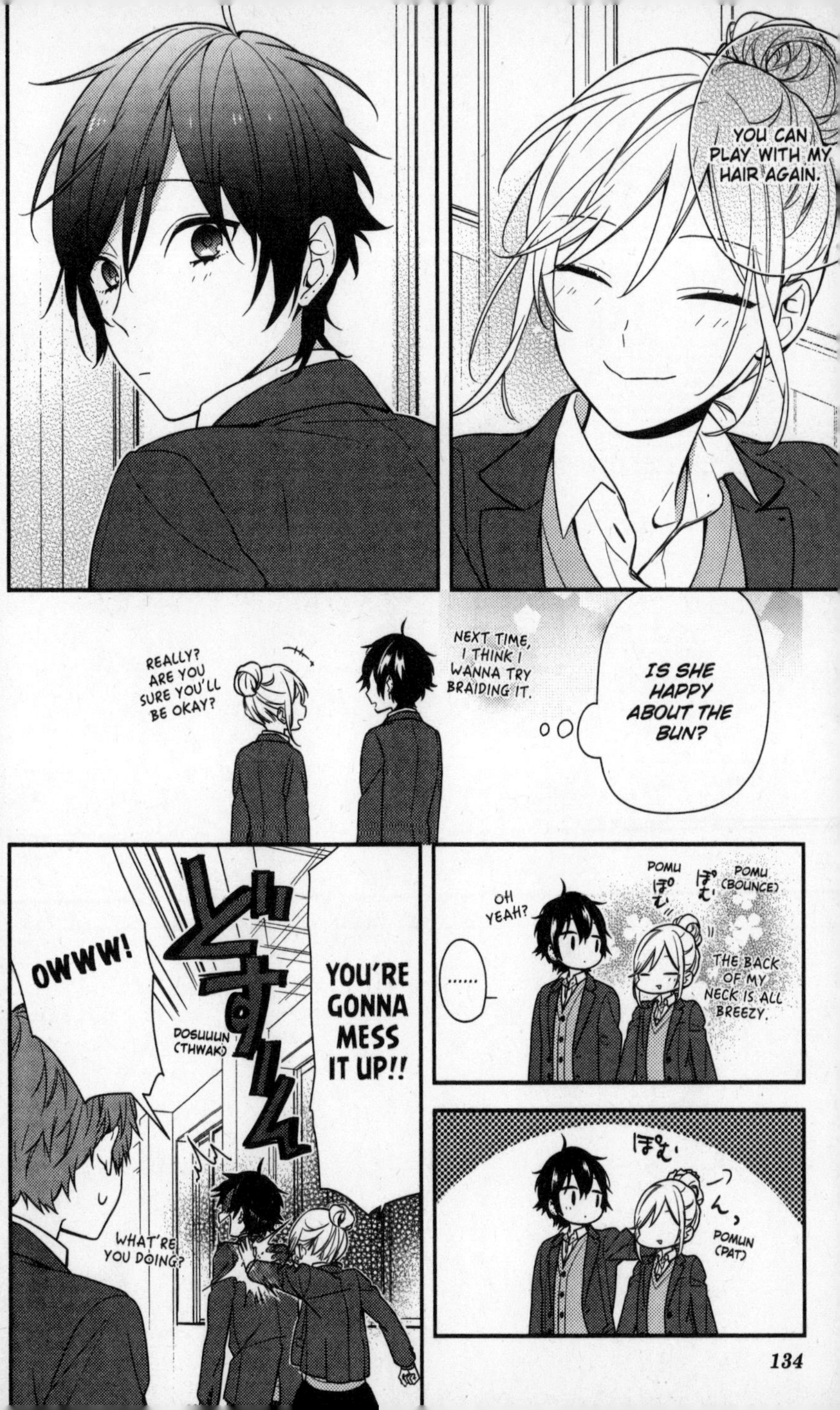

YOU CAN PLAY WITH MY HAIR AGAIN.
IS SHE HAPPY ABOUT THE BUN?
NEXT TIME, I THINK I WANNA TRY BRAIDING IT.
REALLY? ARE YOU SURE YOU'LL BE OKAY?
ぽむ
POMU
ぽむ
POMU (BOUNCE)
THE BACK OF MY NECK IS ALL BREEZY.
OH YEAH?
......
ぽむ
ん,
POMUN (PAT)
YOU'RE GONNA MESS IT UP!!
DOSUUUN (THWAK)
OWWW!
WHAT'RE YOU DOING?

HORIMIYA

HORIMIYA

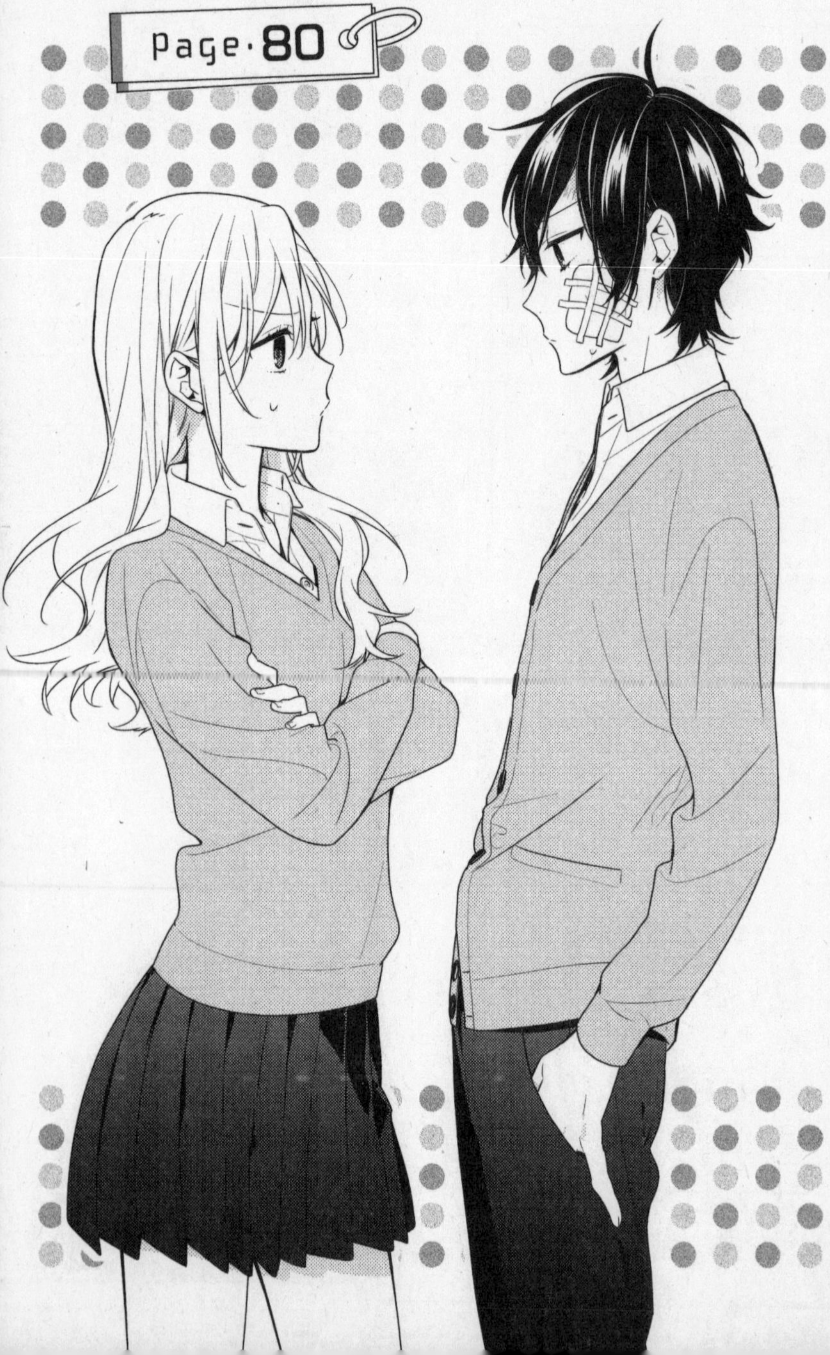
Page・80

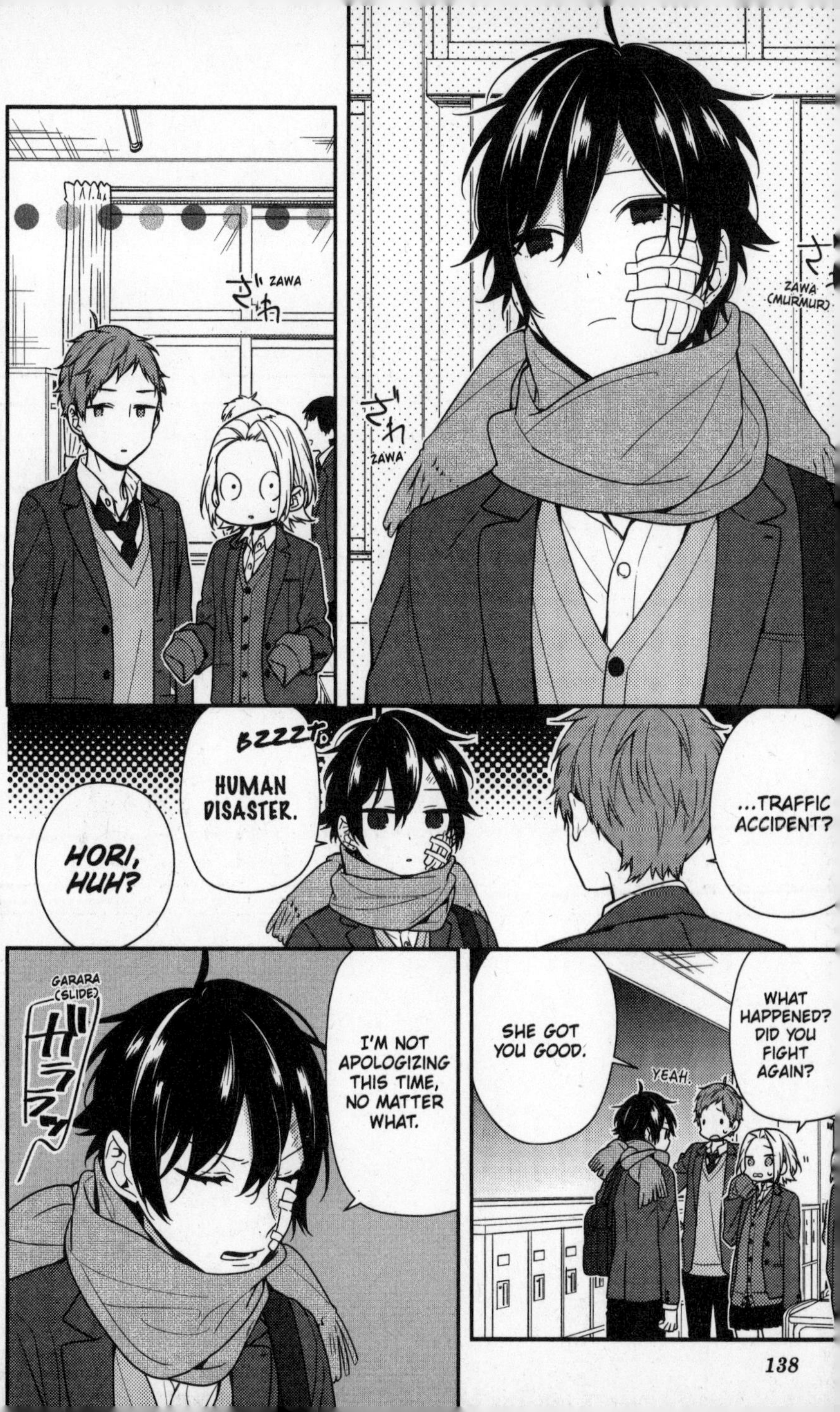
ZAWA (MURMUR)
ざわ
ZAWA
ざわ
ZAWA
...TRAFFIC ACCIDENT?
BZZZT.
HUMAN DISASTER.
HORI, HUH?
WHAT HAPPENED? DID YOU FIGHT AGAIN?
YEAH.
SHE GOT YOU GOOD.
I'M NOT APOLOGIZING THIS TIME, NO MATTER WHAT.
GARARA (SLIDE)
ガラッ

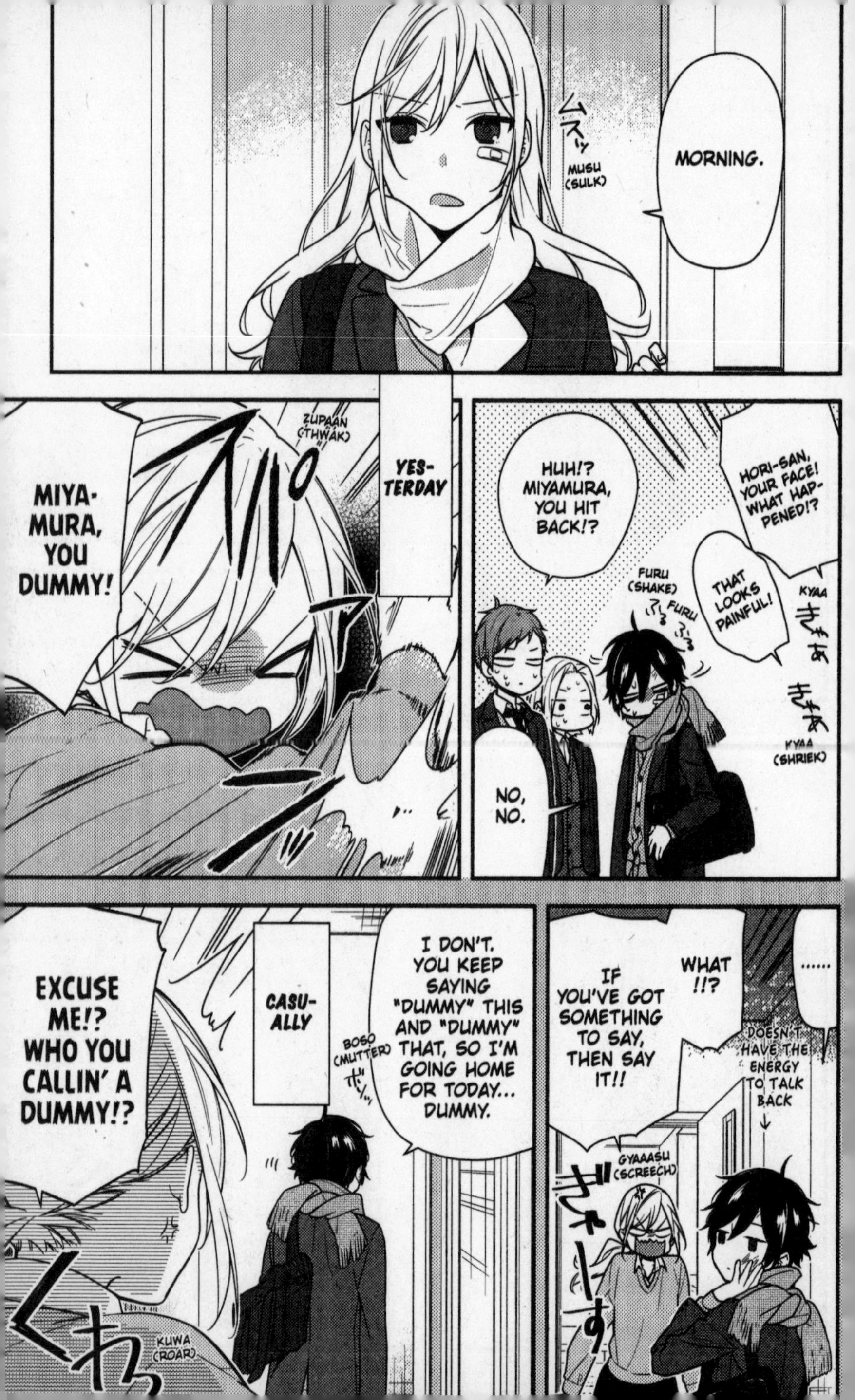

ムスッ
MUSU (SULK)
MORNING.
HORI-SAN, YOUR FACE! WHAT HAPPENED!?
きゃあ
KYAA
THAT LOOKS PAINFUL!
FURU (SHAKE)
ふる
FURU
ふる
HUH!? MIYAMURA, YOU HIT BACK!?
NO, NO.
きゃあ
KYAA (SHRIEK)
YES-TERDAY
ZUPAAN (THWAK)
MIYA-MURA, YOU DUMMY!
......
WHAT!!?
IF YOU'VE GOT SOMETHING TO SAY, THEN SAY IT!!
DOESN'T HAVE THE ENERGY TO TALK BACK
GYAAASU (SCREECH)
I DON'T. YOU KEEP SAYING "DUMMY" THIS AND "DUMMY" THAT, SO I'M GOING HOME FOR TODAY... DUMMY.
CASU-ALLY
BOSO (MUTTER)
EXCUSE ME!? WHO YOU CALLIN' A DUMMY!?
KUWA (ROAR)

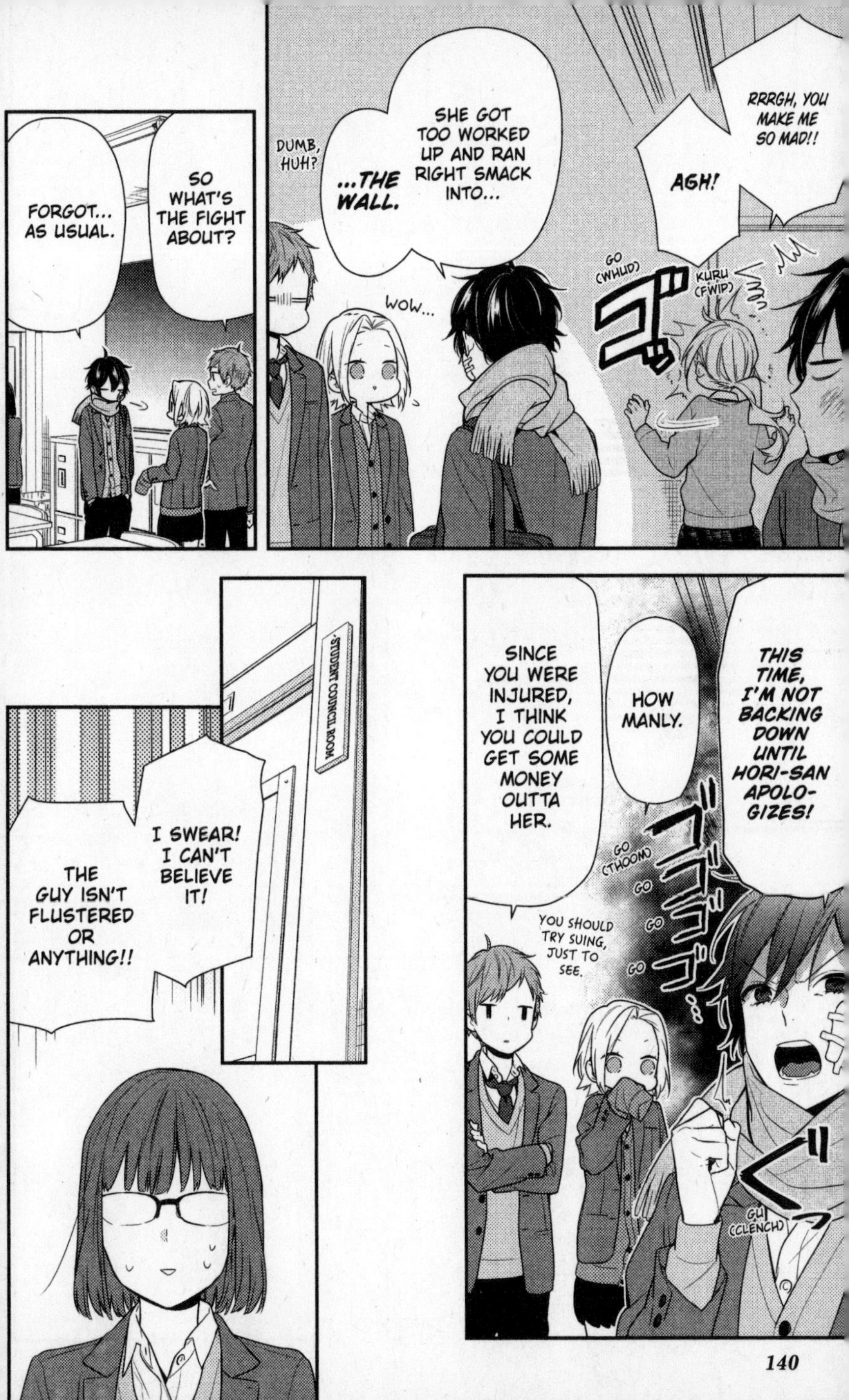
RRRGH, YOU MAKE ME SO MAD!!
AGH!
GO (WHUD)
KURU (FWIP)
SHE GOT TOO WORKED UP AND RAN RIGHT SMACK INTO...
...THE WALL.
DUMB, HUH?
WOW...
SO WHAT'S THE FIGHT ABOUT?
FORGOT... AS USUAL.
THIS TIME, I'M NOT BACKING DOWN UNTIL HORI-SAN APOLOGIZES!
GO (THOOM)
GO
GO
GO
HOW MANLY.
SINCE YOU WERE INJURED, I THINK YOU COULD GET SOME MONEY OUTTA HER.
YOU SHOULD TRY SUING, JUST TO SEE.
GU (CLENCH)
STUDENT COUNCIL ROOM
I SWEAR! I CAN'T BELIEVE IT!
THE GUY ISN'T FLUSTERED OR ANYTHING!!

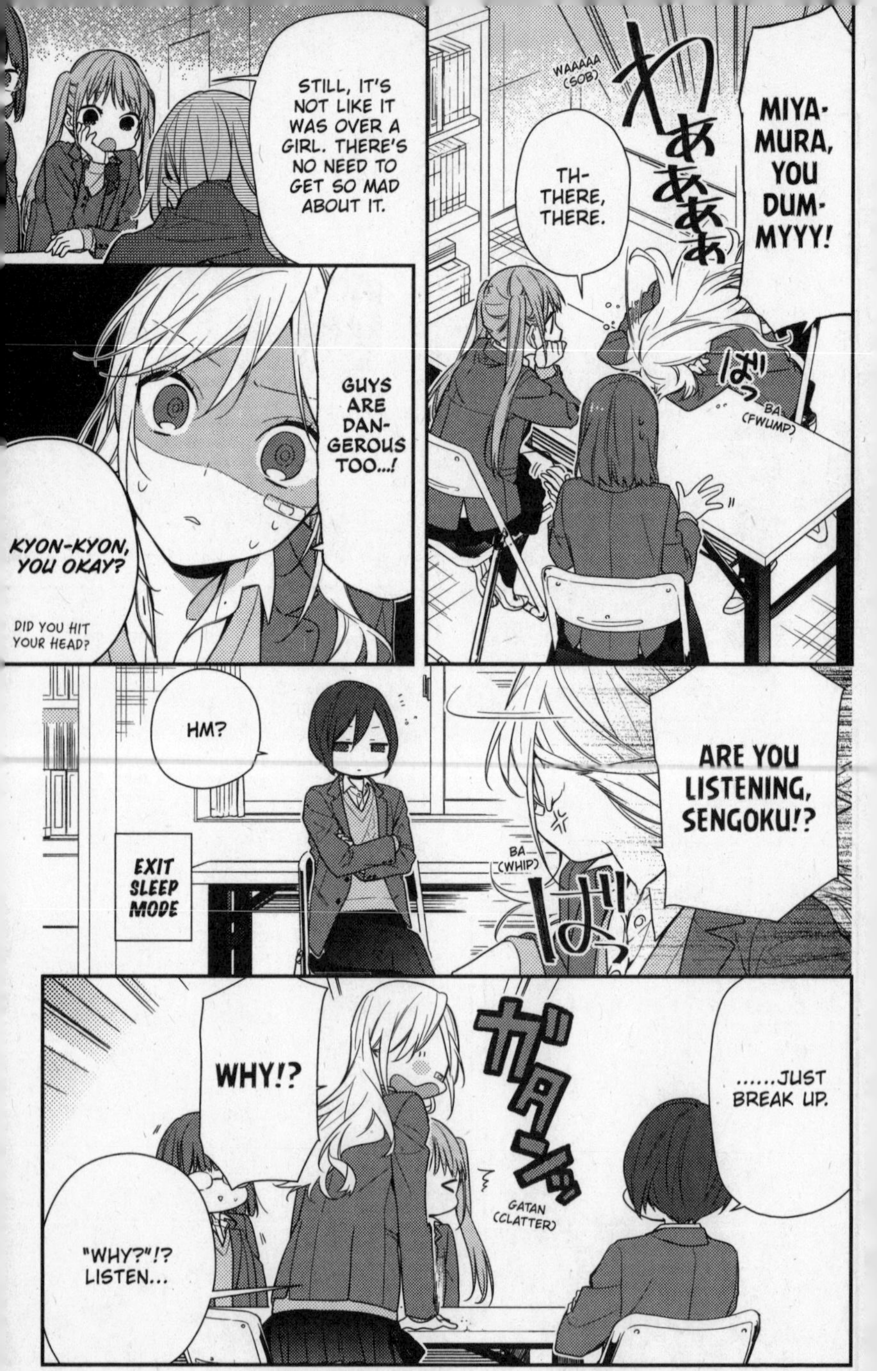
MIYA-MURA, YOU DUM-MYYY!
わぁぁぁ
WAAAAA (SOB)
TH-THERE, THERE.
ばっ
BA (FWUMP)
STILL, IT'S NOT LIKE IT WAS OVER A GIRL. THERE'S NO NEED TO GET SO MAD ABOUT IT.
GUYS ARE DAN-GEROUS TOO...!
KYON-KYON, YOU OKAY?
DID YOU HIT YOUR HEAD?
ARE YOU LISTENING, SENGOKU!?
ばっ
BA (WHIP)
HM?
EXIT SLEEP MODE
......JUST BREAK UP.
ガタンッ
GATAN (CLATTER)
WHY!?
"WHY?"!? LISTEN...

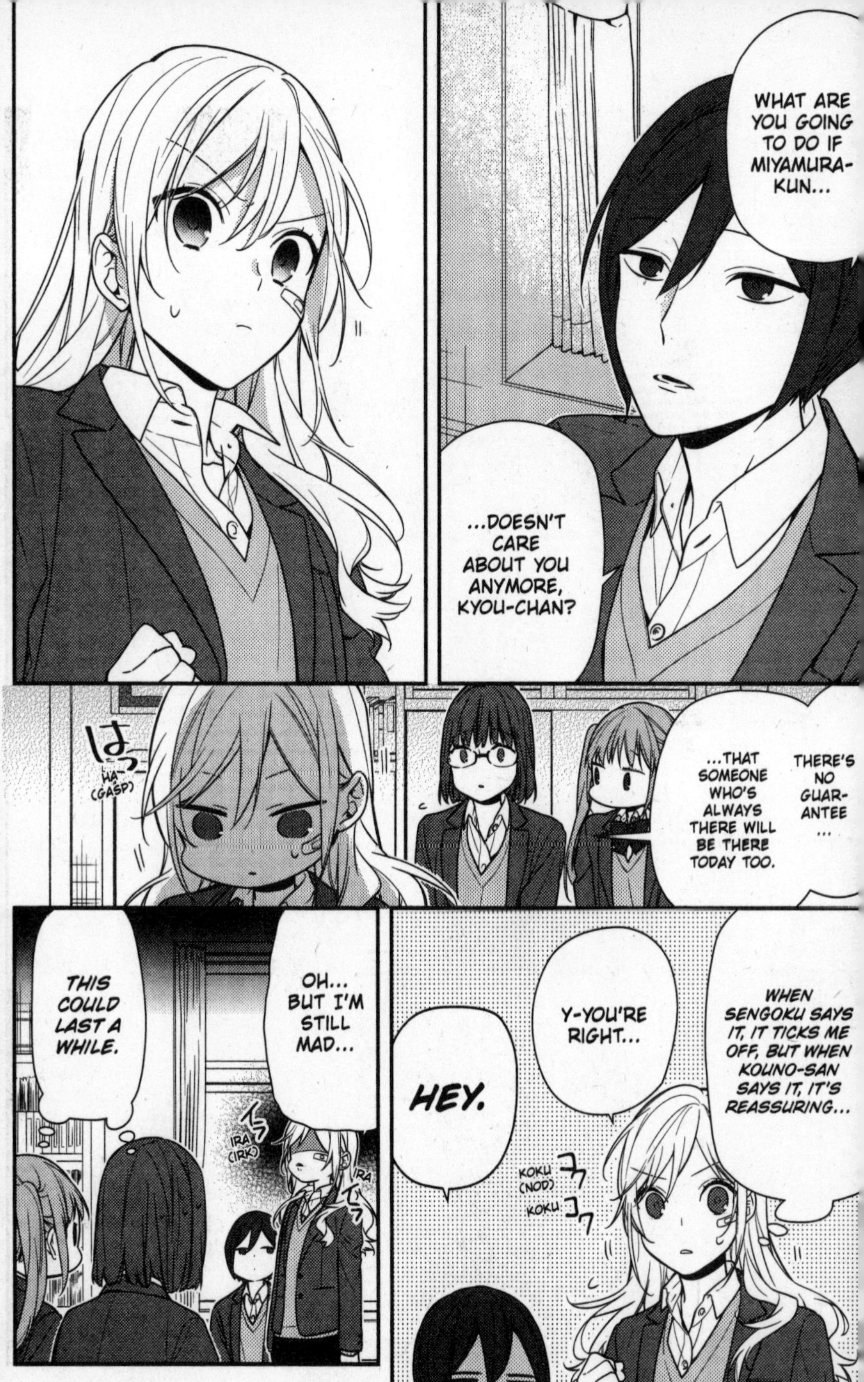
WHAT ARE YOU GOING TO DO IF MIYAMURA-KUN...
...DOESN'T CARE ABOUT YOU ANYMORE, KYOU-CHAN?
THERE'S NO GUARANTEE...
...THAT SOMEONE WHO'S ALWAYS THERE WILL BE THERE TODAY TOO.
HA (GASP)
WHEN SENGOKU SAYS IT, IT TICKS ME OFF, BUT WHEN KOUNO-SAN SAYS IT, IT'S REASSURING...
Y-YOU'RE RIGHT...
KOKU (NOD)
KOKU
HEY.
OH... BUT I'M STILL MAD...
IRA (IRK)
IRA
THIS COULD LAST A WHILE.

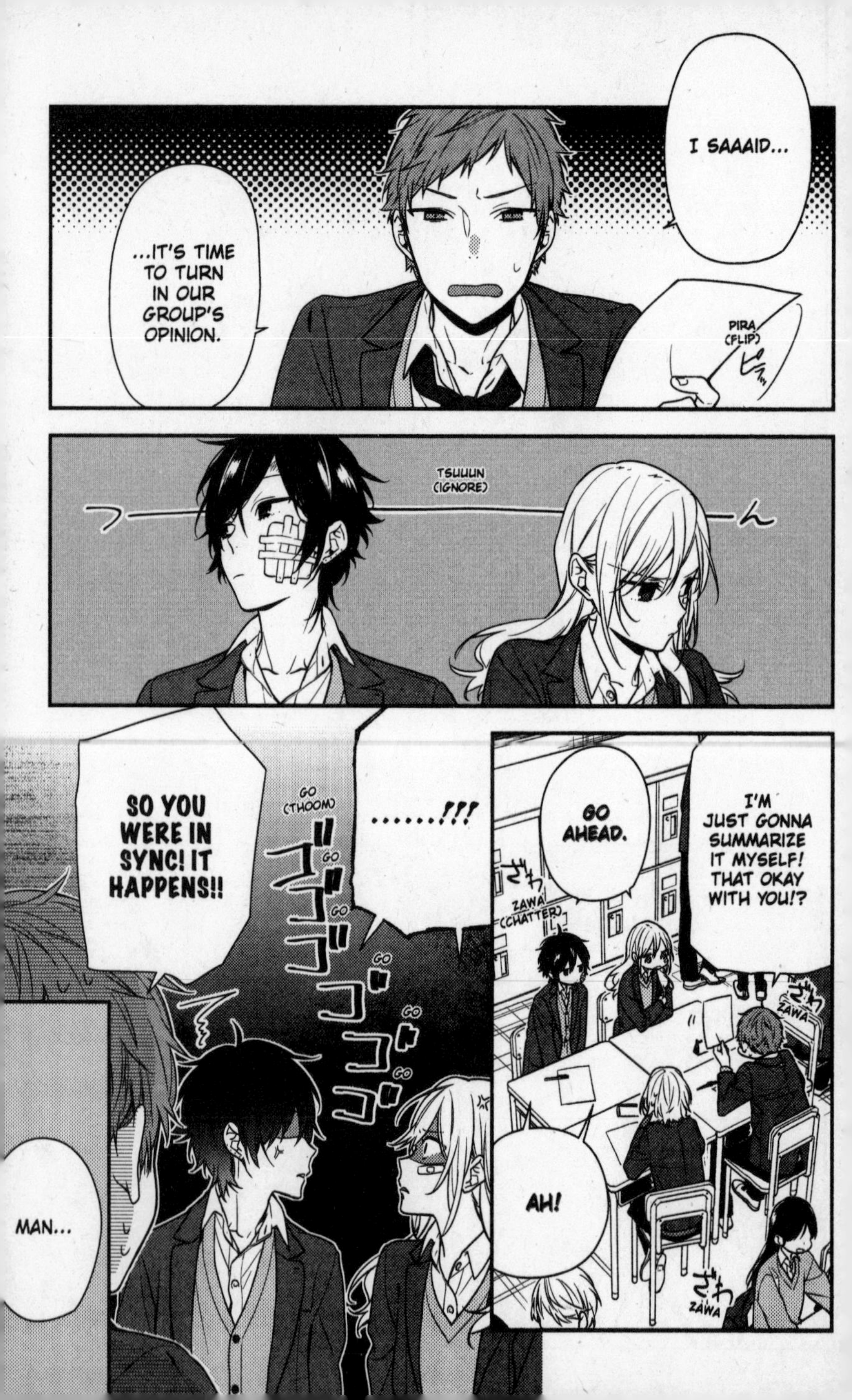
I SAAAID...
PIRA (FLIP)
...IT'S TIME TO TURN IN OUR GROUP'S OPINION.
TSUUUN (IGNORE)
I'M JUST GONNA SUMMARIZE IT MYSELF! THAT OKAY WITH YOU!?
GO AHEAD.
ZAWA (CHATTER)
ZAWA
AH!
ZAWA
.......!?!
GO (THOOM)
GO
GO
GO
GO
GO
SO YOU WERE IN SYNC! IT HAPPENS!!
MAN...

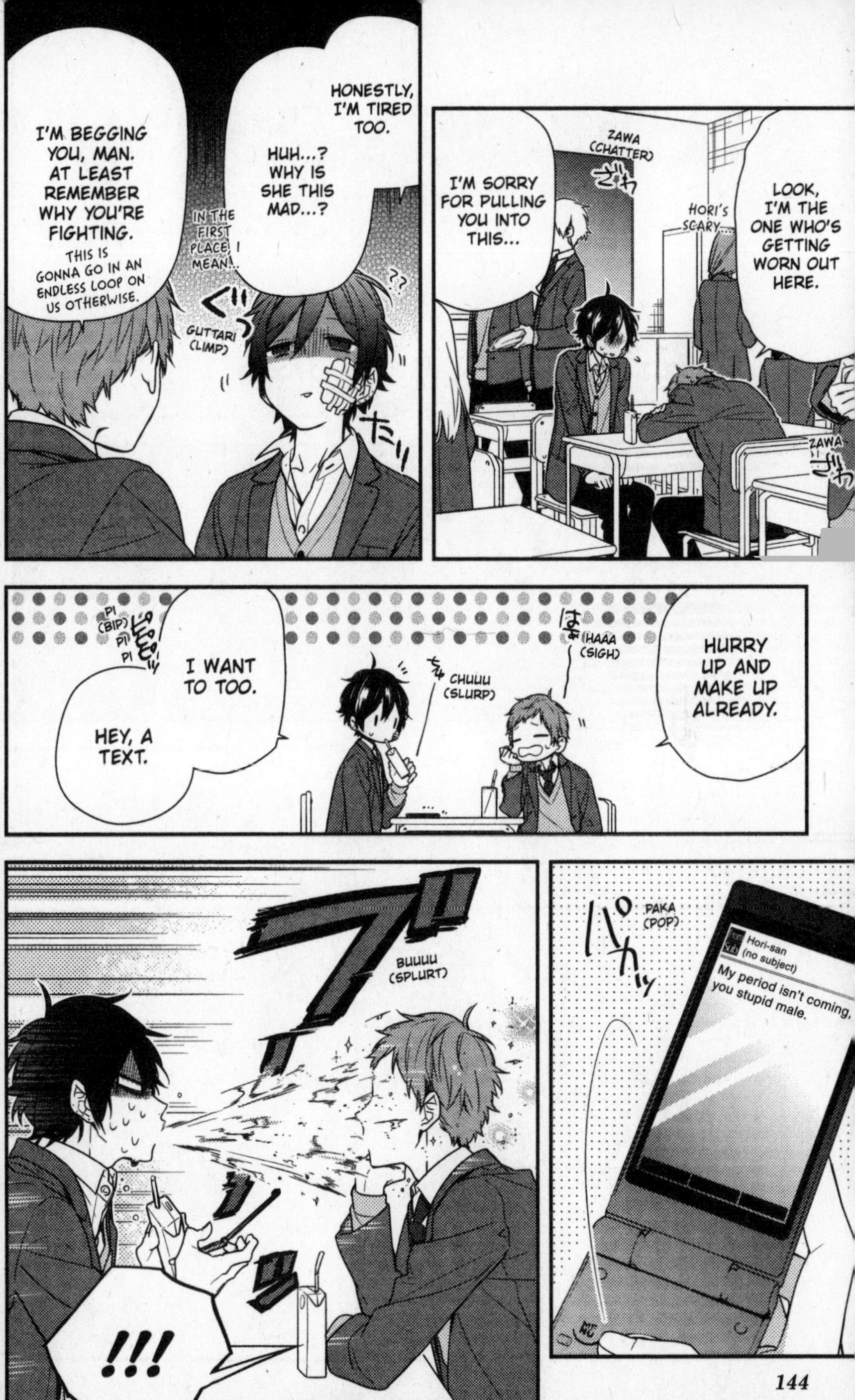
LOOK, I'M THE ONE WHO'S GETTING WORN OUT HERE.
HORI'S SCARY...
ZAWA (CHATTER)
I'M SORRY FOR PULLING YOU INTO THIS...
ZAWA
HONESTLY, I'M TIRED TOO.
HUH...? WHY IS SHE THIS MAD...?
IN THE FIRST PLACE, I MEAN!...
I'M BEGGING YOU, MAN. AT LEAST REMEMBER WHY YOU'RE FIGHTING.
THIS IS GONNA GO IN AN ENDLESS LOOP ON US OTHERWISE.
GUTTARI (LIMP)
HURRY UP AND MAKE UP ALREADY.
HAAA (SIGH)
CHUUU (SLURP)
I WANT TO TOO.
PI (BIP) PI PI
HEY, A TEXT.
PAKA (POP)
Hori-san
(no subject)
My period isn't coming, you stupid male.
BUUUU (SPLURT)
!!!

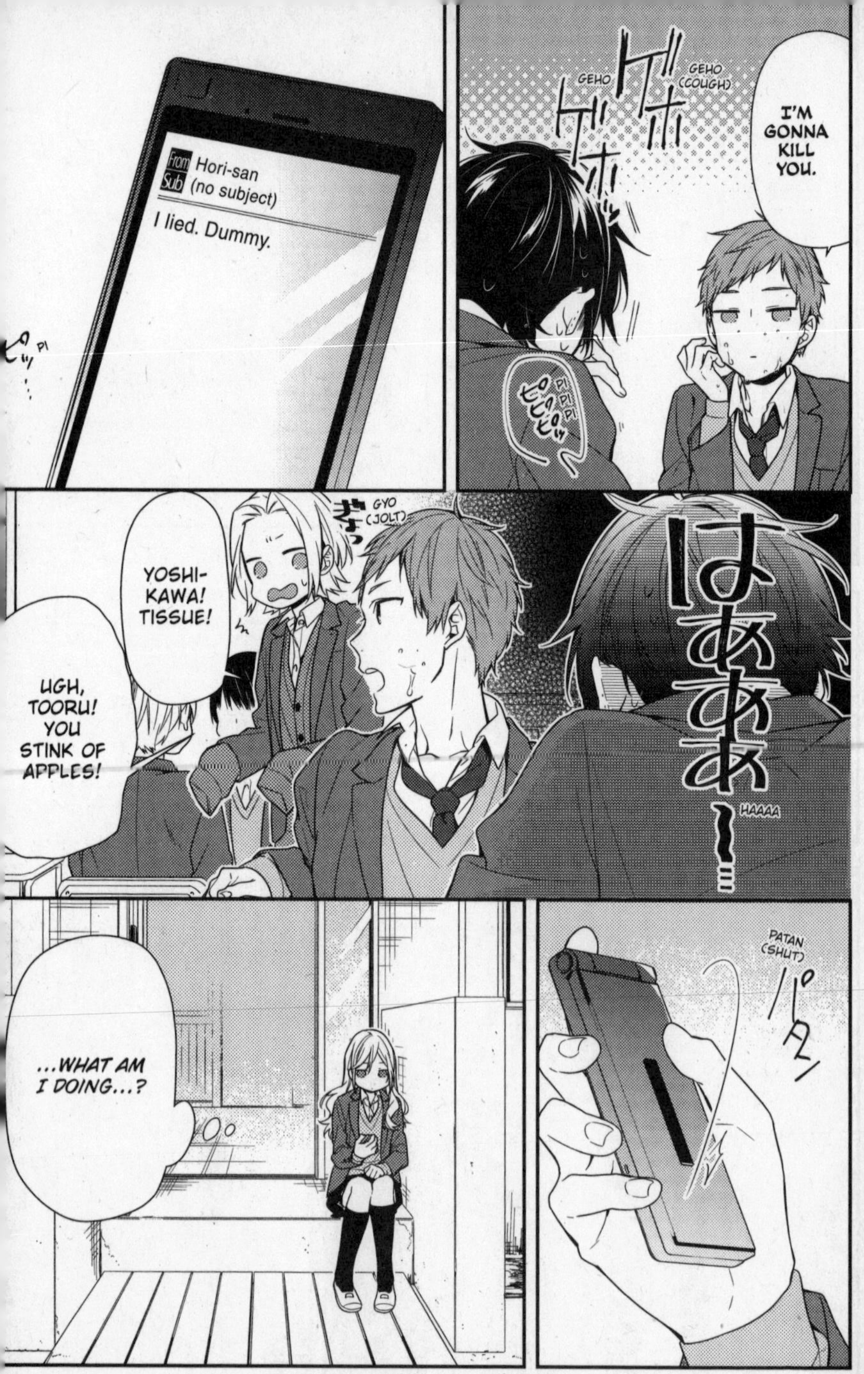
GEHO (COUGH)
GEHO
I'M GONNA KILL YOU.
PI PI PI
From Hori-san
Sub (no subject)
I lied. Dummy.
PI
はあああ～
HAAAA
GYO (JOLT)
YOSHI-KAWA! TISSUE!
UGH, TOORU! YOU STINK OF APPLES!
PATAN (SHUT)
...WHAT AM I DOING...?

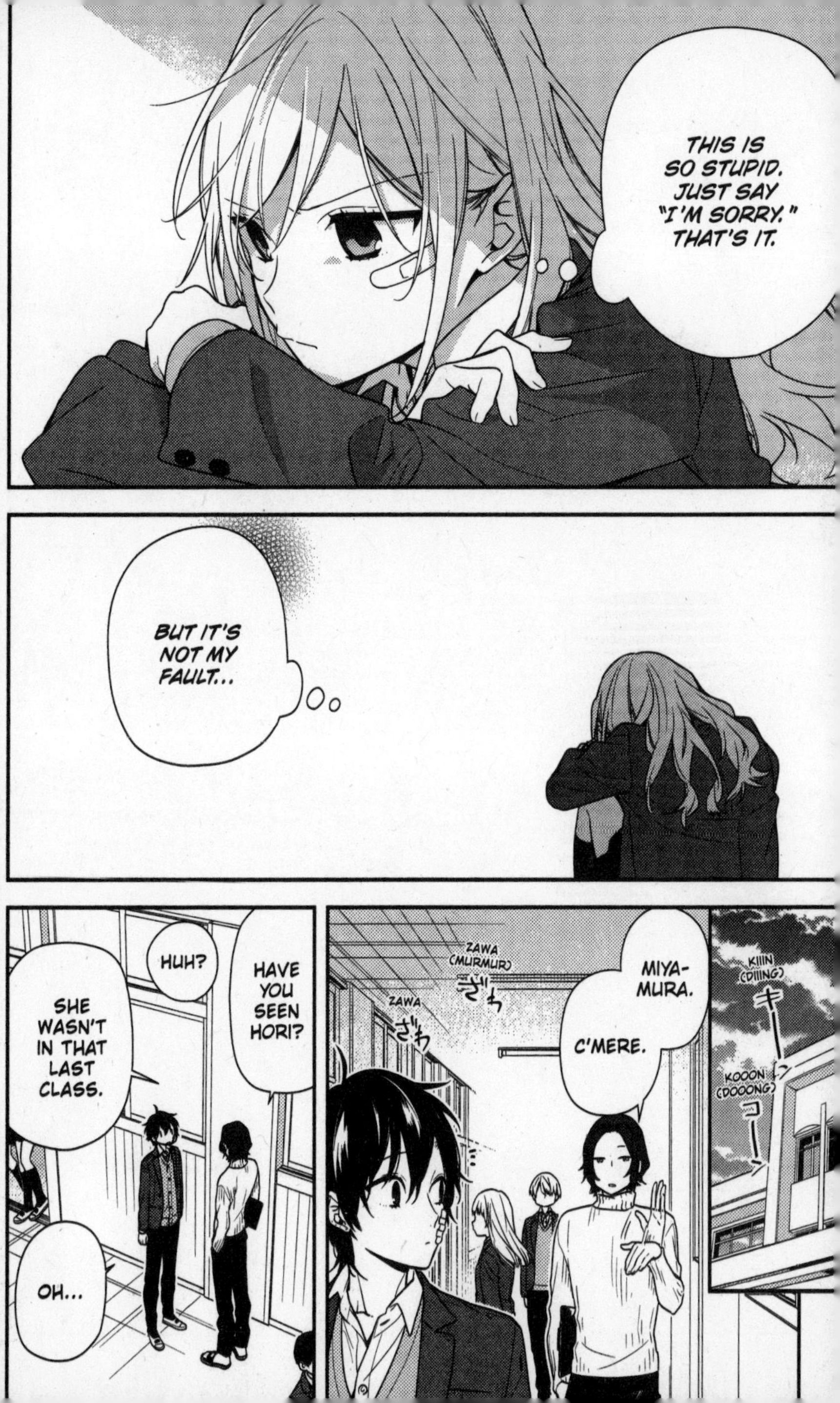
THIS IS SO STUPID. JUST SAY "I'M SORRY." THAT'S IT.
BUT IT'S NOT MY FAULT...
KIIIN (DIIING)
キーン
KOOON (DOOONG)
コーン
MIYA-MURA.
C'MERE.
ZAWA (MURMUR)
ざわ
ZAWA
ざわ
HAVE YOU SEEN HORI?
HUH?
SHE WASN'T IN THAT LAST CLASS.
OH...

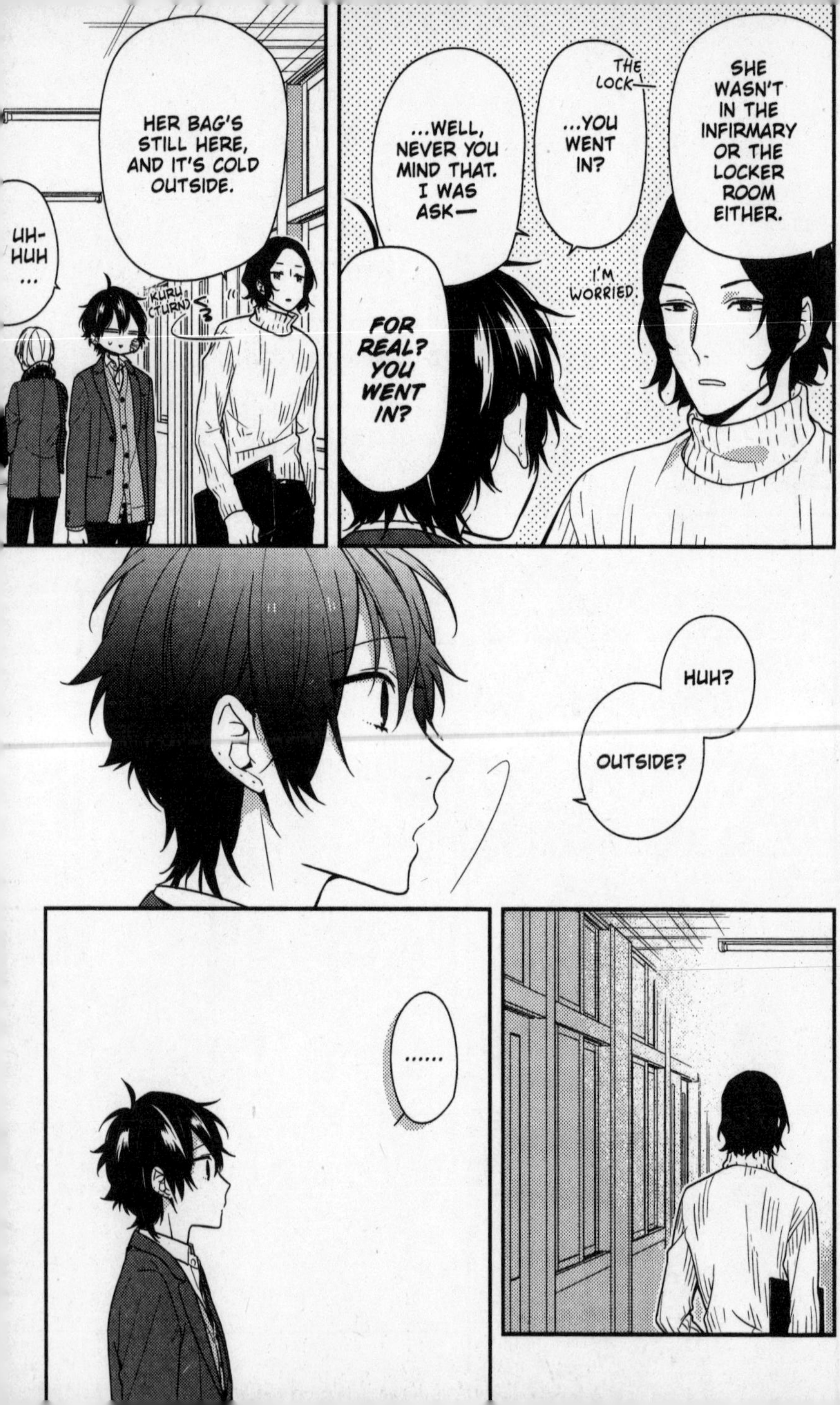
SHE WASN'T IN THE INFIRMARY OR THE LOCKER ROOM EITHER.
I'M WORRIED.
THE LOCK—
...YOU WENT IN?
...WELL, NEVER YOU MIND THAT. I WAS ASK—
FOR REAL? YOU WENT IN?
HER BAG'S STILL HERE, AND IT'S COLD OUTSIDE.
KURU (TURN)
UH-HUH ...
HUH?
OUTSIDE?
......

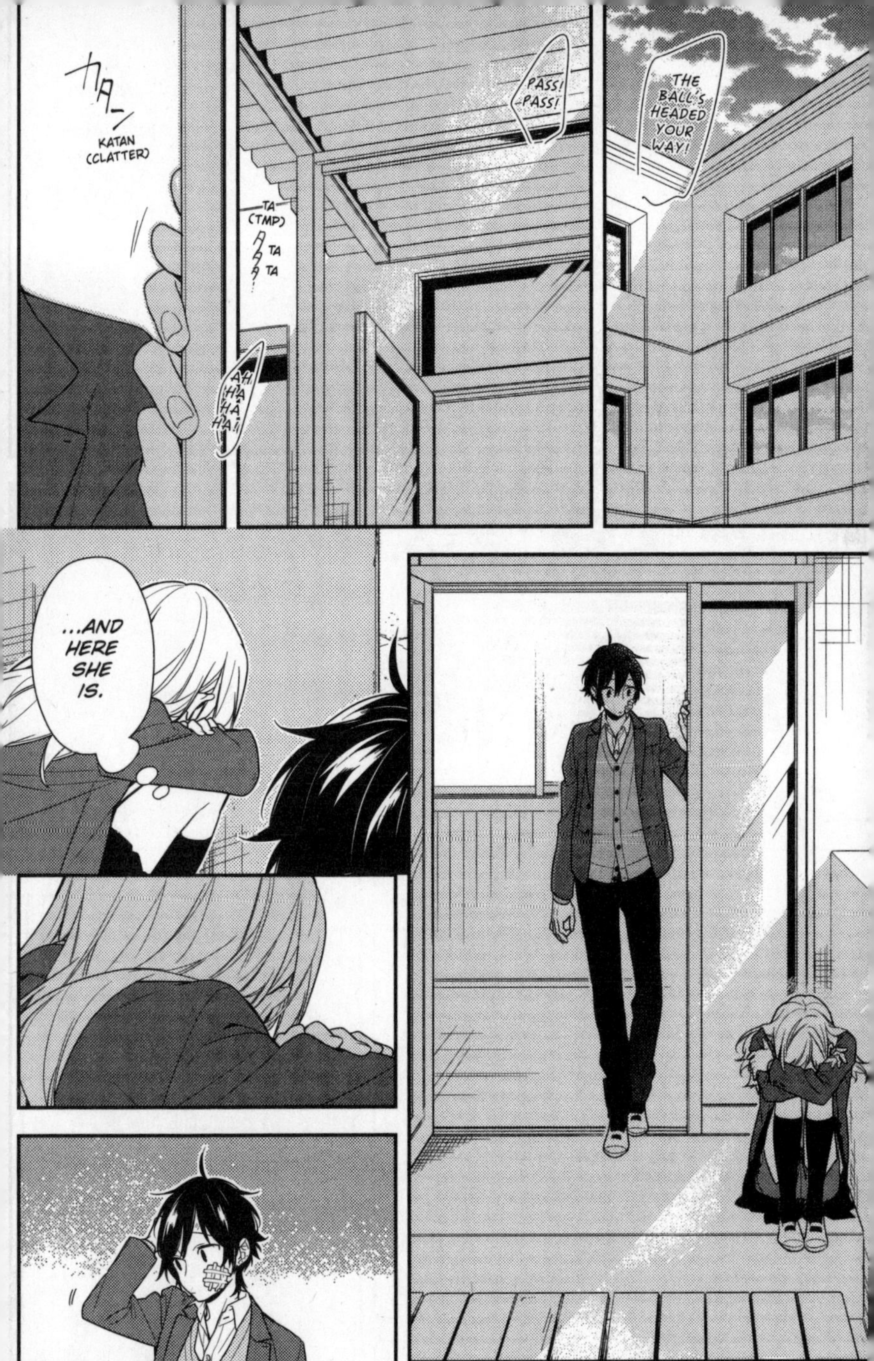
THE BALL'S HEADED YOUR WAY!
PASS! PASS!
TA (TMP) TA TA
AH HA HA HA
カターン
KATAN (CLATTER)
...AND HERE SHE IS.

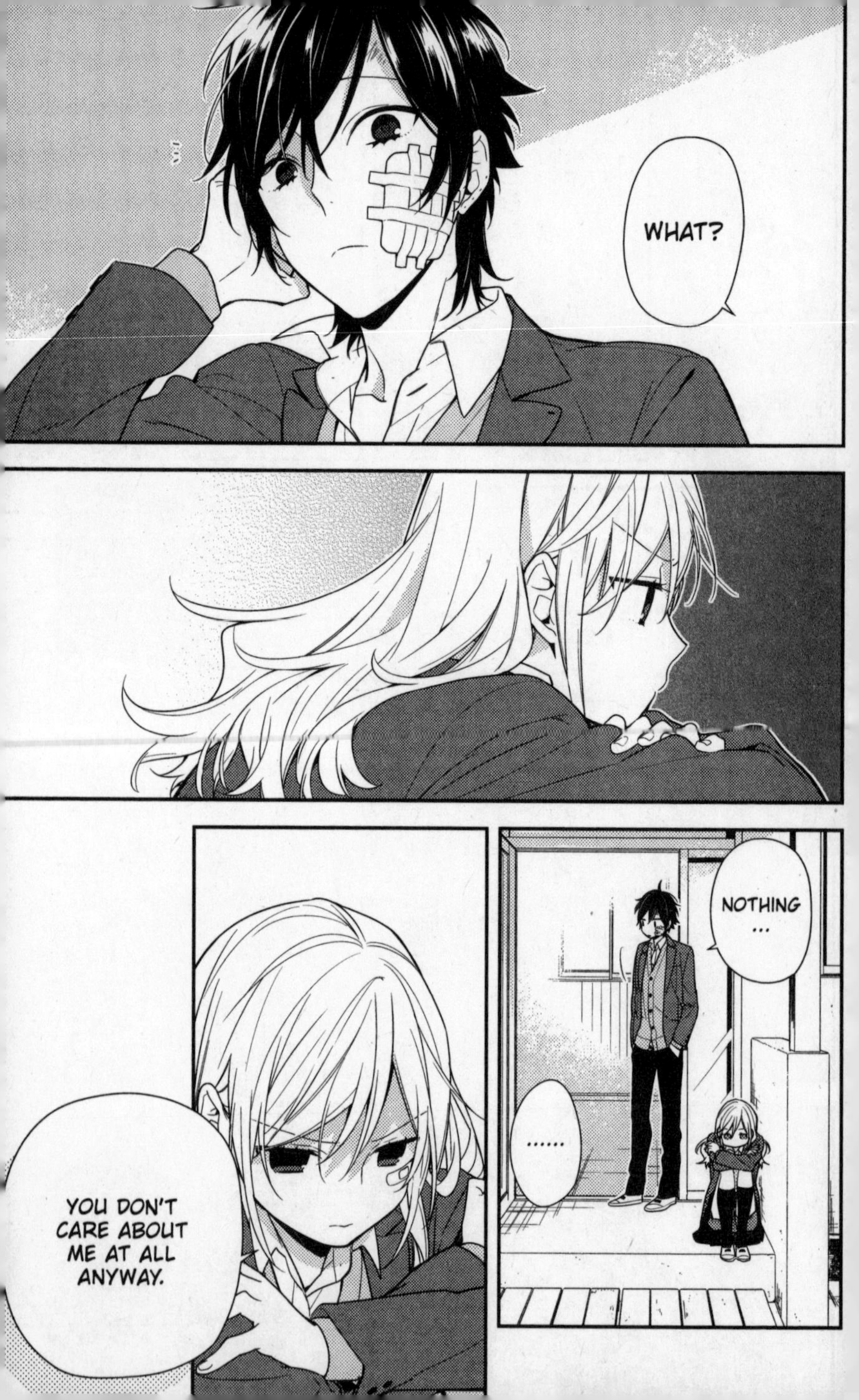
WHAT?
NOTHING ...
......
YOU DON'T CARE ABOUT ME AT ALL ANYWAY.

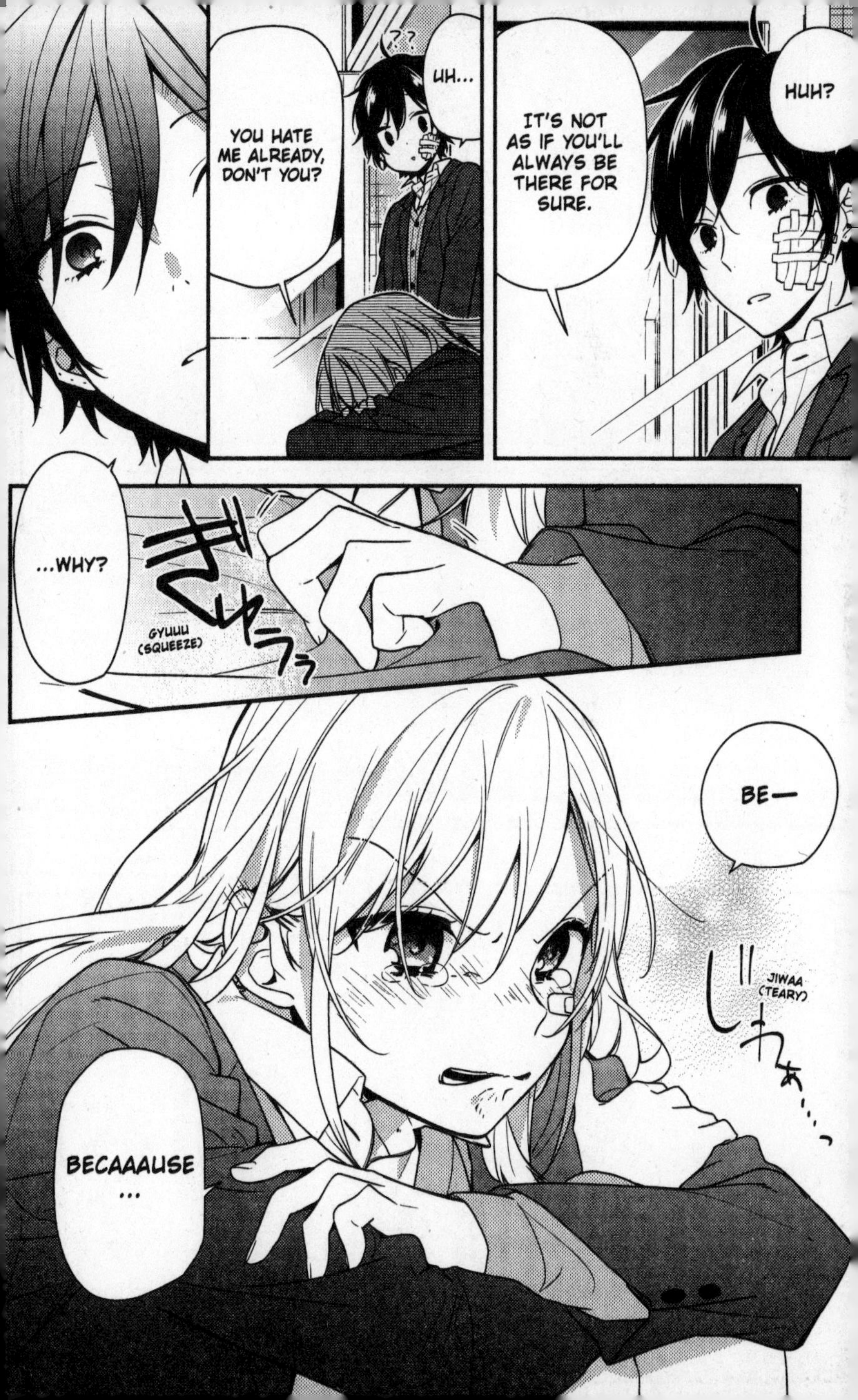
HUH?
IT'S NOT AS IF YOU'LL ALWAYS BE THERE FOR SURE.
UH...
??
YOU HATE ME ALREADY, DON'T YOU?
ぎゅうう
GYUUU (SQUEEZE)
...WHY?
BE—
じわぁ…っ
JIWAA (TEARY)
BECAAAUSE ...

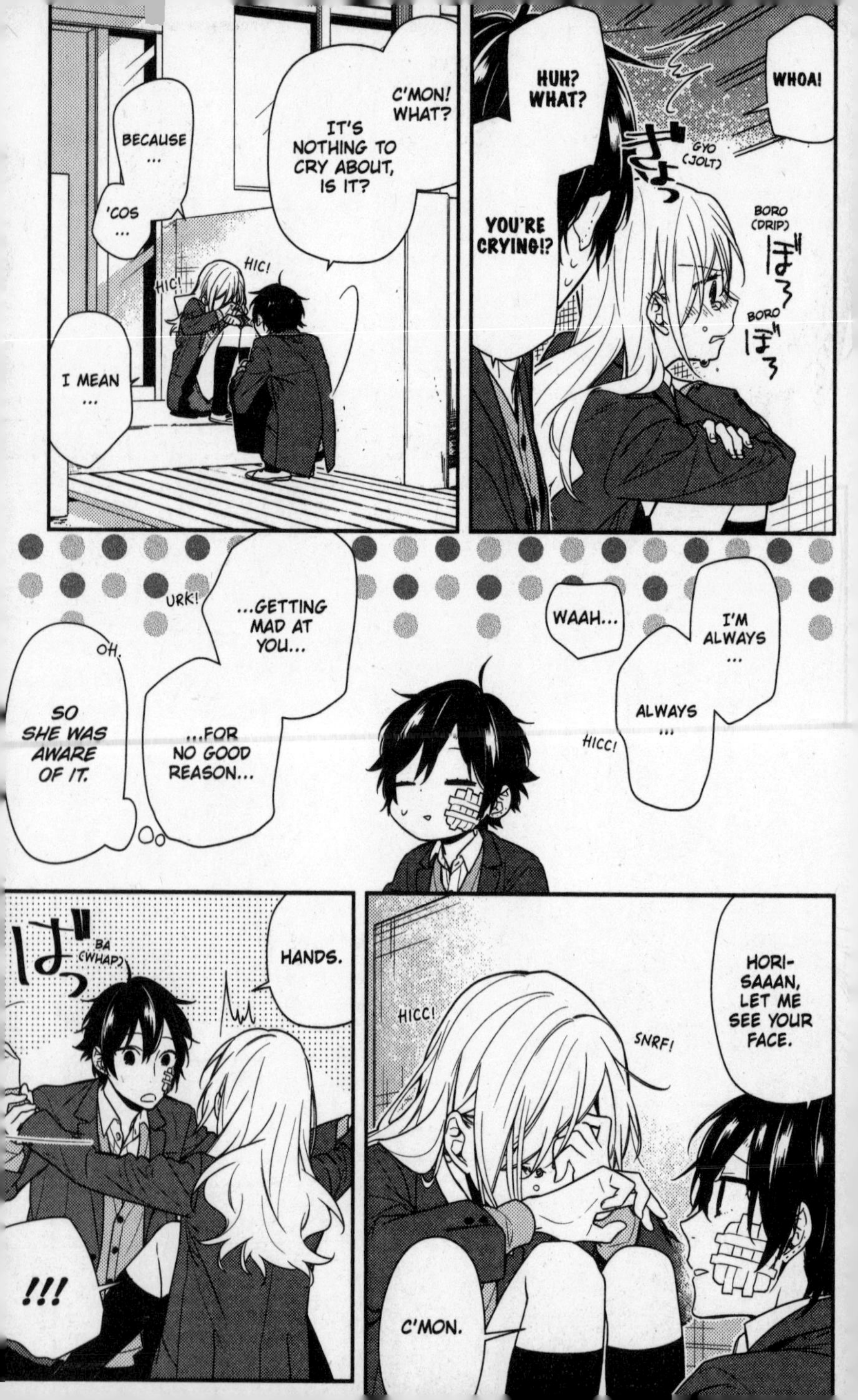
WHOA!
ぎょっ
GYO (JOLT)
HUH? WHAT?
BORO (DRIP)
ぼろ
BORO
ぼろ
YOU'RE CRYING!?
C'MON! WHAT?
IT'S NOTHING TO CRY ABOUT, IS IT?
BECAUSE ...
HIC!
'COS ...
HIC!
I MEAN ...
I'M ALWAYS ...
WAAH...
ALWAYS ...
HICC!
...GETTING MAD AT YOU...
URK!
...FOR NO GOOD REASON...
OH.
SO SHE WAS AWARE OF IT.
HORI-SAAAN, LET ME SEE YOUR FACE.
SNRF!
HICC!
C'MON.
HANDS.
ばっ
BA (WHAP)
!!!

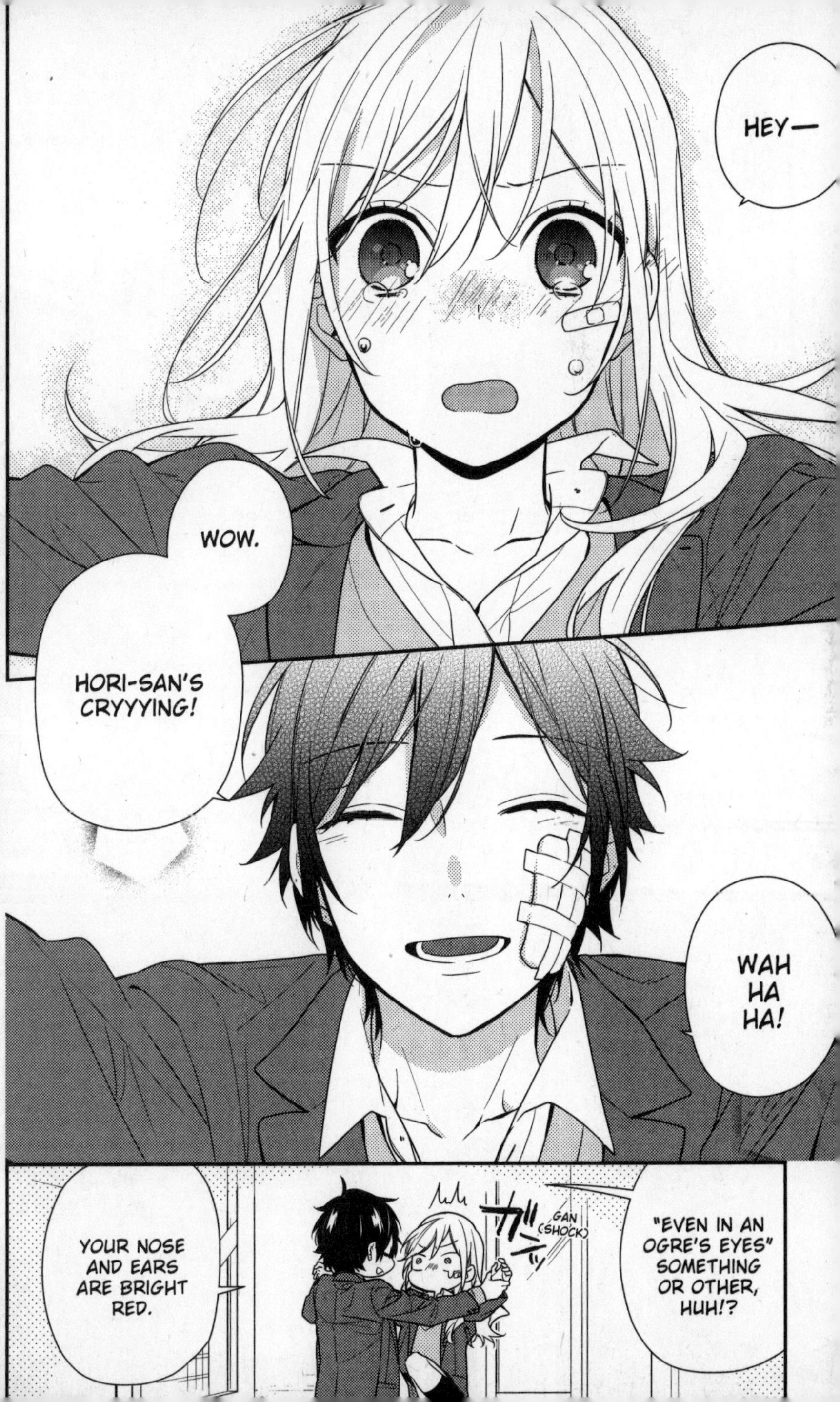
HEY—
WOW.
HORI-SAN'S CRYYYING!
WAH HA HA!
"EVEN IN AN OGRE'S EYES" SOMETHING OR OTHER, HUH!?
GAN (SHOCK)
YOUR NOSE AND EARS ARE BRIGHT RED.

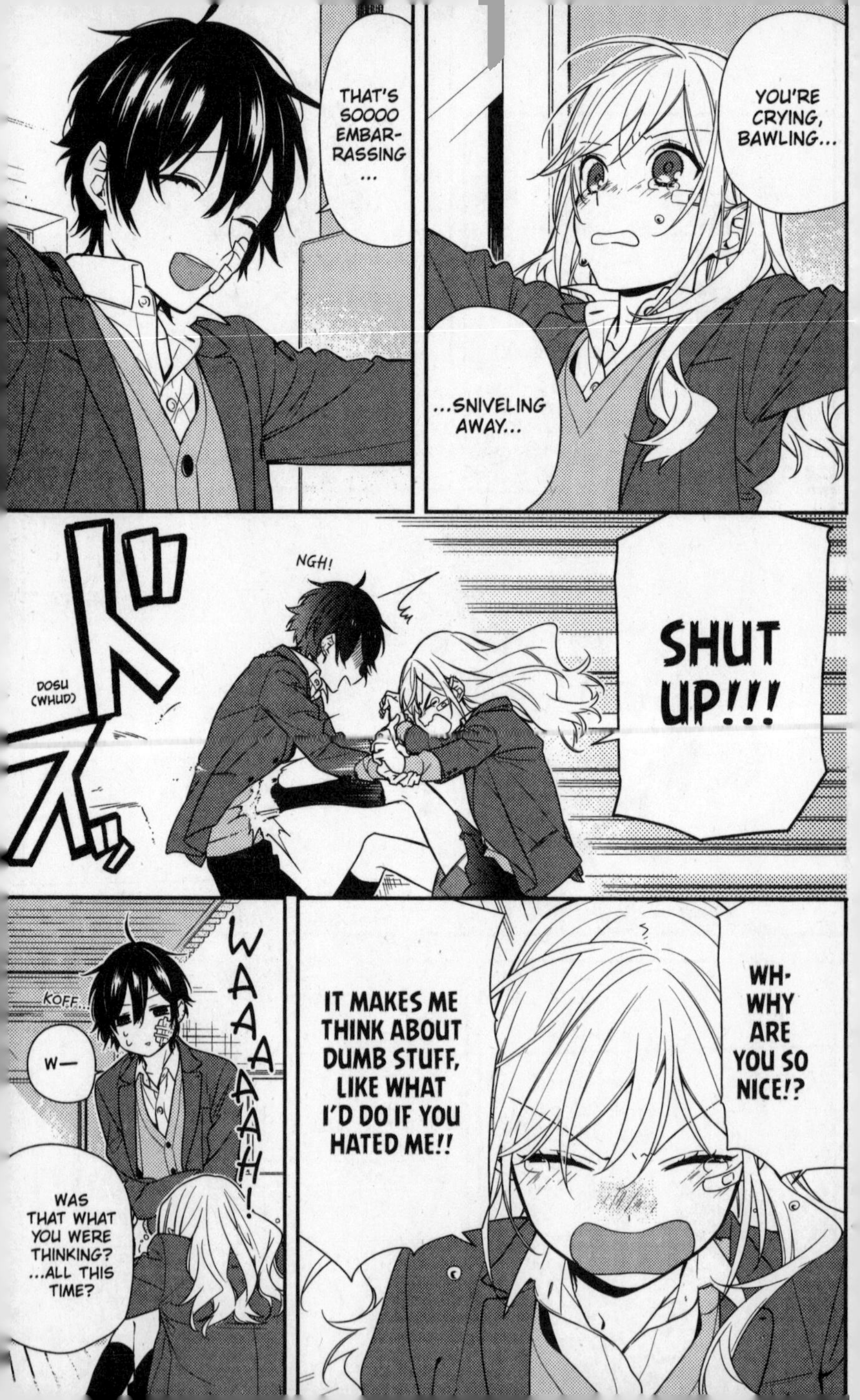
YOU'RE CRYING, BAWLING...
...SNIVELING AWAY...
THAT'S SOOOO EMBAR-RASSING ...
SHUT UP!!!
NGH!
ドスッ
DOSU (WHUD)
WH-WHY ARE YOU SO NICE!?
IT MAKES ME THINK ABOUT DUMB STUFF, LIKE WHAT I'D DO IF YOU HATED ME!!
WAAAAAH!
KOFF...
W—
WAS THAT WHAT YOU WERE THINKING? ...ALL THIS TIME?

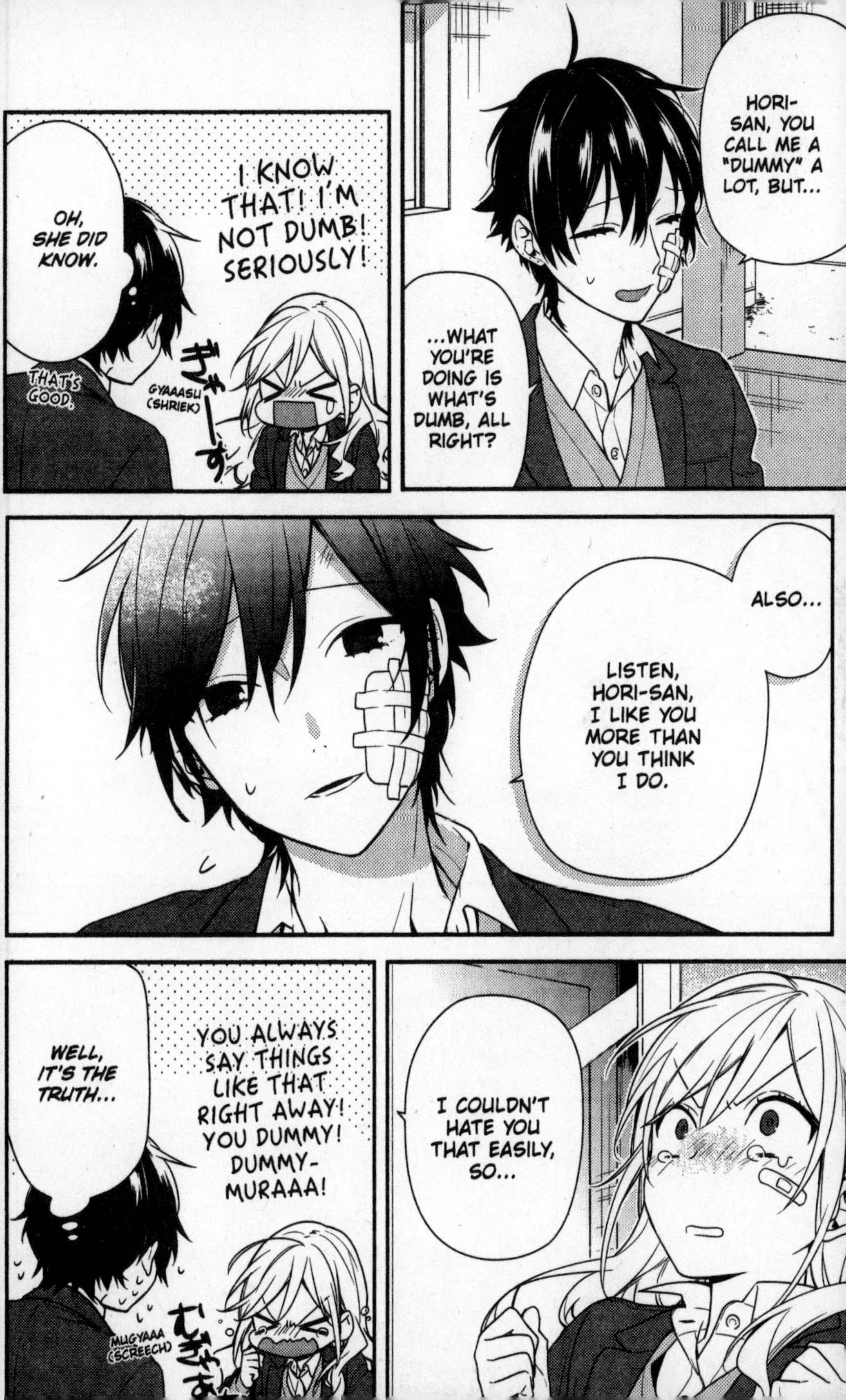
HORI-SAN, YOU CALL ME A "DUMMY" A LOT, BUT...
...WHAT YOU'RE DOING IS WHAT'S DUMB, ALL RIGHT?
I KNOW THAT! I'M NOT DUMB! SERIOUSLY!
ぎゃーす
GYAAASU (SHRIEK)
OH, SHE DID KNOW.
THAT'S GOOD.
ALSO...
LISTEN, HORI-SAN, I LIKE YOU MORE THAN YOU THINK I DO.
I COULDN'T HATE YOU THAT EASILY, SO...
YOU ALWAYS SAY THINGS LIKE THAT RIGHT AWAY! YOU DUMMY! DUMMY-MURAAA!
MUGYAAA (SCREECH)
WELL, IT'S THE TRUTH...

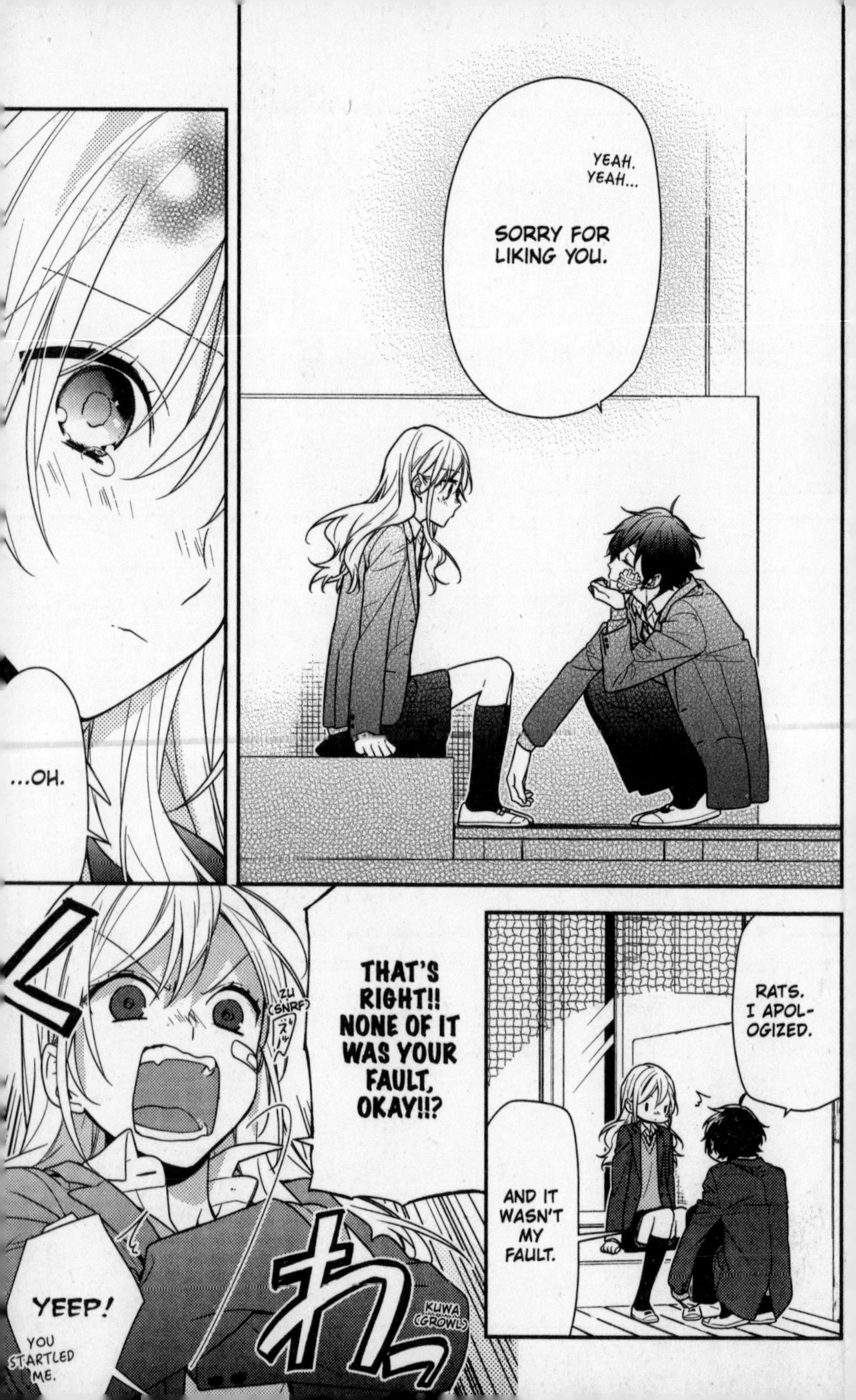
YEAH. YEAH...
SORRY FOR LIKING YOU.
...OH.
RATS. I APOLOGIZED.
AND IT WASN'T MY FAULT.
THAT'S RIGHT!! NONE OF IT WAS YOUR FAULT, OKAY!!?
ZU (SNRF)
KUWA (GROWL)
YEEP!
YOU STARTLED ME.

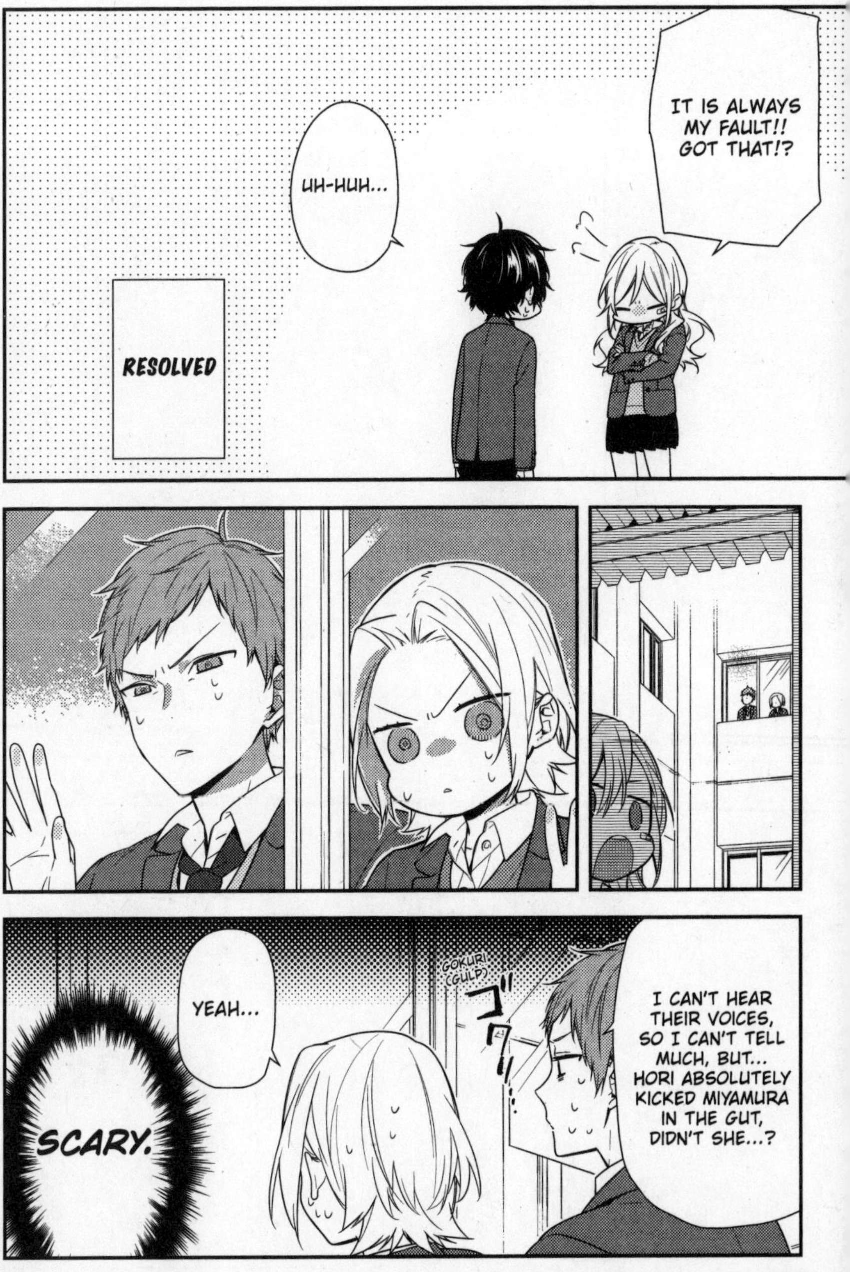
IT IS ALWAYS MY FAULT!! GOT THAT!?
UH-HUH...
RESOLVED
I CAN'T HEAR THEIR VOICES, SO I CAN'T TELL MUCH, BUT... HORI ABSOLUTELY KICKED MIYAMURA IN THE GUT, DIDN'T SHE...?
GOKURI (GULP)
YEAH...
SCARY.

HORIMIYA

HORIMIYA

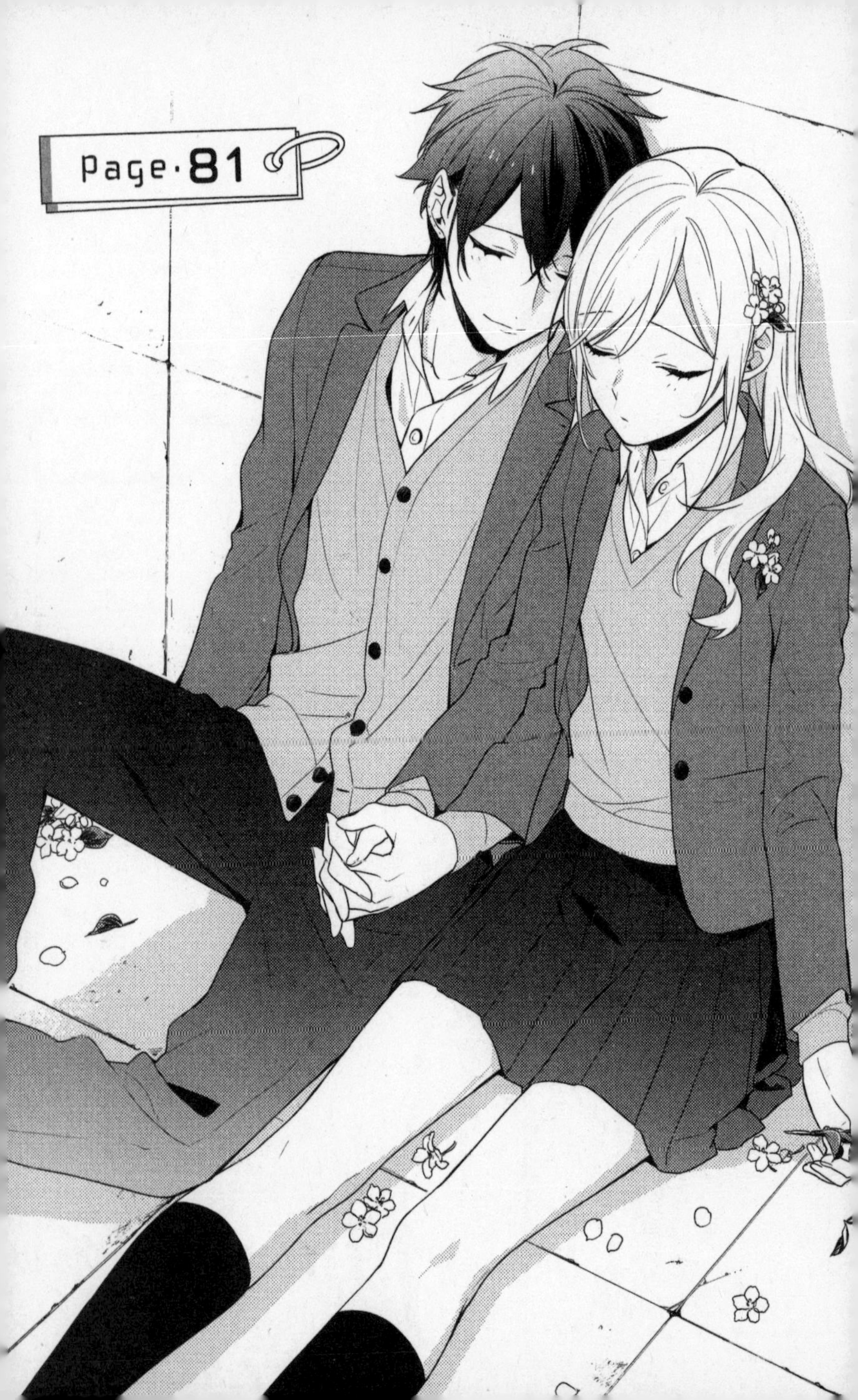
page·81

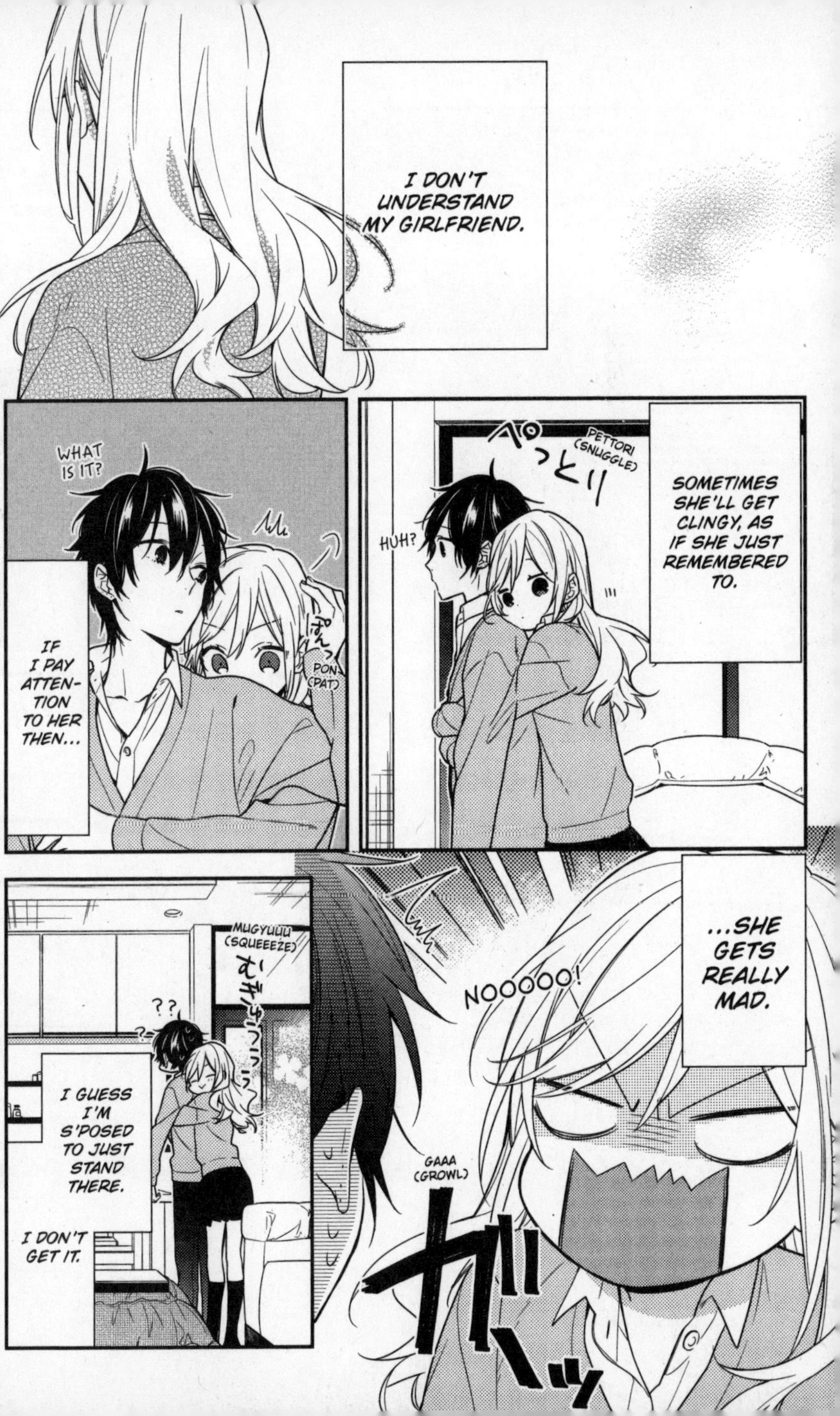
I DON'T UNDERSTAND MY GIRLFRIEND.
SOMETIMES SHE'LL GET CLINGY, AS IF SHE JUST REMEMBERED TO.
PETTORI (SNUGGLE)
HUH?
WHAT IS IT?
PON (PAT)
IF I PAY ATTEN-TION TO HER THEN...
...SHE GETS REALLY MAD.
NOOOOO!
GAAA (GROWL)
MUGYUUU (SQUEEEZE)
??
I GUESS I'M S'POSED TO JUST STAND THERE.
I DON'T GET IT.

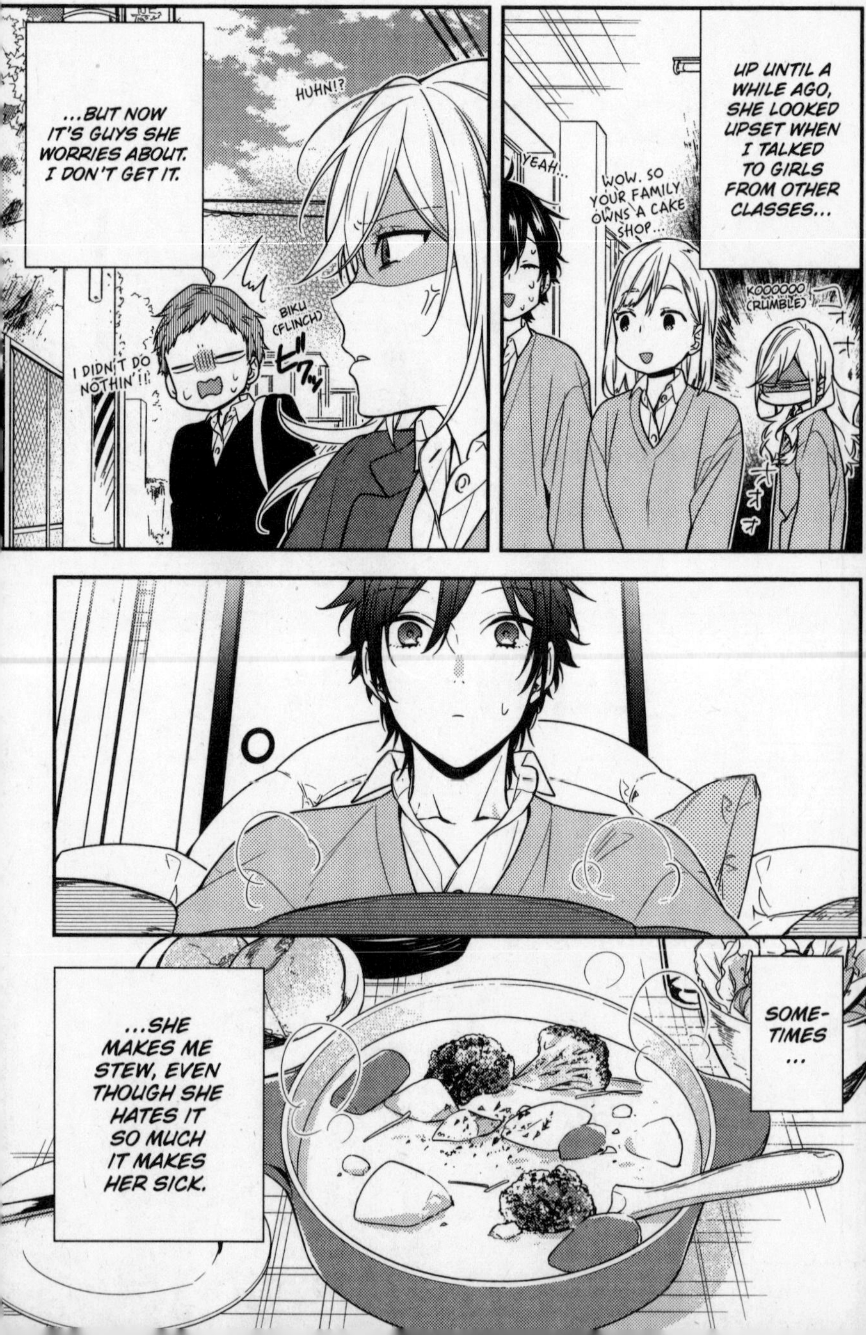
UP UNTIL A WHILE AGO, SHE LOOKED UPSET WHEN I TALKED TO GIRLS FROM OTHER CLASSES...
WOW. SO YOUR FAMILY OWNS A CAKE SHOP...
YEAH...
KOOOOOO (RUMBLE)
...BUT NOW IT'S GUYS SHE WORRIES ABOUT. I DON'T GET IT.
HUHN!?
BIKU (FLINCH)
I DIDN'T DO NOTHIN'!!
SOME-TIMES...
...SHE MAKES ME STEW, EVEN THOUGH SHE HATES IT SO MUCH IT MAKES HER SICK.

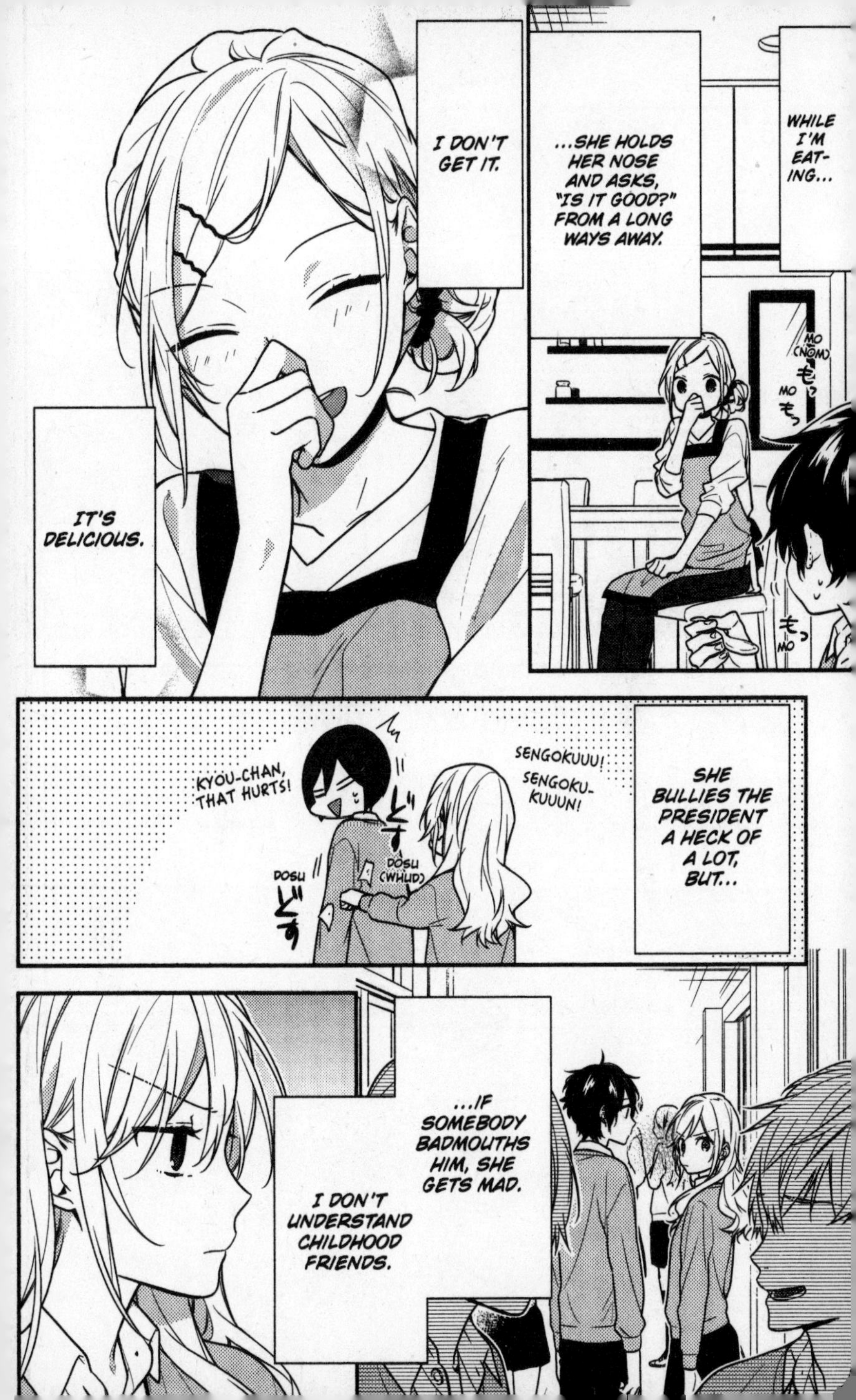
WHILE I'M EATING...
...SHE HOLDS HER NOSE AND ASKS, "IS IT GOOD?" FROM A LONG WAYS AWAY.
MO (NOM) もっ
MO もっ
もっ MO
I DON'T GET IT.
IT'S DELICIOUS.
SHE BULLIES THE PRESIDENT A HECK OF A LOT, BUT...
SENGOKUUU!
SENGOKU-KUUUN!
KYOU-CHAN, THAT HURTS!
DOSU (WHUD) どす
DOSU どす
...IF SOMEBODY BADMOUTHS HIM, SHE GETS MAD.
I DON'T UNDERSTAND CHILDHOOD FRIENDS.

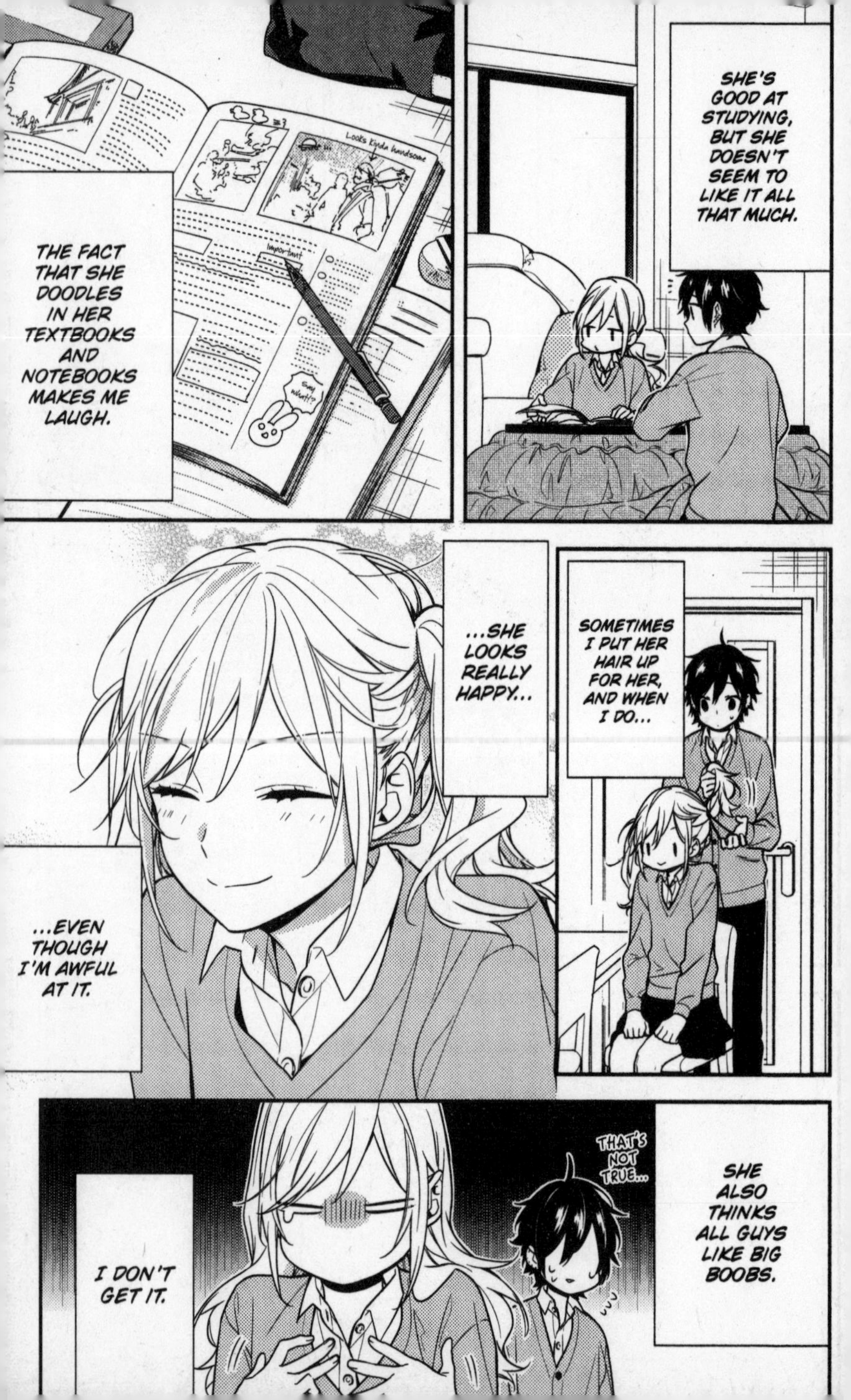
SHE'S GOOD AT STUDYING, BUT SHE DOESN'T SEEM TO LIKE IT ALL THAT MUCH.
Looks kinda handsome
Important
THE FACT THAT SHE DOODLES IN HER TEXTBOOKS AND NOTEBOOKS MAKES ME LAUGH.
SOMETIMES I PUT HER HAIR UP FOR HER, AND WHEN I DO...
...SHE LOOKS REALLY HAPPY...
...EVEN THOUGH I'M AWFUL AT IT.
SHE ALSO THINKS ALL GUYS LIKE BIG BOOBS.
THAT'S NOT TRUE...
I DON'T GET IT.

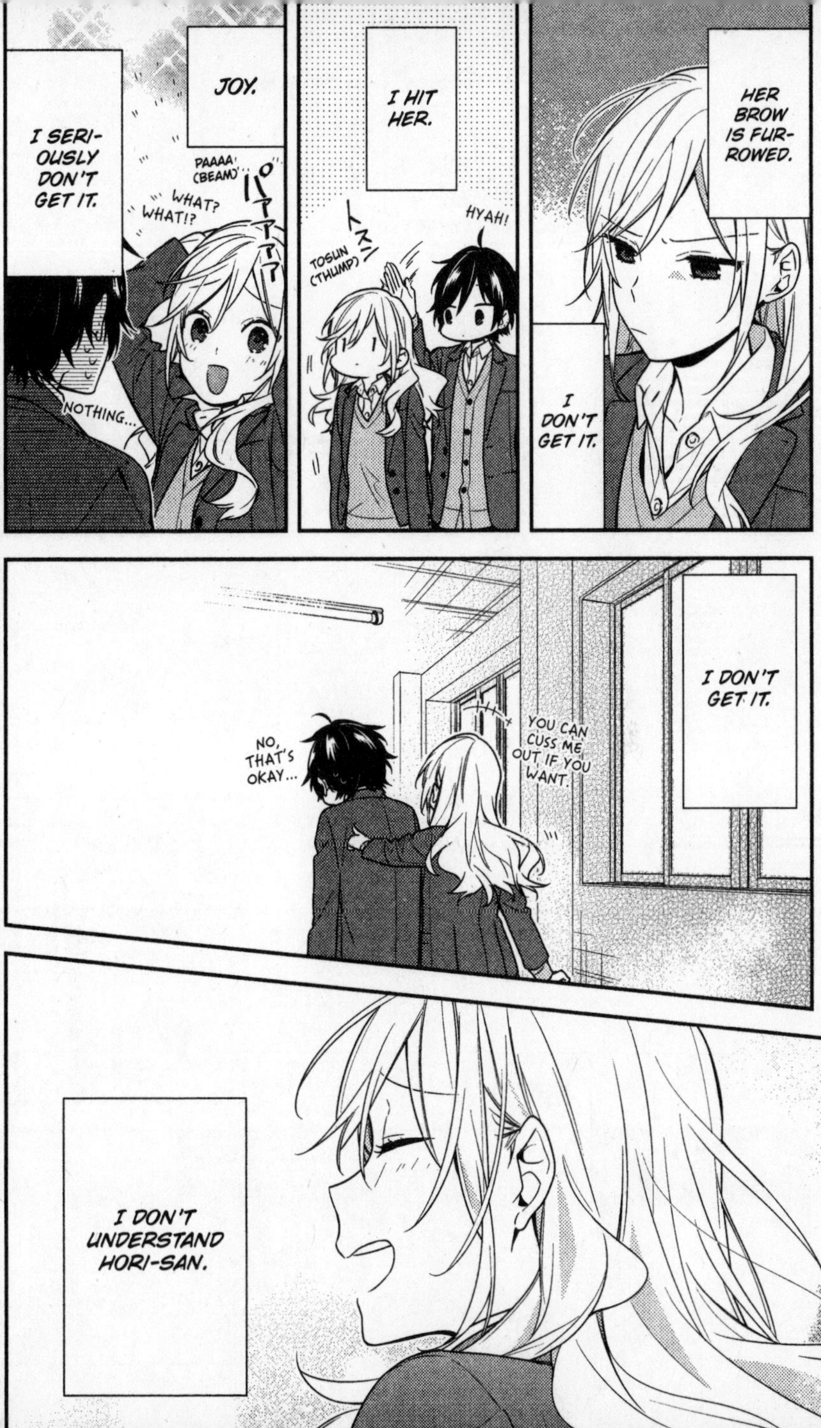
HER BROW IS FUR-ROWED.
I DON'T GET IT.
I HIT HER.
HYAH!
TOSUN (THUMP)
JOY.
PAAAA (BEAM)
WHAT? WHAT!?
I SERI-OUSLY DON'T GET IT.
NOTHING...
I DON'T GET IT.
YOU CAN CUSS ME OUT IF YOU WANT.
NO, THAT'S OKAY...
I DON'T UNDERSTAND HORI-SAN.

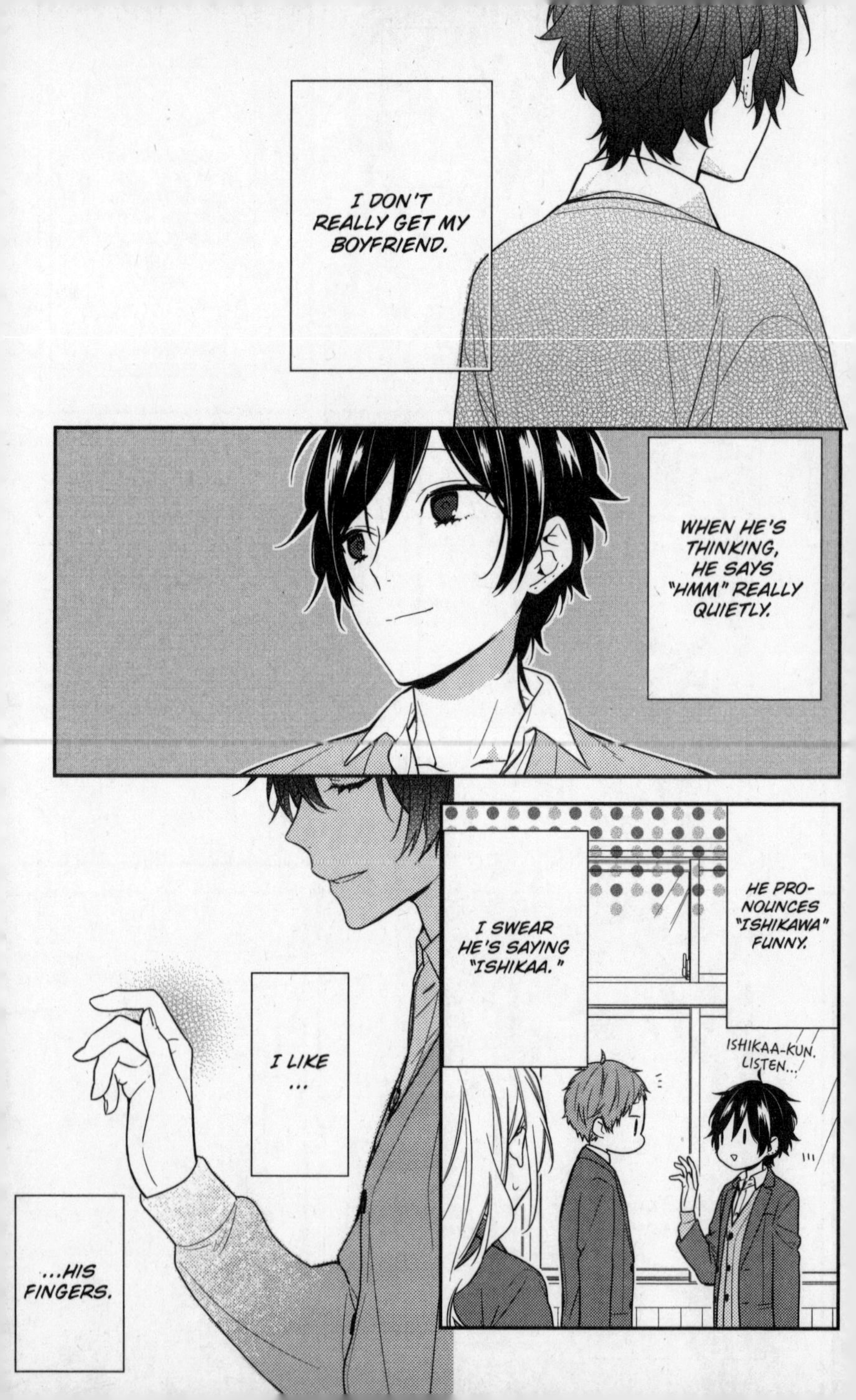
I DON'T REALLY GET MY BOYFRIEND.
WHEN HE'S THINKING, HE SAYS "HMM" REALLY QUIETLY.
HE PRONOUNCES "ISHIKAWA" FUNNY.
I SWEAR HE'S SAYING "ISHIKAA."
ISHIKAA-KUN. LISTEN...
I LIKE ...
...HIS FINGERS.

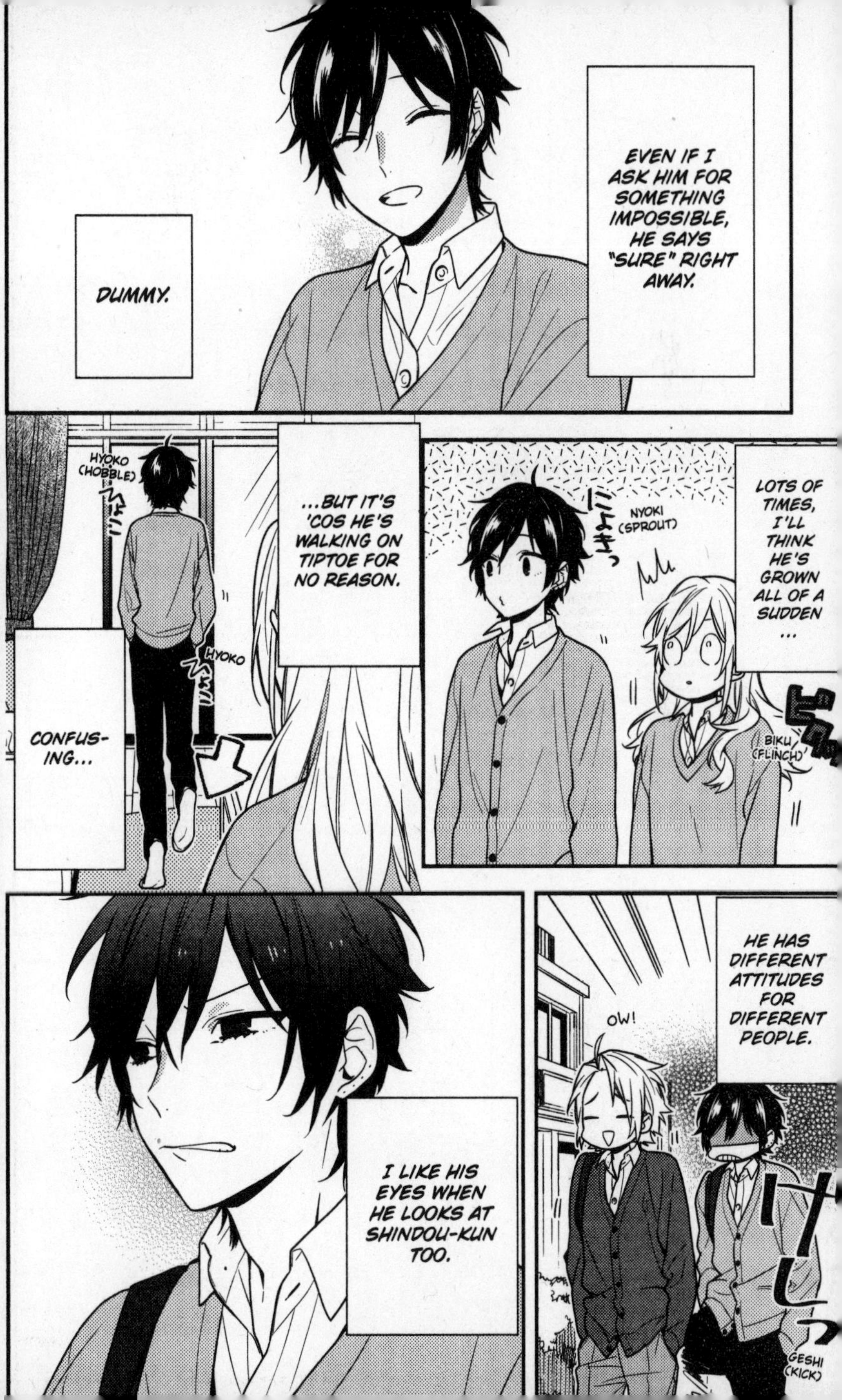

EVEN IF I ASK HIM FOR SOMETHING IMPOSSIBLE, HE SAYS "SURE" RIGHT AWAY.
DUMMY.
LOTS OF TIMES, I'LL THINK HE'S GROWN ALL OF A SUDDEN...
NYOKI (SPROUT)
BIKU (FLINCH)
...BUT IT'S 'COS HE'S WALKING ON TIPTOE FOR NO REASON.
HYOKO (HOBBLE)
HYOKO
CONFUSING...
HE HAS DIFFERENT ATTITUDES FOR DIFFERENT PEOPLE.
OW!
GESHI (KICK)
I LIKE HIS EYES WHEN HE LOOKS AT SHINDOU-KUN TOO.

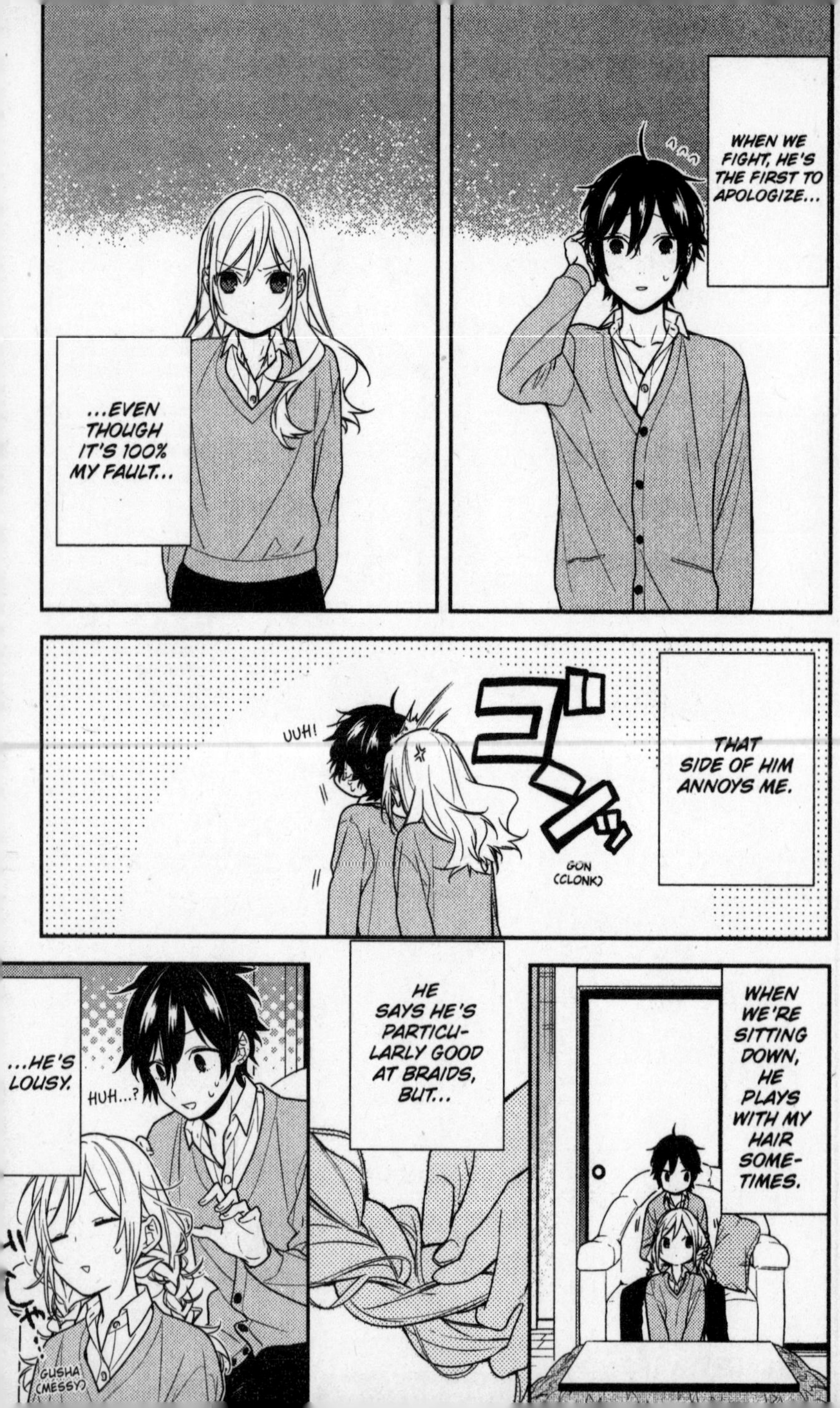
WHEN WE FIGHT, HE'S THE FIRST TO APOLOGIZE...
...EVEN THOUGH IT'S 100% MY FAULT...
THAT SIDE OF HIM ANNOYS ME.
GON (CLONK)
UUH!
WHEN WE'RE SITTING DOWN, HE PLAYS WITH MY HAIR SOME-TIMES.
HE SAYS HE'S PARTICU-LARLY GOOD AT BRAIDS, BUT...
HUH...?
...HE'S LOUSY.
GUSHA (MESSY)

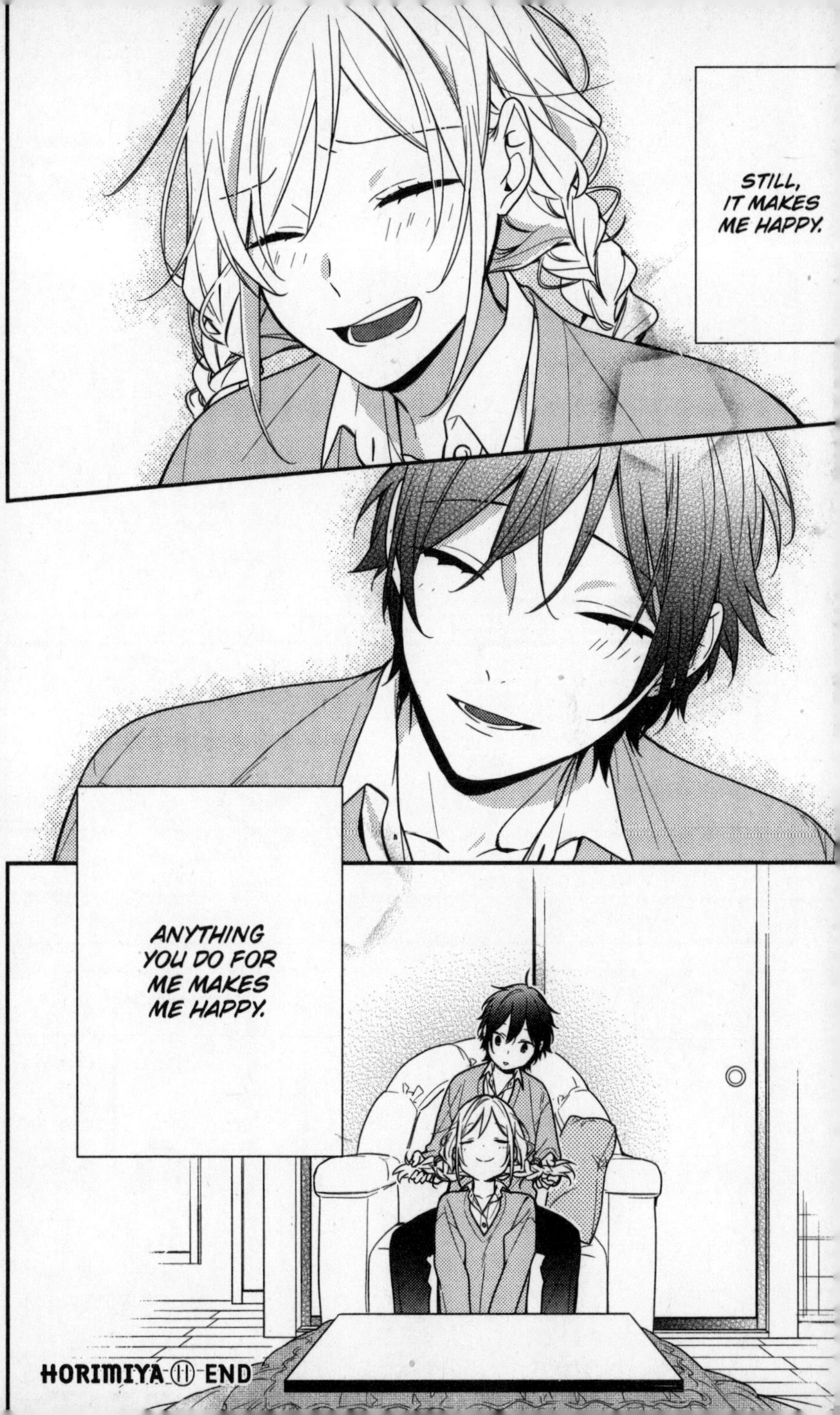
STILL, IT MAKES ME HAPPY.
ANYTHING YOU DO FOR ME MAKES ME HAPPY.
HORIMIYA-11-END

*To Be Continued...*

## Translation Notes

**Page 55 – Savory egg custard**
*Chawanmushi* literally translates to "steamed in a tea cup."
They're savory egg custards prepared in single-serving
dishes and can include additions such as mushrooms,
shrimp, lily root, fish cake, ginkgo nuts, and more.

**Page 101 – *Moe***
*Moe* is an obsession with something cute, usually a certain
category of girl (maids, little sisters) or items of clothing or
accessories (glasses, school uniforms). The term can also be
used as an interjection when something triggers the obsession.

**Page 103 – Penhold, shakehand**
Penhold and shakehand are two different grip styles used
in table tennis. In a penhold grip, the paddle is held the way
you'd hold a pen; in a shakehand grip, it's held like a knife.

**Page 112 – "Like a summer Miyamura moth to the flame..."**
The phrase in the original Japanese translates literally
to "Like the summer insect that flies into the fire."

**Page 152 – "Even in an ogre's eyes..."**
The proverb Miyamura is quoting is "Even in an
ogre's eyes, there are tears," meaning "Even hard-
hearted people can be moved to tears."

# BONUS MANGA: MYAMURA ⑨

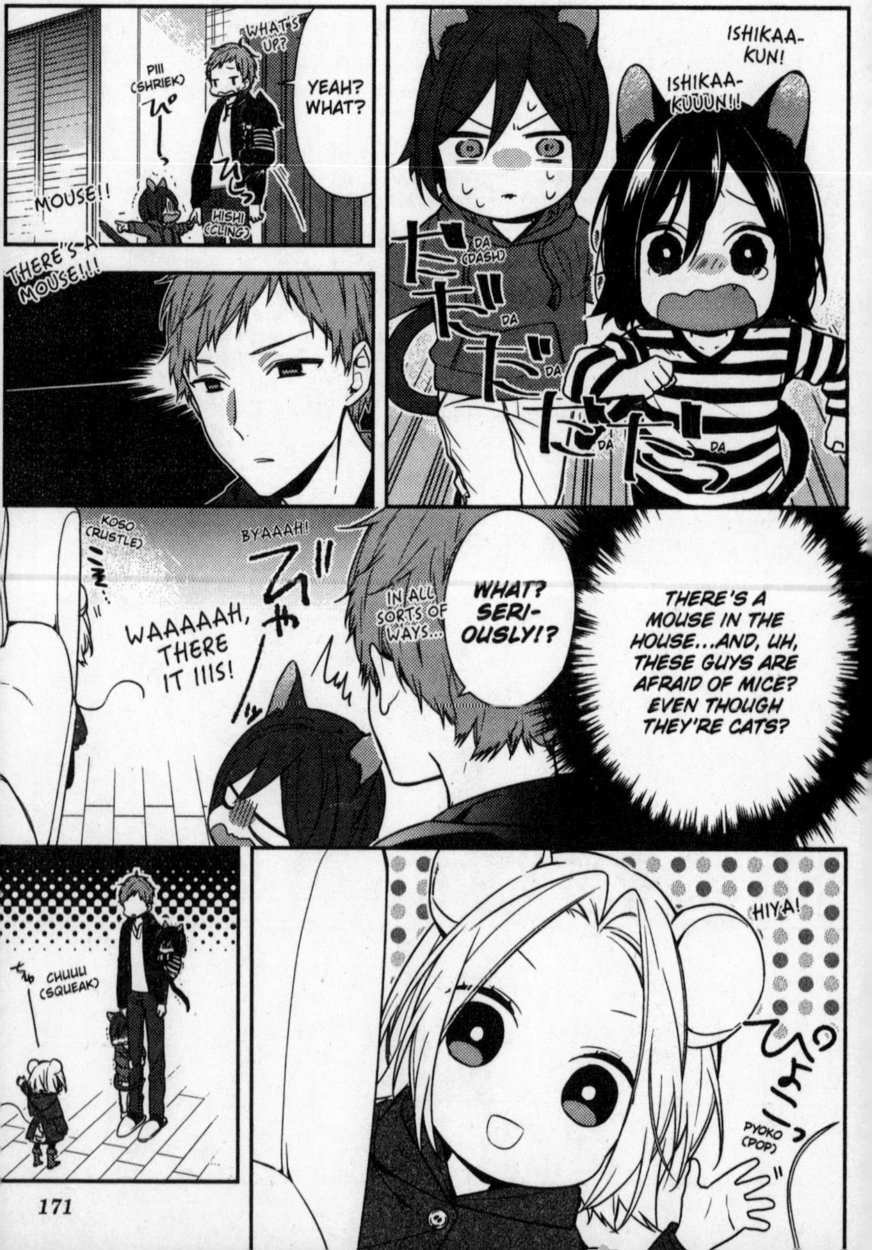
ISHIKAA-KUN!
ISHIKAA-KUUUN!!
DA (DASH)
DA
DA
DA
DA
WHAT'S UP?
YEAH? WHAT?
PIII (SHRIEK)
HISHI (CLING)
MOUSE!!
THERE'S A MOUSE!!!
THERE'S A MOUSE IN THE HOUSE...AND, UH, THESE GUYS ARE AFRAID OF MICE? EVEN THOUGH THEY'RE CATS?
WHAT? SERI-OUSLY!?
IN ALL SORTS OF WAYS...
BYAAAH!
WAAAAAH, THERE IT IIIS!
KOSO (RUSTLE)
HIYA!
PYOKO (POP)
CHUUU (SQUEAK)

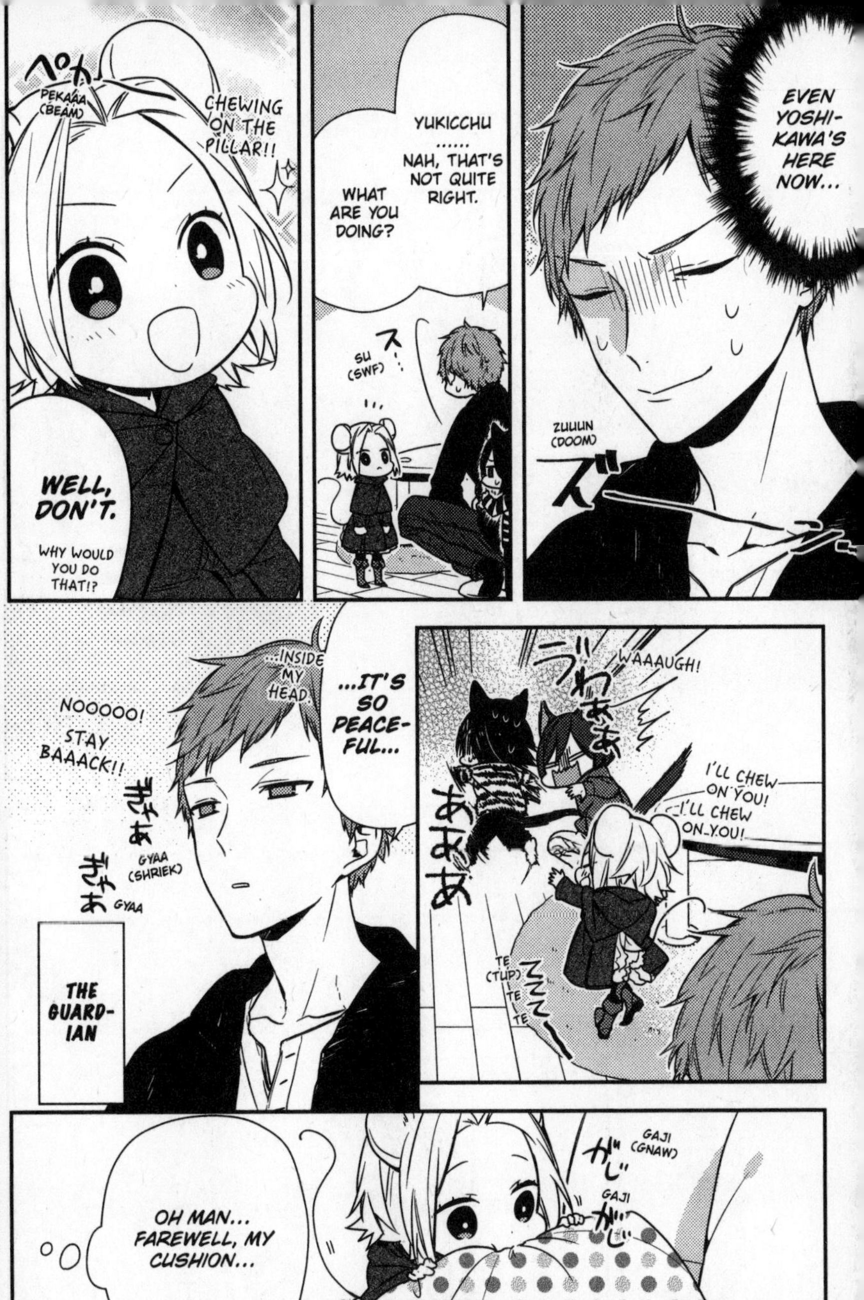
EVEN YOSHIKAWA'S HERE NOW...
ZUUUN (DOOM)
YUKICCHU ...... NAH, THAT'S NOT QUITE RIGHT.
WHAT ARE YOU DOING?
ス
SU (SWF)
ぺかー
PEKAAA (BEAM)
CHEWING ON THE PILLAR!!
WELL, DON'T.
WHY WOULD YOU DO THAT!?
うわあああ
WAAAUGH!
I'LL CHEW ON YOU! I'LL CHEW ON YOU!
TE (TUP) TE TE
...INSIDE MY HEAD
...IT'S SO PEACEFUL...
NOOOOO! STAY BAAACK!!
ぎゃあ
GYAA (SHRIEK)
ぎゃあ
GYAA
THE GUARDIAN
がじ
GAJI (GNAW)
がじ
GAJI
OH MAN... FAREWELL, MY CUSHION...

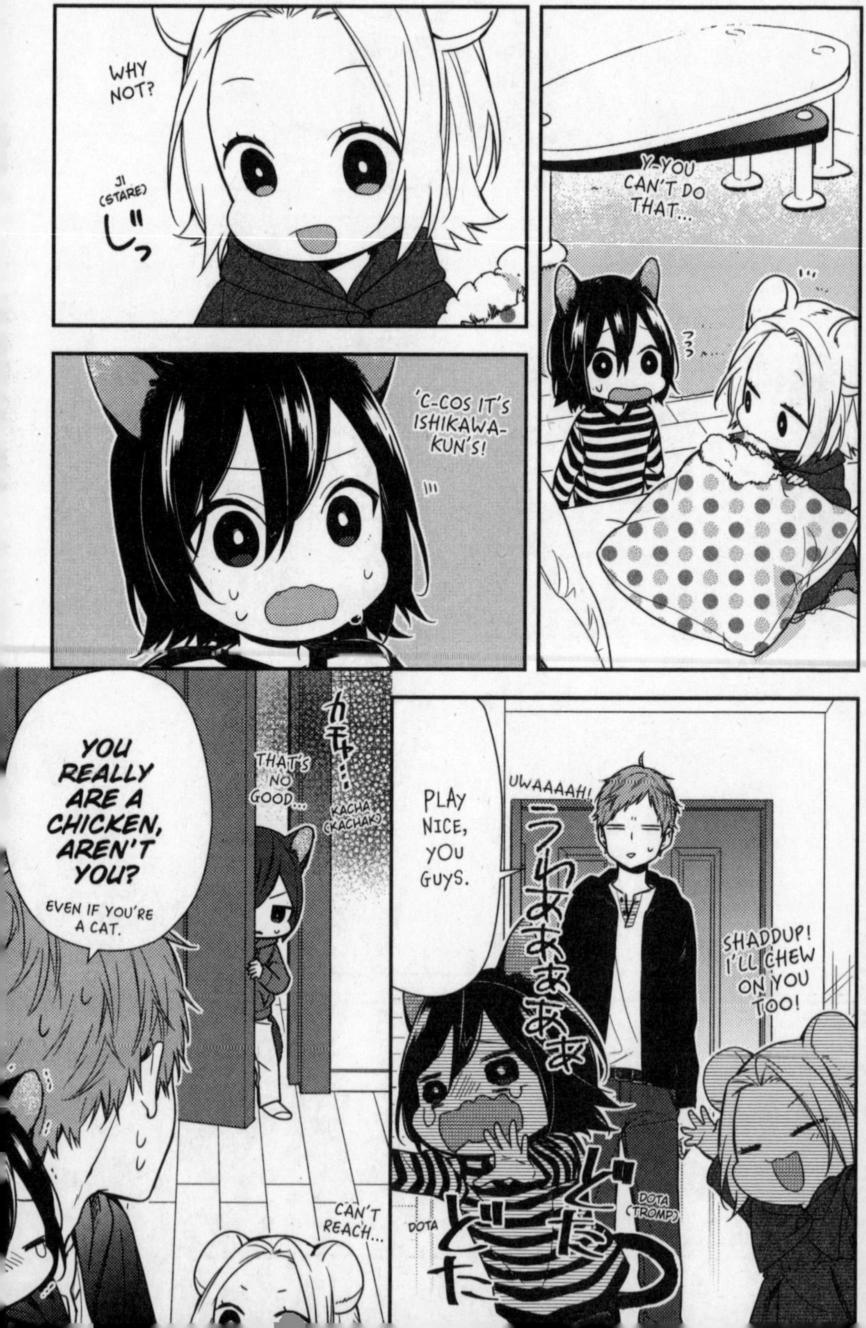
Y-YOU CAN'T DO THAT...
...
WHY NOT?
JI (STARE)
'C-COS IT'S ISHIKAWA-KUN'S!
PLAY NICE, YOU GUYS.
UWAAAAAH!
SHADDUP! I'LL CHEW ON YOU TOO!
DOTA (TROMP)
DOTA
YOU REALLY ARE A CHICKEN, AREN'T YOU?
EVEN IF YOU'RE A CAT.
THAT'S NO GOOD...
KACHA (KACHAK)
CAN'T REACH...

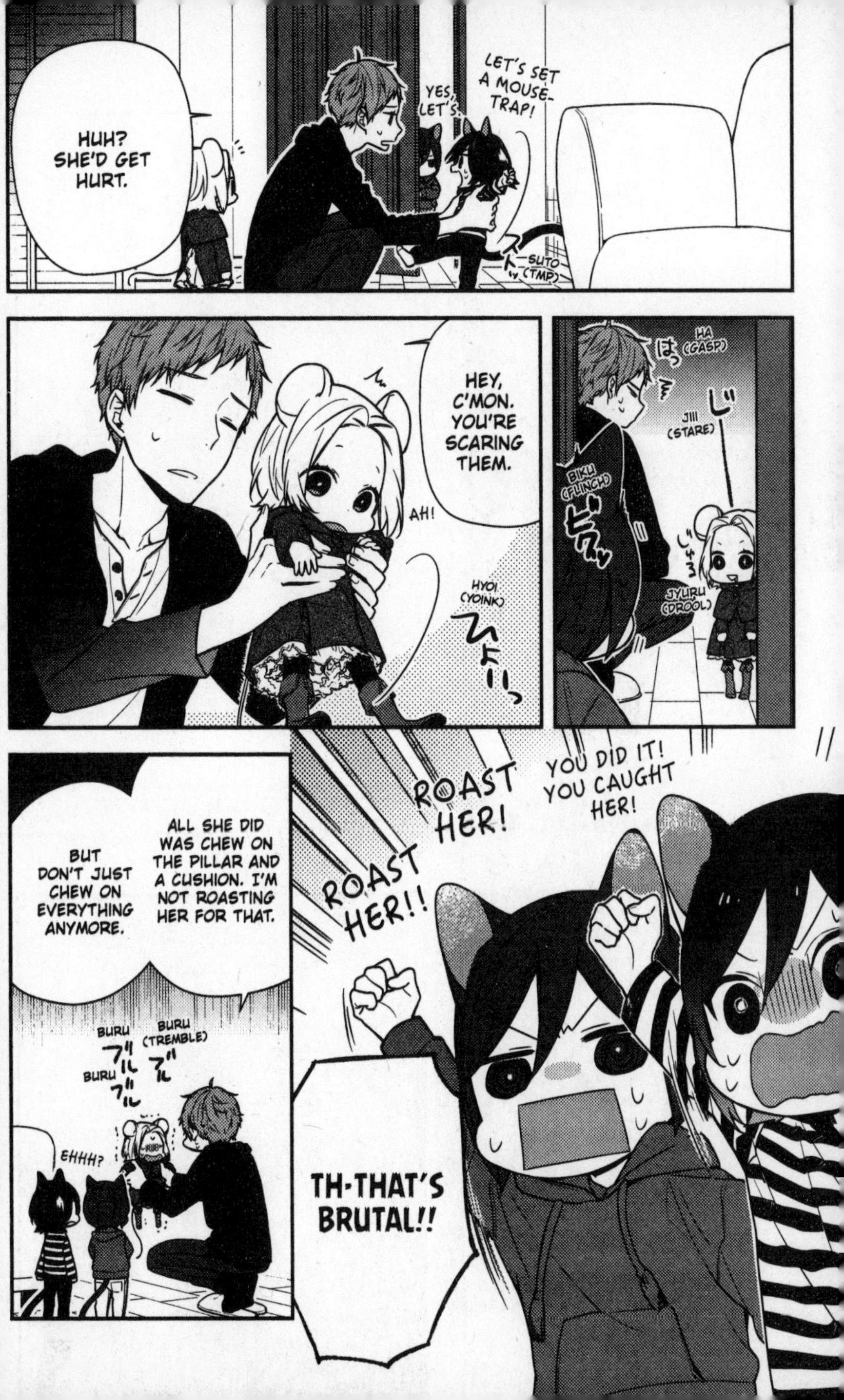
LET'S SET A MOUSE-TRAP!
YES, LET'S.
HUH? SHE'D GET HURT.
SUTO (TMP)
HA (GASP)
JIII (STARE)
BIKU (FLINCH)
JYURU (DROOL)
HEY, C'MON. YOU'RE SCARING THEM.
AH!
HYOI (YOINK)
YOU DID IT! YOU CAUGHT HER!
ROAST HER!
ROAST HER!!
TH-THAT'S BRUTAL!!
ALL SHE DID WAS CHEW ON THE PILLAR AND A CUSHION. I'M NOT ROASTING HER FOR THAT.
BUT DON'T JUST CHEW ON EVERYTHING ANYMORE.
BURU BURU (TREMBLE)
BURU
EHHH?

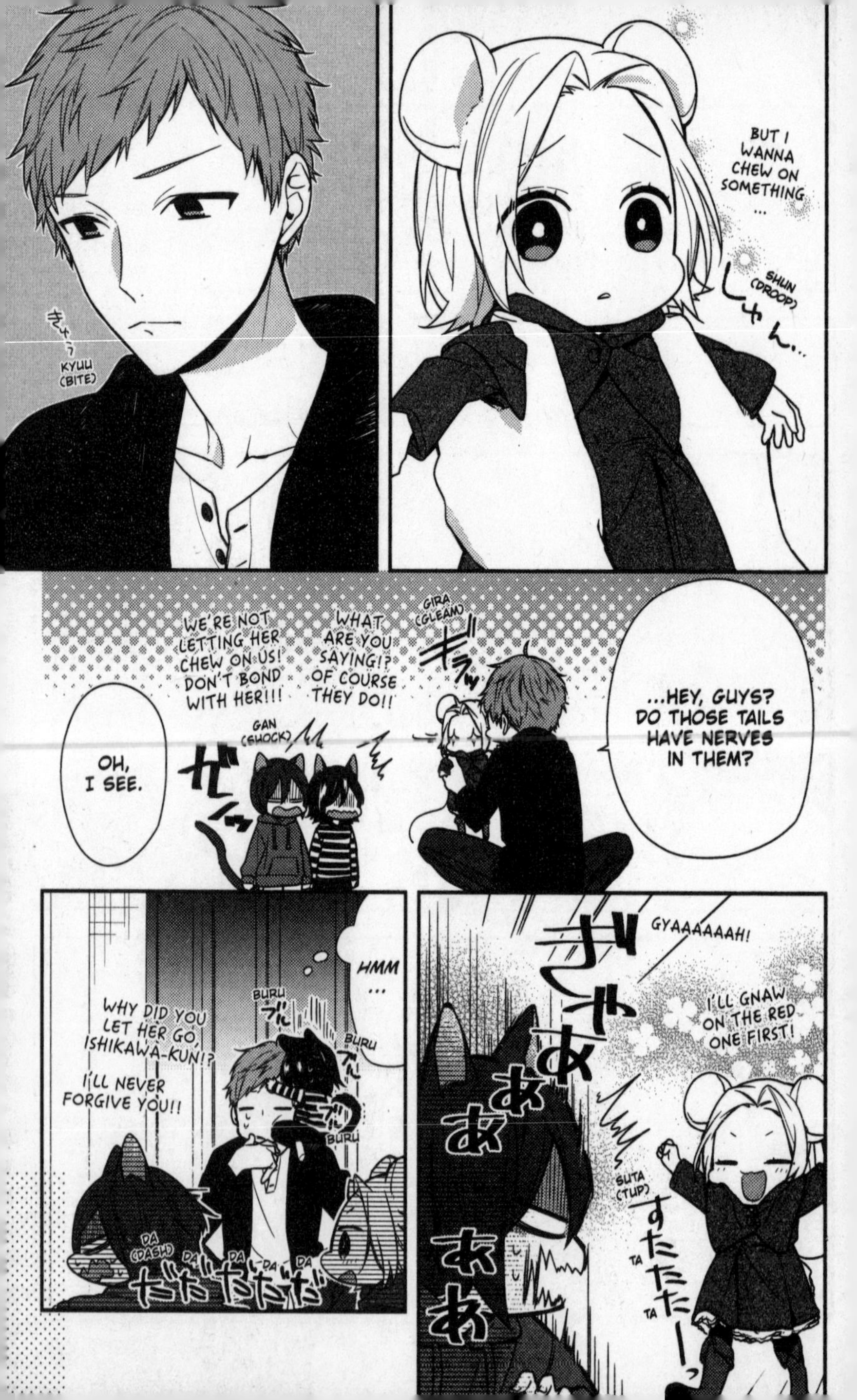
BUT I WANNA CHEW ON SOMETHING...
SHUN (DROOP)
しゅん...
きゅう
KYUU (BITE)
...HEY, GUYS? DO THOSE TAILS HAVE NERVES IN THEM?
GIRA (GLEAM)
ギラッ
WHAT ARE YOU SAYING!? OF COURSE THEY DO!!
WE'RE NOT LETTING HER CHEW ON US! DON'T BOND WITH HER!!!
GAN (SHOCK)
OH, I SEE.
GYAAAAAAH!
I'LL GNAW ON THE RED ONE FIRST!
SUTA (TUP)
TA
TA
HMM...
BURU
BURU
BURU
WHY DID YOU LET HER GO, ISHIKAWA-KUN!?
I'LL NEVER FORGIVE YOU!!
DA (DASH)
DA
DA
DA
DA
だだだだだ

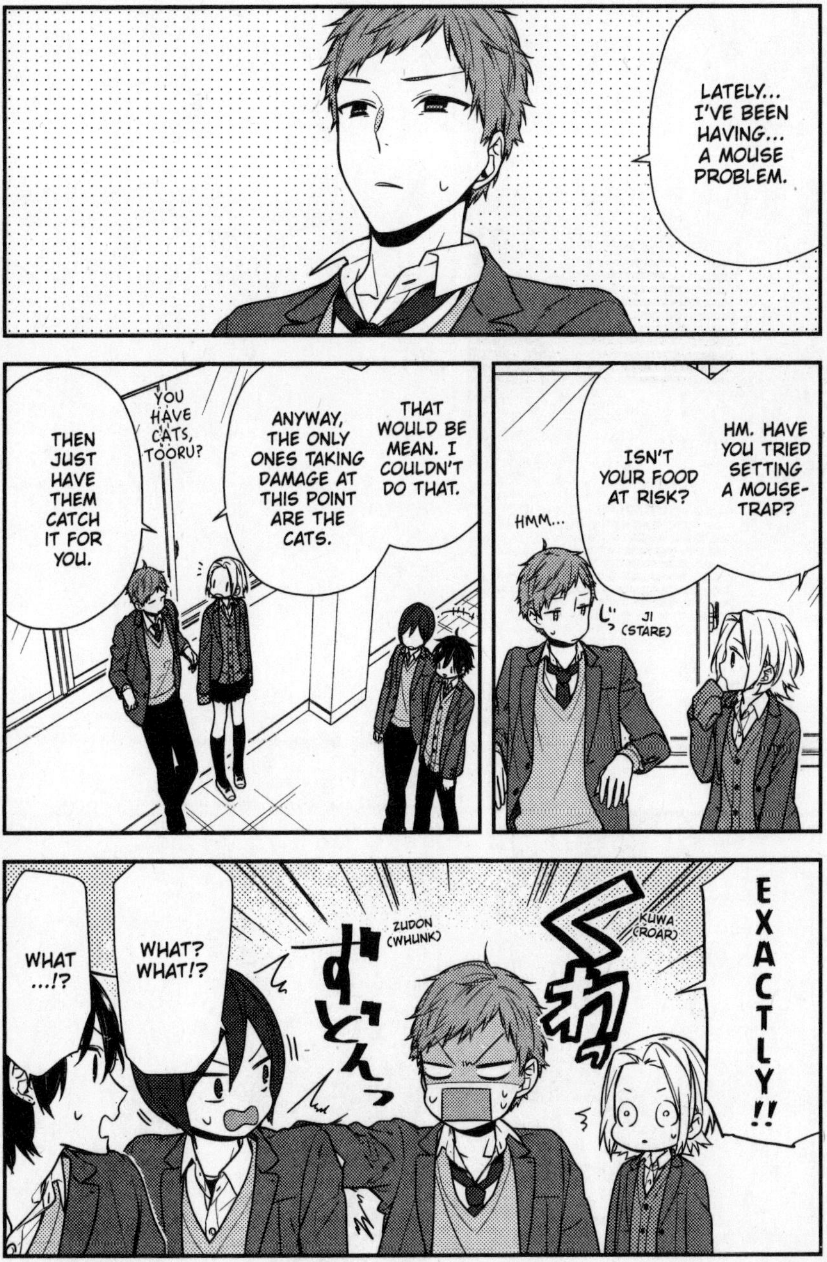
LATELY... I'VE BEEN HAVING... A MOUSE PROBLEM.
HM. HAVE YOU TRIED SETTING A MOUSE-TRAP?
ISN'T YOUR FOOD AT RISK?
HMM...
じっ
JI (STARE)
THAT WOULD BE MEAN. I COULDN'T DO THAT.
ANYWAY, THE ONLY ONES TAKING DAMAGE AT THIS POINT ARE THE CATS.
YOU HAVE CATS, TOORU?
THEN JUST HAVE THEM CATCH IT FOR YOU.
EXACTLY!!
くわっ
KUWA (ROAR)
ずどんっ
ZUDON (WHUNK)
WHAT? WHAT!?
WHAT ...!?

HORIMIYA

## HERO × Daisuke Hagiwara

*Translation: Taylor Engel*
*Lettering: Alexis Eckerman*

*HORIMIYA vol. 11*
© HERO · OOZ
© *2017 Daisuke Hagiwara / SQUARE ENIX CO., LTD. First published in Japan in 2017 by SQUARE ENIX CO., LTD. English translation rights arranged with SQUARE ENIX CO., LTD. and Yen Press, LLC through Tuttle-Mori Agency, Inc.*

*English translation © 2018 by SQUARE ENIX CO., LTD.*

Yen Press
1290 Avenue of the Americas
New York, NY 10104

Visit us at yenpress.com · facebook.com/yenpress ·
twitter.com/yenpress · yenpress.tumblr.com ·
instagram.com/yenpress

First Yen Press Edition: June 2018

Yen Press is an imprint of Yen Press, LLC.
The Yen Press name and logo are trademarks
of Yen Press, LLC.

The publisher is not responsible for websites
(or their content) that are not owned by the
publisher.

Library of Congress Control Number:
2015960115

ISBNs: 978-1-9753-2750-7 (paperback)
978-1-9753-5433-6 (ebook)

10 9 8 7 6 5 4 3

WOR

Printed in the United States of America